INDICES
TO DIATESSARICA

INDICES
TO DIATESSARICA

WITH A SPECIMEN OF RESEARCH

BY

EDWIN A. ABBOTT

"*The Saviour ...... cast into the soul 'a tree that maketh sweet,'
whereby He wrought in us love of toil instead of hate of toil. For
He knew, as being Creator, that nothing that IS can ever be compassed
unless we have a constraining love of it.*"
Philo i. 255
(on the Waters of Marah).

"*So the men toiled away. And the water, exercised by the continuous
strokes and thus purified, was at last drinkable.*"
Josephus Ant. iii. 1. 2
(on the Waters of Marah).

Wipf & Stock
PUBLISHERS
Eugene, Oregon

Wipf and Stock Publishers
199 W 8th Ave, Suite 3
Eugene, OR 97401

Indices to Diatessarica
With a Specimen of Research
By Abbott, Edwin A.
ISBN: 1-59752-891-9
Publication date 9/22/2006
Previously published by Adam and Charles Black, 1907

TO
ORIGEN
PREEMINENT AMONG CHRISTIAN WRITERS
FOR THAT "CONSTRAINING LOVE"
WHICH "SWEETENS" THE TOIL FOR TRUTH
AND WITHOUT WHICH
"NOTHING THAT *IS*
CAN EVER BE COMPASSED"

PREFACE

THESE Indices are published in the belief that they may be of use to a student of the Gospels in ascertaining the truth that lies beneath their often divergent accounts. As they have been composed not by me but by the coadjutor to whom the Johannine Vocabulary and the Johannine Grammar were dedicated I have no scruple in expressing my confidence that they will be found generally accurate. But we shall both of us be grateful for corrections.

Although subsequent study has led me to modify some of the detailed suggestions in the earlier volumes of Diatessarica, my conviction is deepened that the facts on which those suggestions were based will be found of use even to those who differ most from my conclusions.

In fulfilment of a promise made in a previous work (*Notes on New Testament Criticism*, p. xvi) to add a few words about Josephus' version of the Sweetening of the Waters of Marah, I began an investigation into the whole of the story. It proved much more complicated than I had anticipated. But it was also much longer, so that I have not been able to publish it in full. However, I have printed the greater part of it in the pages prefixed to the Indices, as a specimen of research shewing how the Indices might be employed.

Some students of the New Testament may be disposed to put aside such a research as having no sort of utility for them. I think they would be wrong. The stories of water-finding in the exodus of the Hebrews from the bondage of Egypt, stamped anew on the hearts of their descendants the Jews, during the weary return across the desert from the captivity in Babylon, seem to me to have left a permanent impression on their pre-exilic writings (as revised), on their post-exilic writings (as composed), and on all their subsequent traditions. Hence they could not fail to influence all Jews in the first century—of whom our Lord was one.

We shall much better understand the Church as conceived by Christ and the needs and methods of developing the Church as it is into the Church as it ought to be, if we can more clearly realise than at present the continuous passage from the truths and illusions of the Synagogue to the illusions and truths of the Church.

EDWIN A. ABBOTT.

WELLSIDE, WELL WALK,
HAMPSTEAD.
24 *Oct.* 1907.

CONTENTS

A SPECIMEN OF RESEARCH

		PAGE
§ 1.	Water-finding in the Wilderness.	xi–xiii
§. 2.	Marah in the Hebrew narrative.	xiv, xv
§ 3.	Marah according to Ben Sira	xv
§ 4.	Marah according to Philo.	xvi–xx
§ 5.	Marah according to Josephus	xx–xxii
§ 6.	Josephus on the "segment"	xxii–xxvi
§ 7.	Josephus on the "drawing off" of water	xxvi–xxviii
§ 8.	Josephus on "purification" by "strokes"	xxix–xxxii
§ 9.	The Targums	xxxii–xxxiv
§ 10.	Other Jewish Traditions	xxxiv–xxxvii
§ 11.	Rashi on Marah.	xxxvii, xxxviii
§ 12.	Summary of details in Josephus.	xxxviii–xl
§ 13.	The Biblical "tree" still unexplained.	xl–xliv
§ 14.	Outline of an explanation	xliv–lxiii

INDICES TO DIATESSARICA

Contents	2
Indices	3–152

A SPECIMEN OF RESEARCH

§ 1. *Water-finding in the Wilderness*

THE Preface to *Notes on New Testament Criticism* (p. xvi) referred in a footnote to some details in Josephus' version of the Sweetening of the Waters of Marah which is said to have occurred just after the passage of the Red Sea. During the revision of the proof-sheets of that work, an examination of Josephus, Philo, and the Targums, revealed curious variations in the different accounts of this miracle. Taken all together they seemed to furnish a suitable illustration of the way in which the following Indices may be made useful, shewing how divergent traditions may issue from initial metaphor and obscurity.

Further study shewed that Josephus appeared to have included in his narrative some details taken from the Song of the Well, which, though placed in Numbers at the termination of the Wanderings, is connected, according to one reading of the text (and that a reading followed by Onkelos) with the Red Sea[1]. It seemed that Josephus might have recognised the same connection.

The Song of the Well is introduced with these words (Numb. xxi. 16) "From thence [they came] to Well [*i.e.* a place called Well, or, in Hebrew, Beer]. That is the well whereof the Lord said unto Moses 'Gather the people together and I will give them water.'" This seems to refer us back to Numbers xx. 8, where Moses receives a command from God, "Take the rod and assemble the congregation...

---

[1] See below, p. xxviii.

and thou shalt bring forth to them water out of the rock."
But this occurs at Kadesh, not at Well or Beer. Moreover
the Song of the Well says "The well which the princes
digged with the sceptre and with their staves," and does not
mention the name of Moses[1]. The well at Kadesh is clearly
the result of a miracle. The well at Well does not appear to
be regarded as miraculous. The people say to it "Spring up,
O well!" But that is not a prayer for a miracle. It is
a poetic appeal to the well to come forth from the earth in
response to the "digging" of the "princes" and in obedience
to what we call laws of Nature and the Hebrews called the
will of the Lord. In the Benedicite, we read, "O ye wells,
bless ye the Lord: praise him and magnify him for ever."
So, in Numbers, "Spring up, O well," is really a prayer
for a natural blessing, as one might say, "Grow, ye green
things upon the earth."

This leads us on from the miracle of Marah to the whole
question of the miracles of water in the Pentateuch which
have left their stamp upon the Pauline Epistles in the well-
known sentence "They drank of a spiritual rock that followed
them: and the rock was Christ." It will be shewn below that
many Jewish traditions speak as though a real and literal
rock, or fountain, followed Israel through the desert. What
were the facts that originated such traditions?

Beside the miracle at Kadesh in Numbers, there is a
somewhat similar one at Rephidim in Exodus (xvii. 1—7).
The differences between the two would need to be discussed
if the whole subject had to be thoroughly investigated. Here
it must suffice to say that Josephus appears to combine the
two in one, omitting the misdemeanour of Moses which is
peculiar to the narrative in Numbers.

This omission on the part of Josephus may naturally
prepossess his readers against all his evidence. If he is

---

[1] The marg. however substitutes "By [order of] the *lawgiver*" for "with the sceptre."

unscrupulous enough to omit what might discredit the great lawgiver, would he scruple (they may ask) to invent what might be to his credit? or to exaggerate what he regards as a miracle? or to invent facts so as to rationalise what he regards as non-miraculous?

Such a prepossession against the historian is natural and may fairly be called logical; but so far as concerns the present investigation, I believe it is not justified by evidence. Josephus, while here and elsewhere unscrupulously omitting discreditable (or what might seem discreditable) facts, and while occasionally exaggerating, does not appear to invent important details. He has indeed additions, but they do not appear to be his inventions.

At all events, a few of his details seem demonstrably explicable from his peculiar interpretations of Scripture. And the general result of the whole investigation will tend (I think) to shew that verbal similarities and obscurities and the confusion of metaphor with fact have played a large part in developing the poetic literature of the Water-finding of Israel in the Wilderness, and the later legends of the Wandering Well.

It may possibly appear that Josephus' curious hypothesis that the children of Israel were to "draw off" water at Marah in order to make the rest "drinkable," may throw some light on the "drawing" of water at Cana of Galilee. In any case the doctrine of the Fourth Gospel about the Well and the Living Water, and the doctrine of the Epistles about the Rock, will come home to us more forcibly when we have learned to approximate to the position of a Jew with whom it was an axiom that whenever Water was mentioned, the Law was intended[1], and that the Rock of Israel was Jehovah.

---

[1] Comp. *Baba Kamma* 82 a "(Exod. xv. 22) 'And they travelled three days in the wilderness and found no water.' The Haggadists (דורשי רשומות, see Levy iv. 474 a) explained this, '*Water* means nothing but *the Law*, according as it is said (Is. lv. 1) *Come all ye that thirst* etc.'"

§ 2. *Marah in the Hebrew narrative*

Proceeding to quote the narratives of Marah in their chronological order, we find that in the Hebrew the central and most remarkable point is a peculiar phrase correctly rendered by the Vulgate "*docebat lignum*" indicating that Jehovah "*taught Moses a tree*." Our Revised Version translates it "shewed him a tree" as follows :—

Exod. xv. 25—6 (R. V.) "And he cried unto the Lord ; and the Lord *shewed him a tree*, and he cast it into the waters, and the waters were made sweet. There he made for them a statute and an ordinance, and there he proved them ; and he said, If thou wilt diligently hearken to the voice of the Lord thy God, and wilt do that which is right in his eyes, and wilt give ear to his commandments, and keep all his statutes, I will put none of the diseases upon thee which I have put upon the Egyptians: for I am the Lord that healeth thee."

(1) The Heb. rendered by R.V. "shewed him a tree" is a rare construction of the accus. of person and thing. The verb means "taught" much more frequently than "shewed[1]." The causative *horah*, "taught," corresponds to the noun *torah*, "teaching" (found in New Heb. also as *horiah*), which we commonly render "Law." Etheridge renders Onkelos' version of this phrase "instructed him [in the properties of] a tree."

(2) The verb also means "*cast*," and we shall find that Josephus, while omitting the fact that God "*shewed*" Moses

---

[1] Gesen. 435 *a* gives the double accus., with the verb in this sense, only in Exod. xv. 25, Ps. xlv. 5, Job vi. 24. Gesen. also indicates the frequency of its application to "the authoritative *direction* (v. תּוֹרָה) given by priests on matters of ceremonial observance." Comp. in New Heb. הוריה (Levy i. 460) "das Lehren...bes. in ritueller Beziehung.... Morija (Gen. xxii. 2) heisst deshalb dieser Berg weil von da die Belehrung (הוריה) für die Welt ausging."

A SPECIMEN OF RESEARCH

the tree, inserts the statement that something was *"cast at the feet* [of Moses]¹."

§ 3. *Marah according to Ben Sira*

It will be observed above that the miracle of Marah is connected with a mention of healing, "I am the Lord that *healeth* thee." "Healing" is also applied to water in 2 K. ii. 21—2 "I have *healed* these waters...the waters were *healed*," and also thrice in Ezekiel xlvii. 8—11.

Ben Sira alleges the miracle of Marah to illustrate the respect due to a physician or healer, xxxviii. 1 foll. "From God becometh wise (יחכם) *a healer* (רופא).... God bringeth out medicines from the earth.... *Was not water made sweet with a tree* (or, *with wood*) (בעץ) to cause every man to know *his power* (כחו) (marg. *their power,* כוחם)? And he gave men understanding, to glory (התפאר) in *his might* (marg. *their might*)...by them (בהם) doth the *healer* (רופא) assuage *pain* (LXX his pain, ἐν αὐτοῖς ἐθεράπευσεν κ. ἦρεν τὸν πόνον αὐτοῦ, where the sense requires the v.r. αὐτῶν, their pain)."

The Hebrew of Exod. xv. 25 made the "shewing" of the "tree" parallel to the "appointing" of a "statute," חק. Ben Sira is perhaps playing on the assonance of the words חק "statute," חכם "wise," כח "strength," when he speaks of men as becoming "wise (חכם)" and knowing "power" (where it may be noted that the marginal כוחם "their power," if written, as it legitimately might be, כחם, would easily—by a transposition paralleled below—become חכם "wise")². The Cambridge editors also (p. xliv. *n*.) call attention to a possible assonance in התפאר and רופא, the "*glorying*" of men in the "*healing*" of God.

---

¹ Trommius, under ירה, gives βάλλω (3), κατατοξεύω (4), ῥίπτω (the word used by Josephus, s. p. xxii) (1), προβάλλω (1), ἀκοντίζω (3), τοξεύω (8), etc.; meaning "teach," it is διδάσκω (7), νομοθετέω (7), etc.

² Comp. Prov. xx. 29 "their strength," כחם, LXX σοφία, *i.e.* חכמה; *ib.* xxxi. 5 "the law," מחקק, LXX σοφία.

§ 4. *Marah according to Philo*

Ben Sira above regards the healing of the waters in Marah as illustrating the physician's healing of πόνος or "*pain*," using the word in its recognised Greek medical sense, as applied to "pain" in the head, breast etc. implying disease. But the Greeks also use πόνος in a good sense to mean voluntary toil, as in the phrase οἱ γὰρ πόνοι ὄψον τοῖς ἀγαθοῖς, and in connection with γυμνάσια, "exercises[1]." We shall find that both Philo and Josephus use πόνος or πονέω in conjunction with the miracle, and in a good sense. There is no mention of "pain" in the Hebrew, or of πόνος in the LXX. It is perhaps not surprising that Josephus should have followed Philo in drawing this moral. But it is curious that Ben Sira should also have connected πόνος with this miracle— yet in quite a different way.

According to Philo, that kind of πόνος which is the enemy of careless ease is the first and greatest good, the beginning— appointed for men by God—of every good and virtue[2]. When Israel—journeying from Egypt, the region of the flesh—came to the bitter waters of Marah, then the road to virtue, which seemed steep and hard at first, was "made a highway[3]" by God, who "changed to sweetness the bitterness of πόνος." Associating himself with his people, "We had

---

[1] Xen. *Cyrop.* vii. 5. 80. Plato *Legg.* i. p. 646 C γυμνάσια καὶ πόνους. Steph. *Thes.* gives other instances of this connection.

[2] Philo i. 168 ἔστι δὲ ὁ ῥᾳστώνης ἐχθρὸς πόνος, πρῶτον καὶ μέγιστον ἀγαθόν, προσφερόμενος τὸν ἀκήρυκτον πρὸς ἡδονὴν πόλεμον. Ἀρχὴν γάρ, εἰ δεῖ τὸ ἀληθὲς εἰπεῖν, παντὸς ἀγαθοῦ καὶ ἀρετῆς πάσης ὁ θεὸς ἀνέδειξεν ἀνθρώποις πόνον, οὗ χωρὶς τῶν καλῶν παρὰ τῷ θνητῷ γένει συνιστάμενον οὐδὲν εὑρήσεις. Πόνος is as essential as food, comp. i. 169 δοκεῖ γάρ μοι πόνος τὴν αὐτὴν προσφέρεσθαι δύναμιν τροφῇ.

[3] Philo i. 255. Comp. Ps. lxxxiv. 5—6 "Blessed is the man whose strength is in thee; in whose heart are the highways [to Zion]. Passing through the valley of weeping they make it a place of springs; yea, the early rain covereth it with blessings." Instead of "early rain," LXX has ὁ νομοθετῶν, "lawgiver"; מורה means both.

become estranged," says Philo, "from πόνος, as being altogether bitter. We were purposing to return in haste to the licentious life of Egypt, had not the Saviour quickly taken pity and cast into our soul, as a sweetening influence, (Exod. xv. 25) 'a tree' that 'maketh sweet,' whereby He wrought in us *love of* πόνος (φιλοπονία) instead of *hate of* πόνος (μισοπονία). For He knew, as being Creator, that nothing that IS can ever be compassed without a constraining love of it[1]."

Elsewhere Philo tells us what it is that creates this "constraining love." Beginning with an obscure allusion to "*shewing*," he soon explains that he is thinking of the "tree" that was "*shewn*" to Moses : "Now that which is '*shewn*[2]' from time to time, that which is worthy to be seen and to be gazed on and to be passionately loved is the Perfect Good. This, too, can naturally change and 'sweeten' the 'bitternesses' of the soul.... For it is said that 'The Lord *shewed* him a tree and cast it into the water' [that is, into] the confused, fluid, and embittered mind.... Now this tree promises not only food but also immortality. For [the Scripture] says that in the midst of Paradise there grows the Tree of Life, namely, Goodness.... To Goodness has been allotted the midmost and noblest portion of the soul. And he that seeth is the Wise."

---

[1] Philo i. 255—6 σφοδρὸς ἔρως, lit. "a vehement and passionate love." I have ventured to render it "constraining love," in order to bring out a parallelism of thought between Philo and Christian writers, although Philo's words differ from those of 2 Cor. v. 14 "the love of Christ constraineth us," ἡ γὰρ ἀγάπη τοῦ Χριστοῦ συνέχει ἡμᾶς. Philo also calls this feeling φιλία, and σύντηξις πρὸς τὸ ποθούμενον. Comp. i. 542—3 (which includes the story of Marah) ψυχῆς δὲ ἑορτὴ ζῆλος, ὁ τῶν ἀρίστων... πόνος.... Toil, he says, is not enough, there must be *toil* with *sweetening*, λέγει γὰρ "ἐγλυκάνθη τὸ ὕδωρ." Ὁ γλυκὺς δὲ κ. ἡδὺς πόνος ἑτέρῳ ὀνόματι φιλοπονία καλεῖται. Τὸ γὰρ ἐν πόνῳ γλυκὺ ἔρως ἐστὶ κ. πόθος κ. ζῆλος κ. φιλία τοῦ καλοῦ.

[2] i. 441 τὸ μὲν οὖν δεικνύμενον, an allusion to the following ἔδειξεν. It means "what is '*daily shewn*' to us still by God in His present revelations as it was *shewn* to Moses (Exod. xv. 25) in days past."

This really, though not verbally, agrees with Origen, who says, "What then is that 'tree' (lignum *i.e.* ξύλον) which the Lord 'shewed' to Moses? Solomon teaches us, when he says of wisdom that it is (Prov. iii. 18) 'a *tree of life* to those that embrace it[1].'" The "wisdom" mentioned by Origen is not a merely intellectual wisdom. It means that moral or spiritual wisdom which begins in (Prov. ix. 10) "the fear of the Lord" and ends in His love. And Philo indicates this when he says "He that seeth," *i.e.* seeth *Goodness*, "is the *Wise*."

In the *Life of Moses* § 33, Philo treats the subject apart from allegory, and without quoting Scripture. There he says (ii. 110) that the tree was shewn to "the sleepless eye of the soul" of Moses. He leaves it an open question whether the tree "exercised a power that was perhaps not [then] known," or whether the tree was specially made for the occasion. The water, he adds, was "sweetened" and changed so as to become "drinkable[2]." Thus (as we shall see below) he

---

[1] Origen *Hom. Exod.* vii. 1 (Lomm. ix. 74). On the quotation from Proverbs see below, p. xxxv n. 1.

[2] Ὁ δὲ (*i.e.* θεὸς) τῇ ἵλεῳ αὐτοῦ δυνάμει φθάνει προεκπέμψας καὶ διοίξας τὸ τοῦ ἱκέτου ἀκοίμητον ὄμμα τῆς ψυχῆς ξύλον δείκνυσιν, ὃ προσέταξεν ἀράμενον εἰς τὰς πηγὰς καθεῖναι, τάχα μὲν καὶ κατεσκευασμένον *ἐκ φύσεως, ποιοῦν δύναμιν*, ἢ τάχα ἠγνοεῖτο, τάχα δὲ καὶ τότε πρῶτον ποιηθὲν εἰς ἣν ἔμελλεν ὑπηρετεῖν χρείαν. Γενομένου δὲ τοῦ κελευσθέντος, αἱ μὲν πηγαὶ γλυκαίνονται μεταβαλοῦσαι πρὸς τὸ πότιμον, ὡς μηδὲ εἰ τὴν ἀρχὴν ἐγένοντό ποτε πικραὶ δύνασθαι διαγνῶναι, διὰ τὸ μηδ' ἴχνος ἢ ζώπυρον τῆς ἀρχαίας κακίας εἰς μνήμην ὑπολελεῖφθαι.

The underlined phrase ἐκ φύσεως does not occur in Steph. *Thes.* nor in the Indices to Aristotle (Bonitz 835 *b*—9 *b*), Plato (Mitchell), Lucian and Epictetus. Φύσις in Aristotle probably occurs some thousands of times, and φύσει, or κατὰ φύσιν, to represent "naturally," probably some hundreds. Bonitz (838 *b*) gives ἀπὸ τῆς φύσεως...ἡ ἀπόκρισις γίνεται once, and (*ib.*) τὰ ὑπὸ φύσεως συνιστάμενα once : but nowhere ἐκ φύσεως. Even (836 *b*) after οὐκ ἐκ προαιρέσεως, where we might expect an antithetical ἀλλ' ἐκ φύσεως, Aristotle has ἀλλ' ἡ φύσις ἐποίησε : and after τὰ μὲν ἐκ σπέρματος, where we might expect τὰ δ' ἐκ φύσεως, he has τὰ δ' ὥσπερ αὐτοματιζούσης τῆς φύσεως.

In view of the various readings in Josephus (see below, p. xxi) one of

combines the epithet used by Scripture with another which Josephus[1] substitutes for the scriptural one.

Summing up Philo's allegorical view, we may say that the waters of Marah represent the turbid and impure mind imbued with the love of pleasure. The "tree" represents the Supreme Goodness, which, when "shewn" to "the wise," creates in him a passionate love of God and a devotion to His service. This destroys the love of selfish pleasure. Selfishness made toil bitter. The love of God now makes it sweet because the toil is for God's sake.

As to Philo's historical narrative, it leaves us in doubt whether the effect of the tree was miraculous or natural, but inclines to the latter supposition. And here we must note that Moses is apparently instructed to "*lift up* (ἀράμενον) the tree and let it down into the water." The middle, αἴρομαι, (non-occurrent or rare in LXX), when not used with a suggestion of metaphor, is mostly applied to lifting burdens[2]. At all events it is not used simply in the sense of λαμβάνω.

which substitutes "rod" for "tree," and in view of the Jewish legends that represent the rod as being framed "from the six days [of creation]," the question arises whether Philo may have been influenced by a Greek version of some Jewish tradition which might be rendered in Greek "framed *from nature*," but which might have meant, "framed *from the beginning of nature*."

It will be found that Josephus represents Moses as manipulating the tree by "dividing it in the middle lengthwise." This rather suggests that he may have read κατεσκευασμένον as κατασκευασάμενον (the middle being frequently used of architects, sculptors etc.) making it refer to "Moses." In that case, if Josephus borrowed from Philo here (as he certainly does on other occasions) he may have rendered ἐκ φύσεως as "from the starting point of its nature," *i.e.* availing himself of its natural properties.

[1] Josephus (it can hardly be doubted) borrowed from Philo. In addition to the use of πονέω above and the use of πότιμον here, see *Ant.* ii. 12. 1 (267) for his use of πολυπραγμονέω in connection with the bush in Horeb, in which he seems to follow Philo i. 570 μὴ πολυπραγμόνει.

[2] Comp. Steph. *Thes.* 1048—51 αἴρομαι ἱστία, κλιμάκων προσαμβάσεις, φορτίον, ἄχθος etc.

One way of explaining "*lifted up*" applied to a tree would be to say that it had been "blown down"; and, as has been stated above, Josephus describes, not indeed the tree but a "section," presumably of the tree, as " cast at the feet [of Moses]." Neither of the two Philonian passages mentions or alludes to the words " There he made for them a statute and an ordinance." In Scripture, they immediately follow the words " the waters were made sweet " as though they were an integral part of the narrative. But in the *Life of Moses* Philo passes on to (Exod. xv. 27) the palm trees of Elim and descants on the peculiarities of the palm as being " the best of trees " and as having its " living power " not in its roots but " mounting upward like the heart[1]." It almost looks as though he were making up for his silence about the unspecified " tree " of Marah by dilating on the virtues of the trees at Elim. In any case it is strange that in a historical narrative of the Life of Moses he should not only make no attempt to explain what " statute " was made at Marah but also omit all mention of the fact that any "statute " was made at all.

§ 5. *Marah according to Josephus*

In the narrative of which the full text is given below[2], Josephus appears at first sight to be merely working out one

---

[1] Philo ii. 111 φοίνικι τῷ τῶν δένδρων ἀρίστῳ παρεικασθέντες προσηκόντως, ὃ καὶ ὀφθῆναι, καὶ καρπὸν ἐνεγκεῖν ἐστι κάλλιστον, ὅπερ καὶ τὴν ζωτικὴν ἔχει δύναμιν, οὐκ ἐν ῥίζαις ὥσπερ καὶ τὰ ἄλλα κατορωρυγμένην, ἀλλ' ἀνώφυτον (but read ἀνώφοιτον), καρδίας τρόπον, ἐν τῷ μεσαιτάτῳ τῶν ἀκρεμόνων ἱδρυμένην, ὑφ' ὧν οἷα ἡγεμονὶς ὄντως ἐν κύκλῳ δορυφορεῖται. Τοιαύτην δ' ἔχει φύσιν καὶ ἡ διάνοια τῶν γευσαμένων ὁσιότητος. Ἄνω γὰρ μεμάθηκε βλέπειν τε καὶ φοιτᾶν, καὶ μετεωροπολοῦσα ἀεὶ καὶ τὰ θεῖα διερευνωμένη κάλλη χλεύην τίθεται τὰ ἐπίγεια, ταῦτα μὲν παιδιὰν ἐκεῖνα δὲ σπουδὴν ὡς ἀληθῶς νομίζουσα.

See Steph. *Thes.* and comp. ἀνώφοιτος in ii. 513, 612 (where it is again corrupted to ἀνώφυτος) and ii. 621. Steph. (which does not quote this last passage) regards ἀνώφυτος as non-occurrent except as a corruption of ἀνώφοιτος.

[2] *Ant.* iii. 1. 2 (ed. Niese) ἱκετεύειν οὖν τρέπεται τὸν θεὸν μεταβαλεῖν τὸ

A SPECIMEN OF RESEARCH

of the views suggested by Philo in his *Life of Moses*, where the latter speaks of Moses as being commanded to "lift up" the tree, and as possibly having utilised its natural power. But a closer examination shews that he has in view other traditions, and these inconsistent with one another. On the one hand he speaks of "*drawing off*," as though the water as a whole was not purified—but only a residuum, after the impure scum had been removed[1]. On the other hand he speaks of the water as "*purified by strokes.*" These two accounts, not being able to reconcile, he appears to have set down as he found them.

But the strangest feature of all in Josephus' narrative is that he substitutes "*the top of a segment*" for "tree." This it is perhaps impossible (with the evidence at present available) to explain with confidence in detail. But it may be almost assumed—from the extraordinary nature of the phrase itself without further evidence—that the historian did not invent "segment" but found it, and left it as he found it, obscure and possibly corrupt. And the assumption will be converted to something like a certainty if we can shew that other phrases

---

ὕδωρ ἐκ τῆς παρούσης κακίας καὶ πότιμον αὐτοῖς παρασχεῖν. καὶ κατανεύσαντος τοῦ θεοῦ τὴν χάριν λαβὼν τομάδος (vv.ll. ἀποτομάδος, ἀπὸ τομάδος, in marg. ῥάβδου, ἀποκεκομμένου ξύλου) τὸ ἄκρον ἐν ποσὶν ἐρριμμένης διαιρεῖ μέσην καὶ κατὰ τὸ μῆκος τὴν τομὴν ποιησάμενος, ἔπειτα μεθεὶς εἰς τὸ φρέαρ ἔπειθε τοὺς Ἑβραίους τὸν θεὸν ἐπήκοον αὐτοῦ τῶν εὐχῶν γεγονέναι καὶ ὑπεσχῆσθαι τὸ ὕδωρ αὐτοῖς παρέξειν οἷον ἐπιθυμοῦσιν, ἂν πρὸς τὰ ὑπ' αὐτοῦ κελευόμενα μὴ ὀκνηρῶς ἀλλὰ προθύμως ὑπουργῶσιν. ἐρομένων δ' αὐτῶν τί καὶ ποιούντων ἂν μεταβάλοι τὸ ὕδωρ ἐπὶ τὸ κρεῖττον, κελεύει τοὺς ἐν ἀκμῇ περιστάντας ἐξαντλεῖν λέγων τὸ ὑπολειπόμενον ἔσεσθαι πότιμον αὐτοῖς προεκκενωθέντος τοῦ πλείονος. καὶ οἱ μὲν ἐπόνουν, τὸ δ' ὑπὸ τῶν συνεχῶν πληγῶν γεγυμνασμένον καὶ κεκαθαρμένον ἤδη πότιμον ἦν.

[1] Later on, Josephus refers to the miracle in part of a single sentence thus (*Ant.* iv. 3. 2 (45)) "(lit.) O thou that didst prepare, so as to flow fit for drinking, fountains that were before corrupt (ὁ ποτίμους ἡμῖν διεφθαρμένας πηγὰς ῥεῦσαι παρασκευάσας)." Why does he say "prepare so as to *flow*" and not "prepare so as to *be*"? Does he mean that the waters were before stagnant or fed by a mere trickle, and that Moses introduced a new flood of pure running water while draining off the impure water?

in the context must be explained thus, that is to say, as ancient traditions misinterpreted. Many of the details in Josephus are so connected that the explanation of one depends on the explanation of its neighbour; but an attempt will be made to explain each in order and separately as far as possible.

§ 6. *Josephus on the "segment"*

After saying that Moses prayed to God to make the water drinkable, Josephus continues as follows "(lit.) And when God signified that He granted the favour (κατανεύσαντος τοῦ θεοῦ τὴν χάριν), he, having taken the top of a segment (τομάδος[1]) cast at [his] feet (ἐν ποσὶν ἐρριμμένης), divides (διαιρεῖ) [it], having made the section (τομήν) in the middle and along the length[2]."

In this literal rendering the word "segment" is intended to indicate the rarity of the corresponding Greek τομάς, which indeed is not recognised by the Thesaurus as a Greek word at all. Its non-occurrence (at present) in Greek literature is an argument for its being genuine here; for what editor or scribe would alter a text to insert a word either non-existent or of the rarest occurrence? But what does Josephus mean by it?

The first clue to the meaning must be looked for in the expression διαιρεῖν in connection with μέσος. The verb and the adjective occur together in the LXX of Gen. xv. 10 (*and*

---

[1] V.r. ἀπὸ τομάδος and ἀποτομάδος. Steph. *Thes.* does not give τομάς. He gives ἀποτομάς as an adj. applied to rocks in Diod. ii. 13, iv. 78. The noun he quotes only from Hesychius, Pollux, and the present passage in Josephus. Hesychius has ἀποτομάδα. σχίζαν. καὶ ἀκόντιον πεντάθλου.

[2] In διαιρεῖ μέσην καὶ κατὰ τὸ μῆκος τὴν τομὴν ποιησάμενος, there are v.r. μεσηι, μεση, and και om. If καί were omitted, διαιρεῖ μέσην would go together, as in Gen. xv. 10 διεῖλεν αὐτὰ μέσα—the only instance where διαιρεῖν with μέσος occurs in LXX. If καί is inserted, a very strong emphasis indeed is laid on μέσην by the pause necessary after διαιρεῖ. It should be represented by a comma after διαιρεῖ, but Niese does not insert one.

nowhere else in LXX) describing Abraham as "dividing in the midst" the sacrifices that he offered to God when God first (*ib.* 18) "made a covenant with Abraham." The Hebrew verb for "divide" (בתר) occurs there twice, but *nowhere else in O.T.* The corresponding noun occurs only there and in Jerem. xxxiv. 18—19. The LXX renders the verb accurately διαιρεῖν, but fails to render the noun. Aquila renders the noun in Jeremiah by διχοτομήματα (twice).

Rashi illustrates from Jeremiah xxxiv. 18—19 and says that the (Gen. xv. 17) "passing *between the pieces.*" indicates a message from the Shechinah in its highest form. The Jerusalem Targum (on Lev. xxvi. 42) speaks of "the covenant which I covenanted with Abraham *between the pieces*," and still more definitely (on Exod. xii. 40) "The number of 430 years [had passed away since] the Lord spake to Abraham, in the hour that He spake with him on the 15th of Nisan, *between the pieces*[1]." A derivative of בתר occurs in Cant. ii. 17 "the mountains of *Bether*, marg. *separation*," and on this the Targum says "God was mindful of the oath that He sware to Abraham, Isaac, and Jacob...and also of the offering that Abraham offered, namely Isaac his son, on Mount Moriah: and also aforetime he had offered his oblations there *and had divided them equally*[2]." Levy (i. 276) on "*pieces*," בתרים, says that the word is especially used in the phrase "*covenant between the pieces*" referring to the covenant in Genesis (xv. 17—18).

Greek as well as Hebrew influence might facilitate the diffusion of this thought of God's covenant with man as being "*between the divided pieces*"; for it harmonized with the Greek custom of using as *symbola, indentures,* or *tallies*, the two *pieces* of a coin, die, bone etc., by which friends, sending messages to each other, could attest the authority

---

[1] See Levy *Ch.* ii. 276 *a*.
[2] Comp. Gen. xv. 10 (Onkelos) "And he divided them *equally*" as a paraphr. of "divided them *in the midst*."

of the messenger bearing one of the two pieces that exactly "tallied" with the other[1].

Philo devotes more space perhaps to Gen. xv. 10 foll. than to any other text in the Bible[2] in order to shew the meaning of "dividing," διαιρεῖν, and then of dividing "in the middle," μέσος—as being the principle of Justice, the Law underlying all Creation. It is true that he would seem to deny the possibility that Moses could "divide in the middle": for he declares (i. 493) that "no human being can divide anything equally[3]." But he goes on to speak of the "equal division" of the ten commandments into "pentads"; and though he says that these (Exod. xxxii. 16) "were God's work" it is quite possible that he himself, in a different context, might describe Moses, under the influence of God's Spirit, as "dividing" that great section of the Law which contained the Ten Commandments "into equal parts."

This last suggestion—namely, that Josephus' τομάς, or "section," may mean a portion of the Law—may possibly explain why the historian, while giving so much space to the materialistic explanation of the drawing off and purifying of the waters, neither explains nor quotes the words (Exod. xv. 25) "There he made for them a statute and an ordinance." What "statute" and what "ordinance"? We shall presently find Jewish writers giving various answers to these questions. Josephus has perhaps incorporated in his text, not indeed an answer, but the suggestion of an answer, by implying that at Marah there was a renewal of the Covenant of the Pieces, first made when Abraham "divided" a sacrifice "in the middle." On that occasion it had been predicted (Gen. xv. 13—14) that the nation should be afflicted in a strange land

---

[1] See L. and S. on σύμβολα.
[2] See Philo i. 491 foll. Soon after beginning the discussion he implies that it must be a long one, Πολὺν δὲ καὶ ἀναγκαῖον λόγον ὄντα τὸν περὶ τῆς εἰς ἴσα τομῆς καὶ περὶ ἐναντιοτήτων, οὔτε παρήσομεν, οὔτε μηκυνοῦμεν, ἀλλ' ὡς ἔστιν ἐπιτεμόντες, ἀρκεσθησόμεθα μόνον τοῖς καιρίοις.
[3] For the paraphrase "equally," see p. xxiii, n. 2.

four hundred years "and afterward shall they come out."
Now at last Israel had "come out"; and Moses, in this
curious tradition, might be described as having repeated the
act of Abraham.

The circumstances, of course, are quite different. Abraham,
on the occasion referred to, provided his own sacrifice. Moses
provided none. The position of Moses is rather like that of
Abraham afterwards on Mount Moriah. There God "provided" the sacrifice and Abraham "lifted up his eyes" and
saw it. So at Marah, Moses was "made to see," or was
"taught," a "tree." According to Josephus, it was a "section"
which was "thrown down" at his feet. Did Josephus un-
intelligently follow some tradition indicating that the "division
of pieces" made when the exodus was predicted was repeated
when the exodus was fulfilled? That at all events would be
a very interesting and suggestive tradition.

According to this view the "tree" was the Law, not the
whole Law but a part of it, or an introduction to it. The
twofold division might imply the division of the Law into
what Philo calls two Pentads. To do God's will as expressed
in the Pieces of the Law was the sacrifice enjoined on Moses
corresponding to the sacrifice of the pieces of the animals
enjoined on Abraham.

If this suggestion—namely, of the written Law—underlay
the tradition adopted by Josephus, why does he not use some
recognised Greek word, for example τμῆμα or τόμος? Possibly
he (or the authority from whom he derived it) may have
thought that some form suggesting a "writing" was desirable.
Τμῆμα did not suggest this. Τόμος in those days, though
beginning to be used as a "tome" or "section" of a book,
was not yet perhaps recognised in that sense, and in classical
Greek it meant a "slice[1]." Τομάς—a form like Μονάς and

---

[1] See Steph. *Thes.* which quotes no earlier author than Diog. Laert.
for the meaning "volume." But it is used by LXX in Is. viii. 1,
Aq. κεφαλίδα, Sym. τεῦχος, [Theod.] διφθέρωμα, and in 1 Esdr. vi. 23 A

Δυάς, Monad and Dyad, both of which had theological associations—was better adapted to express the divine Principle of Division familiar to the readers of Plato and Philo.

Concerning the mention of "top" ("the top of a segment") and concerning the division "lengthwise," there is no evidence sufficient to establish satisfactory explanations, though possible sources of these details might be suggested[1]. But if it can be shewn that in the main features of his story Josephus is following tradition and not inventing, then a comparatively small amount of evidence will be needed to make it probable that he is doing the same in minor points. So far, the following conclusions are put forward as highly probable:—

(1) The notion that this τομάς was "thrown down" is derived from ירה "teach," taken as ירה "throw."

(2) The word τομάς refers to a tradition about "the Covenant between the Pieces."

(3) Διαιρεῖ μέσην...τὴν τομὴν ποιησάμενος refers also to "the Covenant between the Pieces" and probably to Philo's comment on it.

§ 7. *Josephus on the "drawing off" of water*

Both in the Bible and in Josephus the miracle of Marah is connected with a promise. In the former, however, Jehovah heals the water unconditionally, and then says to Israel, in effect (Exod. xv. 25—6) "If you will observe my statutes

---

(B τόπος) where parall. Ezr. vi. 2 has κεφαλίς. Comp. Jerem. xxxvi. 4 χαρτίον, Aq. κεφαλίδα, Sym. τόμον.

It would be of special interest if we could be sure that τόμος was a rendering for "roll" in Ps. xl. 6—8 (Field, E[1]. ἐν τόμῳ βιβλίου, "nescio an recte τόμος verterim") "mine ears hast thou opened...in the *roll* of the book it is written of me...thy law is within my heart"—where it is implied that the doing of this "law within the heart" is better than "sacrifice."

[1] See below, p. xxxvii, where it is shewn that in Rashi's comment on Exod. xv. 25, מקצה which in New Heb. (Levy iii. 227 a) means "some" might be taken as a form of קצה which is regularly rendered ἄκρον.

I will heal you, too." In the latter, Jehovah, or Moses speaking for Him, makes the healing of the water *conditional on cooperative action on the part of the Israelites*. Moses, he says, first let down into the well the above-named "section," which he had divided in the middle. Then "he tried to persuade (ἔπειθε) the Hebrews that God had listened to his prayers and had promised to give them as much water as they desired if they would unhesitatingly and zealously carry out his orders. Hereon they asked him what they could possibly do to change the water for the better. He then ordered those that were in their prime to take their stand round [the well][1] and to draw off (ἐξαντλεῖν) [water]. What remained, he said, would be drinkable for them when the greater portion had been first emptied out."

What part does Josephus suppose the "section" to have played in purifying the water? None at all in purifying the water at the surface, for that had to be "drawn off." Nor is there the slightest indication that the "section" sank to the bottom and purified the residuum of the water. The mysterious "casting down" of the "section," and its subsequent "letting down[2]" into the water, appear to have merely produced in Moses a conviction—like that produced in him by the sign of the burning bush on Horeb—that God would save Israel in spite of, or by means of, affliction and bitter toil and trial, in other words, πόνος. Having received this conviction, Moses proceeded to impart it to the circle in immediate attendance on him. Then they ἐπόνουν. Thus, though the conviction that the result would be achieved may have been produced by supernatural means, the result (according to Josephus) was achieved by natural means.

This is entirely different from the Biblical narrative. Nor is there anything like it in the two narratives of water-finding

---

[1] See below, p. xxxix. The meaning may be "those that stood round Moses in their prime," *i.e.* the strongest among his attendants.

[2] Μεθίημι in Josephus corresponds to καθίημι in Philo, s. p. xviii n. 2.

in Exodus and Numbers. But it is not altogether unlike the picture suggested by the above-quoted Song of the Well in Numbers xxi. 18 "The well which the princes digged, which the nobles of the people digged, with the sceptre and with their staves." It has already been stated that the Well-Song is connected by Onkelos with a mention of the Red Sea. Josephus may have connected it similarly. And he may have found a tradition that the nobles of the people, who at Beer, or Well, "digged with their staves" so as to *draw pure water* in several directions for the several tribes and families of Israel, cooperated with Moses at Marah in a different way by "*drawing off*" *impure water*, so as to make the rest fit for drinking. This is much more probable than that he should have invented a version that lowers the reader's estimate of the supernatural power of Moses without having any basis at all in Scripture or ancient tradition.

Before quitting the discussion of the "drawing off" of water at Marah, a word must be said about a possible parallel between a tradition of this kind and the "drawing" of water in the Fourth Gospel. The miracle at Marah might be called the "beginning of signs" wrought for Israel when it had first "begun" to be a nation of free men, having passed through the Red Sea[1]. The miracle at Cana is expressly called "the beginning of signs[2]" for the incipient Church of Christ. Both narratives, whatever may be their historical basis, appear to include a symbolical meaning[3].

---

[1] Comp. Justin Mart. *Tryph.* 86 Μωυσῆς...ἐν ἀρχῇ τοῦ λαοῦ διέτεμε τὴν θάλασσαν...καὶ ξύλον βαλὼν εἰς τὸ ἐν Μερρᾷ ὕδωρ, πικρὸν ὄν, γλυκὺ ἐποίησε.

[2] Jn ii. 11. On Exod. xviii. 9 "all the goodness," *Mechilta* gives a tradition that "the good" referred to the well or fountain that the Lord had given to Israel, which supplied wine both old and new: "Dixerunt illi, De fonte quem dedit nobis Deus, nos gustavimus saporem vini veteris, et saporem vini recentis, et saporem lactis, et saporem mellis, saporem omnium liquorum qui sunt in mundo."

[3] If there is any parallelism between Josephus and Jn ii. 6 foll. it would rather confirm Westcott's view (*Johan. Gram.* 2281—2) that the "drawing (ἀντλέω)," in the Gospel, was *from the well* and not from the "waterpots."

§ 8. *Josephus on "purification" by "strokes"*

We should have expected Josephus to continue his account of the "drawing off"—if he thought it worth while to enter into further detail—by describing the digging of the channels of exit. But he proceeds as follows, "And they for their part toiled away; but it [*i.e.* the water] being exercised (γεγυμνασμένον) and purified by the continuous strokes (πληγῶν) was now drinkable."

Nothing in the previous part of the narrative explains this sudden mention of "strokes." But light may be thrown on it by the fact that, in Hebrew, "water" is said to be "*healed*," when it is purified; and there is evidence to shew that Jewish tradition connected a commentary on the waters of Marah with a prophecy about "*healing* from *wounds*, or *strokes*."

Compare *Exod. Rab.* (on Exod. xxxvii. 1) "'He took it [*i.e.* Moses took the tree shewn to him] and cast it into

It would also seem that when Jesus commanded the servants first to "fill the waterpots" (which were not intended to hold drinking water) this corresponded to Josephus' "*drawing off.*" When this was done at Marah what was left was "drinkable water"; when it was done at Cana what was left in the well was to be "good wine," and this the attendants are subsequently commanded to "draw."

Compare Is. i. 22 "Thy silver is become dross, *thy wine mixed with water.*" This is followed by *ib.* i. 25 "I will thoroughly purge away thy dross and will take away all thy alloy [from thy silver]." The parallel in Isaiah would have been completed by "*I will also take away all thy water [from thy wine].*"

This "taking away of water," in a mystical sense, is perhaps the symbolical act contemplated in the Sign of Cana. The wine of the Gospel, "old" wine and "good" (Lk. v. 39, Jn ii. 10), prepared by the Logos from the beginning, was at the bottom of the well, covered by the "water" of the Law. The water was "drawn off" and placed in the "waterpots" (vessels containing the water used for legal purification). Then the Saviour gave the command "*Now* draw (ἀντλήσατε νῦν)," *i.e.* draw the wine from which the water had been removed.

If this view is correct, the νῦν in Jn ii. 8 means "*Now at last*" and is parallel in meaning to the ἤδη in Joseph. *Ant.* iii. 1. 2 ἤδη πότιμον ἦν.

the water, and the water became sweet.' That is the meaning of the words of Jeremiah (xxx. 17) (R.V.) 'And I will *heal* thee of thy *wounds*.'" The English version of the prophecy conceals the similarity of its language to that of Josephus about *strokes*; for the Hebrew word for "wounds" is מכה, "*stripe*" or "*stroke*," regularly rendered πληγή by LXX elsewhere and also here[1].

This at once opens up new possibilities for explaining Josephus' extraordinary statement. It may be one more instance of the manner in which he combines misunderstanding of Jewish metaphor and poetry with misuse of the LXX. The old Hebrew story of Marah connected the healing of the waters with the healing of the nation (Exod. xv. 26 "I am the Lord that *healeth* thee"). Hence it was also connected with such prophecies as that of Jeremiah, "I will *heal* thee from thy *strokes*," i.e. πληγῶν[2]. Josephus recognised no sort of "healing" of the nation, but only a "healing" of water such as he elsewhere finds assigned by the Bible to Elisha[3]. What, then, is he to do when he finds among the numerous traditions about Marah one that described Jehovah as "*healing from strokes* (πληγῶν)"? Having to make some kind of sense of it, he appears to have interpreted it as meaning that Jehovah, through the instrumentality of Moses, who acted with the cooperation of the strongest men of Israel, healed the water *from*, i.e. *as the result of, continuous strokes or blows*—whether with the aid of instruments made from

---

[1] Trommius gives πληγή=מכה 42 times.

[2] In Jerem. xxx. 17 the LXX by error has πληγῆς for πληγῶν.

[3] Comp. *Bell.* iv. 8. 3 ταύταις ταῖς εὐχαῖς πολλὰ προσχειρουργήσας ἐξ ἐπιστήμης ἔτρεψε τὴν πηγήν. Here Josephus indulges a rationalising propensity in two ways. First, he says that Elisha, besides praying, "added many other remedial acts." Secondly, instead of saying "he sweetened," or "changed," the stream, he uses an ambiguous phrase "*turned* it," which might conceivably mean "*turned its course*" (comp. *Iliad* xii. 24, 32). But he does not invent details. He previously mentions the bowl of salt mentioned in Scripture (2 K. ii. 20) and adds nothing more beyond his general assertion that there were "other remedial acts."

the "tree," or not, he does not say. Perhaps he thought that the scum was brought to the surface by flogging the water with rods and that it was then drawn off in troughs[1].

---

[1] In saying that Josephus recognised no sort of healing of the nation, or promise to heal the nation, one ought perhaps to point out suggestions of moral healing although the literal promise is only "to supply them with as much water as they wished," and although the historian himself so confuses matters that we cannot feel sure that he is aware of the latent suggestiveness of the words that he or his Greek secretary commits to paper.

For example, although neither ἐξαντλεῖν in itself, nor ἐπόνουν in itself, implies moral effort, yet, when taken together, the two words suggest the Greek phrase ἐξαντλεῖν πόνον, familiar to the Greek world through Euripides (*Cycl.* 10, and see L.S. for other instances of ἐξαντλεῖν and ἀντλεῖν meaning "draining to the dregs" in the sense of extreme suffering). Thus the whole narrative suggests a lesson in patience, as though God said to Moses and through him to Israel, "Durum, sed levius fit patientia," or "Sweet are the uses of adversity."

And this perhaps may explain the historian's extraordinary statement that the water was *exercised* (γεγυμνασμένον). Comp. Heb. xii. 11 "All chastening seemeth for the present to be not joyous but grievous: yet afterward it yieldeth the peaceable fruit of righteousness to them that are exercised (γεγυμνασμένοις) thereby." In Hebrews, the epithet is in place, applied to people suffering patiently; in Josephus, applied to water, it is not in place unless the intention is to suggest the sufferings of the people.

A somewhat similar remark applies to a sentence (*Ant.* iii. 1. 2) placed before the murmuring of the people, οὐ γὰρ καθαρὸς ἦν στρατὸς ἀλλὰ διέφθειρε τὸ κατ' ἐκείνους γενναῖον παίδων τε κ. γυναικῶν ὄχλος—where note that he uses concerning Israel the same word, "corrupted," that he uses later on (iv. 3. 2 (45)) to describe the "*corrupted* fountains (διεφθαρμένας πηγάς)" of Marah.

What induced Josephus thus to throw all the blame for the murmuring of Israel at Marah on the "corrupting" influence of women and children? Probably he was moved by a desire to avoid an unfavourable inference from Biblical tradition without greatly altering the tradition itself.

Josephus found a mention (Exod. xii. 37—8, comp. Numb. xi. 4) of "the mixed multitude," meaning, as the Targums explain it, and as the sense demands, not the "children"—who are mentioned separately—but "foreigners," those who were not "pure-blooded" Hebrews. Their presence made it impossible to say of the Hebrews what Thucydides (v. 8) said of a certain Athenian military expedition, ὅπερ ἐστράτευε καθαρὸν ἐξῆλθε. On the contrary, truth compelled Josephus to say of his own Hebrew στρατός that οὐκ ἦν καθαρός. But this was a damaging confession. Naturally he would desire to minimize it. Had he been an

After Josephus, the next Greek authority in chronological order would perhaps be Justin Martyr; but owing to Justin's ignorance of Hebrew and of Jewish tradition, his evidence would be of little value even if it were full. As a fact it is scanty and possibly corrupt[1]. So we pass to Jewish tradition.

§ 9. *The Targums*

The Targums on Exod. xv. 25—6 are translated as follows by Etheridge:—

(Onkelos) "And the Lord *instructed him* [*in the properties of*] a tree and he cast it into the waters, and the waters became sweet. There decreed He a statute and a judgment, and there He tried him. And He said, If...I am the Lord thy Healer."

(Jer. I) "And the Lord *shewed* (אחוי) him the bitter tree of Ardiphne and he wrote upon it the great and glorious Name, and cast it into the midst of the waters, and the waters were rendered sweet. And there did the Word of the Lord

---

allegorizer, he might have said that it indicated the temporarily degenerate, slavish, and impure condition of the recently enfranchised Israel. But allegory was not in Josephus' line. He therefore surrounds the word with a context that gives it quite a different meaning from that contemplated by the Hebrew "mixed multitude" or the corresponding Thucydidean phrase.

[1] *Tryph.* 86 "Moses with a rod was sent to redeem the people, and, with this in his hand, in the beginning of the nation [*i.e.* the national life], he cut the sea asunder. *By means of this he received the sight of water sent up gushing from the rock; and having cast a tree*, or *wood* (διὰ ταύτης ἀπὸ τῆς πέτρας ὕδωρ ἀναβλύσαν ἑώρα, καὶ ξύλον βαλὼν) into the water in Marah, [from] being bitter he made it sweet."

Here Justin places the Water from the Rock before the Water of Marah. This might be explained by a wish to mention the two acts performed by the rod, before mentioning that performed by the wood or tree. But he also apparently inserts in the miracle of the Rock a version of a detail belonging to the miracle of Marah, namely that God "shewed," or "taught," or "caused" Moses to "see," something.

Perhaps the text is corrupt and we ought to read ἀνέβλυσεν. ἑώρα καὶ ξύλον [ὃ] βαλὼν...ἐποίησεν. Had ἐρωέω been a prose word, we might have conjectured that ηρωει (= Hesych. ῥέω) had been corrupted to εωρα.

A SPECIMEN OF RESEARCH

appoint to him the ordinance of the Sabbath, and the statute of honouring father and mother, the judgments concerning wounds and bruises, and the punishments wherewith offenders are punished; and there He (Eth. he) tried [them] with the tenth trial, and said, If...I am the Lord thy Healer."

(Jer. II) "And the Word of the Lord *shewed* (חוי) him the tree of Ardiphne (Eth. Ardiphene) and he cast it into the midst of the waters, and the waters were made sweet. There the Word of the Lord *shewed* (חוי) unto him statutes and orders of judgment; and there He tried him with trials in the tenth trial....For I am the Lord who healeth thee by my Word."

The word גזר, used by Onkelos to represent "decreed," means in Hebrew "divide," "cut." It is twice rendered in LXX by διαιρέω[1] (the word employed above by Josephus to describe how Moses "*divided* the section [of wood] in the midst"). Onkelos adds nothing to the original.

Jer. II, which is probably earlier than Jer. I, adds nothing except the name "Ardiphne[2]," and an allusion to "the tenth trial[3]."

Jer. I, besides the additions of Jer. II, adds that the tree Ardiphne was bitter, and that Moses wrote upon it the Name of God. It defines, by instances, "statutes" and "judgments." It also adds "the ordinance of the Sabbath" (perhaps with a view to Exod. xvi. 22—3, where the Sabbath, though

---

[1] Trommius also gives the noun גזר as διαίρεσις (1), διχοτόμημα (1), and גזרה as ἄβατος (1), σύγκριμα (2), τὸ ἀπόλοιπον (6), ἀπόσπασμα (1), διάστημα (1).

[2] "Ardiphne," variously spelt—which is but one of many names given to the "tree" (see p. xxxv)—is said to be the same as the Gk ῥοδοδάφνη. Spelt "hirdophne," it is mentioned in the Talmud as a plant poisonous for beasts (Levy *Ch.* i. 61 *a*).

[3] Comp. *Aboth* v. 4—7 "With ten temptations was Abraham our father tempted.... [Ten plagues brought the Holy One...upon the Egyptians and ten by the Sea.] With ten temptations did our fathers tempt God in the wilderness (Numb. xiv. 22)...." The bracketed words are perhaps an interpolation. The Targumist regarded Israel as being tempted with ten temptations.

not yet mentioned as a legal enactment, is practically observed and referred to in the words, "This is that which the Lord hath spoken").

In Jer. I and Jer. II, the word "shewed" is represented by different voices of הוי which means (Levy *Ch.* i. 242 *b*) "*shew by voice or gesture*," e.g. "the children *made signs* with their fingers." This corresponds to the use of ירה in Prov. vi. 13 "*pointing out* with his fingers." This may explain a remarkable phrase in Josephus in connection with the "shewing" of the tree, "God having *signified assent to* (κατανεύσαντος) the favour, Moses took the extremity of the section *cast* at his feet." Κατανεύω, meaning "shew approval by signs," may be an attempt to render ירה, as applied to God. Josephus may have conflated this with ירה, "cast," which he applies to the tree.

It will be observed that Jer. II applies the same word, "shewed," both to the "tree" and to the "statutes."

§ 10. *Other Jewish Traditions*

In *Exodus Rabba*, a long comment on the tree shewn to Moses at Marah is given in connection with the instruction (Exod. xxxvii. 1) to make the Ark "with the tree, or wood, of Shittim," *i.e.* acacia. Yet no suggestion is offered that the tree "shewn" or "taught" to Moses was actually acacia.

The writer begins by quoting that text of Jeremiah from which, as we have seen above, Josephus appeared likely to have derived his erroneous notion of the healing of the water "from strokes (ὑπὸ πληγῶν)." It runs thus (Wünsche p. 336, on Exod. xxxvii. 1) "*Bezaleel made*. To be connected with Jerem. xxx. 17 'I will lay on thee a *bandage* (אֲרֻכָה) (Verband).'" Then the writer enunciates the law of healing by contraries: "Man wounds with steel and heals with a plaster (Pflaster), but God heals with that wherewith he wounds, even as it is said (Exod. xv. 23) 'They came to Marah and could not drink the water of Marah.' Why?

The water was 'bitter.' R. Levi said, 'The generation was *bitter* in its actions.' Then cried Moses to the Eternal and He taught him to know a tree (or, piece of wood) (er lehrte ihn ein Holz kennen) (Exod. xv. 25). What sort of a tree? Many say it was the olive tree, others say......He took it and threw it and threw it into the water and the water became sweet. That is what is meant by Jerem. xxx. 17 'And from thy *strokes* I will heal thee'......Similarly the Israelites sinned in Shittim (Numb. xxv. 1 'When Israël dwelt in Shittim') and with Shittim (acacia tree) Israel was healed, even as it is said 'Bezaleel made the Ark of the tree of Shittim.'"

Another tradition, from the *Mechilta*, assigns to Simeon ben Jochai (c. 150 A.D.) the assertion that the tree meant "something from the Law" and lays stress on the exact wording of Scripture: "'*The Lord shewed him a tree*' is not the expression used, but '*taught him [a tree]*.'" The writer mentions a great number of trees suggested by different authorities (some on grounds not stated but more or less conceivable); but he says that the general consent of the "Biblical expositors" or Haggadists was that the words meant "God shewed him [Moses] the words of the Law which are as it were likened to a tree, for it is said (Prov. iii. 18) 'She is a tree of life to them that take hold of her[1].'" There are other points of interest in the commentary of the Mechilta[2].

---

[1] This same passage is quoted by Origen *Exod. Hom.* vii. 1 (Lomm. ix. 74—5) in connection with Marah. But he argues that Marah is the bitterness of the letter of the Law and that the tree, or wood, is the Cross.

[2] The following is a transcript of the Latin version of *Mechilta* on Exod. xv. 25 taken from Ugolini's *Thesaurus Antiq. Sacr.* vol. xiv. p. 282. I give it in full (and with some apparent errors of punctuation) as the *Thesaurus* is not so accessible as Wünsche's translation of the *Exod. Rab.* above quoted.

"*Docuitque eum Dominus lignum*, etc.

"R. Jehosua dicit: Hoc est lignum salicis: R. Elieser Amodai dicit; Hoc est lignum oleae, quia nullum est tibi lignum, quod sit amarius ligno oleae. R. Jehosua ben Charcha dicit; hoc est lignum Hirdophne.

xxxvi   A SPECIMEN OF RESEARCH

The following tradition appears to interpret Marah as being (1) the bitterness of adversity, employed by God to try and prove Israel, (2) the bitterness of a rebellious spirit in Israel. It is in *Exod. Rab.* (on Exod. xxxii. 11, Wünsche pp. 302—3) which says that Moses, on first coming to Marah,

---

R. Simeon ben Jochai dicit; Aliquid ex lege monstravit ei; dictum est enim; *Docuitque eum Dominus lignum*: Et ostendit illi Dominus lignum; non dictum est, sed; *et docuit*; Dictum est enim Prov. iv. 4 *Et docebat me, atque dicebat*, etc. [Here it seems necessary to punctuate, *Et ostendit illi Dominus lignum* non dictum est, sed *Et docuit*, i.e. " *The Lord shewed* is not the expression used, but *The Lord taught.*"]

"R. Nathan dicit; Hoc est lignum cedri; et alii dicunt radicem ficus, et radicem malogranati. Expositores Biblici (דורשי רשומות) dicunt (אמרו) *Ostendit illi* (הראהו) verba legis, quae dominantur (?) (שנמשלו) in (?) (ל) ligno (עץ); Dictum est enim Prov. iii. 18 *Lignum vitae est his, qui apprehenderint eam*, etc.

"Raban Simeon ben Gamaliel dicit: veni et vide; quantum differant viae Dei S. B. a viis hominis; Homo dulci sanat amarum; at Deus S. B. sanat amarum amaro. Quomodo? Dedit corrumpens in corruptum, ut faceret illis miraculum; Huic simile tu dicis. *Et jussit Isaias, ut tollerent massam de ficis, etc. Isai. xxxviii.* 21. Atqui erat caro viva: sed quando imposuit illi palatham ficuum, statim foetuit. Quomodo? Dedit corrumpens in corruptum, ut in eo fieret miraculum. Huic simile dictum est 2 *Reg. ii.* 22 *Et exiit haustor aquarum.* Et dictum est *Numer. iv.* 22 *Tolle summam filiorum Gerson.* Ecce si aquae bonae sint, si projiciat in illas salem, statim foetent. Quomodo? Dedit corrumpens in corruptum, ut fieret in eo miraculum."

In par. 2 above, "dominantur in ligno" somewhat resembles the phrase βασιλεύειν ἀπὸ ξύλου, as to which Justin Martyr erroneously declared (*Tryph.* 73) that ἀπὸ ξύλου had been cancelled by the Jews from Ps. xcvi. 10. He said that it applied to Christ, who was to "reign from the tree, or wood, of the Cross." The *Mechilta* in Ugolini's version attributes "lordship in (ל) the tree" to "the words of the Law"; but the correct version is "which are as it were *likened to* the Law."

As regards "aliquid (דבר) ex lege monstravit ei (הראהו)," see Levy iv. 404, who shews that this form frequently means "give in outline" ("zeigen blos den Ort an," מראה מקום), in contrast with "give exactly" (קפידא).

The *Mechilta* adds, as "another tradition," concerning the casting into the water, that the Israelites prayed to God: "*Et projecit in aquas.* Alii dicunt, Israelitae obsecrabant et orabant coram Patre eorum qui est in coelis, et dicebant...."

said to himself, "Why are these bitter waters created?" God replied, "I will teach thee what to say. Say this: 'Make the bitter sweet.'" The writer continues, "And how do we know that God '*taught him*' so to say? It is written (Exod. xv. 25) *Jehovah taught him a tree*. It is not said '*made him see*' (ויראהו) but '*taught him*.' '*Taught him*' means neither more nor less than *instructed him*; comp. Prov. iv. 4 '*And he taught me*' and Exod. xxxv. 34 'And he hath put in his heart *that he may teach.*'" When God is on the point (Exod. xxxii. 11) of destroying Israel for being rebellious—*i.e.* embittered (מרה)—Moses reminds Him of His precept at Marah, as follows: "Hast thou not said to me in Marah, 'Pray and say, *Make the bitter sweet*'? Now therefore do thou make the bitterness of Israel sweet and heal it[1]."

§ 11. *Rashi on Marah*

Rashi's comment on "There made he a statute" is as follows, "In Marah He imparted to them *certain* (lit. *a section of* מקצת) *divisions* (פרשיות) of Torah, wherein they might *toil* (יתעסקו)[2]. Trommius gives קצה as τὸ ἄκρον (22 times) and בקצה as ἐν μέσῳ, so that there is some resemblance between these words and those above quoted from Josephus τομάδος τὸ ἄκρον διαιρεῖ μέσην followed by the mention of "*toiling*."

After giving the substance of what the Midrash says

---

[1] My friend Mr E. N. Adler, to whom I am indebted for the correction of Ugolini given above, sends me the following statement illustrative of Jewish thought concerning Marah: "R. Samuel quoted by the Maharil (Jacob Levi Molin) (died 1427) says he has seen in the Jerushalmi that after the Circumcision they pray over the cup of wine and say May the Lord of Heaven send healing of life and mercy to heal this child that needeth healing and heal him as were healed the Waters of Marah by the hands of Moses and the Waters of Jericho by the hands of Elisha..."

[2] Levy iii. 673 *b* gives עסק as meaning "busy oneself," mostly with the Law, but also with manual labour, such as kneading and baking bread. In Aramaic (Levy *Ch.* ii. 231) it signifies "toil" and is often used where Gk would use πονέω.

concerning Exod. xv. 26 "the diseases of Egypt" and "I am the Lord that healeth thee[1]," Rashi continues, "So says the Midrash. But according to the meaning of the words it runs, 'I, the Eternal, will heal thee; I teach thee Torah and commandments whereby thou mayest *free thyself from them* [*i.e.* from the diseases of Egypt]..."

Rashi appears to lay stress, as Josephus does, on the co-operation of Israel with Jehovah, and his remarks about the Midrash indicate differences of interpretation. Some of these have been given above. But it is probable that many current in the first and second centuries are now no longer extant.

§ 12. *Summary of details in Josephus*

So far, the following peculiarities in Josephus' narrative have been shewn to be explicable not as the historian's inventions but as his interpretations of tradition: (1) οὐ γὰρ καθαρὸς ἦν στρατός, a misinterpretation of the Biblical "mixed multitude[2]"; (2) κατανεύσαντος, possibly a conflation, arising from the various meanings of ירה "teach"; (3) ἐρριμμένης, certainly a misinterpretation of ירה (which means ῥίπτω as well as διδάσκω etc.); (4) διαιρεῖ μέσην...τὴν τομὴν ποιησάμενος, from a tradition comparing the Covenant at Marah with "the Covenant by the divided pieces" made with Abraham (Gen. xv. 10 διεῖλεν αὐτὰ μέσα); (5) ἂν...προθύμως ὑπουργῶσιν, from the Song of the Well which described the joint labour of the nobles in digging the well. One rendering of this includes a statement that they acted (Numb. xxi. 18 (marg.)) "by order of the lawgiver." If Josephus adopted that, it would correspond to his τὰ ὑπ' αὐτοῦ κελευόμενα; (6) ἐξαντλεῖν, a confused version of a

---

[1] "And even if the diseases were laid on thee, I will make them to be as if they had never existed (und wenn sie auch auferlegt wären, werde ich sie als gar nicht vorhanden gewesen machen) (הרי הוא כלא הושמה)."

[2] That it was a misinterpretation, not a correct interpretation from the standpoint of the writer of Exodus, is shewn above, p. xxxi n. 1.

tradition that the "nobles" drew off the water from the well by various channels to the different tribes and families of Israel; (7) ὑπὸ πληγῶν, a confused version of ἀπὸ πληγῶν in a passage of Jeremiah connected by Jewish tradition with the healing of the waters of Marah; (8) γεγυμνασμένον, a confused transference of the word "exercised" from Israel to the waters that typified Israel.

There remain unexplained the two expressions (9) κατὰ τὸ μῆκος τὴν τομὴν ποιησάμενος and (10) κελεύει τοὺς ἐν ἀκμῇ περιστάντας.

As to the former (9) no satisfactory explanation presents itself. But it may be worth noting that in Jerem. xxx. 17—shewn (p. xxxiv) to be connected by *Exod. Rab.* with the healing of the waters of Marah—the word translated by Wünsche "bandage" means literally "extension." Hence, when applied to the extension of the skin over a wound, it may mean "healing," and it is rendered by R.V. "health." But the literal meaning is "lengthening," and ארכה is rendered μῆκος once by LXX, while ארך is thus rendered 81 times. If Josephus misunderstood "*strokes*" in this verse of Jeremiah and took it literally, this suggests that he may also have misunderstood "*lengthening*" in the same literal way—supposing, as has been suggested above (p. xxxi), that the wood was made into troughs. This may have originated his extraordinary tradition in connection with "dividing" "*lengthwise*," κατὰ τὸ μῆκος.

As regards (10) τοὺς ἐν ἀκμῇ περιστάντας, Josephus probably uses τοὺς ἐν ἀκμῇ to mean what Hebrew would call the "chosen men (בחורים)" of Israel, such as are mentioned in 2 S. vi. 1 as assembling with David, to the number of 30,000, to bring the Ark to Jerusalem. These Josephus calls (*Ant.* vii. 4. 2 (78)) τοὺς ἐν ἀκμῇ τῆς ἡλικίας. A frequent rendering of this word in LXX is ἐκλεκτός "chosen" (14 times). The Targum on Is. xii. 3 "drawing water from the wells of salvation" has "deriving new doctrine from the *chosen ones* of the righteous." The Song of the Well says "nobles," and perhaps means a comparatively small number who might be regarded as "standing round" (comp. 1 S. iv. 15 (LXX), 2 S. xiii. 31) the Lawgiver who directs their operations. But Josephus may have considered that for the work at Marah a larger number (not "nobles" but "chosen men") would be necessary; and he seems to mean that they "stand round" the waters of Marah which they are attempting to "draw off."

As regards (11) the use of πονέω (οἱ μὲν ἐπόνουν) it has been shewn that it is in accordance not only with the Greek of Philo, but also with the Hebrew of Rashi, who uses it to express that "toil" (in the performance of commandments) which is implied in the words "If thou wilt diligently hear."

§ 13. *The Biblical "tree" still unexplained*

Concerning the above-mentioned details it may be confidently maintained that at all events several of them are borrowed by Josephus from tradition and not invented by him. But we are not much nearer than before to the answer to the question What historical fact is at the bottom of the tradition about the "tree"? We cannot tell what the author of the Hebrew narrative meant by the "tree." Nay, we cannot tell for certain what Josephus himself meant by his "segment" or "section" which stands in place of the "tree." We may feel sure that he derived it from a gloss, and even from a gloss connected with "the Covenant between the Pieces." But we do not know precisely what meaning Josephus himself assigned to his paraphrase of the gloss.

For example, a marginal reading in the text of Josephus substitutes for τομάδος the word ῥάβδου, and another substitutes ἀποκεκομμένου ξύλου. Did Josephus understand that God cut and cast down from a tree or from heaven a special "rod" as a pledge that He would grant the prayer of Moses? Or did he mean—what seems to have been the view of Ben Sira—

that God cut off a "splinter" of "wood," and that the wood and the water blended together medicinally so as to produce a sweet potion? Or did he mean by τομάς a "section" of the bark of some tree usable for writing, so that (as Targum Jer. I says) the Name of the Lord could be written on it? Or did he use τομάς for the LXX τόμος, a "roll," meaning that the τομάς actually contained the principal commandments of the Law?

And when the answer is given to these questions there remains the further question, What was the result of putting the τομάς in the water? Did it simply produce some result of the nature of an augury, confirming the conviction of Moses that his prayer would be granted? Or did it invisibly act upon the water preparing the way for the success of the efforts of Israel to drain off the impure surface?

So much for the difficulty of merely ascertaining what Josephus meant. But even if that could be settled, it would still remain doubtful what the writer of the Masoretic text meant—whether he meant "tree" or "piece of wood"; whether he meant "*taught* him" or "*shewed* him"; and, if "taught," whether we are to regard Moses as being taught the properties of a literal tree, or whether "tree" was, from the very beginning, a metaphor for the Law.

This last supposition is—it may be said at once—extremely improbable. Although some Rabbinical traditions identify the "tree" with the Law, there is no sufficient Scriptural basis for the hypothesis of an originally metaphorical use of the word. In the case of other words, "rock" for example, we might fairly argue for a metaphorical original. "Rock" is so frequently used for God, that "water from the rock" might very well be, from the first, a poetic phrase for "water from the hand of God." But there is no such evidence for the metaphorical use of "tree."

Moreover the great variety of interpretations of the word "tree," proving, as it does, the early difficulty presented by the word, proves also its genuineness. And the same argument applies to "taught." If there is any corruption, or reading of poetry as prose, it does not seem to be latent in these two words. "Taught him a tree" seems to be a genuine part of the earliest tradition.

But may there not be a corruption, or rather a misinterpretation, in the immediate context? We have seen reason for thinking that Josephus combined the prose story of Marah with the poetic Song of the Well. Such combinations may have occurred, centuries before Josephus, in which prose and poetry were intermingled in the legends of the water-finding in the desert. The result might be that a word meaning one thing in poetry but another in prose might be taken in its wrong meaning with a considerable alteration of the sense.

For example, in Exod. xv. 25 "*into* (אל) the waters," אל, which in prose must mean "*into*," might have meant, in poetry, "*God*[1]." In the same verse, the verb translated "*were made sweet*" would more naturally, and perhaps more correctly, be rendered "*were sweet*[2]." Thus read—as poetry—the original tradition would be to the effect that "*God* cast [forth][3] the waters" that were before hidden[4]

---

[1] In Ps. lxxxiv. 7 "*to* (אל) God," LXX has "*the God* of Gods," and comp. Dan. viii. 16 "Gabriel," *i.e.* "man of God," LXX Γαβριήλ...ὁ ἄνθρωπος ἐπί... (*Clue* 37).

[2] Gesen. 608 *b* gives מתק "be sweet," *i.e.* "taste sweet," in Prov. ix. 17, and "be pleasant" in Job xxi. 33, but "become sweet" only in the present passage. The word is rare.

[3] The verb is used of God in Ps. cxlvii. 17 "He casteth forth his ice like morsels." It would imply more of violence than the verb "send."

[4] "Hidden." Comp. Deut. xxxiii. 13 "for the deep that coucheth beneath," which Onkelos paraphrases as "the fountain springs and the depths which flow from the abysses of the earth beneath." Philo (i. 694) on the Song of the Well, describes the waters as metaphorically "hidden." Jer. I and Jer. II say on Numb. xxi. 20 that the well "*was hidden from them* when on the borders of Moab." But the Targ. uses "hidden" in a special sense. Comp. Jer. I on Numb. xx. 1 "And Miriam died there and was buried there. And as on account of the innocency of Miriam

A SPECIMEN OF RESEARCH

beneath the surface, and "*they were sweet,*" as compared with the bitter waters of Marah.

An objection to this new version of the story is that it is inferior to the old one in moral picturesqueness. It does not distinctly represent God as sweetening the bitter. He sends forth a flood of sweetness which may perhaps be taken as overwhelming and merging the bitterness in its greater volume. But the bitter water itself is not changed. Herein the new version would resemble that of Josephus, according to whom the bitter is not sweetened but "drawn off[1]." This

---

a well had been given, so when she died the well was hidden and the congregation had no water," and Jer. II on Numb. xxi. 1 "Miriam was dead on whose account the well had flowed but had [since] been hidden."

Why was the Water from the Rock that followed Israel associated by Jewish tradition with Miriam? Was it because the tomb of Miriam was conspicuously associated with Petra, the city called Rock, which is mentioned so often in the *Onomasticon*? Josephus (*Ant.* iv. 4. 6) says that Miriam was buried "above, or beyond (ὑπέρ), a certain *mountain* called Sin." Eusebius (*Onomast.* 269) says, "Kadesh Barnea the desert that stretches along by Rock (Petra), the city of Palestine, where Miriam *went up and died, and Moses, having doubted,* (read διστάσας for διαστάς) *strikes the Rock* and supplies water to the thirsty people: and there is shewn to this day *the tomb of Miriam on the spot.*" This connection between the tomb of Miriam on the Rock and the fountain of Moses from the Rock—attested by Eusebius—and the fact that the giving of the fountain closely followed the death of Miriam in Scripture seem sufficient to explain the inference that the water was given "for the merits of Miriam." If the Water from the rock were ever called "Water from the *height* (מרום)" we might suppose that the tradition was favoured by the similarity of this word with מרים "Miriam." But the phrase does not occur in Scripture.

Strabo (779) says "The so-called Rock"—where note καλουμένη, added as also in Joseph. *Ant.* xiv. 1. 4, etc. to distinguish the *place* Rock from the *thing* rock—"is situated on a spot (χωρίον) plain and level in itself but guarded all round by rock [and] abruptly precipitous outside while it abounds with springs inside...." Any traditions that associated such a place with the tomb of Miriam would naturally combine, in the mind of a Jew, two thoughts about the Rock of Israel as being (1) a place of defence, (2) the source of water and life for Israel in the Wilderness.

[1] See also *Aboth* v. 5 "Ten miracles were wrought for our fathers in Egypt; and ten by the sea," *i.e.* by the Red Sea, where Dr Taylor's note says that the *Mechilta* reckoned among the miracles "He gave them fresh

inferiority, so far as concerns the purpose of pointing a moral with a metaphor, must be admitted. But in other respects there is a gain for those who would like to believe that there is a historical and not a merely metaphorical basis for the narrative. For thus this story of water-sweetening would be brought more nearly into line with the two stories of water-finding recorded in Exodus and Numbers and with the Song of the Well.

If space allowed, there ought now to be placed before the reader the results of an investigation of these three stories, with the object of ascertaining what was the original meaning of the mysterious phrase about the "tree." But the details are too lengthy to find a place in this Introduction. Perhaps there may be an opportunity for inserting them in a separate reprint of this research. Meantime the following is presented as a summary of the results of the whole investigation.

§ 14. *Outline of an explanation*

1. Attention was called in § 7 to the Song of the Well as illustrating Josephus' account of the "drawing off" of the waters of Marah, and, at the close of § 13, to "the two stories of water-finding" in Exodus and Numbers.

It must now be added that in the water-finding of Exodus there appears to lie the solution of the greater part of the problem before us. Compare Exod. xvii. 6 "Behold, I [am] standing[1] before thee there upon the rock in Horeb, and thou shalt smite in, or with (בְּ), the rock, and there shall come water out of it."

---

water *out of the midst of salt*," apparently not implying that the salt water was changed. These legends about miracles by the Red Sea harmonize with Onkelos' interpretation of Numb. xxi. 14 (see p. xi).

[1] LXX ἕστηκα, Heb. עֹמֵד, lit. "standing," R.V. "will stand," Onk. קָאֵם, which Walton renders "stabo," Jer. קָאִים, which Walton renders "sto."

2. No rock has been mentioned in the context, and it is left uncertain whether "the rock" means "the rocky ground," or a particular rock supposed to be defined as "the rock" where some definite event has come to pass[1].

3. Rashi and Levy call attention to the remarkable construction "smite *in*, or *with*, the rock." If the preposition means "in," there is no instance in the Bible precisely like this phrase[2]. Rashi even follows the Jerusalem Targum, which takes the preposition as meaning "*with*." To make consistent sense, the Targum goes on to take "rock" as meaning "stone." Thus is obtained the meaning "smite with the stone [of thy rod]," following a tradition that represented the rod of Moses as being made of sapphire. See Levy *Ch.* i. 310 "du sollst daran schlagen mit dem Steine deines Stockes—nach der Sage dass der Stab Mosis von Edelstein war."

4. "Horeb" has not occurred before in the Bible except in Exod. iii. 1 "And he led the flock to the back of the wilderness, and came to the mountain of God, *unto Horeb*."

5. The fact that Moses led his flock to pasture in Horeb implies that he expected to find water there, and accordingly Josephus describes it (*Ant.* ii. 12. 1) as "excellent for pasture," and Philo (ii. 91) as "well watered." Onkelos also calls it "the place of the best pastures in the wilderness." Josephus adds (*Ant.* ii. 12. 3) that Moses "took *some of the water that was near him* and poured it on the ground."

6. When God is described as saying to Moses "I [am]

---

[1] Comp. Mk iv. 5, 16, and parallels in Mt. and Lk. for "the rocky [ground]," "the rocky [places]," "the rock," as parallel expressions. Targ. Jer. has "Behold I stand (Eth. will stand) before thee there on the spot where thou shalt see (Eth., wrongly, sawest) the impress of the foot on Horeb."

[2] The nearest approach given in Gesen. Oxf. 645 *b* is 1 S. ii. 14 "Give a thrust *into* a pot." Could the meaning be "thrust and probe in the rocky ground"? If so, is the rocky ground, or rock, regarded as a receptacle of water, like one of the "cup-oases" described below?

standing before thee there upon the rock in Horeb," Moses is not said to be in Horeb, but at a place called (Exod. xvii. 1) Rephidim, afterwards called (*ib.* 7) Massah or Meribah. It is nowhere stated that Rephidim is in Horeb or Horeb in Rephidim[1].

7. Philo explains "before thee there upon the rock" as expressing the ubiquitousness of God; so does the *Mechilta* ad loc., "In omni loco in quo invenies vestigium pedis humani, ego sto coram te[2]." But it may be explained by Deut. xxxiii. 16 "him that dwelleth[3] in the bush," as being a title of the God worshipped by Moses under the name of Jehovah, after He had revealed Himself through the fire in the bush in Horeb. According to this view, "He that standeth on the rock in Horeb" would express another aspect of the revelation that might be expressed by the words "Him that dwelleth in the bush in Horeb."

8. The words "Him that dwelleth in the bush" come at the end of the Blessing of Joseph, which begins thus, "Blessed of the Lord be his land; for the precious things of heaven, for the dew, and *for the deep that coucheth beneath*...." These last words are paraphrased by Onkelos and Jer. I severally as follows, (1) "*from the fountain springs and the*

---

[1] Hastings' *Dict. Bib.* ("Rephidim") after quoting Exod. xvii. 6 as R.V. "I will stand" and Exod. xviii. 5, says "The difficulty of harmonizing these statements with those introduced with reference to the situation of Rephidim is apparent."

[2] It may be added that Philo—who appears (like Josephus) never to use the name "Horeb"—on one occasion (i. 687) reads ἐγχωρεῖν (so Mangey) for ἐν Χωρήβ. As regards "pedis humani" in *Mechilta*, see p. xlv, n. 1 for a different version in Targ. Jer. on Exod. xvii. 6.

[3] This form of the participle (שֹׁכְנִי) occurs only in Deut. xxxiii. 16, Jerem. xlix. 16, Ob. 3, Mic. vii. 14. In the last three instances R.V. has the present tense. The present of the same verb is also used to describe Jehovah as "dwelling in the height" or in "eternity" or in "the high and holy place," Is. xxxiii. 5, lvii. 15. In Deut. xxxiii. 16 R.V. has "him that *dwelt* in the bush." But it seems better to translate here as elsewhere by the present.

depths which flow from the abysses of the earth beneath," (2) "*from the bounty of the founts of the deep which rise up and flow to water the herbage from beneath.*"

9. The "deep that coucheth beneath" is thus divided by Onkelos into two classes of water supply, (1) "fountain springs," (2) "the depths which flow from the abysses of the earth beneath." The former might well include what has been called in a recent work[1] a "cup-oasis." The water oozing up from below, invisibly sustains the life of a tree which, if the fountain were cut off, would speedily perish in the burning sun. Thus, concerning the date palm, the mainstay of life in the desert, the Arabs have a proverb that it flourishes best when it has "*its feet in water and its head in fire*[2]."

---

[1] "*In the Desert*," by L. March Phillips (Arnold, London, 1905), p. 164.
[2] *Ib.* p. 166. The following extract gives an account of another kind of water supply in the Desert (p. 128) " Though, when in the midst of the desert and surrounded by blinding white sand-dunes, the very idea of water seems absurd, and its existence impossibly remote, yet it is often present at a distance of only a few yards underfoot.

This secret reservoir—so tantalisingly close, so difficult of attainment —of what in the desert are veritably the waters of life, is a phenomenon which has always haunted the Arab imagination, and has expressed itself in all kinds of legends and quaint theories and explanations. One tradition relates, what was no doubt the case, that the earliest oases grew round springs of naturally flowing water. These in time became gradually exhausted, and on this happening the Marabouts, or priests, confronted with a danger that menaced the existence of the tribes, united in offering up solemn prayers to the Almighty for guidance. It was in answer to these prayers that the existence of the underground supply of water was revealed, and the idea of tapping it by boring wells was suggested as a direct inspiration from heaven. Further south the tradition varies somewhat. It is there believed that a servant of the Prophet, having been inhospitably received by the people of the Rir, invoked a curse upon them, which sealed up the natural springs of their oases. In consequence of this ten of the most aged and venerable of the priests were chosen to go on a pilgrimage to Mecca to expiate the sin of the whole country. Their piety was rewarded. The springs were set going, and, in addition, the knowledge of the hidden water and the means of

10. Some have attempted to explain the fire of the burning bush by the phenomena of electricity. But such phenomena, whether of the nature of lightning or otherwise, do not, for this purpose, commend themselves theologically or scientifically so well as the explanation suggested by the Arabian Proverb. The latter harmonizes with the doctrine in the Parable of the Sower. If there is not what Mark and Matthew call a "root," but Luke calls "moisture," there is no abiding life for the plant when the sun beats on it. But if there is this supply of invisible life below, then the burning sun strengthens and develops what it would otherwise have destroyed[1].

11. Most commentators—however they might differ as to the material basis of the lesson—would agree that the revelation of Jehovah in Horeb was such a one as might teach a shepherd in exile that the fire of God's trial does not consume but strengthens men and nations that have in themselves that spring of life which comes from a trust in Him as the One Eternal Righteousness. Writing about the Bush, Philo says very much what Horace says about Rome ("ab ipso ducit opes animumque ferro"). Only Philo recognises this truth, not about one favoured nation alone, but about all nations (presumably righteous) unrighteously oppressed. The

---

reaching it was revealed. In both cases, it will be seen, the art of well-sinking is supposed to have had its origin in a suggestion from heaven."

How slight an effort may sometimes draw forth water from unexpected places appears from a story of the origin of what was called the Well of the Dog (pp. 140—1).

"There returned from Mecca a pious Marabout, on foot and followed by his dog, and finding no tent to shelter or person to succour him, he laid himself down exhausted and dying of thirst on the parched ground. His dog thereupon, seeing his master on the point of death, and guided by a divine instinct, set to work to scratch in the sand, and by and by a clear spring of water gushed out, and the pilgrim was quickly restored."

[1] Comp. Jerem. xvii. 5—8 which likens the man that "trusteth in man" to the heath in the desert and to one that "inhabiteth parched places in the wilderness," whereas the man that "trusteth in the Lord" is like "a tree planted by the waters."

fire itself, he says, *becomes "food"* for the branches that it is apparently attempting to burn[1]. This then appears to be the Lesson of the Tree in Horeb.

12. We can hardly exaggerate the influence that must have been exerted on the newly enfranchised Israelites by their dependence for their daily supply of water on the God revealed to their Lawgiver Moses. They came from Egypt, where each man (Deut. xi. 10) "watered" with his "foot," into a land that was no land but a desert, where water was felt in a peculiar way to be the source of life[2]. To be able to find water might well seem almost a religious power. The Bible says in one place that Moses is bidden to "speak to the rock," and in another that all Israel sings together "Spring up, O well[3]." These statements appear easily credible in view of life in the desert passed by a nation beginning to be a nation[4], under

---

[1] Philo ii. 91 "not being itself fuel for fire but using the fire for food (τροφῇ χρώμενος τῷ πυρί)." The same context says "Being encompassed wholly from root to top in a great *blaze, as though from some* [*mysterious*] *fountain oozing upward*, it [*i.e.* the bush] remained unharmed and unburned." Understand by "*blaze*" the blaze of sunlight, and leave out "*as though*," and then this sentence may express the scientific fact.

[2] See above, p. xlvii n. 2.

[3] Numb. xx. 8, xxi. 17. On the religious character of well-finding in the desert, see p. xlvii n. 2. As to the rejoicing for the opening of a well, see *In the Desert*, p. 137 "The night is passed in dancing and festivity. A goat is sacrificed at the mouth of the well. The Sheyks and Marabouts of Tamerna, and the leading men of the neighbouring villages, gather round it to recite their prayers. The musicians of Tuggurt and Temacin range themselves in the midst. The young girls surround them dancing. The men, according to their wont, fire their guns in the air. All the inhabitants give themselves up to a manifestation of triumph and delight, such as only those, perhaps, who are acquainted by experience with what the word water means in the desert can understand."

[4] "Beginning to be a nation." May we not add "and, later on, resuming its national existence when the mixed multitude of returning exiles passed across the Syrian desert from Babylon to Jerusalem"? Comp. Is. xxxv. 6 "Then shall the lame man leap as an hart, and the tongue of the dumb shall sing : for in the wilderness shall waters break out, and streams in the desert." Commenting on these words, Ibn Ezra implies that "the dumb" are

a lawgiver whose experience in pasturing his flocks on Horeb may have given him not only a knowledge of actual water supplies but also a faculty of finding others—a faculty that some would call miraculous and others a gift of God through nature. Many, more competent than the author to give an opinion on the subject, believe that this faculty still exists.

13. According to this view, the words in Exod. xvii. 6 "Behold I am standing before thee there upon the rock in Horeb," come to Moses not as a statement of locality but as an encouragement based upon the original revelation: "I am, as of old, still standing there upon the rock in Horeb, making the tree burn yet live through the spring of life below." In that case there is an implied connection between the vision of Horeb and the gift of water. This makes the mention of Horeb appropriate. Without some such link it seems inappropriate.

14. It would follow that whenever Moses found water for Israel during their wanderings in the wilderness, he might be said to do it "in the presence of Him that standeth on the rock in Horeb." Then, for brevity, he might be said to do it "in presence of the rock." And then, "rock" being personified, it might be said that the Rock, like the pillar of fire, followed Israel in all its wanderings. And Paul, accepting this, would explain it by saying "the Rock was Christ."

15. This legend of the Following Rock might be fully illustrated by comparing the Song of the Well and the

---

those who cannot speak because the tongue cleaves to the roof of the mouth through thirst. The gift of water makes them "sing" for joy. This is not to be wholly rejected as the comment of a pedant reducing poetry to prose. The miseries of the parched mothers and little ones of returning Israel may well have inspired a contemporary prophet to sing of God's kindness to the afflicted, and may also have influenced in no slight degree the historians of Israel in their task of revising and supplementing the Books of the Law when they realised from recent experience their debt to the Rock of Israel for the waters of life.

context in the versions of R.V., Onkelos, Jer. I and Jer. II.
Space can be found here for no more than the following
extracts :—

Numb. xxi. 18—19

R.V.	Onkelos
"And from the wilderness [they journeyed] to *Mattanah* : and from *Mattanah* to *Nahaliel*"	"In the wilderness *was it* [*i.e.* the Well] *given to them*; and from [*the time*] *that it was given to them* it descended with them to *the rivers*"

There is no "they journeyed" in the original. Neither Mattanah nor Nahaliel is mentioned in the list of the Stations of Israel in Numb. xxxiii. 1—49. The omission is in favour of the view that there were no such places. No one in modern times claims to have identified them. According to Onkelos "to Mattanah" is an error for "it was given." This view has recently been revived. If it is true, then the name "Mattanah" is an instance of the development of quasi-history out of poetry[1].

16. Returning from these remarks about the lesson of Horeb to the problematic phrase in the story of Marah (Exod. xv. 25) "And the Lord taught him a tree," we are led to this as the most probable conclusion, that on the first occasion when the nation appealed to their leader for water, Moses received anew the revelation of Horeb, or a divine message reminding him of it.

17. Regarded morally and spiritually, this repetition would have an obvious fitness. The vision in Horeb shewed God to Moses as symbolically "proving" a nation. The vision at Marah shewed God to him as actually "proving" a nation (Exod. xv. 25) "there he proved them."

18. But even when it is admitted that the words "the Lord taught him a tree" may mean "the Lord taught him

---

[1] As to Nahaliel, comp. *Mechilta* on Exod. xv. 17 "Lex vocatur haereditas ; dictum est enim Num. xxi. 19 *Et e Mattanah Nahaleel*," taking " Nahaleel." as " haereditas."

the lesson of a tree such as He had taught before in Horeb," it appears difficult, if not impossible, to interpret, consistently with this view, the following Hebrew words, as long as אל is rendered "into," "and he cast [it] into the waters[1]."

19. There remains the suggestion above-mentioned (p. xlii) that the text contains an obscure combination of prose with poetry, so that the poetic אל "God" has been misunderstood as "into" ("*into* the waters"). Restoring the former, we should interpret the narrative as meaning that at Marah God repeated for Moses the teaching of the tree at Horeb. This indicated not only a moral lesson but also the material fact that water was close beneath the surface, or, in other words, that God was ready to give it if man would take it. "*And he cried unto the Lord; and the Lord taught the lesson of a tree, and God cast forth waters, and the waters were sweet*[2]."

---

[1] In *Itinera Hierosolymitana* (Geyer p. 183) Antoninus Placentius (c. 570 A.D.) says that while his companions were on the way to Horeb (ch. 36) the water in their water-skins grew as bitter as gall, and "mittebamus in ea harenam et indulcabatur." Castell (סנה rubus) has the following extraordinary statement "(סיני) Sinai mons, *Ruborum plenus, in quo lapides inveniuntur, quorum si frangantur partes habent imaginem Rubi, More,* I. c. 66. *Ephodeus, qui hoc se vidisse scribit.*" Have these two stories any connection with each other, implying that the smallest particles of Mount Sinai had in them the image of the miraculous "bush," סנה, from which Mount Sinai, סיני, was supposed to derive its name? Or can the statement of Placentius be ascertained to be in accordance with facts? Concerning the tradition that the rod of Moses was made of stone, s. above, p. xlv. For a legend that Moses caused the coffin of Joseph to emerge from the Nile by throwing a stone (? his rod) into the water, see *Mechilta* on Exod. xiii. 19.

[2] Although this appears the most probable explanation it may be worth while to note some peculiarities in Josephus' account of the "bush" in Horeb, which indicate that it may have had, or may have been believed to have had, sweetening properties in its fruit. He does not call it βάτος but (*Ant.* ii. 12. 1) θάμνος βάτων, and on another occasion (*Ant.* iii. 2. 5) θάμνος. In the first passage he says (lit.) "The fire(?) of the bush of bramble-berries (or, of brambles) while feeding on the foliage round it, passed by its blossom, and destroyed none of the fruit-laden branches

A SPECIMEN OF RESEARCH

(πῦρ γὰρ θάμνου βάτων, νεμόμενον τὴν περὶ αὐτὸν χλόην, τό τε ἄνθος αὐτοῦ παρῆλθεν ἀβλαβές, καὶ τῶν ἐγκάρπων κλάδων οὐδὲν ἠφάνισε)." This suggests that he may have taken βάτων as the pl. of βάτον, "a berry." Βάτος in LXX (apart from Job xxxi. 40 "noisome weeds") never occurs except as a rendering of סְנֶה, Exod. iii. 2—4, Deut. xxxiii. 16. Hastings' *Dict.* ("Bush") says "The translation, βάτος, in the LXX, gives the opinion of the scholars of that time in favour of the *bramble* (*Rubus*, blackberry)" but proceeds to say "*Rubus* has not been found wild in Sinai, which is south of its range, and climatically unsuited to it." The only instance of βάτον given by L.S. is from Diod. Sic. i. 34 "what are called βάτα (τὰ δὲ βάτα καλούμενα)" "are gathered at the subsidence of the river [Nile] and on account of their natural lusciousness are consumed as sweetmeats (διὰ δὲ τὴν γλυκύτητα τῆς φύσεως αὐτῶν ἐν τραγήματος μέρει καταναλίσκεται)."

It would appear from *Enc. Bibl.* and Hastings that no one professes to know with certainty what the Heb. סְנֶה, Gk βάτος, really was; and the latter states the facts fairly when it says that "bramble" merely "gives the opinion of the scholars of that time."

Hence we may fairly ask whether these scholars—being in Egypt, and being presumably familiar with the extremely sweet βάτον that grew near the waters of the Nile—might not be influenced by their Egyptian associations when they came to interpret a passage mentioning a divinely indicated "tree," and "casting," and "sweetening of waters." If so, might they not be induced by prepossession to render אֵל "*God*" as אֶל "*into*," thus turning "*God* cast forth the waters" into "cast *into* the waters," suiting the meaning to their Egyptian experiences? Jewish interpretation might follow so early and authoritative an error.

In modern times it has been proposed to read Deut. xxxiii. 16 "He that dwelleth in *Senah* i.e. Bush," as "He that dwelleth in *Sinai*." In the following extracts from Josephus and Clement of Alexandria there appears at all events a curious parallelism between what Josephus says about the lambent fire on the Bush and what Clement says about the lambent fire on Sinai.

(1) Joseph. *Ant.* ii. 12. 1 πῦρ γὰρ θάμνου (v.r. θάμνον) βάτων (v.r. βάτον) νεμόμενον τὴν περὶ αὐτὸν (v.r. αὐτὸ) χλόην τό τε ἄνθος αὐτοῦ παρῆλθεν ἀβλαβὲς καὶ τῶν ἐγκάρπων κλάδων (v.r. δένδρων) οὐδὲν ἠφάνισε.

(2) Clem. Alex. 755 τῇ θείᾳ ἐπιφανείᾳ περὶ τὸ ὄρος τὸ Σινᾶ, ὁπήνικα πῦρ μὲν ἐφλέγετο [comp. *ib.* 215 ἐπὶ φλεγομένῃ βάτῳ] μηδὲν καταναλίσκον τῶν φυομένων κατὰ τὸ ὄρος.

It looks as though Clement followed some tradition like that of Josephus, only (1) with a comma after νεμόμενον, (2) rendering νεμόμενον "spreading" (not "devouring"), (3) taking *Senah* as *Sinai*. According to this view Josephus meant "A fire on Sinai, spreading, left unharmed all the herbage, flower, and fruit," and the last words may have been paraphrased by Clement as "all that grew on the mountain."

20. The course of this investigation has led us to digress—for the purpose of illustration—from the Waters of Marah to the Fire in the Bush[1]. But the results of the

> Josephus himself seems to see some sort of parallelism between the "fire" round the Bush, and the lightnings on Sinai. He associates both with "graciousness." Comp. *Ant.* ii. 12. 4 (about the Bush) ἐξ ὧν ἀπάντων πλέον περὶ τῆς ἀληθείας τῷ πυρὶ νέμων, καὶ τὸν θεὸν <u>εὐμενῆ</u> παραστάτην ἕξειν πιστεύων with *ib.* iii. 5. 2 (about Sinai) ἄνεμοί τε σφοδροὶ λάβρον κινοῦντες ὑετὸν κατήγιζον, ἀστραπαί τε ἦσαν φοβεραὶ τοῖς ὁρῶσι, καὶ κεραυνοὶ κατενεχθέντες ἐδήλουν τὴν παρουσίαν τοῦ θεοῦ οἷς Μωυσῆς ἔχαιρεν <u>εὐμενοῦς</u> παρατυχόντος.

In this last passage the connection of violent "*rain,*" first with the giving of the Law at "*Sinai,*" and then with "*graciousness,*" may be illustrated (1) by Judg. v. 4 " Lord, when thou wentest forth out of Seir, when thou marchedst forth out of the field of Edom...the heavens also dropped, yea, the clouds dropped water, the mountains flowed down [in cataracts] (Gesen. 633 *b*) at the presence of the Lord, even yon *Sinai*, at the presence of the Lord," and (2) by Ps. lxviii. 7—9 " When thou didst march through the wilderness...the heavens also dropped at the presence of God, even yon Sinai...thou, O God, didst send a *gracious* rain, thou didst confirm thine inheritance when it was weary." Comp. *Mechilta* (on Exod. xx. 2—3) "Tribus rebus data est lex, sc. in deserto, igne, et aquis," and *ib.* (on Exod. xx. 18) quoting Judg. v. 4, Ps. lxviii. 9.

In Ps. lxviii. 9, R.V. "*plentiful* rain" is an inadequate and erroneous rendering of נדבות, a word that means (Gesen. 621 *b*) "voluntariness," or "noble graciousness," especially manifest in "generous offerings." It corresponds well to the εὐμενής of Josephus, who thus appears to be justified by Judges and Psalms in connecting God's gift of water with God's gift of the Law as a connection based on Scripture.

We have inferred also from many other considerations, both *a priori* and documentary, that this connection is probably based on actual fact. When God "*marched*" or "*strode*" through the desert with His people, water sprang up repeatedly beneath the staff of His servant Moses. This and other deliverances Moses may well have connected with the vision of the Tree, seeing continually before him the revelation of the God that "dwelleth in the Bush," or what the Jerusalem Targum (on Exod. xvii. 6) calls "*the impress of the foot* on Horeb" (see p. xlvi n. 2).

[1] As to the actual nature of the "bush," Hastings' *Dict.* (i. 334) says that it cannot be the *senna* because this "is not thorny and is too insignificant a bush (not more than 2 to 3 ft. high) to have been chosen for the theophany." The latter argument seems to assume in the Eternal a predilection for bigness that is not justified by the Bible in

digression may be more important than those of the direct investigation. The Revelation of the Fire in the Bush appears to be at the bottom of the deepest Hebrew theology. We may almost say that the Bush on Horeb is to Jews what the Cross on Golgotha is to Christians.

Moreover the story is of special interest to us because Christ Himself asked the Sadducees whether they had not "read" it, appealing to it as a proof of the Resurrection. His appeal would be reason enough—were there no other reason—for closely and reverently studying the Mosaic narrative and its context. If we do this we shall find that several considerations justify us in attaching to it much more importance than can be attached to the narrative of the two confirmatory "signs" that follow it at a little distance (Exod. iv. 1—9), (1) the rod converted to a serpent and restored to its original shape; (2) the hand first made leprous and then restored to health.

21. The Bible says that the sign of the rod-serpent is given that the *Israelites* (Exod. iv. 5) "may believe that...*the God of their fathers*" had appeared to Moses. This phrase excludes, or does not include, the Egyptians. The persons to be convinced by the second sign are not mentioned. Then it is said (*ib.* 8—9) "And...if *they* will not believe thee, neither hearken to the voice of the first sign, they will believe the voice of the latter sign. And...if *they* will not

---

general or Jonah's gourd and worm in particular. R. Elieser says about "the bush" that it is "the humblest (niedrigste) of all the trees in the world" (Wünsche *ad loc.* p. 34). "Trees" in Hebrew might include shrubs. Eratosthenes (Strabo 767—8 διαμμός ἐστι γῆ κ. λυπρά, φοίνικας ἔχουσα ὀλίγους κ. ἄκανθαν κ. μυρίκην κ. ὀρυκτὰ ὕδατα) speaks as though the sandy deserts of Arabia had only one kind of thorn. Wünsche (p. 35) quotes a saying that "the thornbush grows by every collection of waters." We ought not to be surprised if we should have to admit that the course of empires, and of the whole of the civilised and uncivilised world, has been greatly influenced by a divine lesson taught through an object "not more than 2 to 3 ft. high."

believe even these two signs, neither hearken unto thy voice, thou shalt take of the water of the river [Nile] and pour it...."

22. There are obvious possibilities of confusion here. In the first place "the voice of a sign," which might originally mean "the *report* of a sign," might be loosely taken as "sign" ("voice of" being dropped as metaphorical or unmeaning). Moreover "they,",which in the last-quoted extract ought grammatically to mean Israelites, would seem (from vii. 19, where the sign is apparently worked with the Egyptians in view) to mean, or to include, others besides Israelites. "The others" are expressly included by Philo, and perhaps by Josephus who mentions "all[1]."

23. The third "sign" (Exod. iv. 9 "thou shalt take of the water of the river...and the water shall become blood...," comp. Exod. vii. 19) presents special difficulty. Philo (ii. 93) carefully explains that this was merely a promise of a future sign. The promise was rendered credible, he says, by the other two signs, which were on quite a different footing, being, so to speak, "confidential instructions given by God to Moses (ὑπὸ μόνου μόνος ἐπαιδεύετο)." Josephus (*Ant.* ii. 12. 3) entirely dissents. According to him a third "sign," too, was performed on the spot, and Moses "*took water from the neighbourhood*" for the purpose of turning it into blood!

24. Since in this last point Philo is more accurate than Josephus, we naturally ask with interest what account the two give of the actual performance of the signs. Here are some remarkable divergences :—

(i) The Bible says (Exod. iv. 29—30) "And Moses and Aaron went and gathered together all the elders of the children of Israel: and *Aaron* spake all the words which the Lord had spoken unto Moses, and *did the signs in the sight of the people.*"

---

[1] Philo ii. 92 ἀπιστήσοντας τούς τε ὁμοφύλους καὶ τοὺς ἄλλους ἅπαντας, Joseph. *Ant.* ii. 12. 3 παρεκελεύετο...σημείοις πρὸς τὸ πιστεύεσθαι...παρὰ πᾶσι χρῆσθαι.

(ii) Philo says (ii. 94) "They, *i.e.* Moses and Aaron, having come to Egypt with one mind and soul, first gathered together the elders of the people in secret and revealed to them *the divine utterances* (χρησμούς) and how God, having taken compassion on them, promised them freedom..., and after this they were emboldened to speak to the king."

(iii) Josephus says (*Ant.* ii. 13. 1) "When they, *i.e.* Moses and Aaron, approached, the most notable of the Hebrews came to meet them....To them Moses—*since it was impossible to indicate the signs by mere words so as to produce conviction—gave the* [*actual*] *sight of them.* And the Hebrews, amazed by their extraordinary nature, took confidence...[1]."

25. It will be observed that, according to the Bible, Moses repeated no signs at all, *in act*, not even to Aaron. He repeated them to Aaron, *but merely in word* (Exod. iv. 28) "And Moses *told* Aaron *all the words* of the Lord [with] which He had sent him and *all the signs* [with] which He had charged him."

26. What would naturally follow—and what did follow according to Philo—would be that Aaron, who was to be (Exod. iv. 16) "a mouth" to Moses, should *repeat these words and signs to the people, not in act but in word*, and that they should believe, as had been predicted by the Lord (Exod. iii. 16—18) "Go, and gather the elders of Israel together, *and say unto them,...And they shall hearken to thy voice*: and thou shalt come, thou and the elders of Israel, unto the king of Egypt...." This is Philo's view. He says that Moses and Aaron "*with one mind and soul*" informed the assembly of the "divine utterances." He means that there was perfect unity between the two. Moses revealed them to Aaron, and Aaron, as being the "mouth" of Moses, passed them on to the people.

---

[1] Οἷς Μωυσῆς τὰ σημεῖα ἐπεὶ πιθανῶς οὐκ ἦν λέγειν παρέσχεν αὐτῶν τὴν ὄψιν. οἱ δ' ὑπ' ἐκπλήξεως τῶν παρὰ δόξαν αὐτοῖς ὁρωμένων ἀνεθάρσουν.

27. The writer, whoever he was, of the present Hebrew text of Exod. iv. 30 *b* "*and did the signs in the sight of the people*," was not content with Philo's view. He did not perhaps realise the truth expressed in the saying "Blessed are they that have not seen and yet have believed." He felt, with Josephus, that it was "impossible to indicate the signs by mere words so as to produce conviction," and he consequently appears to have added something to make it clear that Aaron did more than talk—"And Aaron spake all the words that the Lord had spoken unto Moses and [DID] the signs [IN THE SIGHT OF THE PEOPLE]." But in making this addition he has destroyed the Biblical and consistent view of Aaron as the "mouth" of Moses. He compels us to suppose that Aaron "*did*," before all the people, what Moses did in Horeb. Aaron, it seems, changed and rechanged his own rod, and made his own hand leprous and non-leprous—and according to Josephus must have also changed water into blood—while Moses stood by saying nothing, and doing nothing! It is not surprising that Josephus, perceiving the difficulty of this supposition, drops Aaron altogether out of the narrative rather than sacrifice the ocular demonstration afforded by the repetition of the "signs" before the Israelites ("Moses...gave them the sight of them").

28. Philo, as we have seen, uses the word ἐπαιδεύετο about the two confirmatory "signs" given to Moses. Παιδεύω in Biblical Greek sometimes means "scourge" and regularly means "chasten." *Exod. Rabba* reveals a general Jewish belief that the rod-serpent and the leprous hand indicated a "chastening" of Moses for some fault.

29. The fault would seem to be a diffidence and unwillingness to go to the aid of the flock of Israel and to stretch out his hand in their behalf. Instead of using his shepherd's staff, he throws it down; instead of stretching out his hand in action, he places it in his bosom. This is

what his conscience makes him see himself doing in two separate visions. The consequences severally follow. The rod, thrown down, becomes a serpent to sting his conscience. His hand, voluntarily isolating itself from duty to his people, as a leper is perforce isolated, is punished with leprosy[1].

30. That these signs, like those given to Gideon to encourage him for his enterprise, are on a different footing from the theophany itself, is admitted perhaps even by Josephus who says "These signs, however, came to pass for Moses at his will not only then, but all through, whenever he begged [for them]. And (?) of all these [signs] giving more weight to the Fire [than to any other] in respect of the [essential] truth and believing that he would find in God a gracious Champion, he continued in the hope that he would save his countrymen and shipwreck Egypt[2]." Whatever may be his exact meaning, he seems to recognise that the Theophany of the Fire was in the mind of Moses throughout his career.

31. This and previous considerations lead us to a conclusion on which, if it is true, it seems desirable to lay

---

[1] The prospective sign of the water changed to blood is more difficult to explain and there is no space to attempt an explanation. *Exod. Rab.* (on Exod. iv. 9) associates it with the water from the rock in Numb. xx. 11 (see *Numb. Rab.* ad loc.). On this there was a tradition that the first blow of Moses on the rock produced drops of blood, the second a deluge of water.

Origen (*Comm. Johan.* xxxii, Lomm. ii. 449) says "Now if a man will not believe these two signs, *the former being the leprosy, the latter being the restoration* (τῷ μὲν προτέρῳ ὅτι λεπρὰν ποιεῖ τὴν πρᾶξιν, τῷ δὲ δευτέρῳ ὅτι ἀποκαθίστησιν αὐτὴν εἰς τὸ κατὰ φύσιν) the water becomes blood to him."

[2] *Ant.* ii. 12. 4. Μωυσεῖ μέντοι τὰ σημεῖα ταῦτα οὐ τότε μόνον, διὰ παντὸς δὲ ὁπότε δεηθείη συνετύγχανεν. ἐξ ὧν ἁπάντων πλέον περὶ τῆς ἀληθείας τῷ πυρὶ νέμων καὶ τὸν θεὸν εὐμενῆ παραστάτην ἕξειν πιστεύων τούς τε οἰκείους σώσειν ἤλπιζε καὶ τοὺς Αἰγυπτίους κακοῖς περιβαλεῖν.

Whiston and Hudson take ἐξ ἁπάντων, as above, partitively. But if it means "in consequence of these signs," the meaning would be that Moses "attached more weight to the theophany than he otherwise would have done in consequence of these confirmatory signs."

emphasis, namely, that to the mind of Moses the revelation of "Him that dwelleth in the Bush" was of a permanent character meaning something more than "Him that once manifested Himself in the Bush."

It was on these grounds that it was stated above that the Bush for Jews might almost be said to correspond to the Cross for Christians. Those who accept the personality of Moses may say that to Moses[1] God revealed Himself in the Bush that burned yet did not perish in somewhat the same way in which Jesus revealed Himself to Paul as the Crucified[2]. Christ on the Cross was to the latter a permanent revelation, though the crucifixion was a thing of the past. So to Moses God, "dwelling in the Bush," manifested Himself as the Giver of Life amid Fire. This was a revelation of a permanent attribute of the One Permanent Being, better called the Eternal.

32. What was the precise meaning attached by the best Jewish thought to this revelation?

In Josephus, the fire is the prominent notion: "*the fire,*"

---

[1] Some (with whom I am quite unable to agree) regard Moses as little more than a mythical character. These will consistently deny the historical existence of any such theophany to Moses. Even for them it is of some importance to ascertain what was the meaning of the writer who conceived this tradition about the mythical Moses, and what influence it exerted on Jewish thought at the beginning of the Christian era.

[2] *Acts of John* xii. (ed. James 1897) καὶ ὅτε τῇ σταυροῦ βάτῳ ἐκρεμάσθη, "and when He was hung upon the bush of the cross," would afford an interesting illustration at this point, if βάτῳ were correct. But Dr James (*Journal of Theol. Studies*, vol. vii. p. 567) is now of opinion that τῷ ἀρουβάτῳ, the reading of most of the MSS. (which he had conjecturally corrected to τῇ σταυροῦ βάτῳ) means (as Hilgenfeld had previously suggested) *the 'arûbhtâ, i.e.* the Friday, "When on the Friday He was hung (on the cross)." This is supported by the *Book of the Bee* (13th century) *Anecdota Oxoniensia* (1886) (p. 99) "As regards the name of 'arûbhtâ [*i.e.* the eve of the Jewish Sabbath], it was not known until this time [that is, the time of the Passion], but that day was called the sixth day. And when the sun became dark, and the divine care also set and abandoned the Israelitish people, then that day was called '*arûbhtâ.*"

he says, "emitted a voice and called Moses by name"; "thus marvellous were the divine utterances that he heard *from the fire*"; "*to the fire* Moses attached most weight[1]." He seems to have had in view Deut. iv. 24 "the Lord thy God is *a devouring fire*"—only not devouring the chosen people of Israel. This view, of course, contains a truth, and it is claimed as a truth for Christians as well as for Jews in the Epistle to the Hebrews "We, too, have a God that is a consuming fire[2]."

33. Jewish traditional comment recognised two kinds of fire, one from above and one from below. It applies the vision to Egypt attempting to consume Israel[3]. So does Philo. He says that the bush was the symbol of the oppressed; the fire, of the oppressor; the angel was the symbol of "God's providence," which, "in great stillness," tames the powers of terror. By "stillness" he means the voice with which the angel spoke, "a stillness," he says, "clearer than any voice" (τρανοτέρα φωνῆς ἡσυχίᾳ). Philo seems to have in his mind the "still small voice" that spoke to Elijah on Horeb, centuries afterwards. There was fire, too, but he implies its inferiority to the light (φῶς αὐγοειδέστερον τοῦ πυρός)[4]. On the whole, Philo gives us the impression that he would have said, with the author of the story of Elijah (rather against the view of Josephus), "the Lord was not in the fire[5]."

---

[1] *Ant.* ii. 12. 1 φωνὴν τοῦ πυρὸς ἀφιέντος κ. ὀνομαστὶ καλέσαντος αὐτὸν κ. ποιησαμένου λόγους, *ib.* τοσαῦτα μὲν ἐκ τοῦ πυρὸς θεοκλυτεῖται, *ib.* ii. 12. 4 πλέον...τῷ πυρὶ νέμων.
[2] Heb. xii. 29 καὶ γὰρ ὁ θεὸς ἡμῶν *i.e.* "our God as well as the God called by the Jews their God." See Westcott's note.
[3] See *Exod. Rab.* on Exod. iii. 2 (Wünsche p. 35) as to what "they" *i.e.* "the ancients," said.
[4] Philo ii. 91.
[5] Josephus in his account of the theophany to Elijah (*Ant.* viii. 13. 7 (351—2)) σεισμοῦ τε ἐπακούει κ. λαμπρὰν πυρὸς αὐγὴν ὁρᾷ. κ. γενομένης ἡσυχίας φωνὴ θεία μὴ ταράττεσθαι τοῖς γινομένοις αὐτὸν παρακελεύεται, omits

34. This seems to be the truth. In the revelation to Moses as in the revelation to Elijah, the Lord was not in the fire but in the principle of life that made the fire harmless. This principle of life was revealed to Moses in the saying I AM, or rather I WILL BE—which occurs here for the first time in the Bible. At the first utterance, the word is modified so as to be a private or individual revelation (Exod. iii. 12) "I WILL BE *with thee*[1]." Then it is used without any reference except to a repetition of itself, I WILL BE WHAT I WILL BE. This revelation is morally and spiritually neutral—for it might denote futurity of anything—unless we read it in the light that comes from the Bush. But, read in that light, it teaches that God who is on the side of the afflicted, and who may be said to be in the midst of the affliction (*i.e.* the bush)[2], WILL BE ever the Champion of the good, ever the Eternal Life, even in the midst of fires that seem to imply death.

35. This view of the I AM and of what may be called the "baptism with fire" of the bush in Horeb, must be kept in view throughout our study of the four gospels. It indicates a connection, vital yet easily passed over, between (1) "baptism with fire" and (2) baptism (not outward but inward) with the living water that sustains the roots of spiritual life.

---

the statements that "the Lord was not in the earthquake, fire etc." Note that in connection with the "voice" he uses ἡσυχία, the word used by Philo—but not as Philo uses it to denote the characteristic of the voice, and as the Hebrew ("still small voice") might lead us to expect it to be used. Josephus, possibly by some confusion, takes it to mean "when the elements were still."

[1] Mandelkern's Concordance indicates that its first occurrence is in Exod. iii. 12 and its second in iii. 14. Aquila and Theod. render it in iii. 14 ἔσομαι. Both R.V. and LXX render it "will be," ἔσομαι, in iii. 12. In iii. 14, R.V. text has I AM, but with several marginal variations.

[2] Exod. iii. 14 says "*out of the midst of the bush*" and Deut. xxxiii. 16 "dwelleth *in the bush*" (not "*out of the midst of the fire*" nor "*in the fire*"). Comp. Is. lxiii. 9 "In all their affliction He was afflicted."

Clement of Alexandria[1] indicates a parallelism between the theophany of the thornbush and the theophany of the crown of thorns. There is more justification for it than might be supposed. Interpreted and developed by Jewish teachers, the phrase in the Law "He that dwelleth in the Bush," might fairly be said to correspond to an expression adapted from Prophecy, "He that is afflicted in our afflictions." This again corresponds to the Christian conception of Him who "so loved the world that He gave His only begotten Son" to die for the world—surely an act that betokens some "affliction" in the Father, who gave so much for an afflicted world.

Why is it that the Fourth Gospel alone speaks of "being born from above," and lays so much more stress than the synoptists lay on "life"—not "life eternal," but "life"—as the gift of the Son? Why does it alone tell us that this life cannot be sustained without support from inner sources, the "bread of life," the "flesh and blood" of the Son, "the living water"—none of which are so much as mentioned by the earlier Gospels? And why does this Gospel alone represent Jesus as saying—with apparent allusion to the theophany of the Bush—I AM?

May it not be because the fundamental doctrine of the Mosaic theophany, as interpreted by Isaiah and taught by Jesus, had been obscured by the thaumaturgic element in the earliest gospels and needed to be emphasized even at the cost of departing from the words actually used by Jesus in order to convey the thoughts that spiritually underlay His teaching?

---

[1] Clem. Alex. 215 ὅπως ὁ διὰ βάτου τὸ πρῶτον ὀφθείς, ὁ Λόγος, διὰ τῆς ἀκάνθης ὕστερον ἀναληφθεὶς μιᾶς ἔργον τὰ πάντα δείξῃ δυνάμεως.

INDICES TO DIATESSARICA

CLUE AND CORRECTIONS OF MARK

		PAGE
I.	New Testament Passages.	3
II.	English	9
III.	Greek.	17
IV.	Hebrew	21

FROM LETTER TO SPIRIT

I.	New Testament Passages.	35
II.	English and Greek.	38
III.	Hebrew	51

PARADOSIS

I.	New Testament Passages.	53
II.	English and Greek.	56
III.	Hebrew	63

JOHANNINE VOCABULARY

I.	New Testament Passages.	67
II.	English	83
III.	Greek.	88

JOHANNINE GRAMMAR

I.	New Testament Passages.	94
II.	English	108
III.	Greek.	119

NOTES ON NEW TESTAMENT CRITICISM

I.	New Testament Passages.	130
II.	English	137
III.	Greek.	148

CLUE AND CORRECTIONS OF MARK

I. NEW TESTAMENT PASSAGES

[*The references are to paragraphs, indicated by black numbers, which, in this Index, run from* 1 *to* 552[1].]

MATTHEW			MATTHEW			MATTHEW		
		PAR.			PAR.			PAR.
2	8	456 (iii)	8	23	244–8, 381	10	41	272 (i)
	20	334 *b*		25	382–6		42	268–72
3	5	18, 71, 334–5		26	134–6	11	1	350, 438 (v) *c*
	11–12	336–42, comp. 333		27	137–40, 387		9	272 (i)
				28	147–8		11	429 (vi)
	16	343, 455–6		29	455–6	12	1	211–18, 360 (i)
4	1	344–6		31	152–5		4	361
	1–2	192–5, 345–6		34	149, 155, 455–6		10	456 (ii) *a*
	12	129	9	2	195–209, 259–63, 352, 354		14	466 (ε) *b*
	13–15	438 (v)					15–21	397 *a*
	17	129		7–8	355–6		22–3	363 *a*
	18	347–9		11	357		25	364–6
	21	347–9		16	358		31–2	367–9
	23	350		17	359–60		38	466 (δ)–(ζ)
	24	362		18	352, 455–6		39	408–12
	24–5	157–8		20	388		43	150 *a*, 390 (i) (α) *a*
5	13	432–7 (i)		32–3	363 *a*			
	14	435–6		35	389–90		47	531
	15	186, 372–3		36	401–3	13	4	210
	47	254–8	10	1–14	390 (i) (α)–(ε), 390 (ii) (ε)		5	131–3
	48	161–2					5–6	378 *a*
6	19–20	390 (ii) (ε)		2–3	363		9	459 (iii) *a*
	24	318 (ii)		7	243		10	370
7	28	438 (v) *c–d*		9–10	263–7, 390 (ii) (α)–(ε)		17	272 (i)
8	2	351–2					19	370 (i)–371
	5	154		10	390 (ii) (ε) *a*		21	447 (iii) *a*
	8	107 *a*, 198 *a*		26	373 (i)–(ii)		22	390 (ii) (γ)
	16	130		28	249		31–2	374–80
	20	385		29	79, 224–5, 250–3		35	366 *a*, 436
	21	248					53	438 (v) *c*

[1] *Clue* includes 1–272, *Corrections* 273–552.

CLUE AND CORRECTIONS OF MARK

MATTHEW			MATTHEW			MATTHEW		
		PAR.			PAR.			PAR.
14	1	391-3	21	17	116 a, 390 (i)	27	31	505
	9	56			(δ), 450-3		33	505
	12	394-9		21	372, 454		35-6	506
	13	76, 165-71,		24	456 (i)-(iv)		36	506, 506 (iii) b
		394-400		26	372, 454		37	506 (i)-(iii)
	14	401-3		33	459 (iv)		40	507-8
	15	372		38	457-8		42-3	507-8
	17	403 (i)		40-2	459 (i)-61		46	81-3
	20	404-5	22	12	188		50	509-14
15	16	136 b		16	466 (ε) a		54	172-7, 415 a,
	29	171 a		18	466 (β)			514
	39	498 g		19	449		55	506 a, 515-16
16	1	466 (δ)-(ζ)		22	83 b		57-8	517-19
	3	439, 466 (ε) c		28	459 (v)		59	520-1, 527 e
	4	372, 406-12		34-6	462-9		61	498 f, 506 a
	6	413, 466 (ε)		45	459 (v)	28	2	527 a-d
	8	136 c	23	1	470		2-3	522 (i)-(iv),
	14	487 (i) (β)-(γ),		4	466 (η) a			523-7
		487 (i) (ζ) e		5-7	471-2		8-9	528-33
	16	414-17		8-11	429-31 (ii)		10	531
	21	226-7, 418		29	272 (i)		16-17	487 (i) (ε)
	22	460 (iii) a, c		35	438 (v) a			
	27	428		39	485 a			
	28	522 (ii) a	24	6	428			MARK
17	1-2	419-21		21	436			
	2	522 (i)-(iv) and		27	522 (ii)-(iv)	1	2	160
		(vii), 527		36	361		5	13, 18, 71,
	3	352		51	466 (ε) c			334-5
	5	123 a, 417 a,	25	34	436		8	336-42, comp.
		422-4	26	1	438 (v) c			333
	9	141-4		2	223		9	13
	11	426		27	141, 243		10	343, 455-6
	17	425, 425 (i),		29	485		12	344
		449		34	219-22		13	192-5, 345-6
	22	426-8		47	352-3		14	129
18	1	431 (ii)		48-50	473-7		16	347-9
	5	270		50	189-91		19	347-9
	19-20	224		51	478-82		22	438 (v) d
	21	232 a		55	178		26	137 a, 387 a
	22	228-32		58	178-85		27	140
19	1	438 (i)-(v)		63	372, 414-17,		28	128-9
	3	466 (γ)			483		32	130
	21	162-4		64	484 (i)-5		38	350, 389, 390
	22	392 a, 439-42		67-8	486-93			(i) (γ)
	24	444 (i)-(ii)		69	178, 493,		39	350
	25	443			494 a-8		40	351-2
	27	447 (iv)		70-4	494-8	2	1	223 a
	29	445-7 (iv)		75	499-501		3	352, 354, 449
20	13	188	27	2	449		3-5	195-209
	19	418, 488		14	56-60		5	259-63
	22	427		15	502 (i)		12	355-6
	26-7	429-31 (ii)		16	502 (vi) c		14	418 a
	30	61-8, 448		17	56, 502-4		16	357
21	2	237-9, 449		20-2	502-4		21	30, 358
	7	449		26	493 b, 502 (v)		22	359-61

Clue includes 1-272, *Corrections* 273-552.

NEW TESTAMENT PASSAGES

MARK		MARK		MARK	
	PAR.		PAR.		PAR.
2 23	211–18, 360 (i)	6 7	233–6, 535 a	9 35	429–31 (ii)
25–6	65	7–13	390 (i) (a)–(ε),	37	270
26	359 a, 361		390 (ii) (ε)	41	268–72
27	459 (iii) a	8	263–7, 390 (ii)	48–9	434
3 6	466 (ε) b		(a)–(ε)	50	432–7 (i)
7	397 a	8–9	264 a	10 1	438 (i)–(v),
8	156–8	9	390 (ii) (ε) a		466 (γ)
9	73	10	459 (iii) a	2	466 (γ)
10	362	11	369 b	10	466 (γ)
14	350, 394 a	11–12	243	21	162–4
14–18	363	14	56, 391–3	22	392 a, 439–42
19–21	363 a	20	391–3	24	259
21–6	363 b	29–32	394–9	25	444 (i)–(ii)
23	364–6	32	167–71	26	443
28	137 a, 387 a,	33	76, 165–6, 400	28	447 (iv)
	409 a	34	401–3	29	446
28–9	367–9	37	372	30	445–7 (iv)
32	531	38	403 (i)	34	418, 488 a
4 4	210	43	404–5	38	427
5–6	131–3, 378 a	7 6	466 (ε) c	43–4	429–31
9	459 (iii) a	11	456 (iv)	46	61–8
10	370	18	136 b	46–7	448
12	387 a	19	342	51	351 b
15	370 (i)–371	20	459 (iii) a	11 2	237–9, 449
17	447 (iii) a	24	438 (ii) a	7	449
19	390 (ii) (γ)	31	171 a	11	452 a, 453
21	186, 372–3,	8 8	405	17	459 (iii) a
	459 (iii) a	9	56	19	390 (i) (δ),
22	373 (i)–(ii)	10	498 g		450–3
24	432 a, 459 (iii) a	11	466 (δ)–(ζ)	19–20	116 a
26	459 (iii) a	12	371 a, 372,	22	372
30	459 (iii) a		406–12	22–3	454
30–2	374–80	15	413, 466 (ε)	29	456 (i)–(iv)
34	370 b	17–18	136 c	32	372, 454
36	244–8, 381	21	459 (iii) a	12 1	459 (iv)
38	382–6	28	487 (i) (β)–(γ)	7	457–8
40	134–6	29	414–17	9–10	459 (i)–61
41	137–40, 356,	31	226–7, 418	12	83 b
	387	38	428	13	466 (ε) a
5 2	146 a	9 1	459 (iii) a	15	449, 466 (β)
3–4	147–8	2	419–21	23	459 (v)
5	145–7	3	522 (i)–(iv) and	26	487 (i) (β) c
6	455–6		(vii), 527	28	459 (vi), 461 d,
10	150–2	4	352–3		462–9
10–12	152–5	6	123 a, 422–4,	32	459 (vi), 462–7
14	455–6		540	34	459 (vi), 462–7
15	149	7	417 a	35	459 (iii) a
17	155	9	141–4	37	393 a, 459 (v)
19	395 (i) a	11	357 a	37–8	470
22	352, 455–6	12	426	38	413, 459 (iii) a,
27	388	19	425, 425 (i),		471–2
37	515 a		449	40	472 a
42	137 a, 387 a,	28	357 a	41	390 (ii) (δ)
	418 a	31	426–8, 459 (iii) a	43	409 a
6 6	389–90	34	431 (ii)	13 7	428

Clue includes 1–272, Corrections 273–552.

CLUE AND CORRECTIONS OF MARK

MARK		MARK		LUKE	
	PAR.		PAR.		PAR.
13 32	361	16 10	531	8 9	370
35	222 a	13	531	12	370 (i)–**71**
14 1	223	14	487 (i) (ε) a	13	447 (iii) a
19	535 a			14	390 (ii) (γ)
23	141, 243			16	186, 372–3
25	409 a, 485		LUKE	17	373 (i)–(ii)
30	219–22			18	432 a
36	459 (iii) a	1 3	456 (iii)	20	531
43	352–3	19	479	22	244–8, 381
44–5	473–7	3 3	18, 71, 334–5	23–4	382–6
47	478–82, 491 b	11	390 (ii) (ε) a	25	134–40, 387
49	178	16–17	336–42, comp.	27	146 a, 147–8
51	515 a		333	28	455–6
54	177–85	21	455–6	31	150–2
61	372, 414–17,	21–2	343	31–2	152–5
	483	4 1	192–5, 344	35	149, 455–6
62	484 (i)–485	2	192–5, 345–6	37	155
65	482 c, 486–93	14	129	39	395 (i) a
66	178, 493	18	149 a	41	352, 455–6
67–8	494–8	32	438 (v) d	44	388
69–70	479, 494–8	36	140	55	418 a
71	494–8	37	128	9 1–6	390 (i) (α)–(ε),
72	499–501	40	130		390 (ii) (ε)
15 1	449	43	350, 389	2	243
2	503 (i)	44	350	3	263–7, 390 (ii)
5	56–60	5 2	347–9		(α)–(ε)
6	502 (i), (iv)	10	347–9	5	369 b
7	502 (vi) c	12	351–2	7	391–3
8	502 (i), (iv)	17	223 a	10	167–71, 394–9
9	56, 502–4	18	352, 354	11	76, 165–6,
10–11	503 (ii)	18–20	195–209		400–3
11–12	502–4	20	259–63, 497 b	12	167
15	490, 493 b, 502	25–6	355–6	13	372, 403 (i)
	(v)–(vii)	30	357	17	404–5
20	505	36	30, 358	19	487 (i) (β)–(γ)
22	505	37–8	359–60	20	414–17
24–5	506	6 1	211–18, 360 (i)	22	226–7, 418
25	81–3	4	361	26	428
26	506 (i)–(iii)	9	456 (ii) a	29	419–21, 522 (i)–
32	507–8	11	466 (ε) b		(iv) and
34	81–3, 137 a	13–14	363		(vii), 527
35	479	17	157–8, 362,	30	352
37	137 a, 509–14		438 (v)	32–4	422–4
39	172–7, 415 a,	33	254–8	34	123 a
	479, 514	36	161–2	35	417 a
40	506 a	42	466 (ε) c	36–7	141–4
41	515–16	7 2	107 a	41	425, 425 (i),
42–3	517–19	3	154		449
46	520–1, 527 e, k	4	360 a	44	426–8
47	506 a	6	198 a	45	527 h
16 1	527 g–k	21–2	360 a	46	431 (ii)
3–4	527 a–d	28	429 (vi)	48	270, 429–31 (ii)
5	522 (i)–(iv),	8 5	210	58	385
	523–7	6	131–3, 378 a	59	248
8	528–33	8	459 (iii) a	10 1	233–6

Clue includes **1–272**, *Corrections* **273–552**.

NEW TESTAMENT PASSAGES

	LUKE PAR.			LUKE PAR.			LUKE PAR.
10	4	390 (ii) (ε) a	18	35-7	448	23 25	502 (v)-(vii), 503 (iii) a
	4-5	266 a	19	24	479		
	11	390 (i) a, 390 (i) (γ) and (ε)		30	237-9, 449	26	505
				35	449	33	505-6
	19	192	20	3	456 (i)-(iv)	35	466 (β) a, 507-8
	24	272 (i)		6	372, 454	37	507-8
	25-8	462-9		14	457-8	38	506 a, 506 (i)-(iii)
	25 foll.	466 (η) c		15-17	459 (i)-61		
	28	459 (vi)		19	461	46	137 a, 509-14
	37	466 (η) d		20	466 (ε) a	47	172-7, 415 a, 514
11	14	363 a		23	466 (β)		
	16	466 (δ)-(ζ)		24	449	49	515-16
	17	364-6		33	459 (v)	50-2	517-19
	24	150 a, 390 (i) (a) a		39	459 (vi), 462-7	53	520-1, 527 e
				44	459 (v)	56	527 g-k
	29	372, 406-12		45	470	24 1.	527 g-k
	45-6	466 (η) a		46	471-2	2	527 a-d
	47	272 (i)		47	472 a	4	522 (i)-(iv), 523-7
	51	438 (v) a	21	1	390 (ii) (δ)		
12	1	413, 466 (ε)		9	428	9	487 (i) (ε) a
	2	373 (ii)		37	116 a, 390 (i) (δ), 450-3	9-11	528-33
	5	249				33	487 (i) (ε) a
	6	79, 224-5, 250-3	22	1	223		
				18	485		
	10	367-9		26	429-31 (ii)		JOHN
	14	259		28	480 b		
	46	466 (ε) c		32	501 a	1 33	383
	56	466 (ε) c		34	219-22	34	417 a
13	9	456 (iv)		36-8	480	36	459 (vi)
	15	466 (ε) c		47	352-3	42	459 (vi)
	18-19	374-80		47-8	473-7	51	343
	22	389-90		49	491 b	3 16-21	342
	35	485 a		49-50	478-82	22	334 b
14	1	466 (β) a		55	178-85, 493 d	31-6	342
	34	432-7 (i)		56	178-85, 493-8	4 46	107 a
15	25-32	429 (v)		57-60	494-8	6 1	171 a
16	13	318 (ii)		61	459 (vi)	13	405
	14	466 (β) a, 466 (γ)		61-2	499-501	15	397 a
				63-5	486-93	31	167
	22	449		67-70	483-5	68-9	414, 417 b
17	3	232	23	1	449	7 25	334 b
	4	228-32		2	503 (i)-(ii)	9 8-9	487 (i) (γ)
	6	372, 454		4	506 (iii) a	11 55	71, 334 b
	11	438 (i)-(v)		5	503 (i)-(ii)	12 6	527 f
	24	522 (ii)-(iv)		6-12	503 (iii) a	38	129, 470
18	22	162-4		9	56-60	13 27	191, 477 a
	23	392 a, 439-42		11	487 (i) a	33	259
	25	444 (i)-(ii)		12	503 (iii) a	18 2	476
	26	443		14	506 (iii) a	5	476, 484 (i) c
	28	447 (iv)		14-15	503 (iii)	8	484 (i) c
	29	446		16	56, 502-4	10	480
	30	445-7 (iv)		18	502-4	17	494-8
	32-3	488 a		20	502-4	18	177-85
	33	418 a		22	493 b, 502-4, 506 (iii) a	22	479, 487 (i) (a), 493 a
	35	61-8					

Clue includes 1-272, *Corrections* 273-552.

JOHN

	PAR.	
18	23	493 c
	25	179 a, 494-8
	26	498
	27	494-8
	30	503 (i) a
	33	503 (i) a
	38	506 (ii)
	39-40	502-4
19	1	493 b, 502 (v)
	3	487 (i) (a)
	4	506 (iii) a
	6	506 (i) a, 506 (iii) a
	14	81-3
	15	56, 504 b
	16	487 (i) (a)
	19	506 b, 506 (i)-(iii)
	30	509 a, 514
	38-40	527 g-l
	40	521
20	1	527 c
	7	521, 527 d
	9	527 h
	15	527 f
	18	531
21	18	143
	20	501 a

ACTS

1	5	338
	26	487 (i) (ε) a
2	14	487 (i) (ε) a
3	13	107 a
	22	487 (i) (β) d
	26	107 a
4	13	317 a
	27	107 a
	30	107 a
5	35	506 (i) b
7	6	429 (ii)
10	39	334 b
11	16	338
	19	506 (i) b
12	2	480 a
	8	390 (ii) (ε) a
13	28	506 (i) a
	50	519
	51	390 (i) a, 390 (i) (ε)

ACTS

	PAR.	
15	17	159
17	12	519
	23	506 (i)
23	2	479
28	4-5	192
	18	506 (i) a

ROMANS

8	29	417
9	12	429 (i)-(v)
	12-31	429 (v)
10	16	470
11	20	433 a
13	4	480 a
15	19	390 d

1 CORINTHIANS

1	20	465
4	11	489 a
15	6	487 (i) (ε) a
16	9	343

2 CORINTHIANS

2	12	343
3	7	420
	10	420
	15	527 h
11	19	393 a
12	7	362 a, 489 a

GALATIANS

2	9	480 b
6	9	446

EPHESIANS

4	3	437
6	14	390 (ii) (ε)
	15	390 (ii) (ε) a

PHILIPPIANS

2	15	435

COLOSSIANS

	PAR.	
1	15	417
	18	417
3	15	437
4	3	343

1 THESSALONIANS

5	13	437

2 TIMOTHY

8	9	466 (ε) b

HEBREWS

1	6	417
3	11	371 a, 408
4	3	371 a, 408
	5	408
12	1	272 (i)
	6	502 (v)
13	2	272 (i)

JAMES

5	3-4	390 (ii) (ε)

1 PETER

1	10	272 (i)
	12	272 (i)
2	20	489 a
	25	501 a
5	6	446

2 PETER

1	19	522 (iii) a

REVELATION

1	5	417
	12-15	522 (v)-(vii)
	13	390 (ii) (ε)
2	18	522 (vi)
3	4	526 a
	8	343
	18	390 (ii) (ε)
4	1	343
	4	526 a
7	9	526 a
14	13	485 c
16	13-14	390 (i) (a) a
17	3	449
19	14	526 a
21	10	449
	12	506 (i)

Clue includes 1-272, *Corrections* 273-552.

CLUE AND CORRECTIONS OF MARK

II. ENGLISH

[*The references are to paragraphs, indicated by black numbers, which, in this Index, run from* 1 *to* 552[1]. "*C. w.*" *means* "*c(onfused), or c(onfusable), w(ith).*" *For details, the context must be consulted.*]

A (*i.e.* Codex Alexandrinus) compared with B (*i.e.* Codex Vaticanus) **306–14**; more accurate than B as rendering of Hebrew **33**
Abiathar **65**[2]
Abridgments **276** foll.; in Josh. **276–9**; in Layamon's *Brut* **279**; a. and additions, in Chron. (compared with Sam.) **280–9**; a. and additions in LXX version of Dan. **290–2**
Abruptness in Mk **534** (ii)
"Abyss," parall. to "country" **150–2**
"Accomplish," c. w. "peace" **477** *a*
"Acquit," in Gk, c. w. "release" **503** (iii)
"Across," c. w. other words **12**
Active (voice) c. w. passive **19, 89**; c. w. causative **19**
Acts, the, Petrine portions of **390** (ii) (*e*) *a*
Additions, marginal and interlinear **31** *a*; Gk, to O.T. **290, 296**; a. and abridgments, in Chron. (compared with Sam.) **280–9**, in LXX version of Dan. **290–2**
"After," c. w. "afterwards" **193** *a*, "with" **193**, "other" **245**, "brother" **348** *a*; "after him" c. w. "another," *Corrections* p. **322** n.
"Afterwards," c. w. "after" **193** *a*
"Against," c. w. "to" **369** *b*; "against," "upon," or "went up" **506** (i)

"All," ins. or om. by LXX **380** *a*, **390**
"Amazed," c. w. "keep" **392** *a*
"And," Heb., errors arising from **237–9**; may mean "for" **532** *a*; particip. substituted for indic. w. "and" **535** (iv)
"Angel" or "messenger" **105**; c. w. "king" **105** *a*; "angel" and "man" **526**
"Another," c. w. "after him," *Corrections* p. **322** n. (comp. **245**)
"Answering" **456** (i)
Anthropomorphism, Heb., corrected by LXX **24**
Antoninus, connected with Esau **429** (iv)
Apostles, the, naming of **363**; the term used once in Mk **394** *a*
Aquila, his translation of Scripture **15, 32, 315**
Aramaic, conflations arising from **126–7**
Araunah, the story of **285–6**; his "four sons" **105–12**
"Arise," applied to "seed" and "sun" **131–3**; "a." and "be raised" **418**
Article (Heb.) c. w. interrog. prefix **372** (comp. **409**), **476**; c. w. voc. prefix **476** *a*, **497**
"Ask," c. w. "beg" **448** *b–c*
"Assemble," in R. V. **397** n. 3
"Astonish," c. w. "hear" **443**
Awake, "keep awake," c. w. "yet" **424**

---

[1] *Clue includes* **1–272**, *Corrections* **273–552**.
[2] The suggestion in **65** might be improved by supposing the original to be "*the* House," *i.e.* the House of God (Levy i. 224 *b*) and that "Habaith" became "Abiathar." Comp. Ezek. xx. 29 "*the* high place," LXX "Abana" or "Habana."

B and M, in Heb. inscriptions of Christ's time, almost identical 516 a
B (*i.e.* Codex Vaticanus) compared with A (*i.e.* Codex Alexandrinus) 306–14; less accurate than A as rendering of Hebrew 33
Bacon, Francis, on preferring the more difficult reading 30
Baptism, Christ's, the place of 13–14
"Bar-," "son of" 61–2
Barabbas, "Jesus Barabbas" 502 (vi) c
Bartimæus 61–8; s. also *Fourfold Gospel*
Beasts, "wild b." parall. to "hungered" 192 foll.
"Become," c. w. "behold" 484 (iii)
Bed, "on a b." parall. to "by four" 195 foll.
"Befall" (or "meet") c. w. "call" 472 c, 474
"Before," c. w. "inner," *Corrections* p. 322 n.
"Beg," c. w. "ask" 448 b–c
"Begin," Mk's use of 535 a
"Behold," c. w. "behold!" 455–6; "behold" c. w. "become" 484 (iii); s. also "see"
"Behold!" parall. to "cometh" 352–3; parall. to "behold" 455–6; "b.!" rendered "straightway" 455 a; "b.!" c. w. "those" 457
Bethabara 13–14
Bethany 13–14, 453
Betharaba 13–14
Bethsaida, "a city called B." 167 foll.
"Beyond the river," ambig. 301
Bezae, Codex, see D
Binding of Isaac, the 521
"Blessed," c. w. "first-born" 417; "the B.," parall. to "God" 483
"Boat" in Mk 167–71; "other boats" mentioned by Mk alone 245; s. also *Fourfold Gospel*
Border (of garment) 388, 472
"Boundary," c. w. "Galilee" 438 (ii)
"Brother" or "brothers" 347 foll.; "b." c. w. "after" 348 a
"But," c. w. "for" 428
"Buy," c. w. "pure" 527 e

"Call," c. w. "(draw) near" 386 a, 474 a; c. w. "befall" (or "meet") 472 c, 474
Cardinal numbers, c. w. ordinal 78, 226
"Cast," parall. to "destroy" 249
Causative forms, c. w. non-causative 8, 19, 140, 142, 154, 244, 381, 505, 510 foll.
"Chastise," c. w. "imprison" 502 (vi) c

"Chiefs of the priests," c. w. "rulers" 59
"Chosen of God, the" 417 a
"Christ, the," a term familiar to Gentiles 417
Chronicles, compared with Samuel 280–9, with Esdras and Ezra 294 foll.
Chrysostom, on "shaking off dust" 390 (i) (ε)
"City," c. w. "beacon" 436 a; c. w. "mountain" 452 a; "cities and villages" parall. to "villages" 389–90
"Clothed," c. w. "return" 149
"Come," parall. to "light," "kindle" 186, 373 b–c; parall. to "behold!" 352–3
Command and statement, confused 28, 85–6, 141, 240 foll., 390 (i) (γ); *Corrections* p. 7
"Companion," Mt.'s use of 187–91
"Compassionate," parall. to "perfect" 161–2
Conditional prefix, c. w. interrog. 372, 409, 454
Conflation, the nature of 20–155; rules for discovering 30–1; the sign of an early translation 32–5; caused mostly by obscurity 24–9, 300–1, by prejudice 104, by variation of grammatical form 84–94; of dates 77–80; of names 36–68; of technical terms 69–76; Hebrew 100–3; longer 95–9; in Synoptic gospels 128–55
Conflative versions 113–27
Confusions, of words 156–218; of idioms 219–72
Consistency, errors springing from desire of 176 a
"Convey," c. w. "gardener" 527 f
"Councillor," c. w. "rich" 519 n. 3
Counterchange, *e.g.* D simultaneously conforms Lk. to Mk and Mk to Lk. 16 a
"Country," parall. to "abyss" 150–2; "the surrounding c." 128–9; "the c. round about Jordan" 334–5
"Covering," c. w. "myrrh" 527 g; "covering the face" 489 b
Crucifixion, the, predicted only in Mt. 488 a; the hour of 81–3
"Cry," c. w. "evil" 147
"Cure" and "heal," parall. to "teach" 401–3
Custom, of "releasing prisoners," the 502 (i)–(iv)

D and R confused in Heb. 90, 406, 424; in Heb. books as well as in transl. from Heb. 5

Clue includes 1–272, *Corrections* 273–552.

D (*i.e.* Codex Bezae) conforms Mk to Lk. and Lk. to Mk **16** *a*; comp. *Fourfold Gospel*, Index, "Counterchange"
Dalmanutha **498** *h*
Daniel, two versions of **17**, **290–3**; the LXX version **32**, **118–25**; exceptional nature of **24** n. 1
"Darius the Mede" **49**
Dates, conflation of **77–80**
"Daughters," meaning "villages" **40**
"Dawn," c. w. "lightning" **522** (i)–(ii)
Day, "on the third day" parall. to "after three days" **226–7**, comp. **418**, **447**; "after two days" parall. to "drawing nigh" **223**
Definiteness, corrections for **390** (i) (δ), **534** (i); comp. **110**
"Desire," c. w. "come" etc. **430** *a*
"Destroy," parall. to "cast" **249**
Dialogue, verbs of speech om. and ins. **459** (i)–(iv), comp. **475** n. 2; verbs of speech om. and name of speaker ins. **459** (iii) *b*
Disciples, "other seventy-two d." **232–6**; may be meant by "hearers" **443**; parall. to "in his teaching" **470**
"Disputant," *i.e.* teacher **464**
Double Tradition, the **318** (i)–(iii)
"Dove," or "Jonah" **412**
"Draw nigh," s. "near"
"Drought," c. w. "mountains" **20**
Dual, c. w. plural **220**, **223**

"Each," in Heb. **390**; c. w. "man" **139**
Earthquake, the, recorded by Mt. alone **172–7**
Ecclesiasticus, written in Heb., *Clue* p. xviii, **20** *a*
"Edom" (*i.e.* Idumæa) c. w. "Aram" (*i.e.* Syria) **6**; "E." c. w. "man" **159**; meaning "Rome" **429** (iv); Amos on E. **159**
El-, prepos., treated as part of name **498** *h*
"Elder, the" **429** (i)–(vii); "elders of," in Ezra, c. w. "captivity" in Esdras **92**
"Eleven, the" **487** (i) (ε) *a*
Elision, rare in MSS. of N.T. **502** (ii) *b*
Esau and Jacob **429** (i)–(vii)
Esdras, first book of, comp. w. Ezra **113–17**, w. Ezra and Chron. **294–304**; less accurate than Ezra **32**, **314**
"Eternal life" **417** *b*
Evangelists, would naturally adopt language of O.T. **522** (vii)

"Even," c. w. "and" **237** foll.
"Evil," c. w. "cry" **147**; c. w. "know" **7**, **406**; c. w. "neighbour" **551** n. 3
Experiments in LXX **353**, **455** *a*
Ezra, comp. w. Esdras **113–17**, w. Chron. and Esdras **294–304**; more accurate than Esdras **32**, **314**

Face, "from the f. of" **413**; "lift up my f. to thee" parall. to "before thy f." **420** *a*; "see my f.," marg. for "appear before me" **420** *a*; "covering the f." **489** *b*
"Fall to the ground without," parall. to "forgotten in the sight of" **250–1**
"Fame," parall. to "preaching" **129**
Farthing, "two for a f." parall. to "five for two f.'s" **224–5**
"Fasting" and "praying" **304–5**
"Fear," connected with "wonder" **138**; "fear" c. w. "see" **532**
"Filled themselves against," *i.e.* "gathered themselves against" **466** (ε) *b*
"Finish," c. w. "go forth" **509** *a*
"Fire," c. w. "whose" **339**; c. w. "man" **434**; "the Holy Spirit" and "fire" **336–42**; two kinds of f. **434**; answering by f. **287–9**
"First," c. w. "one" **293** n. 2; "first" and "last" **429** (i) foll.; "first" meaning "the greater" **429** (vii)
"First-born," c. w. "blessed" **417**
Foot, "on foot" (an error, **165–6**) parall. to "followed" **76**, **400**; "at his feet" c. w. "with their feet" **75–6**
"For," in Heb., c. w. "but" or "when" **428**; c. w. "and" **532** *a*
Forget, "forgotten in the sight of" parall. to "fall to the ground without" **250–1**
Four, "by f." parall. to "on a bed" **195** foll.
"From," c. w. "in" (or "into") **151**, **158** *a*, **371**, **516**; c. w. "who?" **491**
"Fuller," c. w. "lamb" **522** (vii)
Future (tense) c. w. past **19**, **84**, **87**, **240** foll.

"Gabri-el," conflated as (1) "Gabriel" (2) "man to" **37**
Gadarene, the, story of **145–55**
"Galilæan," possible confusion of **498**
"Galilee," *i.e.* "surrounding country" **128**, **438** (i) 10ll.; c. w. "boundary" **433** (ii); "in G." parall. to "from G." **515–6**

Clue includes **1–272**, *Corrections* **273–552**.

"Garden," interpolation of 498 f; "g." c. w. "over against" 498 f
"Gardener," c. w. "convey" 527 f
"Gather" (Heb.) various senses of 396
Genesis, style of, followed by Mk 455 a, 456 (ii) a
Glorified, "was g." c. w. "had horns or rays" 420
"Go," c. w. "pass the night" 116 (comp. 450-2); c. w. "send" 154; parall. to "receive" 244
"Go forth," parall. to "pass the night" 450-2; c. w. "finish" 509 a
"Go up," c. w. "kindle" 373 b-c; c. w. "against," "upon" 506 (i)
God, "Living God" 416
Gold of Ophaz 522 (v) b
Good, "do g. to," parall. to "salute" 254-8
"Great," i.e. "greatest" 467
"Greater, who is" 429 (i) a
Greek additions in O.T. 290, 296; Gk words transliterated in Heb. 519
Greeks, "are always children" 429 (iv) n. 2

"Heal" and "cure," parall. to "teach" 401-3
"Hear," c. w. "wonder" 11, comp. 443; c. w. "keep" 392 a; "hearers" may mean "disciples" 443
"Hearing," parall. to "teaching" 470
"Heaven," c. w. "name" 446; "heaven" meaning "God" 252 a, 446 n. 1; "the heavens opened" 343
Hebrew letters, some, hardly distinguishable 5-7; Heb. corruption may produce Gk corruption 498 c; Heb. conflations 100-3; parallels, differing 241; reduplication 137; variations in Sam. and Chron. 280-9
"Here" and "hither," ins. for clearness in LXX 425 (i); "here" and "to me" 425 (i)
Herod (Antipas) 466 (a) b; Luke's misunderstanding about 55-60; "the tetrarch" 391-3; called "king" in Mk 502 (iii); "the leaven of H." 466 (ε); s. also 503 (iii) a
Herodians, the 466 (ε)
Him, "to him" c. w. "not" 151, 403 (i), 423 a, 529
Historic Present, freq. in Mk 534 (iii), avoided by Mt. and Lk. 505, 534 (iii)
Holy Spirit, the, blasphemy against 367-9; "the Holy Spirit" and "fire" 336-42
Homoeoteleuton 131 a

"Honourable," c. w. "wealthy" 518-19
"Horns," assigned to Moses 420
"Hour" (Aram.) may mean (Heb.) "look" 127
"Household," c. w. "wife" 447 (iv) a
Hundred, a 445 a, 527 k
"Hundredfold, a" 445
"Hungered," parall. to "wild beasts" 191 foll.
"Hypocrisy," "hypocrite" etc. 466 (a)-(ε)

"I," changed to "the Lord" 176 a
Idiom, confusions of 219-72
"Idumæa" (i.e. Edom) c. w. "Syria" (i.e. Aram) 6; parall. to "Syria" 156-8
"If," used interrogatively 363 b, 372; in Heb. adjuration 408; "if" c. w. "ye" 456 (iv); c. w. "say" 456 (iv) n. 2
Imperative, c. w. indicative 28, 243, 390 (i) n. 1, 390 (i) (γ)
Imperfect tense, in Gk 195; in Mk, corrected by Mt. and Lk. 535 a
"Imprison," c. w. "chastise" 502 (vi) c
"In" (or "into") c. w. "from" 151, 158 a, 371, 516; c. w. "through" 444 (i)
Indicative, c. w. imperat. etc. 28, 240-3, 390 (i) n. 1, 390 (i) (γ)
Infinitive, sign of, c. w. negative 529
"Inner," c. w. "before," Corrections p. 322 n.
Insertions (or interpolations), caused by literalism 21, by desire of clearness 22, by incompleteness 21, 447 (iii) a
Interrogative 371-2, 409; exclamatory 357; expressed by "if" 363 b, 372, 409; parall. to conditional 454; expr. by Heb. article 476; c. w. participle 490-1 (comp. 374 a); neg. interrog. 409
"In(to)," c. w. "from" 151, 158 a, 371, 516; c. w. "through" 444 (i)
Is, "there is" (emph.) 435
Isaac, the binding of 521
Israel, "king of I." 508

Jacob and Esau 429 (i)-(vii)
"Jeremiah" 487 (i) (β) d
Jeroboam, traditions about 26
Job, exceptionally interpolated 24 n. 1
John the Baptist, naming of 448 b
"Jonah," or "dove" 412; "the sign of J." 408-12

Clue includes 1-272, Corrections 273-552.

ENGLISH

Jordan, "on the other side of J." and "the surrounding country of J." 70–1, 438 (ii)–(v)
Joseph of Arimathæa 517–19
Joshua, abridgments in 76–9
"Judges," c. w. "men of war" 57
Justin Martyr attacks the Jews for "corrupting" the scriptures 15

"Keep," c. w. "amazed" 392 *a*
"Kindle," parall. to "come" 186, 373; c. w. "go up" 373 *b*–*c*
"King," c. w. "messenger" (or "angel") 105 *a*, 272 (i); parall. to "righteous [man]" 272 (i); parall. to "went" 466 (η) *d*, 502 (iii) n.; "your k." c. w. "what for you?" 502 (iii); "K. of Israel" 508
"Know," and "cause to know," c. w. several other words 7; c. w. "say" 8, 464; w. "evil" 90, 406; w. "yet" 422

"Lacking," parall. to "perfect" 163–4
"Lambs," c. w. "fullers" 522 (vii)
"Last," c. w. "one," *Corr.* p. 42 n. 2; "first" and "last," 429 (i) foll.
Legend, to be distinguished from falsehood 288
"Less, the" 429 (i)
"Life, eternal" 417 *b*
"Light" (n.) c. w. "see" 184
"Light" (vb) parall. to "come" 186; c. w. "go up" 373 *b*–*c*
Lightning, beneficent 522 (ii); c. w. "dawn," "hail," "morning," or "morning-star" 522 (i)–(iii)
Literalism, interpolations caused by 21
"Living God" 416
Logos, the, called "first-begotten" 417
"Look" (Heb.) c. w. "hour" (Aram.) 127
"Lord, the," substituted for "I" 176 *a*
Lucianus of Antioch, his transl. of O.T. 34
Luke, his misunderstanding about Herod Antipas 55–60; never writes "beyond Jordan" 438 (v); nor "sea of Galilee" 438 (v) n. 1; Luke and Matthew borrow from Mark 314–20; minor agreements of Luke and Matthew 534–41

"Man," c. w. "each" 139; w. "Edom" 159; w. "fire" 434; w. "woman" 497 *b*; parall. to "angel" 526; parall. to "son" 259–63; "men"

c. w. "nations" 429 (iv) n. 1; "son of m." 368 foll.
"Manifest" (vb) c. w. "remove" 373 (ii)
Mark, redundancy of, apologized for by Papias 23; conflative tendency apparent in 145 foll.; his style follows that of Genesis 353 *a*, 455 *a*, 456 (ii) *a*; influenced by Isaiah 459 (iv) n. 1; contains no precept to preach the gospel or the kingdom 243; includes late interpolations 325 *a*; termination of his gospel, "they feared" 528–33; names in, omitted in later gospels 36; priority of, to Matthew and Luke 314–30; corrections of, adopted by Matthew and Luke 323, 331 foll.; corrections of, adopted by Matthew and Luke, complete table of 542–4
Matthew, Papias on, *Clue* p. xviii; why alleged to be author of first gospel 317 *a* (comp. 2879); Matthew and Luke borrow from Mark 314–20; minor agreements of Matthew and Luke 534–41
Me, "to me" and "here" 425 (i)
"Meet," c. w. other words 7; "meet" (or "befall") c. w. "call" 472 *c*, 474
"Men of war," c. w. "judges" 57
"Messenger" or "angel" 105 *a*; c. w. "king" 105 *a*, 272 (i)
Messiah, the, identified with Israel 417
"Metamorphose," avoided by Luke 421
"Mock," parall. to "spit" 488
"Morning," c. w. "hail" or "lightning" 522 (i)
"Morning-star," c. w. "lightning" 522 (iii)
Morrow, "on the m." rep. as "on the mountain" 144
"Mountains," c. w. "drought" 20; c. w. "city" 452 *a*; s. "morrow"
"Myrrh," c. w. "covering" 527 *g*

Name, "in the n. because ye are Christ's" 268–72; "n." and "heaven" 446; "*the* NAME" 446; father's name not given to the son 448 *d*
Names, conflations of 36–68; eleven, made into twenty-four, by conflation 45; originated by phrases, prayers etc. 63 foll., comp. 498 *h*
Narrative, c. w. speech 19, 28, 141, 240 foll., comp. 503 (i)–(ii)
"Nations," c. w. "men" 429 (iv) n. 1

Clue includes 1–272, *Corrections* 273–552.

"Near," "draw near," c. w. "call"
386 a, 474 a; "drawing near," parall.
to "after two days" 223
Negative, inserted, omitted, or confused
151, 529, 530; implied from previous
neg. 265 a; c. w. "to him" 123 a,
151, 403 (i), 423 a, 529; neg. interrog.
409
"Neighbour," c. w. "evil" 551 n. 3
Nicodemus Ben Gorion 519
"Nigh," s. "near"
"Not," s. "negative"
"Now," c. w. "in [due] time" 447 (i);
c. w. "thou" 484 (iv) a

Object and subject reversible 19, 335 b,
Corrections p. 142 n. 2; object
defined by Mt.-Lk. 534 (i)
"One," c. w. "first" 293 n. 2; w.
"last," Corrections p. 42 n. 2; w.
"take" 487 (i) (ʃ); w. "some"
463-4; "[one]" meaning "people"
506
Ophaz, gold of 522 (v) b
"Or," variations in LXX where Heb.
omits 226
Oral tradition 545 foll.
Ordinal numbers, c. w. cardinal 78, 226
Origen, on the place of Christ's baptism
14; on the "axe" and the "fire"
341
"Other" 245, 348 a; "other boats"
in Mk 245, s. also Fourfold G.;
"others" c. w. "spices" 527 j; s.
also "another"
"Over against," c. w. "garden" 498 f;
c. w. "tower" 498 g

Papias, on Matthew, Clue p. xviii;
apologizes for Mark's redundancy
23
"Parables," parall. to "thoughts" or
"purposes" 364-6
Parallel books, e.g. Kings and Chronicles
15-16
Paralytic, healing of the 195-209
Parentheses, a source of corruption
503 (ii)
Participle, c. w. interrog. 490-1, comp.
374 a, 527 b; s. also 491 a; substituted
for indic. with "and" 535 (iv)
"Pass the night," c. w. "go" 116,
450-2[1]
Passive (voice) c. w. active and causative
19, 89
Past (tense) c. w. fut. 19, 84, 87,
240 foll.

Peace of Christ, the 437
"Peace," c. w. "accomplish" 477 a
People, meaning "[one]" 506; "his
p." c. w. "with him" 246
"Perfect," parall. to "compassionate"
161-2; to "lacking" or "wanting"
163-4
Peter, "sitting" or "standing" 178-9;
"warming himself" 180 foll.; his
confession 417
Pharisees 466 (ε)
Philo 315
Phylacteries 472 n. 2 and 472 a
"Pillar," metaph. 480 b
Pluperfect tense, non-existent in Heb.
83 a, 241 a
Poetry, how affecting translation 306
foll.
Pray 421 b; "praying" and "fasting"
304-5
Prayers, "making long p." 472 a
"Preaching," parall. to "fame" 129
Prediction, c. w. statement of fact
242 a; s. also "future"
Preposition, see Heb. Index ב, כ, ל,
על, מ
Present, historic, in Mk, avoided by
Mt. and Lk. 505, 534 (iii)
"Priest," c. w. "man of understanding"
466 (η) c
"Proclaim," Mk's use of 350; s. also
2839 a foll.
"Pure," c. w. "buy" 527 e
"Put," c. w. "sit" and w. "there"
506

R and D confused 90, 406, 424, in
Heb. books as well as in transl. from
Heb. 5
Rab "great," c. w. "Rabbi" 468;
c. w. "judge" 472 c
Raise, "be raised" and "arise" 418
Read, "how readest thou?" 469 a
"Receive," parall. to "went" 244
Reduplication, Heb. 137, 387 a;
dropped in LXX 373 (ii) a
"Rejoice," c. w. "together" 470 (iii)
Relative, freq. om. in Heb. 370 (i);
om. after Heb. "man" 476 b, comp.
87 n. 2, 497 c
"Release," in Gk, c. w. "acquit"
503 (iii)
"Remove," c. w. "manifest" 373 (ii)
"Repeat," c. w. "sit" 9, 11
"Return," c. w. "sit" 9, 149; c. w.
"clothed" 149

[1] Add Josh. viii. 13 R.V. txt "went," marg. "lodged."

Clue includes 1-272, Corrections 273-552.

"Reveal," c. w. "roll" and "gravestone" 527 d
"Rich," c. w. "councillor" 519 n. 3
"Righteous [men]," parall. to "kings" 272 (i)
"River," parall. to "young man" 304–5
Robes, "walking in r." 472
"Roll," c. w. "reveal" and "gravestone" 527 d; "stones of rolling," i.e. "great stones" 527 b
Rome, signified by Edom 429 (iv)
"Rubbing with their hands," parall. to "making a way" 210–18
"Rulers," c. w. "chief priests" 59

Sadducees 466 (δ)–(ζ)
"Salt" 432–7; metaph., use of 434 foll.; salting of sacrifices 434
"Salute," parall. to "do good to" 254–8
Samuel, the book of, compared with Chronicles 280–9
"Say," c. w. "know" 8, 464; c. w. "if" 456 (iv) n. 2; "saith Jesus" in Oxyr. Logia 535 (v); s. also "dialogue" and "speech"
Scribes, the 466 (η)
"See," c. w. "light" 184; w. "those" 457; w. "fear" 532
"Send," c. w. "go" 154
Septuagint, the, errors in 3, 15 foll., 32 foll., 314, 466 and see *passim* *Clue* and *Corrections*; abridges and amplifies 290; dislikes anthropomorphism 289; deviated from by later translators 15; experiments in 353, 455 a
"Serve oneself with," i.e. "employ for service" 429 (ii)
Seven, "s. times turn," parall. to "seventy times s." 228–32
Seventy, "s. times seven," parall. to "seven times turn" 228–32; "other seventy [two] disciples" 233–6
"Shall be," ambig. 431 (i)
"Sheol" 548 (3)
Sirach 20 a
"Sit," c. w. "repeat" 9, 11; w. "return" 9, 149; w. "put" 506; Peter "sitting" or "standing" 178–9
"Skin," c. w. "aspect" or "colour" 421 a
"Some," c. w. "one" 463–4
"Son," parall. to "man" 259–63; "son of," conflated as part of name 37; "son of man" 368 foll.; "Son

of God, a, or the," 415 a; a son not called by the father's name 448 d; "a son of sixty-two years," i.e. "sixty-two years old" 125 b
Speech, c. w. narrative 19, 28, 141, 240–3, comp. 503 (i)–(ii); variously assigned 459 (i)–(iv)
"Spices," c. w. "others" 527 j
"Spit," parall. to "mock" 488
Staff, "nothing except a s." parall. to "nor a s." and "neither a s." 264–6; but see also 2888
"Stand," Peter "sitting" or "standing" 178–9; "they that stood by," i.e. attendants 479
Statement of fact, c. w. command 28, 85–6, 141, 240 foll., 390 (i) (γ)
Stone, "s. of rolling," i.e. "great s." 527 b
"Straightway," c. w. "Behold!" 455 a
Subject and object reversible 19, 335 b, *Corrections* p. 142 n. 2; defined by Mt.-Lk. 534 (i)
Subjunctive, Heb., non-existent 240
"Such and such," conflated as "God's Faith" 44
"Surrounding country, the" 128–9
Swords, not habitual for pilgrims 480 n. 1
Symmachus, his transl. of scripture 15 n. 2
Synoptic Gospels, the, conflations in 128–55; confusions of words in 156–218; confusions of idioms in 219–72
Synoptists, the, relation between 322
Syria (i.e. Aram) c. w. Idumæa (i.e. Edom) 6; parall. to Idumæa 156–8

"Take," c. w. "one" 487 (i) (ζ)
Tarshish 522 (v) c
"Teach," parall. to "cure" and "heal" 401–3
"Teacher," c. w. "man of understanding" 466 (η)
"Teaching," parall. to "hearing" 470; "in his t." parall. to "disciples" 470
Technical terms, conflation of 69–76
"Tempting" 465
Tetrarch, Herod the 391–3
"That," c. w. "verily" and w. "when" 459 (v)
Them, "to them" c. w. "therefore" 432
Theodotion, his transl. of scripture 15, 32, 315
"There," c. w. "put" 506

Clue includes 1–272, *Corrections* 273–552.

CLUE AND CORRECTIONS OF MARK

"Therefore," c. w. "not thus" 94; w. "to you" and "to them" 432
"Thing," c. w. "word" 369 a
"Third day, on the," parall. to "after three days" 226-7
"This [woman]," c. w. "thus" 311 n. 1; "those" c. w. "Behold!" and w. "see" 457
"Thou," c. w. "now" 484 (iv) a
Three, "after t. days" parall. to "on the third day" 226-7
Thrice, "before the cock crow twice thrice..." 219-22, s. "twice"
"Through," c. w. "in(to)" 444 (i)
"Thus," c. w. "this [woman]" 311 n. 1
Time, "in [due] t." c. w. "in this t." (*i.e.* "now") 447 (i)
"To," c. w. "against" 369 b
"Together," c. w. "rejoice" 470 (iii)
Tradition, oral 545-52
Transfiguration, the 419-21
Translation, the evidence needed to prove 1-2; specimens of Gk error in 7-12
Transliteration, s. "Greek"
Triple Tradition, the 318 (i)-(iii)
"Tunics, two" 390 (ii) (ε) a
Twelve, instructions to the 390
Twice, "before the cock crow twice thrice...[1]" 219-22
Two 220 a, 224 foll., 234; "after t. days," parall. to "drawing nigh" 223

"Understanding, a man of," c. w. "teacher" 466 (η); w. "priest" 466 (η) c
"Upon," c. w. "against" and w. "went up" 506 (i)

"Valley," conflated as part of name 38
Vaw (Heb.) meaning purpose 474 b
"Verily," c. w. "that," and w. "when" 459 (v); w. "verily I say" 409
"Villages," transl. of Heb. "daughters" 40; parall. to "cities and villages" 389-90

Vocative prefix, c. w. article and w. interrog. 476 a; confused by LXX 497 b
Vowel-points, introduced in 6th or 7th century 4

"Wanting," parall. to "perfect" 163-4
Warm, Peter "warming himself" 180 foll.
Way, "making a w." parall. to "rubbing with their hands" 210-18
"Wealthy," c. w. "honourable" 518-19
"What," c. w. "who?" 502 (ii) b
"When," c. w. "who" 370 b; w. "but" and "for" 428; w. "that" and "verily" 459 (v)
"Where is your faith?" *i.e.* "ye have no faith" 134-6
"Who," (rel.) c. w. "when" 370 b; "whose" c. w. "fire." 339
"Who?" c. w. "from" 491; w. "what?" 502 (ii) b
"Why?" the rhetorical 548 (3)
"Wife," c. w. "household" 447 (iv) a
Wise, the 466 (η)
"With," c. w. "after" 193, 245; "with him" c. w. "his people" 246
"Woman," c. w. "man" 497 b
"Wonder," c. w. "hear" 11; wonder connected with fear 138
"Word," c. w. "thing" 369 a
Words, confusions of 156-218
"World, of the," ins. or om. 436

"Ye," c. w. "if" 456 (iv); "to you" c. w. "therefore" 432
"Yet," c. w. "keep awake" 424; w. "know" 422
"Young man," parall. to "river" 304-5
"Younger, the" 429 (i) foll.

Zacharias, the name of, why proposed to be given to his son 448 b

---

[1] The interpretation suggested in 219 foll. is now confirmed by the recently discovered Heb. of Sir. xiii. 7 (Heb.) "Times two [nay] three," Gk "twice or thrice," Syr. (Walton) "una aut altera vice."

Clue includes 1-272, *Corrections* 273-552.

CLUE AND CORRECTIONS OF MARK

III. GREEK

[*The references are to paragraphs, indicated by black numbers, which, in this Index, run from* 1 *to* 552[1]. *The reasons for combining two Gk words, e.g.* (1) ἀγοράζω *and* καθαρός, *and* (2) ἄγω *and* φέρω, *may be quite different, and must be ascertained from the context.*]

Ἀγοράζω and καθαρός 527 e
ἀγράμματος 317 a, s. also 2879
ἄγω and φέρω 449
ἀδικία and ἀναβαίνω 506 (iii)
αἰνέω and εὐφραίνομαι 460 (ii)–(iii)
αἰτέω and πυνθάνομαι 448 b
αἰτία 506 (i) a, 506 (iii) a
ἀκοή i.e. "teaching" 470; s. also 129
ἀκούω, confused in transl. from Heb. 392–3; ἀκούσαντες ins. 461 d
ἀλλήλων : μετ' ἀ. 437
ἄλλοι and ἕτεροι 487 (i) (β) a
ἅμα and εὐφραίνομαι 470 (iii)
ἀμήν, how used 409
ἀναβαίνω and ἐμβαίνω 244 n. 1; ἀ. and ἀδικία 506 (iii)
ἀνάβασις, Heb. "leaf" 378 a
ἀναβλέπω 527 a
ἀναιρέω act. and mid. 125 a
ἀνακυλίω and ἀποκυλίω 527 c
ἀνασείω 503 (i)
ἀναχωρέω and ὑποχωρέω 397 a
ἀνήρ and ἕκαστος 139 n. 2
ἄνθρωπος and ὅς 497 c, comp. 87 n. 2
ἀνίστημι, ἐγείρω, and ἐξεγείρω 418 a
ἄνοια and ἀνομία 466 (ε) b
ἀνομία and ἄνοια 466 (ε) b
ἀπ' ἄρτι 485 a–c
ἀπό, ἐκ, and ἐν 516 a ; ἀπὸ τότε and ἑκατόν 445 a
ἀποδέχομαι and εἰσδέχομαι 401 a
ἀποκρίνομαι 456 (i)
ἀποκυλίω and ἀνακυλίω 527 c
ἀπόλλυμι 460 (i) ; ἀπολύει and ἀπολλύει 504

ἀπολύω "release" or "acquit" 503 (iii) ; ἀπολύει and ἀπολλύει 504
ἀπορέω and ποιέω 393 b
ἀποσπάω act. and mid. 481 a
ἀποστέλλω and φέρω 449
ἀπώλεια 460 (i)
ἄρτι and νῦν 485 b
ἄρχομαι in Mk 535 a
ἄρχων and ἀπὸ παντός 502 (iii) n.; ἄ. and παιδεύω 502 (vi) a–c
ἀσεβής 434 n.
αὐλή, *Corrections* p. 322 n.
αὐλίζομαι and πορεύομαι 450–2
αὐτός : αὐτή and ἔρχομαι 448 a ; αὐτοῖς and ἑαυτοῖς 437 ; αὐτῷ and οὐ 423 a
ἀφίστημι : ἀποστῆναι "rebel" and παιδεύω 502 (vi) a

Βάλλω : βαλεῖν and λαβεῖν, ἔβαλον and ἔλαβον 377 a, 486 a
βαστάζω and κλέπτω 527 f
βλασφημέω 493 b
βλέπω : βλέπετε 413 a
βοάω and λέγω 475
βραχίων and σπέρμα 121 n. 4

Γῆ 334 b
γίνομαι and ζάω 484 (iii) n. 1 ; γ. and ὁράω 484 (iii) ; ἐγένετο and ἰδού 456 a
γόνατα and σιαγόνα 487 (i) (ζ) a

Δέ : adopted agst Mk by Mt.-Lk. 536 (vi) ; δέ and καί in LXX 537-9 ; εἶπεν δέ discontinued in LXX from Exod. xx. 22 to end of Chron. 538

---
[1] *Clue includes* 1-272, *Corrections* 273-552.

A. 2

δέρω 493 c
δέσμιος and παιδεύω 502 (vi) c
διαμένω 480 b
διαπορεύομαι 390
διὰ τί, and τί, parall. to ὅτι 357 a
διδάσκαλος, διδάσκω, and συνίημι 466 (η)
δίδωμι ἐν φωνῇ 511 a
διέρχομαι and εἰσέρχομαι 444 (i)
διώκω "tremble at," *Corrections* p. 321 n.
δοῦλος, παῖς, and υἱός 107 a
δουλόω 429 (ii)

ε, ο, and c interchanged 493 c
ἐάν interrog. 409 d; ἐάν and λέγω 456 (iv) n. 2; ἐάν and πλήν 484 (ii) a
ἑαυτοῖς and αὐτοῖς 437
ἐγείρω 487 (i) (β) d; ἐ., ἐξεγείρω, and ἀνίστημι 418 a
ἐγώ : ins. and om. 456 (iii); ἐγώ εἰμι 484 (i) a foll.; ἐγώ and εἶπεν 484 (i) b
εἰ interrog. 409
εἰ μή 361, comp. 359 a
εἶδον and εἶπον 482 b; εἶδον and ἰδού 456 a–b
εἰμί : ἐγώ εἰμι 484 (i) a foll.; οὐκ εἰμί 496 a; τὸ ἐσόμενον, only once in N.T. 482 a
εἶπον : εἶπεν etc. om. or ins. in dialogue 459 (i)–(ii); εἶπεν substituted for λέγει 535 (v); ἐ. and οἶδα 464 a; εἶπον and εἶδον 482 b; ἐμβλέψας and εἶπεν 459 (vi); ἐγώ and εἶπεν 484 (i) b
εἰρηνεύω 437
εἰς and ἐπί interchanged in LXX 369 b
εἷς and τινές 463; εἷς and κατέχω or κρατέω 487 (i) (ζ) b
εἰσδέχομαι and ἀποδέχομαι 401 a
εἰσέρχομαι and διέρχομαι 444 (i)
ἐκ, ἀπό, and ἐν 516 a
ἕκαστος and ἀνήρ 139 n. 2; ἑκάστη πόλις, Heb. "city and city" 390 a
ἑκατόν and ἀπὸ τότε 445 a
ἐκεῖ and καί 506 a; ἐ. and τίθημι 506 b
ἐκκεντέω and κατορχέομαι 488 b
ἐκμυκτηρίζω 466 (β) a
ἐκπορεύομαι and ἐξέρχομαι 390 (i) (δ)
ἐκτινάσσω 390 (i) a, s. also *Fourfold Gospel*
ἔκφοβος, *Corrections* p. 315 n.
ἐλάττων 429 (i) foll.; parall. to ἥττων 379 n. 2
ἐλεέω in LXX, Heb. "gather" 401 b
ἐμβλέπω : ἐμβλέψας and εἶπεν 459 (vi)
ἐμπτύω 488
ἐν, ἀπό, and ἐκ 516 a
ἐνειλέω 520

ἐντυλίσσω 521
ἐνώπιον, *Corrections* p. 322 n.
ἐξαίρετος 525 b
ἐξαίρω, v. r. for ξηραίνω 402 a
ἐξεγείρω, ἐγείρω, and ἀνίστημι 418 a
ἐξέρχομαι and ἐκπορεύομαι 390 (i) (δ)
ἐξολεθρεύω 460 (i)
ἑορτή : κατὰ δὲ [τὴν] ἑορτήν 502 (i) n. 1
ἐπερωτάω and ἐρωτάω 456 (ii) a, 466 (δ) a
ἐπί : interchanged w. εἰς in LXX 369 b; w. dat. of pers. 506 (i) b; confused w. ἔτι 422 a
ἐπιβαλών, meaning of 499
ἐπιβλέπω and ἐπιστρέφω 501 a
ἐπιγραφή 506 (i) n. 2
ἐπιγράφω 506 (i) n. 2
ἐπιρράπτω 358[1]
ἐπίσταμαι 497 a
ἐπιστρέφω and ἐπιβλέπω 501 a
ἔρχομαι in Theod., αὐτή in LXX 448 a; ἐ. and φέρω 505 a
ἐρωτάω and ἐπερωτάω 456 (ii) a, 466 (δ) a
ἔσχατον as prep., *Corrections* p. 319 n.
ἔσω and ἕως, *Corrections* p. 322 n.; ἔσω and κατὰ πρόσωπον ib.; ἐσώτατος ib.
ἑταῖρος, Mt.'s use of 187–91
ἕτεροι and ἄλλοι 487 (i) (β) a
ἔτι and ἐπί 422 a
εὐθύς, Heb. "behold !" 353 a, 455 a
εὐσχήμων 519
εὐφραίνομαι and αἰνέω 460 (ii)–(iii); ἐ. and ἅμα 470 (iii)
ἕως and ἔσω, *Corrections* p. 322 n.; ἐ. and νεανίσκος 524
ἑωσφόρος 522 (iii) a

Ζάω and γίνομαι 484 (iii) n. 1

"Ηττων parall. to ἐλάττων 379 n. 2

Θέλω : τί θέλεις; 502 (ii)
θεραπεύω and ἰάομαι 400–403 a

Ἰάομαι and θεραπεύω 400–403 a
ἴδιος : τὰ ἴδια and οἶκος 447 (iv)
ιδον (sic) and ιπον (sic) 482 b
ἰδού, never used by Mk in narrative 455; ἰ. and ἐγένετο 456 a; ἰ. and εὐθύς 455 a; s. also 482 b
ἱερεύς and συνετός 466 (η) c
Ἰησοῦν, spelt ῡ, ins. or om. after ιν 504 a
ἵλεως and μηδαμῶς 460 (iii) a
ἵνα in LXX, καί in Theod. 474 b
Ἰουδαία 438 (iv) n. 1
ιπον (sic) and ιδον (sic) 482 b

---

[1] Add ref. to Steph. *Thes.* 1754, shewing that in Nonn. *Dion.* ix. 3 ἐπέρραφε is prob. corrupt for ἐνέρραφε.

Clue includes 1–272, *Corrections* 273–552.

GREEK

Καθαρός and ἀγοράζω 527 e
καί in Theod., ἵνα in LXX 474 b; καί and ἐκεῖ 506 a; καί and δέ in LXX 537–9
καιρός: πρὸς καιρόν 447 (i) a
κακός and φίλος 551 n. 3
καλέω and κλαίω 313 a
καλῶς 432 a, 433 a
κατέναντι and κῆπος 498 f
κατέχω, s. κρατέω
κατορχέομαι and ἐκκεντέω 488 b
κῆπος and κατέναντι 498 f
κλαίω and καλέω 313 a
κλέπτω and βαστάζω 527 f
κονιορτός and χοῦς 390 (i) (e)
κράσπεδον 388
κρατέω (or κατέχω) and εἰς 487 (i) (ζ) b
κρίνω and μέγας 472 c
κύκλῳ 390 b–d
κύριε: om. and ins. 351; parall. to Ῥαββουνεί 351 b

Λαμβάνω ῥάπισμα 486 a, 492, 492 a; λαβεῖν, ἔλαβον etc. confused with βαλεῖν, ἔβαλον etc. 377 a, 486 a
λέγω: om. and ins. in dialogue 459 (i)–(ii); ἔλεγεν in LXX and Mk 459 (iii) a, 535 (v); λέγει in Mk replaced by εἶπεν in Mt.-Lk. 535 (v); λ. and βοάω 475; λ. and ἐάν 456 (iv) n. 2
λίτρα 527 k
λόγος and συντέλεια 422 a, comp. 123 a
λυπέω in LXX and N.T. 440 n. 2

Μᾶλλον in LXX 503 (iv) a
μανθάνω and πειράζω 466 (η)
μαρτύριον: εἰς μ. αὐτοῖς parall. to εἰς μ. ἐπ᾽ αὐτοῖς 369 b
μαστιγόω and φραγελλόω 493 b
μάστιξ and νόσος 362; s. also 490
μάχαιρα 480 a
μέγας and κρίνω 472 c
μείζων 429 (i) foll.
μέλλω inserted 427.
μέσος: ἐν μέσῳ = Heb. οἰκία 355 a
μετά 193 a; οἱ μ. 495 b
μηδαμῶς and ἵλεως 460 (iii) a

N abbreviated in Gk MSS. 360 a
νεανίσκος and ἕως 524
νομικός 466 (η)
νόσος 390 (i) (β); ν. and μάστιξ 362
νῦν and ἄρτι 485 b; νῦν and σύ 484 (iv) a

Ξηραίνω, v. r. ἐξαίρω 402 a

Ο, Ε, and C, interchanged or dropped 493 c
ὅ, τίς, and vocative 476 a; οἱ δέ, meaning of 487 (i) (β) b, 487 (i) (δ)–(ζ)
ὁδοποιέω and ὁδὸν ποιέω 211 b
οἶδα and εἶπον 464 a
οἰκία, Heb. ἐν μέσῳ 355 a
οἶκος and τὰ ἴδια 447 (iv); ὁ. and πάντα 447 (iv)
ὀλέθριος 460 (i)
ὀλιγο- in compounds 135
ὁράω and γίνομαι 484 (iii)
ὅρια in LXX 438 (ii) a
ὅς and πῦρ 339; ὅς and ἄνθρωπος 497 c, comp. 87 n. 2
ὅτι, parall. to τί and διὰ τί 357 a
οὐ and αὐτῷ 423 a; οὐκ εἰμί 496 a
οὐκέτι 485
οὖν rare in Mk 459 (v) n. 2
οὗτος: ταῦτα = Heb. "before them" 484 (iii) n. 2
οὕτως: οὐχ οὕτως = Heb. "ought ye not?" 461 a
ὄψις 421

Παιδεύω 493 b, 502 (v); π. and ἀποστῆναι 502 (vi) a; π. and ἄρχων 502 (vi) a–c; π. and δέσμιος 502 (vi) c
παιδίον "first-born" 417 a
παίζω and ῥαπίζω 487 (i) (ζ) a, 493 a
παῖς, δοῦλος, and υἱός 107 a
παίω and πατάσσω 478; π. and ῥαπίζω 487 (i) (ζ) a
παράνομος and ὑποκριτής 466 (a) b
παρίστημι, in perf., "stand by," i.e. "attend" 479
πᾶς: πάντα and οἶκος 447 (iv); πᾶς and σύ 551; ἀπὸ παντός and ἄρχων 502 (iii) n.
πατάσσω and παίω 478
πεζῇ 75–6, 165–6
πειράζω 465 foll.; π. and μανθάνω 466 (η)
περί: οἱ π. 370
περιάπτω 180 a, 493 d
περιβόλαια prob. = "phylacteries" 472 n. 2
περίσσευμα 404–5, but see *Fourfold Gospel* πλήρωμα
περίχωρος 335 a
πλεονάκις and πολλάκις 445 a
πλήν and ἀλλά 484 (ii) a
ποδήρης 522 (v) a
ποία "soap" 522 (iv) a
ποιέω and ἀπορέω 393 b
πορεύομαι and αὐλίζομαι 450–2[1]; ἐπορεύετο meaning "increased" 442

[1] See footnote in English Index, "pass the night."

Clue includes 1–272, *Corrections* 273–552.

2—2

πρᾶγμα parall. to ῥῆμα 369 a, comp.
119 a
πρεσβύτερος 429 (i) c
προπορεύομαι implying "more and
  more" 442
προσεγγίζω and προσσιελίζω 488, *Corrections* p. 233 n. 1
προσέρχομαι and συνίημι 365; π. and
  συνετίζω 466 (η)
προσκεφάλαιον 382–5
πρόσωπον 420 a; κατὰ π. and ἔσω,
  Corrections p. 322 n.
προτερέω 429 (vii)
πρόφασις and αἰτία 506 (iii)
πυνθάνομαι and αἰτέω 448 b
πρωτόγονος and πρωτότοκος 417 n. 1
πρῶτος 429 (i)–(vii)
πρωτοτόκος 429 (vii) a; π. and πρωτόγονος 417 n. 1

Ῥαββουνεί parall. to κύριε 351 b
ῥαπίζω, παίζω and παίω 487 (i) (ζ) a,
  493 a
ῥάπισμα 486 a, 492 a, 493 a
ῥάπτω and ῥίπτω 358
ῥαφίς 444 (ii)
ῥῆμα and πρᾶγμα 369 a, comp. 119 a
ῥίπτω and ῥάπτω 358

c, ϵ, and o, interchanged or dropped
  493 c
σανδάλιον and ὑπόδημα 390 (ii) (ϵ) a
σιαγών : σιαγόνα and γόνατα 487 (i) (ζ) a
σοφός and φιμόω 462
σπάω act. and mid. 481 a
σπέρμα and βραχίων 121 n. 4
στέγη 198 a
στολή 525
στόμα and σῶμα 522 (v) c
στυβή = στοιβή (comp. Mk xi. 8 στιβάδας) 311
στυγνάζω 439
σύ and νῦν 484 (iv) a; σύ and πᾶς 551

συνάγομαι and ὑποχωρέω 396–7
συνακολουθέω τινι 515 a
συνετός and ἱερεύς 466 (η) c
συνίημι and διδάσκω 466 (η); σ. and
  προσέρχομαι 365
συντέλεια and λόγος 422 a, comp. 123 a
σῶμα and στόμα 522 (v) c

Τί, s. τίς
τίθημι and ἐκεῖ 506 b; τ. and φυλάσσω
  506 c
τίς, τί : τίς, ὁ, and voc. 476 a; τίς =
  Heb. participial prefix 491 a; τί
  θέλεις ; 502 (ii) ; τί ἐστίν σοι; and τί
  σύ ; 502 (ii) a ; τί or τίνα 502 (ii) b;
  τίνα in N.T. perh. only once before
  vowel 502 (ii) b ; τί and διὰ τί parall.
  to ὅτι 357 a
τις : τινές and εἷς 463
τρυμαλιά 444 (ii)

Ὑπόδημα and σανδάλιον 390 (ii) (ϵ) a
ὑποκριτής and παράνομος 466 (a) b
ὑποχωρέω and ἀναχωρέω 397 a; ὑ. and
  συνάγομαι 396–7

Φέρω and ἄγω 449; φ. and ἀποστέλλω
  449 ; φ. and ἔρχομαι 505 a
φεύγω (?) once used of Jesus 397 a
φίλος and κακός 551 n. 3
φιμόω and σοφός 462
φραγελλόω and μαστιγόω 493 b
φυλάσσω and τίθημι 506 c
φῶς 435
φωστήρ 435
φωσφόρος 522 (iii) a

Χαλκολίβανον 522 (vi)
χαλκός *i.e.* "money," perh. "pelf"
  390 (ii) (β) n. 2 [1]
χοῦς and κονιορτός 390 (i) (ϵ)
χώρα 150 n. 1, 334 b

---

[1] See *Fourfold G.* κέρμα, similarly used in Jn ii. 15.

Clue includes 1–272, *Corrections* 273–552.

CLUE AND CORRECTIONS OF MARK

IV. HEBREW

[*The references are to paragraphs, indicated by black numbers, which, in this Index, run from 1 to 552¹. "C. w." means "c(onfused) or c(onfusable) w(ith)." For details, the context must be consulted. "Hebrew," in this and the following Indices, includes Aramaic.*]

א c. w. ה and ע 4 *a–b*, 186 *a*, 484 (iv) *a*

אבד, s. האביד

אביתר "Abiathar," c. w. אל־בית "to the house of" 65

אדם "Edom," "Idumæa," "man" 159; c. w. אמר "Amorite" 114; c. w. ארם "Syria" 6, 159, 329

אהיה "I shall be," c. w. אחרי "behind me" 96 *a*

אהל "tent," c. w. הלך "go" 444 (i)

או "or," c. w. אל "not," "to," "God" 529; לו "not" or "to him" 529

אופז "Uphaz," c. w. אפוד "Ephod," אזור "light" (*q. vid.*), "girdle" 522 (v) *b*

אור "flame" or "light" 181 *a*, "kindle" 493 *d*; c. w. אזר "gird round" 493 *d*, אזור "girdle" 148 *a*; w. אופז "Uphaz," אפוד "Ephod" 522 (v) *b*; w. ראה "see"

181–4; w. עור "skin" 421 *a*; w. בוא "come" etc., s. בוא

אז "then," c. w. אני "navy" and אני "*I*" 487 (i) (ך) *d*; c. w. אחז "take" 487 (i) (η) *a*

אזור "vinculum" or "cingulum" 148 *a*; s. אור and אזל

אזל "go," c. w. אזר "gird," "bind," ἐνισχύειν, κατισχύειν, אזור "vinculum," "cingulum" 148 *a*

אזר, s. אזל and אור

אח "brother," c. w. אני "*I*," which = אני "shipping" 349 *a*; אחיך "thy brothers," c. w. אני "*I*" 96 *a*; אחיך "thy brother," c. w. אחריך "after thee" 348 *a*; אחיו "his brother" or "his brothers," אחי "my brother" or "my brothers" 347

אחד "one," Aram. for Heb. אחז "grasp," c. w. אחר (*q. vid.*)

Clue includes 1–272, *Corrections* 273–552.

or אַחֲרֵי 487 (i) (𝑔) foll.; w.
אֶחְדָּל "I will cease" 311 n.;
w. אַחַר "after" 223, 245;
pl. אֲחֵרִים "few," c. w.
אֲחֵרִים "last" 487 (i) (𝑔) g;
אֲחֵרִים "a few," c. w.
אַחַד מִ־ "one of" 463;
אֲחֵרִים "certain persons,"
c. w. אֲחֻזִים "taking" 487
(i) (𝑔) foll.

אָחַז "grasp," "take," "hold," is
in Aram. אֲחַד (q. vid.); c. w.
אַחַר "hinder" (q. vid.) and
w. אַחֲרֵי "after" 487 (i) (𝑔)
foll.; c. w. אָז "then" 487
(i) (η) a

אַחַר "after," c. w. אֶחָד "one"
223 a, 311 n.; c. w. אֵת
"with" 193 a; = "other,"
"after," "behind," "back-
wards," "followers," etc.
245, 348 a, 381; = "hinder"
487 (i) (𝑔) b; c. w. אָחַז
"grasp" 487 (i) (𝑔) foll.;
אַחֲרֵי "after" 487 (i) (𝑔) foll.;
אַחֲרֵי "behind me," c. w.
אֶהְיֶה "I shall be" 96 a;
אֲחֵרִים "others," c.w. אִכָּרִים
"husbandmen" 460 (i);
אַחֲרֶיךָ "after thee," c. w.
אָחִיךָ "thy brother" 348 a;
אֲחֵרִים "last," c. w. אֲחֵרִים
"few" 487 (i) (𝑔) g; אַחַר
"at the last," c. w. אֶחְדָּל
"I will cease" and אַחַר
"one" 311 n.

אַחַת "one thing," c. w. אֵת "with"
or "in" 164 n.

אֵי "where?" hence "not" 136 a

אֵינֶנִּי "I am not" 496 a

אִיסֹר "I will chastise," c. w. אָסִיר
"prisoner" 502 (vi) c

אִישׁ "each," "man," "men" 139;
אִישׁ or אֱנוֹשׁ (q. vid.), c. w.
אֵשׁ "fire" or w. אִשֶּׁה "fire-
sacrifice" 289 a, comp. 434;
c. w. rel. pron. אֲשֶׁר 97 n.,
476 b, 497 c

אִכָּרִים "husbandmen," c. w. אֲחֵרִים
"others" 460 (i)

אֶל־ or לְ־ "to," becomes part of the
foll. name 498 h

אֵל = "God" or "to" 37, comp.
529; hortative negative 151
n.; interchangeable w. עַל
369 b

אֶל־בֵּית, s. אֲבִיתַר

אֱלָהּ (Aram.) "God" = (Heb.) אֱלוֹהַּ
or אֱלֹהִים, c. w. אֵל־חַי
"living God" 416

אֵלֶּה "these," c. w. לֵוִיא "Levites"
38

אֱלֹהִים = "God" or "the judges" 74;
c. w. אֲלֵיכֶם "to you" 278
n.; God = (Heb.) אֱלוֹהַּ,
(Aram.) אֱלָהּ, c. w. אֵל־חַי
"living God" 416

אֲלֵיכֶם "to you," s. אֱלֹהִים

אִם "if," adjurative, interrogative,
and negative 371 a, 409, esp.
409 c-d; c. w. אֶחָד "one,"
אָמַר "say," and אַתֶּם "ye"
456 (iv); אִם יֻתַּן "if there
shall be given," c. w. אֲמַרְתִּי
"I have said," and אָמֵן
"verily" 409 b

אָמֵן "verily," s. אִם

אֱמֹר "Amorite," s. אֱדֹם

אָמַר "say," c. w. רָאָה "see" 459
(vi), 464 a; w. אָנֹכִי "I"
484 (i) b; w. אִם "if" 456
(iv) n.; s. יָדַע

אֱנוֹשׁ "man," "woeful," "incurable"
261 a; s. also אִישׁ and אֱנָשׁ

Clue includes 1-272, *Corrections* 273-552.

HEBREW 23

אֲנִי "*I*" or "shipping" **349** *a*, **487**
(i) (ʓ) *d*; c. w. אָח "brother"
and אָחִיךָ "thy brother"
96 *a*, **349** *a*; w. אִן "then"
487 (i) (ʓ) *d*

אָנֹכִי "*I*" **94** *a*; c. w. אָמַר "say"
484 (i) *b*; s. esp. **484** (i) *a–c*

אָנַשׁ "sick unto death," "afflicted,"
c. w. נָשָׂא "lift up," "bear"
(*i.e.* "forgive.") **262** *a*,
263 *a*; s. also אֱנוֹשׁ and אִישׁ

אָסִיר "prisoner," c. w. אִסֵּר "I will
chastise" **502** (vi) *c*

אֵפוֹד "Ephod," s. אוֹפָז and אוֹר

אַרְבָּה, s. אַרְבַּע

אַרְבַּע "four" **106**; c. w. אֲרֻבָּה "roof-
window" **204**; w. שֶׁבַע
"seven" **234**; s. also דָּבָר

אָדָם, s. אֲרָם

אַרְעָא (Aram.) "land," "landward,"
"inferior," "less," "smaller"
379

אֵשׁ "fire," c. w. אִשֶּׁה "fire-offering," and אִישׁ or אֱנוֹשׁ
"man" **289** *a*, **434**; c. w.
rel. pron. אֲשֶׁר **339–40**

אִשָּׁה, s. אִישׁ

אֲשֶׁר relative, or "in order that"
373 (i); c. w. אֵשׁ "fire"
339–40; w. אִישׁ "man"
97 n., **476** *b*, **497** *c*

אֵת "with" or "in," c. w. אַחַת
"one thing" **164** n.; c. w.
אַחַר "after(wards)" **193** *a*;
אִתִּי "with me" = "Ittai"
38; אִתָּךְ "with thee," and
אֹתָךְ "thy signs," c. w. אַתָּה
"thou" **417** *b*

אַתָּה "thou," c. w. אֹתָךְ "with thee"
or "thy signs" **417** *b*; c. w.
עַתָּה "now" **484** (iv) *a*

אֹתָךְ "thy signs," s. אֵת

אַתֶּם "ye," c. w. אִם "if" **456** (iv)

בְּ c. w. כְּ **4** *a–b*, **114** *a*, **351** *b*; c. w.
מִ **9** *a*, **144** *a*, **151** *a*, **158** *a*,
253, **371**, **516** *a*

בְּ (s. above) prepos. **444** (i); means
"through" **444** (i) *b*; superfl.
in English "know *in*," etc.
365; "gave *with* a cry" **510**,
511 *a*; "*B*ishlam" interpr.
as "*in* peace" **46**

בְּבֶל "Babylon," ? c. w. כָּבֵד "glory"
122 n.

בִּגְלַל "for the sake of," c. w. גָּלָה
"manifest" **373** (ii)

בַּגַּנָּה "in the garden," c. w. נִגְלָה
"uncovering" **498** *d*

בַּד "white linen," c. w. בָּחוּר
"chosen," "young man,"
בַּר "pure," בָּהַר "bright"
525

בְּדָוִד "in David," c. w. בְּכוֹר "first-
born" **91**

בַּדִּים, s. **522** (v) *a*

בָּהַר "on the mountain," and מֵהַר
"from the mountain," c. w.
מָחָר "on the morrow,"
"next day" **144** *a*

בּוֹא "came," c. w. בָּהּ "in that"
125; c. w. בָּחַן "tempt,"
which is c. w. בִּין rt. of
"instruct," "teach" **466** (η);
הֵבִיא "cause to go," c. w.
הֶאֱבִיד "destroy" **249** n.;
s. also **186** *a*, **373** *a*, *b* foll.
373 (ii) etc.

בָּחוּר "young man," "chosen" **417** *a*,
525–6; c. w. בֹּקֶר "morning
light" or "oxen" **524**; c. w.
בַּר "white linen," בָּהַר
"bright," בָּרָד "hail," בָּרָק
"lightning," קֶבֶר "sepul-

Clue includes **1–272**, *Corrections* **273–552**.

chre" 525; c. w. בָּרוּךְ "blessed," בַּר "son," דָּבָר "word" 417 *a–b*; s. *passim* 522 (ii)–524 foll.

בָּחִיר "elect," "chosen," c. w. בָּחוּר "young man" 526 *a*

בָּחַן "tempt," c. w. בּוֹא "approach," and בִּין "teach" 466 (η)

בִּין "teach," s. בָּחַן

בֵּין "between," c. w. בַּיִת "house" 355 *a*; c. w. בְּנֵי "sons of" 438 (v) *a*

בַּיִת "house," rendered "all," "own" 447 (iv); meaning "wife" 447 (iv) *a*; c. w. בֵּין "between," "among" 355 *a*

בָּכָה "weep" 313 *a*

בְּכוֹר "firstborn" 417 *a*; c. w. בָּדָד "in David" 91; c. w. בָּחוּר "chosen," "young man," בַּר "son," בָּרוּךְ "blessed" 417 *a*; בְּכֹרָה "first born-ship," c. w. בְּרָכָה "blessing" 417 n.; s. also 417 *b*

בְּכֹרָה, s. בְּכוֹר

בֵּן "son," in pl., c. w. יוֹם "day," מַיִם "water," יָמִין "right hand" 230 n.

בְּנֵי "sons of," "Baani" etc. 37, comp. 368–9; c. w. בֵּין "between" 438 (v) *a*

בְּעֳנִי "in, or with, affliction," c. w. בְּעִתּוֹ "in its time," "in due time" 447 (iii)

בָּרָד, s. בַּעַר

בְּעִתּוֹ, s. בְּעֳנִי

בֹּקֶר "morning light," or "ox" 524; c. w. בָּרָק "lightning," בָּרָד "hail," בָּחוּר "young man," "chosen," קֶבֶר "sepulchre," בַּר "son," "pure" etc. 522

(ii)–526; c. w. בַּקֶּרֶן "with rays" 522 (vii)

בַּר "Bar-," "son" 61 foll., 417, esp. 417 *a–b*; c. w. בְּכוֹר "firstborn," בָּחוּר "chosen," "young man," בָּרוּךְ "blessed" 417 *a*; בַּר "lye," "soap" 522 (iv); דָּבָר "word" 417 *b*; s. also כָּבַר

בְּרַגְלָיו "on foot," or "following after" 75–6, 166

בָּרָד "hail," c. w. בָּעֲרוּ "were kindled," עָבָיו "his thick clouds," עָבְרוּ "passed" 101; c. w. בַּר "lye," "soap," בָּרָק "lightning," בֹּקֶר "morning-light" or "ox," בָּחוּר "chosen," "young man" etc. 522 (ii)–526; s. also בֹּקֶר

בְּרָכָה "blessing," c. w. בְּכֹרָה "first-bornship" 417; s. בְּכוֹר

בְּרַע "on evil," c. w. עֲבֵרָה ὁρμήματα, עָבַד "do" 191 *b*

בָּרָק "lightning" etc., c. w. בֹּקֶר "morning-light" or "ox," בָּחוּר "chosen," "young man" 522 (ii)–526; s. בָּחוּר

בָּתוֹת "desolate," c. w. תֵּבֵל "habitable land" 150 n.

גְּבוּל "boundary" 438 (ii) *a*; s. also גְּלִילָה

גּוֹי "nation," c. w. עִיר "city" (*q. vid.*), נֵר "beacon" 436 *a*; גּוֹיִם "nations," c. w. "men" 429 (iv)

גּוֹלֵל "gravestone," c. w. גָּלָה "reveal," גָּלַל "stone of rolling" 527 *b, d* foll.

גּוֹיִם "men," s. גּוֹי

Clue includes 1–272, *Corrections* 273–552.

גל "spring," c. w. גן "garden" 498 d

גלה "reveal," "manifest," "betray" 373 (ii) b–c; c. w. ב גלל "for the sake of" 373 (ii) b; גלילי "Galilæan," גלל "roll" 498 foll.; נגלה "uncovering," בגנה "in the garden" 498 d; נגלתה "is revealed," LXX ἐπέβλεψεν 498 d; גולל "gravestone," גלל "stone of rolling" 527 b, d foll.

גלילה "region," "circuit," "Galilee" 128, 438 (ii) foll.; c.w. גבולת "boundaries" 438 (ii) a–b

גלילי "Galilæan," גלל "roll," גלה "reveal," "betray" 498 foll.

גלל "roll," "stone of rolling" etc., s. גלה; "sake" (in בגלל), s. גלה

גן, or גנה "garden," c. w. גל "spring" 498 d; c. w. נגד "over against" 498 f; בגנה "in the garden," c. w. נגלה "uncovering" 498 d

גנב "convey," c. w. גנן "gardener" 527 f

גן, s. גנה

גנן "gardener," c. w. גנב "convey" 527 f

ד c. w. ר 5, 90 foll., 106, 125 b, 161, 191 b, 403, 406

דבר "word" or "thing" 119, 369 a; parall. to עבד "servant" 417 b; c. w. בר "son" 417 b; c. w. דרך "way" 369 a; מדבר "more than word [can express]," c. w. מבר "more than soap" or מברד "more than purifying" 522 (iv);

על־דבר "because of" 391 n.; רביעה דברה "Debir," c. w. "fourth part" 391 n.

דוד, s. בדור

דע imperat. of ידע "know" (q. vid.), c. w. רע "friend," "companion," "evil" etc. 10, 90, 188

דק "dust," c. w. רק "spittle" 488 b

דקק "crush," "pound," "beat" 214; once = "champ," "eat" 213–15; c. w. דרך "way," "trample" 211 foll.; c. w. רק, רקד etc. 488 b

דקר "pierce," fig. "curse," "contemn," c. w. רקד "dance over," "insult" 488 b; how transl. 488 b

דרך "way," "trample" etc. 211 foll.; c. w. דקק (q. vid.); w. דבר "word" 369 a

דרש 465 n., comp. 466 (η); "seek," interchanged w. שאל "ask" 255

ה c. w. ת 4 b, 5, comp. 185 b

ה article, or vocative, or interrog. prefix 372, 476 a, 497 b; interrog. sometimes rendered el or où 409 a foll.

הוא, or הנה, "behold," c. w. הוא "this," or היה "be" 456 a

האביד "destroy," c. w. הביא "cause to go," "bring" 249

האיר "kindle," c. w. הביא "bring" 186 n., comp. 373 a foll.

הביא "cause to come," "bring," c. w. האביד "destroy" 249; c.w. האיר "kindle" 186, comp. 373 a foll.

הוא "this," s. הא

היה "be," "was," c. w. חיה "live"

Clue includes 1–272, Corrections 273–552.

and חזה "behold" 484 (iii);
w. הנה "behold" 455 a,
456 a; w. הוא "this" 456 a;
יהי or יהיה "be," c. w.
יהוה "the Lord" 297 n.
הכהן "the priest," c. w.
המבין " teacher," " man of understanding " 466 (η) c
הלא "nonne?" 461 a
הלך "go," "went," c. w. המלך
" the king " 466 (η) d ; c. w.
אהל " pitch tent " 444 (i) n.
הלל "praise," c. w. חלל "enjoy,"
" profane," "make com-
mon " 460 (ii), comp. 461 a
הלם "hither," c. w. לחם "bread"
403 (i)
הכהן, המבין, s.
המה "those," c. w. הנה "behold"
457 n.; הנה "those" (fem.),
also "behold" 457 n.

הלך, s. המלך
הנה "behold," also הא 456 a ; c. w.
הוא " this " 456 a; w. היה
"be," "was" 455 a, 456 a;
means "those" (fem.) 457 n.;
c. w. המה "those" (masc.)
(LXX ἰδού) 457 n.; means
"hither" 425 (i) b; rendered
"straightway" in Genesis but
not in later books 353 a, 455 a
הר "mountain," c. w. עיר "city"
(q. vid.) 436 a, 452 a ; הרים
" mountains," c. w. חרב
"drought" 20 a

ו (vaw) c. w. י (yod) 4 a (iii);
meaning " for " or " now "
47; "but" or "so" 102;
"and" or "(in order) that"
142, 474 b, comp. 240; "and"
or "even" 237-9, 447 (ii),

comp. 283 n.; "since" 82 ;
other English conjunctions
102, 532 a ; "city and city,"
i.e. " each city " 390 a ; s.
also 224-6
ויוצא " and brought out," parall. to
ויצו " and commanded "
154 n.
ויחדו " and rejoiced," c. w. יחדיו
"together" 470 (iii)
וילך " and went," c. w. וילן "and
passed the night " 116 a,
comp. 450-1, 451 a
ויראם "and looked on them,"· c. w.
ויאמר " and said " 459 (vi)
ושבעה " and sevenfold," c. w. ישב
"he shall turn" 231 a

זה "this," and זנה " adulterous"
407 a
זרע "arm," also "seed" or "off-
spring " 121

ח c. w. ה (q. vid.) 4 b, 5, 185 b ;
w. א and ע 4 b; interchanged
w. ק 524
חדה "rejoice," and יחד " unite,"
forms of, c. w. יחדיו " together " 470 (iii)
חזה " behold," s. חיה
חיה " live," היה "be," "was," and
חזה "behold" 484 (iii)
חכם "wise," "do wisely," and חסם
" muzzle " 462 a
חלה " be sick," Greek renderings of
390 (i) (β)
חלילה (lit.) " profanation " 460 (ii),
460 (iii) a
חלל " enjoy," " profane," " make
common " 460 (ii) ; c. w.
הלל "praise" 460 (ii),
461 a

Clue includes 1-272, *Corrections* 273-552.

חנף "hypocrite," "profane" 466 (a) foll.

חסד "(is a) reproach," "merciful" 161–4; c. w. חסר "lacking" 161–4

חסם "muzzle," and חכם "wise," "do wisely" 462 a

חסר, s. חסד

חרב "drought," c. w. הרים "mountains" 20 a

חרם "utterly destroy," and כרם "vinedresser" 460 (i)

טימי "profit," טמא "unclean," "defiled," and תימה "admiration" 67–8

י (*yod*) and ו (*vaw*) 4 a (iii)

ידע "know" 7; c. w. יעד "appoint a meeting" 7; w. עוד "still," על "upon" 123 a, 422; w. רוע "cry out" 7, comp. 147; w. רע "evil" 7, 90, 406 a; w. רעה "feed" 7; w. רעע "break," "crush" 7, 147; rendered "say" 464 (esp. 464 a, and comp. 8); s. also 496 b

יהוה "the Lord," c. w. forms of היה "be" 297 n.

יום "day," forms of, c. w. ימין "right hand," מים "water," בנים "sons" 230 n.

יונה "Jonah" or "dove," c. w. ינה "oppress," יתן "shall be given" 412 a

יחד "unite," יחדיו "together," c. w. ויחדו "and rejoiced" 470

יכח "will scourge," c. w. יכח "admonish," "reprove" 493 b; s. also 502 (vi)

יכל "be able," c. w. forms of כלה

כל "come to an end," comp. כל "all" 363 b

וילך, s. ילך

יום, s. ימין

יונה, s. ינה

יסר "chastise," c. w. סר or שר "governor" 502 (vi); s. also איסר

יעד "appoint a meeting," c. w. ידע "know," רוע "cry out," רע "evil," רעה "feed," רעע "break," "crush" 7

יצא "go forth," c. w. יצת "light" 373 d

יקרב "will draw near," c. w. ירק "spit" 488 n.

ירא "fear" 138, 356; means "he feared" or "he will see" 533

ירמיה "Jeremiah" 487 (i) (β) d; c. w. forms of רום "lift" and אמר "say" 487 (i) (β) d

ירק, or רקק, "spit," c. w. יקרב "will draw near," דק "dust," רקד "dance over," and דקק "break" 488 n.

יש "*is*" 435; c. w. ישר "right" 435; rendered ἔσται 437 n. 2; ambig. 487 (i) (β) d

ישב "sit," c.w. forms of שוב "turn," "return," "do again" 9, 149; meaning "abide" 178 foll.; s. also 231 a, 448 c

ישר "right," s. יש

יתן "shall be given," s. יונה

כ c. w. ב 4 a–b, 351 b; hence כ "like," c. w. ב "in" 114 a

כבד "glory," c. w. כבר "like a son" 125 b; s. also כבד "rich" 518

כבסים "fullers," c. w. כבשים "lambs" 522 (vii) n.

Clue includes 1–272, *Corrections* 273–552.

כבר "like a son of" (*i.e.* "aged"), c. w. כבר "renowned" 125 *b*

הכהן, s. כהן

כון "prepare," "set," c. w. כן ("right" 433 *a*) 434 *b*

כזית "like this" (fem.) conflated 311 n.

כי "for" or "when" 98 *a*; "but" or "for" 115 n.; "but" or "when" or "for (indeed)" or "assuredly" 428; "when" or "that" or "verily" or equiv. to inv. commas 459 (v); s. also 102

כי אם "that if" or "except" 411; "but if," "only," "however" 484 (ii) *a*

ככר "plain," "circle" 335 *a*

כל "all," ins. or om. 380 *a*; c. w. כלה "come to an end" and יכל "be able" 363 *b*

כל, s. כלה

כן "well," "good," "right" 433; c. w. לכם "to you," and לכן "therefore" 433; c. w. להם "to them" 433 *a*; c.w. כון "prepare," "set" 434 *b*; s. also 432 *a*, 502 (ii)

כנף (lit.) "wing," hence "border (of garment)" 388 n.[1]

כף "palm" of hand, "sole" of foot 218

כרמים "vinedressers" or "vineyards," c. w. חרם "destruction" 460 (i)

כשל "fall," "stagger," and שכח "forget" 250–1

ל c. w. ר 148 *a*, 351 *a*; sign of infin. 529; c. w. part of a name 498 *h*

לא "not" (sometimes written לו 94 *a*, 403 (i)), c. w. לו "to him" 123 *a*, 423 *a*; c. w. ־ל sign of infin., w. אל "God" (or "to"), w. או "or" 529 n.

לכן, or לא כן, לאכן "not thus," c.w. "therefore" (*q. vid.*) 94 *a*

לב "heart," and קרב "midst," s. 370 (i)–371

לבן "white(n)," c. w. Heb. of "Lebanon" 522 (vi) *c*, 525 *c*

להם "to them," "for themselves," c. w. לחם "bread" 267 (iii); w. לכם "to you" and לכן "therefore" or "to you" (fem.) 432 *a*; w. כן (*q. vid.*) 433 *a*; s. also 502 (ii)

לחן "therefore," c. w. להם "(to) them" 432 *a*; w. לכן (*q. vid.*) "therefore," or "to you" (fem.) 432 *a*

לו "to him" 351 *a*, also "not" 94 *a*, 403 (i); c. w. לא "not" 123 *a*, 423 *a*; s. also 529 n.

לויא "Levites," conflated as אלה "these" 38

לוט "covering," c. w. לט "myrrh" 527 *g*

לחם "bread," c. w. הלם "hither" 403 (i); w. להם "for themselves" or "to them" 267 (iii)

לוט, s. לט

לכם "to you," c. w. לכן "there-

---

[1] The view taken in 388 is confirmed by the fact that כנף—the word there suggested as the original in Mk v. 27, Mt. ix. 20, Lk. viii. 44—occurs in Mt.-Lk. in the Curetonian, rendered "skirt" by Prof. Burkitt, and also in Ezek. v. 3 where it is rendered by LXX "mantle," Aq. "fringes," Sym. "borders," al. Sym. "the border of thy cloak."

Clue includes 1–272, *Corrections* 273–552.

HEBREW

fore" or "to you" (fem.) and w. לָהֶם "to them" 432 a; לָהֶן "therefore" (LXX "(to) them") 432 a; s. also 432-5, 502 (ii) לָכֵן "therefore," also "to you" (fem.) 432 a; c. w. לֹא כֵן "not thus" 94 a; s. also לָכֶם

לֵעָג "mock," and מָעוֹג "cake" 466 (a) a

־מ (particip. prefix) 490; c. w. מָה or מִי interrog. 374 a, 490-1, esp. 491 a, 527 b

־מ (prepos. prefix) "from," c. w. ־בְּ "in," "into," "with" 9 a, 144 a, 151, 158 a, 253, 371, 516 a; c. w. מִי or מָה interrog. 491 a, 527 b; c. w. final ם (sign of pl.) s. ם final below; c. w. ם 309 n.; "more than" 522 (iv); ambig. 310 n. 1; comp. 380, 380 a

ם final, written ־ם, pl. suffix, c. w. ־מ "from" 487 (i) (ζ); repeated as ־מ "from" 155 n.; causes omission of foll. ־מ "from" 114 n.; s. also 522 (iv)

מְאֹד "exceedingly," c. w. מֵאָה (or מְאַת) "a hundred," "a hundred times" 445 a; w. מֵאָז "from then" 445 a

מֵאָה, מְאַת, "a hundred," s. מְאֹד

מֵאָז "from then," s. מְאֹד

מִגְדָּל "tower," c. w. מִנֶּגֶד "over against" 498 g

מַדּוּעַ (lit.) "knowing what?" i.e. "why?" 357 a; c. w. מֵרַע "evil" 406 a; w. מֵידַע "acquaintance" 496 b

מִדְרָשׁ, meaning of 465 n., 466 (η)

מָה "what?" "why?" c. w. מִי "who?" 493 c, 502 (ii) b; w. particip. prefix 374 a; מָה לָכֶם "what will ye?" c. w. מַלְכְּכֶם "your king" 502 (iii)

מָחָר "next day," c. w. מֵהַר "from the mountain" 144 a

מִי "who?" s. ־מ and מָה

מֵידַע "acquaintance," c. w. מַדּוּעַ (q. vid.) 496 b

מַיִם "water," c. w. forms of יוֹם "day," יָמִין "right hand," בָּנִים "sons" 230 n.

מַכִּים "smiters," נָכִים "abjects," and נָכְרִים "aliens" 490

מָלֵא "fulfil," c. w. מִלְתָא "word" 123 a, 422 a

מַלְאָךְ "angel" (or "messenger") c. w. מֶלֶךְ "king" 105-6, 272 (i), 285 foll.

מִלִּים "words," c. w. סָלַח "forgive" 403 a

מַלְאָךְ and מָה, הָלַךְ, s. מֶלֶךְ

מָלֵא, s. מִלְתָא

מִנֶּגֶד "over against," c. w. "tower" 498 g

סַנְדָּל "shoe," "boot," diff. fr. "sandal" 390 (ii) (ε) a

מָעוֹג "cake" 466 (a) a, s. לֵעָג "mock"

מְעִילִי "my mantle," c. w. מָעַר "tremble," "totter" 113 n.

מַעַל "treachery," and מָשָׁל "parable" 366 b

מִפְּנֵי "from the face of," "away from," because of" 413 a; פָּנָה (vb.) "turn the face [to, or, from]" 413 a

מָצָא "find," "be able" 209

מֵרַע "evil," s. מַדּוּעַ

Clue includes 1-272, Corrections 273-552.

מרפא "remedy," c. w. מאמר "saying," 403 a
משל "parable," and מעל "treachery" 366 b

נגד "against," "over against," c. w. גן "garden" 498 f; s. also מנגד
נדיב, meanings of 272 (i)
נהר "river," c. w. נוה "habitation," נר "beacon," עיר "city" 436 a
נוה, s. נהר
נחש and נחשת, meanings of 390 (ii) (γ)
נטה "stretch," c. w. נטל "hoist" 196
ניר, rare for נר (q. vid.)
נכה "scourge," 3rd pers. fut. יכה, c. w. יכח "admonish" (fut. יוכח) 493 b
נכים "abjects," c. w. נכרים "aliens," מכים "smiters" 490
נעל "shoe," "boot," diff. fr. סנדל i.e. "sandal" 390 (ii) (ϵ) a
נער "shake out" 390 (i) (ϵ)
נערה "maid," c. w. נר or ניר "lamp" 373 c
נפל "fall," c. w. תפל "untempered" 437 (i) a
נצה "end," c. w. יצת "burn," "kindle" 185 b
נר "beacon," "lamp," "light," c. w. עיר "city" (q. vid.) 436 a; c. w. נערה "maid" 373 c
נשא "lift up," "bear," "forgive" 262 a–b; c. w. אנש "afflicted" 262 a, 263 a

ס c. w. מ 309 n.; w. שׁ 502 (vi) a, 522 (vii) n.

סבב "travel round," rendered "go through" 390 c
סגן "governor" 502 (iv) b
סכן "benefit," "am in the habit" 502 (iv) b
סלח "forgive," LXX "heal" 403 a
סנדל, translit. of Gk "sandal," diff. fr. "shoe," "boot" 390 (ii) (ϵ) a
סר, or שר, "prince," "governor" 502 (vi) a, c. w. יסר "chastise" 502 (vi)

ע c. w. א 4 a–b, 186 a, 484 (iv) a; w. ח 4 b; w. שׁ 366 b; om., e.g. בעל for בל, and בי for בעי 4 a
עב, s. עביו
עבד "minister," "serve," "servant," c. w. עבר "pass," "cross" 72, 95–6, 106; w. דבר "word" 417 b; pl. rendered οἱ περὶ 370 a; s. also 191 b
עביו "his thick clouds," c. w. עברו "passed," בערו "were kindled," and ברד "hail" 101
עבר "pass," "cross," "across," c. w. ערב "evening," "west," ערבה "wilderness," עברות "ferry-boat," "fords," ערבות "plains" 12, 13, 70–3; s. also עבד, עביו
עברה "ferry-boat," pl. עברות "passages," "fords," s. עבר
עוד "still," c. w. ידע "know" 123 a, 422; w. על "upon" 123 a
עולה "iniquity" or "burnt-offering" 506 (iii); s. על
עור "skin," c. w. עין "colour" and אור "light" 421 a

Clue includes 1–272, Corrections 273–552.

עִין, meanings of 421 a; s. עוּר

עִיר "city," c. w. (or substituted for) גּוֹי "nation," הַר "mountain," נָהָר "river," נָוָה "habitation," נֵר "beacon" 436 a, 452 a; c. w. עֲרָבָה "wilderness," עֲרָבוֹת "plains" 169 foll.

עַל "upon," c. w. עוּר (q. vid.) 123 a; interchanged w. אֶל 369 b; c. w. עָלָה "go up," עָלָה "occasion," עָלָיו "about him (or, it)," "above him (or, it)," עוֹלָה "iniquity" or "burnt offering" 506 (i)–(iii); s. also עָלָיו

עִלָּאָה "high," c. w. צְלָא "pray" 421 b

עָלָה "go up," ἀναστῆναι (only (4) in LXX) 438 (v) b; hiph. "cause to go up," "light" 373 b–c; rendered in LXX "come," "come into" 373 b; "shoot" or "leaf," ἀνάβασις 378 a; s. also עַל

עָלָיו "towards him," c. w. עִמּוֹ "with him" 108; s. also עַל

עִם "with," or "people" 246

עָמַד "stand," "stand fast," "pillar," "attendant," "guard" 479–80; "make to stand up," ἀναστῆσαι, parall. to ἐγεῖραι 418 a

עִמּוֹ "with him," or "his people" 246; c. w. עָלָיו "towards him" 108

עֶרֶב "evening," "west," c. w. עֵבֶר "on the other side of," and עֲרָבָה (q. vid.) 12, 13, 70 foll.

עֲרָבָה "Arabah," "waste region," "desert," pl. עֲרָבוֹת "plains" 70; c. w. עֶבְרָה

"ferry-boat" 12, 13, 73, 171; pl. c. w. עִיר "city" 169 n.

עָשָׂה "do," c. w. שָׁעָה "look to" and שׁוֹעַ "cry out" 174 n.; c. w. שָׁמַע "hear" 393 b

עֲשִׁית (Aram.) "intended" (? c. w. שׁוּת q. vid.) 293 n.

עֶשְׂרִים "twenty," c. w. שִׁבְעִים "seventy" 234

עֵת "time," and עַתָּה "now" (447 (i)–(ii)) c. w. אַתָּה "thou" 484 (iv) a; בְּעִתּוֹ "in its time" 447 (i)–(ii), and esp. 447 (i) a

פָּנָה "look upon," "turn towards" 501 a; s. also מִפְּנֵי

פְּעָמִים "times," dual or pl. 219 foll.

צִוָּה "command," parall. to forms of יָצָא "go out" 154 n.

צוֹם "fast," c. w. צִיִּים "wild beasts," "demons" 192, 346

צֵידָה "provision," c. w. צִיָּה "drought" 167 foll.

צִיָּה "drought," s. צֵידָה

צִיִּים a rare term for "wild beasts" 192 n.; c. w. צוֹם "fast" 192, 346

צְלָא "prayer," "pray," c. w. עִלָּאָה "high" 421 b

צָלַח "shine" 421 b

צֵלֶל "shadow," LXX "branches" 380 n.

צָעִיר "younger," "inferior" 429 (i) foll.

ק interchanged w., or c. w., ח 524

קָבַץ "receive" 401 a

קָבַר "sepulchre," c. w. בָּרָק "light-

ning," בחור "young man,"
"chosen," בהר "bright
shining," בקר "morning
light," בד "white linen,"
בר "pure" 522-7; s. also
146 a

קדד "bow down," c. w. קרן
"become horned" 421 b

קדם "ancient," c. w. קום "stand
up" or רום "be high"
487 (i) (β) d

קום "stand up," or "stand fast"
363 b; c. w. רום "be
high" and קדם "ancient"
487 (i) (β) d; s. also 418 a

קטל "slay" 125 a
קלל "flash" 522 (v)-(vii)
קצף "wrath" 440 n.

קרא "call," c. w. קרה "befall,"
"meet" 472 c, 474 a; w.
קרב "draw near," "be
near" 386 a, 474 a; s. also
313 a

קרב "draw near," "be near," c. w.
קרא (q. vid.); w. קרב
"midst" 370 (i); w. רק
or ירק "spit" 488 n.

קרה "befall," "meet," c. w. קרא
"call" 472 c, 474 a

קריה "city," c. w. קברת "graves"
146 a

קרן "horn," or "be horned"
419-21, 522 (vii); c. w. קדד
"bow down" 421 b; w.
בקר "dawn," ברק "light-
ning" 522 (vii)

ר c. w. ד 5, 90 foll., 106, 125 b,
161, 191 b, 403, 406; c. w.
ל 148 a, 351 a

ראה "see," c. w. אמר "say" 459 (vi),
464 a; w. אור "light"

181-4; ירא "he feared"
or "he will see" 533

רב "great[er]," "elder" 428-31,
467-8; c. w. ריב "plead-
ing" or "contending" 472 c

רגל "foot," "on foot," c. w.
"following after" 75-6, 166

רוח "breath," "spirit," "wind,"
c. w. רחת "winnowing-fan"
340 a

רום "be high," c. w. קום "stand"
or "arise," and with part of
"Jeremiah" 487 (i) (β) d

רוע "cry out" 7, 147, s. רע, ידע,
יער

רחת "winnowing-fan" c. w. רוח
"spirit," "breath," "wind"
340 a

ריב "plead," "pleading," "contending," c. w. רב "great"
472 c, comp. 57

רע "evil," or "companion" or
"friend" 10, 90, 188 foll.;
c. w. דע imperat. of ידע
"know" 7, 90-1, 406, 406 a;
w. רעה "feed," "pasture,"
"shepherd" 7; w. יעד
"appoint a meeting" 7;
w. רוע "cry out" 7, 147;
w. רעע "break," "crush"
7, 147

רעה and רעע, s. רע

רקד "dance over," i.e. "insult,"
c. w. דקר "pierce," דקק
"break in pieces," רקים
"vain fellows" 488 b

קרב or ירק "spit," c. w. רקק,
"draw near"; רק "spittle,"
דק "dust," דקק "break in
pieces," רקד "dance" 488-9
(notes, passim, and s. esp.
488 b)

Clue includes 1-272, *Corrections* 273-552.

HEBREW

שׁ and שׂ 92
שׂ c. w. ס 502 (vi) a, 522 (vii) n.;
  w. ע 366 b
שׁאל "beg" or "ask" 448 b; interch.
  w. דרשׁ "seek" 255
שׁבי "elders of," c. w. שׁבי "captivity" 92
שׁבע "seven," c. w. ארבע "four"
  234; שׁבעה "sevenfold,"
  c. w. שׁבעים "seventy"
  228 foll.; w. ישׁב "he shall
  turn" 231 a; שׁבעים "seventy," c. w. שׁלשׁים "thirty"
  234 n.
שׁבת "sitting," "rest," "sabbath"
  9 n.
שׁ ב "turn," "return," "do again,"
  "again" 9, comp. 85; c. w.
  ישׁב "sit" 9, 149, comp. 506;
  w. ושׁבעה "and sevenfold"
  228 foll.; w. שׁום "set [the
  mind on]" 500 n.; s. also
  506
שׁובב variously rendered 440–1; c. w.
  שׁמם "wonder" 440 n.,
  comp. 443
שׁום "set," "put," c. w. שׁם "there"
  or "name," שׁמע "hear,"
  and שׁמם "wonder" 11,
  comp. 506; c. w. שׁוב
  "return" 500 n., comp. 506,
  506 d
שׁוע "cry out," c. w. שׁעה "look,"
  which is c. w. עשׂה "do"
  174 n.
שׁות "appoint," c. w. שׁנית "the
  second time" 234 n.; s. also
  293
שׁכח "forget," c. w. כשׁל "fall,"
  "stagger" 250–1
שׁלישׁ "three" or "thrice" 221
שׁלם "peace," "recompense" 255–8;

"man of my peace" i.e.
"intimate friend" 477 a;
  meaning "accomplish,"
  "complete " 477 a
שׁלשׁים "thirty," c. w. שׁבעים "seventy" 234 n.
שׁם "name," also "there," c. w.
  שׁום "put," שׁמם "wonder,"
  and שׁמע "hear" 11, 506;
  s. also below
שׁם, שׁמא, "name," c. w. שׁמיא or
  שׁמים "heaven," and שׁמע
  "hear" 446; שׁמי "my
  name," rendered "me"
  446; s. also above
שׁמי and שׁמא, s. שׁם
שׁמח "rejoice," c. w. שׁמע "hear"
  393 a
שׁמים "heaven," c. w. causative
  שׁמע "hear," i.e. "pro
  claim" 446; in Dan., freq.
  שׁמיא, c. w. שׁמיא "name"
  446; paraphr. as "king-
  dom of God " 446
שׁמם "wonder," "be dismayed"
  439 foll.; c. w. שׁמע "hear"
  392 a, 441 n. (2) and 441 a,
  comp. 443; c. w. שׁובב
  "turning" 440 n. and foll.;
  c. w. שׁמר "keep" 392 a
שׁמע "hear," c. w. שׁמם "wonder,"
  "be dismayed" 392 a, 441 n.,
  comp. 443; w. שׁובב 439
  foll. (esp. 441 n.); w. שׁמר
  "keep" 392 a; w. שׁמח
  "rejoice" 393 a; w. עשׂה
  "do" 393 b; causative, "proclaim (the kingdom),"
  "preach," c. w. שׁמי "my
  name" and w. שׁמים
  "heaven" 446
שׁמר "keep," c. w. שׁמע "hear" and

Clue includes 1–272, *Corrections* 273–552.

שמם "am perplexed" 392 a;
שמר in S., parall. to שום
"put" in Ps. 506
שנא, s. שעה
שנה "sleep," "be changeable,"
"fickle" 487 (i) (ε) a
שני "two," c. w. ישב "sit" 448 c
שנית "the second time," c. w. שות
"appoint" 234 n.
שעה "look," c. w. עשה "do" and
שוע "cry out" 174 n.
שעה "hour," "season," c. w. שער
"shudder" and שנא "alter"
127 b
שער "shudder," c. w. שעה "hour,"
"season" 127 b
שערים "porters," c. w. שרים "rulers"
93

שר or סר "prince," "governor,"
c. w. יסר "chastise" 502 (vi)
שר־הרבע "tetrarch" 391
שרי "princes," "rulers," applied
to priests, LXX "rulers" 59
שרים "rulers," c. w. שערים "porters"
93

תבל "habitable land," c. w. בתות
"desolate" 150 n.
תימה "admiration," c. w. טימי "profit," and טמא "unclean,"
and תימיא (for סימיא
"blind") 67-8
תפל "untempered," c. w. נפל "fall"
437 (i) a; parall. to פתל
437 (i) a
תפר "sew" 358

Clue includes 1-272, *Corrections* 273-553.

FROM LETTER TO SPIRIT

I. NEW TESTAMENT PASSAGES

[*The references are to paragraphs, indicated by black numbers, which, in this Index, run from* **553** *to* **1149**]

MATTHEW			MATTHEW			MARK		
		PAR.			PAR.			PAR.
3	3	830 a	16	23	891 a, b	1	1	851
	11	856 a		24	928 (i) a foll.		1-3	830-5, 839 a
	13	553-724, esp.		28	646 a, 660		2	837 b, 839 a
		610-6	17	1	630 a		4	851
	13-16	597-609		2	864 b, comp.		9	597-605; 610-6
	14	581 c, d, 588 a, 606-9			880-1		9-11	553-724
	15	575 a, 609 a, 1062, 1066		2-4	876		10	617-52; 662-84
				4	865 foll., 891-5			
	16	617-52; 662-84		5	786 foll., -907		11	786-816; 850-864
				6	885 a			
	16-17	553-724	19	29	928 (iv)			
	17	786-816; 850-864	20	21	1021 b	2	24	939 a
				22-3	978 b	3	13	630 a
				28	925		19	928 a
4	11	609 a	22	37	928 (ii)	4	11	660
5	16	969, 1022	23	13	944 a	5	12	680 a
6	9-10	965-71 (viii)		34	831 a		13	680 a
	13	940 d, 970, 971 (i)	25	31	838 a	6	3	558 b
			26	24	983 a, 985		15	872-4
	14	1021 b		29	934-6		46	630 a
10	4	928 a		36	942 foll.	8	12	931 b
	29	748 a		38	917-24, 942 foll., 1003 a		28	841, 873-4
	37-8	928 (i) a foll.					29	789-90
11	9-10	830-1		39	929-31 i foll., 975-6, 1010 c		33	891 a, b
	10	839					34	928 (i) a foll.
	14	1062		40	941 b	9	1	646 a, 660
	25	923 a, b, 984, 1003 a, 1014		41	941 a, 960 e		2	630 a, 864 b, 875
				41-47	941 foll.			
	29	928 (iii)		42	932, 955-6		3	864 b, 901 b, 907 a
12	18	672 b, 787, 802-11, 813 a		44	932			
				53	979		4	875 foll.
13	11	660	27	40	788		5	865 foll., 875, 885 foll.
	16	660		42	788			
14	23	630 a		45-50	1052-69		6	885 foll.
16	4	931 b		46	1066		7	786-849
	14	841, 873-4		49	1066, 1069	10	30	928 (iv)
	16	789-90		50	1066		37	1021 b
	17	719, 849 a		54	790 a		38	978 b
	18	891 a					45	925
	22	979 d				12	15	933 h

3—2

MARK		LUKE		JOHN	
	PAR.		PAR.		PAR.
12 30	928 (ii)	9 27	646 a, 660	1 23	830 a
14 20	978 b	28	630 a	25	829
21	983 a, 985	29	864 b	26	558 a
25	934-6	30-33	877-9	28	610-6
32	942 foll.	31	878	28-34	553-724; 854-64
33	941 b	32	879 b, 884		
34	917 foll., 942 foll.	33	865 foll., 883 b, 885 foll.	29	576, 577 a
				31	863 a
35	955-6	34	885 a	32	594
35-6	929-31, 952-6 foll., 1003 b	35	786 foll.	32-3	646-52; 662-84; 723-4
		62	928 (iii) b		
36	931 d-i, 975-9; 1010	10 1	1015 b	33	593-4; 855-61
		17-21	922 a	34	593, 791, 815-6
37, 38	960 c, e	21	923 a, b, 984, 1003 a, 1014	36	904
38-43	941-56 foll.			38	653
39	932, 946 a, 949 foll.	24	660	41	894
		27	928 (ii)	42	719, 891 a
15 32	788	29-33	928 (ii)	45	1026
33-7	1052-69	11 1	967	50	653
34	1051-68	2	965-71 (viii)	51	640-61
35	1069	29	931 b	2 21	1019
36	1066, 1069	49	831 a	3 7	883 b
37	1064-7	12 49-50	978 a-f; 1010 d	8	722
39	790 a	14 26-7	928 (i) a, 928 (iv), (x)	13	722
43	598 b			4 29	894
16 12	896 d	15 17	680 a	5 39	892
		17 6	764	6 15	630 a
	LUKE	18 7	933 c	37	934
1 5	578	30	928 (iv)	66	891 b
54	809	19 42	1013 a	67	891 b
69	809	22 3	680 a, 986 a	67-9	870
2 24	594 a, 685 b	16, 18	934-6	68	892-5
46	709 b	22	983 a, 985	69	789, 816 a, 893-4
3 2	850	27	925		
4	830 a	31	891 a	70	891 a, 986 a
21	579, 597-605; 610-52	40	942 foll.	7 19	937
		42	929-31 foll., 976 foll.	30	937
21-2	554-724			45	939 b
22	662-84, 717, 786-816; 850-64	43-4	958 foll., 989	8 35	724
		46	960 c	43, 46	939 b
		46-7	941 foll.	55	937
23	709 c, d	51	1062, 1066	59	558 a, 1013 a
6 12	630 a	53	947 a	10 16	1016
16	928 a	23 26	928 (x) c	11 9	979 d
36	1022	34	1056, 1066-8	33	920
7 2	809	35	788	51-2	1016
7	809	37	788	12 1	1120
26-7	830-1	44-6	1052-69	5	939 b
27	839	45	1066	19	1016
8 10	660	47	790 a	24-6	928 (x)
30	680 a	24 19	841	27	917 foll., 920, 933, 937-40, 954 b, 1010 f
32	680 a	25	841		
9 8	872-4				
19	841, 873-4		JOHN	27-33	1003 foll.
20	789-90			28	913, 1011, 1020, 1024
23	928 (i) a foll., 928 (viii)	1 1	793 c, 851 b		
		6	593	28-9	728 a

NEW TESTAMENT PASSAGES

		JOHN			ROMANS			2 THESSALONIANS
		PAR.			PAR.			PAR.
12	29	775 a, 954 a	4	25	927 a	3	3	940 d
	36	1013	8	15	979			
	38	971 (vii) a		26	685 c			1 TIMOTHY
	41	1020		32	927 a			
13	3	983 a		38	658	1	7	1146 d
	21	920, 986	11	11	1014	3	16	655
	27	680 a		25	1014	4	8	665 b
	37	939 b		35	928 a	6	16	1021 b
14	2	998	12	1	883			
	8	1027						HEBREWS
	9	939 a			1 CORINTHIANS			
	30–1	947 a				1	5	793 c
15	20	928 (x)	2	8–10	641		6	655–6
16	32	937	4	4, 9	605 a, 658	3	5	807 c
17	1	913, 970	6	3	658	5	5–7	957–964
	2	970	9	4, 5	979 c	7	9	1015 f
	6	970	11	10	658	10	37	839 a
	8	970		23	928	12	21	885 a
	11	672, 894 a						
	12	970, 983 a, 987			2 CORINTHIANS			1 PETER
	15	940 a, d, 970	1	10	940 c			
	17, 19	970	3	3–13	882	1	1	1016
	25	672, 894 a		17	724, 883 b		12	659 b
18	8	1066	5	21	605 a		24	850 b
	11	933–6, 979 c, d,	11	14	962	2	9	1126
		1007				4	12	978 b
20	22	671			GALATIANS		14	660 a
	31	990 foll.	2	9	764 c	5	11	1021 b
21	2	1015 b		20	927 a			
	15–17	913 a	4	4	587			"2 PETER[1]"
	24	1118		6–7	979			
	25	990 foll.		25	1015 f	1	18	981 b
			5	1	928 (vii) a		19	785 b
		ACTS		13	928 (iii) a	3	5	879 b
2	17	672 b			EPHESIANS			1 JOHN
3	13	809						
	22–5	845 foll.	5	2	927 a	3	2–3	907 a
	26	809		14	884	5	16	987
4	25	800, 809		25	927 a		18	940 d
	27	809	6	12	962 a			
	30	809						JUDE
6	5	1015 b			PHILIPPIANS			
	15	880 (n.)	2	6, 7	601, 810 a,		14	839 a
7	37	842			896 d, 928 (vi)			
	56	646 a		9	915			REVELATION
8	26	1015 d						
	39	1015 d			COLOSSIANS	1	4	668 a
	40	1015 d				2	20	1064 a
9	7	775 a	1	17	879 b	3	1	668 a
15	10	928 (vii) a		19	571 a, 665		8	646 a
20	35	997 b	2	9	571 a, 665	4	5	668 a
21	8	1015 c				5	6	668 a
22	9	775 a			1 THESSALONIANS	12	5	704 b
26	14	928 (iii)	1	10	940 c			

[1] See also Appendix V, *passim*.

FROM LETTER TO SPIRIT

II. ENGLISH AND GREEK

[*The references are to paragraphs, indicated by black numbers, which, in this Index, run from* 553 *to* 1149]

Aaron, "the Saint of the Lord," 812 *c*, 893
Abide, Jn prefers "a." to "rest", in describing the resting of the Spirit, 714
Abraham, "a voice as from A.," 795
Aenon, 615, 616 *a*
Akibah, 675, 783; his martyrdom, 928 (v)
"And", Heb. *vaw*, "but", 937; "in order to", 598; "even", 818, 834
"Andrew", typical meaning of the name, 1015 *e*, *f*
"Angel" = "Messenger" in Heb. and Gk, 817 *a*; altered to "Holy One", 839; angel of the Lord, "an" or "the", 663; "an a. hath spoken to him," 954; the a. strengthening Jesus, 958; wrestling with Jacob, 959; an a. called the Prince of Esau, *i.e.* Edom or Rome, 961 *a*; "an a. of the Lord " (Acts viii. 26), 1015 *d*
Angels, in bad sense, 658; in Heb. i. 6 corresponds to Ps. xcvii. 7 "[? false] gods", 656; "a. of the face," 567 *a*; "of God", 655, 659–61; "seven", 668 *a*; "seventy", 668 *a*; agents of God's wrath, 900
Answered, parall. to "rejoiced", 923 *a*
Antiochus, confused with Antioch, 730 *a*

Apocryphal works, early, 994
Apostles, 1015, 1136 foll.
Appearance, "in its a.", rendered (R.V.) "in his eyes" (Lev. xiii. 5, 37), 717
"Appeared (as)", ambiguity of, 849, 871–2
Aramaic, said to have been used in the temple, 730 *a*
Arians, the, 1001
Arm of Jehovah, the, 971 (vii)
Article, the, in Gk or Heb., 663, 669 *a*
Axe, the, metaphor of, 704 *a*
Azotus, 1015 *d*

ἀγάπαις, confused with ἀπάταις, 1129
ἀγαπητός, 786–816, 811 *a*
ἀειδής, 558 *a*
ἀήρ, 643
-αι interchanged with -ε, 976 *a*, *b*
αἱρετίζω, 813 *a*
ἀλλά, "but", read as ἄλλο, "another", 978 *d*; ἀλλά in Mk = πλήν in Mt.-Lk., 1010 *c*
ἀναβαίνω, "go up" in Mk iv. 7, 8, 32 = "grow up", 704 *e*; ἀνέβη interchanged with ἀνήφθη, 634 *b*
ἀνάβασις, 629 *b*
ἀναπαύομαι, "rest" or "cease", 712
ἀνέξω, parall. to συνέχομαι, 1010 *d*

ENGLISH AND GREEK 39

ἀνήφθη, 978 c; interchanged with ἀνέβη, 634 b
ἀνοίγω, 641 a; ἀνεῳγότα, 640 a, 646 a
ἀνυπόδετος, 901 c
ἀπάταις, confused with ἀγάπαις, 1129
ἀπό and ἐκ, primary distinction between, 940 c; ἀπὸ Ναζαρέτ = "*of* (not *from*) N.," 598 b
ἀρετή applied to God, 1135 a
ἄροτρον, 928 (iii) b
ἀροτρόπους, 928 (iii) b
ἄρχω, "begin" or "reign", 709 d
ἀφείς, the regular meaning of, 1064
ἄφες, adopted as a Heb. word, 1066 b; confused with ἄφεσις, 1066 b
ἄφεσις, "forgiveness", confused with ἄφες (Ezek. xlvii. 3), 1066 b
ἀφίημι = "forsake", "forgive", "let go", "utter (a cry)", 1056, 1065-6; parallel to ἐῶ, 1066 a

Back, the, of God, 896, 901 a
Backward or behind, to go, 891 b
Baptism, The Baptism of Christ symbolical of the bestowal of priesthood, 797 b; "b. by fire", not a Jewish phrase, 856 a; "b. with the Holy Spirit," not a Jewish phrase, 856; b. synonymous with "cup" and "fire", 973 b
Baptize with the Holy Spirit, not a Jewish phrase, 856
Barabbas, 928 (i) e
Bar Kochba or Koziba, 667, 783
Bath Kol, 725-85; from the midst of the earth, 741; seldom described as simply *Kol*, 741 a; said to be substituted for "Holy Spirit", 743; words of Scripture uttered by, 743 d; Jewish definition of, 780; as an echo, 780-5; subjective in Jn xii. 29 and Acts xxii. 9, but never in the Talmuds, 775 a; chiding Solomon, 825; regarded by Jn as an inferior sign, 1005; "One does not trouble oneself about Bath Kol," 762-75
Beautify, Exod. xv. 2 "I will beautify him (God)," how explained, 1022

"Beloved Son", 786-816
Beloved, a mistranslation of "chosen", 802-4
Ben Zoma, 687-8, 913
Bethabara, 555, 612-6
Bethany, 555, 612-6
Bethara, 612-6
Betharabah, 555, 613 a, 616 a
Bethel, 960 a
Beth Gadia, 616 d
Betrayed, in 1 Cor. xi. 23, should be "delivered up", 928
Bodily, Lk. iii. 22 "in a b. form," 717; "the fulness of the Godhead b.," 571 a, 665
Boy, (?) "son" or "servant", 806-11
Branch, The, a name of the Messiah, 1019, comp. 570, 704
Brocken apparitions, 866
Build, the Messiah to "build the Temple", 1019
"Building", in Jewish tradition, 1019
"But" or "and", Heb. *vaw*, 937; "but" confusable with "for" in transl. from Heb., 1068 a

βαλών, substituted for ἐπιβαλών, 928 (iii) b

Caiaphas, like Balaam, 1016
Caleb and Joshua at the Assumption of Moses, 897
Caligula, alleged Bath Kol concerning, 732
"Called" confusable with "was called", 638 a
"Came", confusable with "upon" in Heb., 851
Carpenter, Christ "being supposed a c.," 558 b
Celsus, on the Baptism of Christ, 560-5
Cephas, a name preserved by no Gospel but the Fourth, 891 a
Cerinthus, on "the Dove", 584, 589, 689, 722
Choose, interchangeable with "be well pleased", 863; first Biblical mention of God's "choosing", 812 c

"Chosen", a title of Messiah, 786–816; retained by Luke alone in the Transfiguration, 791; mistranslated as "Beloved", 802–4; how explained by Epiphanius, 815 a; might represent Heb. בר "son", 860; in the Book of Enoch, 864; a name of Tabor, 981 a; "Saul, the Chosen of the Lord," 783 a, 803 b

Christ, "the Christ" a title likely to supersede unfamiliar terms, 790

Chrysostom, on the miraculous phenomena of the Baptism, 648

Conquest, meaning of in O.T. and N.T., 1015 d, 1018

Constrained, "I am c.", confusable with "hasten", 1010 e

Cross, "taking up the C.," 926, 928 (i)—(x)

Crown, "stones of a c.," 1018; "four crowns", 742

Crucifixion, not a Jewish punishment, 928 (i)

Crying, "strong c. and tears" imputed to Jesus, 957

Cup, (?) paraphrased by "hour", 956; (?) conflated with "hour", 1003 b; synonymous with "baptism" and "fire", 978 b, f, 1001, 1010 a; confusable with "furnace", 978 b; the Synoptic and Johannine traditions about "not drinking the cup," 933–6, 1007

Daniel, praying "about the time of the oblation," 628

Daughter, "d. of the desert"="ostrich", 716; "d. of voice", 716, 725 (see also *Bath Kol*)

David, anointed by Samuel, 650, 797

Day, "to-day", perh. meaning "endless and inexhaustible time," 793 c

Deacons, the seven, 1015 b

Delivered-up, LXX "was d."=Heb. "made intercession", 927; 1 Cor. xi. 23 R.V. "was betrayed" should be rendered "was d.", 928

Demas, 891 b

Dew, an angel of, 624; a wind of, 624; "d. of God", 625; the Holy Spirit compared to d., 625

Diatessaron, the Arabic, its relation to Tatian's work, 556

Divine, "d. nature, virtue" &c., a periphrasis for "God", 1127

Dove, the, 685–724; "[turtle] dove" distinguished from "pigeon", 594 a, 685; pictures of, in the Catacombs, 689; connected with Polycarp's death, 690; introduced by Aquila without any warrant in the Hebrew, 696; Mary reared "as a dove", 698; "dove" confusable with "resting", 695–6; Wetstein on, 686–7

Doxology in the Lord's Prayer, the, in the *Didaché* and the *Acts of John*, 1021 b, c

δέ, perh. changed to ἀλλά read as ἄλλο, 978 d

δέομαι, "beseech" or "need", 602

διαγρηγορῶ, 884 a

διὰ τί, never used by Jn except with negative, 939 b

διηλλαγμένον, used of the Son's Will, 1001

δίκρουν, 928 (vii) e foll.

δόξα, 896 c; "glory" interpr. as "opinion" by Diatess., 878

δοξάζω, 1022 a

δόξασον, perh. corrupted to δοξα σοι, 964 b

δοῦλος, interchanged with παῖς, 807 d

δύναμις, inserted after δόξα, 660 a

Ear, a slave's, why pierced, 928 (iv) b

Ebionites, the, Gospel of, 578 foll.

Echo, Bath Kol as an, 780–5

Eclipsed, "to be e.", confusable with "forsake", 1060

Edifying, a Pauline term, 1023

Edom meaning Rome, 961 a

Eldad and Modad, 837

Elders, mentioned by Papias, 995; an Elder identified with Papias, 998

"Eli, Eli", 1053, 1057 foll.

Eliezer, Rabbi, 763-75; the prayer of, 966, 1011 b
Elijah, "Messenger" or "Prophet", 818, 826-9, 834; with Moses at the Transfiguration, 848-9, 872-4; E., Moses, and Enoch, as precedents, 836; E. praying "at the offering of the oblation," 627; "Elijah" confusable, in Gk, with "the sun", 1057-60. See also 1027
Elisha, 1027
"*Eloi, Eloi*", 1053, 1057 foll.
Enoch, date of the Book of, 812
Enoch, Elijah, and Moses, as precedents, 836
Ephrem (or Ephraemus) Syrus, date of, 573
Epictetus, the doctrine of, 920
Eusebius, the Promise of, 1136-49
Evangelist, Philip the, 1015 a foll.
[Evening] oblation, the, 627 foll., 724 d
Eyes, "in his e." (R.V. Levit. xiii. 5, 37) rendered (Gesen.) "in its appearance", 717
Ezra, praying "at the offering of the oblation," 628

-ε interchanged with -αι, 976 a, b
ἐγλείπω = ἐκλείπω, 1060
ἐγρηγορῶ, 945 c
εἰς, the Heb. for εἰσῆλθεν εἰς wrongly rendered ἦλθεν ἐπί, 680 a; εἴς τινα (after ἔρχομαι &c.) does not mean *to* (or, *on*), but *into* a person, 680 a
εἰ, meaning "not", 931 b; "if only", "would that", 978 g; interchanged with εἴθε, 978 c, g
εἴθε, 978 c, g
εἰσῆλθεν εἰς, the Heb. for ἐ. ἐ. wrongly rendered ἦλθεν ἐπί, 680 a
εἰσφέρομαι, 1129 d
ἐκ and ἀπό, primary distinction between, 940 c; σώσον ἐκ &c., 940 a
ἐκλείπειν, 1060 b
ἐκλεκτός (ἐκλελεγμένος), 786-816; a name of Tabor, 981 a
ἐκτενέστερον, 959 a
ἔκφοβος, 885 a, 896 b
ἐμπλήσει = Is. xi. 3 (R.V.) "his delight shall be," 666 a
ἐνανθρώπησις, 587
ἐνισχύω, 959
ἐξέραμα, 1130
ἐπείγομαι, 978 d, 1010 d, e
ἐπεσχόμην, 1010 e
ἐπί, ἦλθεν ἐπί wrongly substituted for εἰσῆλθεν εἰς, 680 a
ἐπιβαλών, read as βαλών, 928 (iii) b
ἐπιστολαί, 1137 a
ἑπτὰ τό, error for ἔπτατο, 668 b
ἔπτατο, read as ἑπτὰ τό, 668 b
εὐλάβεια[1], Heb. v. 7 "was heard

[1] Εὐλάβεια means "taking good heed to avoid offence," sometimes in a good sense, as when Philo (i. 476-7) praises Abraham for his combination of free speech (Gen. xv. 2 "What wilt thou give me?") with "godly fear" (Gen. xv. 2 "O Lord (ὦ δέσποτα, *i.e.* Master)"); but often in a bad sense, as in Wisd. xvii. 8 (of the Egyptian "*fear worthy to be laughed at*"), and the verb is often thus used with negatives (" Be not *afraid*" &c.). In Prov. xxviii. 14 "Happy is the man that *dreadeth* alway," LXX has καταπτήσσων, "crouching down", softened by the addition of δι' εὐλάβειαν. And so a Greek translator might use εὐλάβεια instead of φόβος to imply that the fear was not cowardly, but the "fear of *doing evil*." But would "fear", *in this negative sense*, be attributed to Christ by an early Evangelist except under a misunderstanding?
    Note that in Prov. xxx. 5, Nahum i. 7, Zeph. iii. 12, LXX has εὐλαβοῦμαι as a rendering of a form of חסה "*trust*", confusing it with חסה "*be silent before*", "*be afraid of*". This suggests that the text might be a misinterpretation of "He was heard because he *trusted*."
    Westcott says "For the use of ἀπό see Luke xix. 3; xxiv. 41; Acts xii. 14; xxii. 11; John xxi. 6." But *all these have a negative* ("could *not* for the crowd", "*dis*believed for joy" &c.); *and a negative, or some notion of constraint* (as with the Latin *prae*), occurs in most of the instances of מן "from", meaning "by reason of", referred to in Gesen. 580 a, 583 a. More to the point would be Josh. xxii. 24 "we did it *from* carefulness," ἕνεκεν εὐλαβείας, but Aq. ἀπὸ μερίμνης "from anxiety": but neither this, nor any of the instances, is exactly parallel to the present. The preposition points to literal translation from Hebrew, in which case a participial may have been taken for the prepositional prefix (-מ), as in Ps. lxxii. 12, Job xxix. 12 &c.

(R.V.) for (ἀπὸ) his godly fear (τῆς ἐ.)," 964 a
ἐχέτλη, 928 (iii) b
ἑῶ, parall. to ἀφίημι, 1066 a

ἡλί, or ἠλί, 1053 a_1, and see "Eli"
ηλιου, may mean "sun" or "Elijah", 1057-60, esp. 1060 q

θ, see below T

Face, "f. of God", opposed to "back", 898-901
Face (verb), Mal. iii. 1 (lit.) "shall face", i.e. "shall clear from before my face," 830
Fan, "the winnowing f.", 858
Father, "Our Father", not freq. in Jewish Prayers, 966 b
Fiery (trial), (?) confused with "cup", 978 b
"Fire" or "light", 617-25; fire a hostile element, 624; "the immaterial f.", 625; confusable with "fire-offering", 634; baptism by f., not a Jewish phrase, 856 a; interchangeable with "cup", 978 b, f, 1001, 1010 a
Firmament, the, 644
Firstborn of God, the, 797; connection between "chosen" and "firstborn", 799
Flock of the Gentiles, the, 1018
"For" (conjunction) and "but", confusable in transl. from Heb., 1068 a
"For" (prep.) (Heb. לְ) rendered "to", 927 b

Forsake, confusable with "be eclipsed", 1060
Fountain, "the whole f. of the Holy Spirit," 665; (Deut. xxxiii. 28) "fountain of "=(Onk.) "according to the likeness of," 717 a; "fountain", (?) a name given to a "summary" of prayers, 717 b
Freedom, "the spirit of f.," 724; in 2 Cor. iii. 17, 883 b-c
Fuller, (Mk ix. 3) "no f. on earth," 864 b, 901 b
Fuller's soap, 901 b
Fullness, "the f. of the Godhead," 571 a, 665
Furca (Lat.), the yoke of punishment, 928 (i) foll., 928 (vi) (vii) foll.
Furcifer (Lat.), 928 (vi), 928 (vii) b foll.
Furnace, confusable with "cup", 978 b

φ, see under P

Gadia, "the House of G.," 616 d, 734
"Gaza¹", "G. this is desert," 1015 d
Gennesaret, rabbinical derivation of, 860 b; perh. erron. for Gethsemane, 877, 960
Gentiles, "the Court of the G.," 981 b; "the coming in of the G.," 1014
Gethsemane, 1004, 1008; Gennesaret perh. erron. for G., 877, 960 b
Gibeonites, the, 783 a
Glorify, "them that glorify me I will glorify," 913; "g." interchanged with "hallow", 969-71, comp. 1011;

---

[1] Beside other conflations (1015 d), Acts viii. 26-7 appears to have conflated (1) εὐνοῦχος with δυνάστης (comp. Jerem. xxxiv. 19 "eunuchs", δυνάστας); (2) εἰς γάζαν "to Gaza", with "over [all her] treasure" ἐπὶ [πάσης τῆς] γάζης [αὐτῆς]. The Eunuch, being (Euseb. ii. 1. 13) "the first" convert "from the Gentiles", appropriately comes from "Aethiopia", because Ps. lxviii. 31 (LXX) "*Aethiopia shall be the first* (προφθάσει) to stretch out her hand unto God." In Zeph. ii. 3-4 ("Azah (*i.e.* Gaza) shall be *Azubah*, i.e. *forsaken*") the Targ. has (1051-6) *sabach* (for *azab*), which might suggest that "the man of Gaza" was "*forgiven*". Also, instead of "noonday", Targ. has a deriv. of טהר, which may mean "*purify* [*with water*]", suggesting "baptism". The Eunuch, no longer lamenting over himself as (Is. lvi. 3) "*a dry tree*", but being guided to the Man who is (Is. xxxii. 2) "as rivers of *water in a dry place*," exclaims (Acts viii. 36) "Here is water". Receiving life, he departs after God has (Is. lvi. 7) made him "joyful". Philip (Acts viii. 40) "is found in *Azotus*," (?) the city of "No-Life" (L.S. recognize ἄζωτον only as "ungirt", but Hesych. adds ἀβίωτον): where he continues his life-giving career.

ENGLISH AND GREEK

"Glorify thy Name", 913, 970, 1011, 1020, 1022
Glory, of Moses, of the Lord &c., 882-4; of God, 898; substituted for "goodness", 660 a, 899; paraphrased as "hosts of angels", 900; the Heb. for, may mean "weight" or "riches", 660 a, 1021 b; a LXX rendering of Heb. "goodness", 660 a, 899; a periphrasis for "God", 660 a; "a weight of g.", 660 a; the Gk "glory" interpr. "opinion" by Diatess., 878; glory, in Jn, regarded as following trouble, 986; "the power and the glory," 1021 a-b; Mk x. 37 "in thy glory", parall. to Mt. xx. 21 "in thy kingdom", 1021 b; see also 1021 c
Goad, mistranslated "plough", 928 (iii) b; "kick against the g.," 928 (iii)
God, periphrases for, e.g. "Glory", "Heaven", "Name" &c., 660 a
Gods, false, 658
Going up, confused with "offering", 629 c
Goodness, rendered by LXX "glory", 660 a, 899
Gospel of the Ebionites, 578; of the Hebrews or Nazarenes, 570 foll.; the Arabic Gospel of the Infancy, 658; (?) "according to the Apostles," 600 b
Greece, called Javan, 696 a; (Zech. ix. 13) "thy sons, O Greece," 1018
Greeks, come to Jesus, 921, 1014-6, comp. 1020 c

γινώσκω, aorist of, 1068
γραφαί, meaning of, 1145-6
γρηγόρησις, 635 a
γρηγορῶ, 945

Hallow, interchanged with "glorify", 969-71, comp. 1011
Hands, "lay h. on", 611 b
Hasten, confusable with "be constrained", 1010 e
"Hate", applied to parents, 928 (iv), (x)
"Hear ye him", 817-49

Heaven, a periphrasis for "God", 660 a; "of Heaven" interchanged with "Most High", 971 (vi); "the heaven opened", 641
Hebrews, the, Epistle to, 1139; Gospel of, 570
(H)eli, aspiration of, 1053 a_1
Hellenists, the, 1015 a
Hermon, 867 a, 981, 1060 c
Herod, erroneously mentioned, 578 a
Hezekiah, his prayer, 989
Hide, Jesus "was hidden", 1013
High, "Most High", 971 (vi), interchanged with "of Heaven" (ib.)
Highpriesthood, 893 a
Hillel, 734-8; the Bath Kol for H. against Shammai, 756-62; "the House of H.," 616 c
Holy, "the Holy One" in Clem. Rom. substituted for "angel", 837; "the Holy One of God," 893-4; see "hallow"
Horns (Exod. xxxiv. 29, 30, 35), 882, 896
Hour, (?) a paraphrase of "cup", 956; (?) conflated with "cup", 1003 b
House of, meaning "the followers of", 616 c

I AM, how expanded by Jer. Targum, 1024 a
If, implying a negative, 956; meaning "if only", "would that!" 978 g
Intercession, Heb. "made i.", LXX "was delivered up", 927
Interrogative pronouns, variation of, 1146 c
Isaac, the Sacrifice of I., 928 (i) b; 1069 (i)-(v); carrying the wood, 928 (i) b
Isaiah, his martyrdom, 928 (v); Mark's use of the name, 833, 839 a
Israel, "the hardening of I.," 1014

ἵκριον, 928 (vii) d, 928 (x) b
ἵνα τί, not used in Jn, 939 b

Jabneh, 735; the synedrion of J., 761

Jacob at Bethel, **659**; wrestling with the angel, **959**; accused by Satan, **961**

Javan, *i.e.* Greece, **696** *a*

Jesse, the name, confusable with "aged", **706** *c*; "a weaver of the veil of the house of the sanctuary," **709** *a*

"Jesus" interchanged with "John" in the Ebionite Gospel, **581**; Jesus, or Joshua, son of Nun, **832, 846**, cp. **961** *a*

Jews, Christian, prepossessions of, **963**

John (the Baptist), described himself as being a Voice, **864**

John (the Evangelist), his style, **1120**; its apparent simplicity, **913** *a*; he does not dislike ambiguity, **939** *c*; intervenes where Luke omits or alters Mark, **656**

"John" (the name), interchanged with "Jesus" in the Ebionite Gospel, **581**; interchanged with "Jona(h)", **719**; rendered "Ὀνίας", **616** *c*; perh. an error for "Jordan", **563** *a*, **565, 610, 611** *b*, **1039** *a*

John Hyrcanus, **566, 569, 730**

"Jonah", a Heb. noun for "dove", **719**; interchanged with "John", **719**

Jonathan ben Uzziel, **739** *a*

"Jordan", perh. corrupted to "John", **563** *a*, **565, 610, 611** *b*, **1039** *a*; perh. taken as "going down", **611**; the water of J. to be rejected, **615**

Joseph, his "rod", **697–710**

Joshua, **897, 961** *a*; one of "the former Prophets", **797** *e*; Joshua or Jesus, the son of Nun, **832, 846**, cp. **961** *a*

Joshua ben Chananya, **763–75**

Judas Iscariot, **985** foll.

Kingdom, "the K. of God is within you," **971** (iv); "the yoke of the K.," **928** (ii); "No blessing in which there is not the K.," **1005** *a*; Mt. "in thy kingdom" parall. to Mk "in thy glory", **1021** *b*

καθαρὸν πῦρ, **625** *a*

καθεύδεις[1] (Mk xiv. 37), corrupted, **960** *c*

καθώς, confused with καλῶς, **951**

καί might mean (Heb. *vaw*) "and" or "even", **818, 834**; "and" or "but", **933** *a*, **937**; "for" or "but", **1068** *a*

καιρός, "time of trial", **956** *a*

καλῶς, confused with καθώς, **951**

κρίσις βλασφημίας, "a charge of blasphemy," **1129**

Laban, the egotist, **928** (iv) *a*

"*Lama*" or "*Lema*", *i.e.* "why?" possible corruptions of, **1061**

Lamb, "the L. that taketh away sin," **636**

Legend, Jewish, **1069** (i)–(v)

Leper, purifying of a, **585**

"Lifting up", in John, **928**; comp. **1003** *c*, **1018, 1020** *b*

Lightfoot, Bishop L.'s interpretation of the Promise of Eusebius, **1136** *a*

Likeness, Deut. xxxiii. 28 (Onk.) "according to the l. of,"=(R.V.) "fountain of", **717** *a*

Luke, his style, **850**

Lulab, a, **1022**

λ, *i.e.* "thirty", perh. dropped, **587** *a*

λάκκος, name of Tabor, **981** *a*

λῃσταί, **928** (i) *e*

---

[1] As an illustration of (960) John's feigning sleep, comp. the story (no doubt as true as it is beautiful) about Bernard of Quintavalle (*Little Flowers of St Francis*, p. 2) "first companion of St Francis," who was at that time reckoned "the fool of Assisi." Bernard was entertaining Francis as his guest for the night, and (*Sons of St Francis*, p. 31) "the host fought against sleep, also feigning unconsciousness, watched, and saw his guest rise and spend the night in prayer, ...till morning broke. By the light of the little chamber lamp *he had seen the fool transfigured*. Bernard that night left all his former life behind him." The narrative also illustrates what might have happened to the two guests of the Lord Jesus who (Jn i. 39) "abode with him that day, it was about the tenth hour"; and it suggests how some kind of physical "transfiguration"—but very different from the common conception of it—might be combined with special spiritual energy.

ENGLISH AND GREEK

Macarius, his comment on the accounts of the Crucifixion, 1051 *a*
Mahanaim, 659 *a*
Majority, vote of the (Exod. xxiii. 2), 763, 767
Malachi, his reference to the "Temple", 862; on the "Messenger", 818, 826-9 foll.
Marcosians, the, 978 *d*
Mark writes what may be called "a note-book Gospel", 996; said to have been Peter's "interpreter", 997
Martyrdom, of Akibah, 783, 928 (v), of Isaiah, 928 (v)
Mary (the Lord's mother), referred to as "the root" in Is. xi. 2, 669 *b*; reared "as a dove", 698; makes a veil for the Temple of the Lord, 709 *a*; the "choosing" of, 815 *a*
Matthew, prepossessed by prophecy, 996; said to have written his Gospel in Hebrew, 997
Maxims, "not maxims wanted, but men," 1000
Melchizedek, 893 *a*
Menahem, name of the Messiah, 704 *b*
"Messenger" and "Angel", identical both in Heb. and in Gk, 817 *a*
"Messenger" and "Prophet", 817-49; Mal. iii. 1 "Behold, I send my m.," 818, 826-35 foll.; Exod. xxiii. 20 "I send a m.," 820-4; Philo on, 822
Messiah, the, titles of, 790; builder of the Temple, 1019
Metamorphose, 883 foll., 896, 896 *c*, *d*; rarity of the word, 883
Metamorphosis of Satan into a sparrow, 688
Metatron, the, 824
Michael, 961 *a*
Minchah, oblation, 633-6, 627 *a*, 724 *d*
Misinterpretation in the synagogue, 997 *a*
Misquotation, in Mk i. 1-3, Mt. xi. 9-10, Lk. vii. 26-7, 830-1; in Acts iii. 22 foll., 845
Moses, "a prophet like unto M.," 825-46; the Assumption of M., 897; the Mosaic Theophany, 896-907; M. "received the Torah from Sinai," 1136; the name, alleged to mean "a great teacher", 871 (but see 871 *a*); the glory of M., 882; Moses with Elijah at the Transfiguration, 848-9; "Moses and the Prophets," 870
Most High, interchanged with "of Heaven", 971 (vi)
Mountain, the, connected with prayer, 630 *a*; the M. of the Transfiguration, 867 *a*, 981; "the M. of the House," 981 *b*; "a rooter up of mountains," 764 *a*
"My", the freq. use of, rebuked by Philo, 928 (iv) *a*

μεσημβρία, "south" or "noonday", 1015 *d*
μετασχηματίζεσθαι, 896 *d*
μή interrogative, 933 *e* foll., 979 *c*
μοναί (Jn xiv. 2), 998
μορφή, "essential form", contrasted with σχῆμα, "fashion", 810 *a*, 896 *d*; in Theod. means (Heb.) "brightness", 896 *c*

Nail, a, used as a charm, 778
Name, a periphrasis for "God", 660 *a*, 1022; the Name, 915, 964 *b*; Name or Shechinah, 971 (iii); "thy (or, the) Holy Spirit" substituted for "thy (or, the) Name", 968, 971 (iii); Name of Glory, 660 *a*; "Name" compared with "Son", 1005; "in my n.", a corruption from Exod. xxiii. 21, 823
Nathanael, 661
Nations, seventy, 668 *a*
Nazarene, a, 571; "Gospel of the Nazarenes," 570 foll.
Nazer or Branch, the, 570, 704
Negative, Heb., confused with personal pronoun, 779 *a*

Oblation, "the [evening] o.", 627 *a*, 724 *d*; "the going up of the o.," 629-39; connected with Ezra, Daniel, and Elijah, 627-30

Offering, confused with "going up", 629 c. See also "oblation"
Omens, 778
"Opinion", substituted for "glory" by Diatess., 878
Origen, on the place of the Baptism, 612-3; on the Transfiguration, 869-74
"Original", the term, how used in this book, p. xxxvi (c)
Oven, "the o. of a snake," 765

ο, interchanged with ω, 960 a, d, 966 a, 1015 c
ὅ, (?) replaced by τί, 1010 c
οἰκειότερον, (?) "more particularly" or "more suitable", 1143 a
ὄνομα, ins. for, or with, πνεῦμα, 660 a; Phil. ii. 9 τὸ ὅ. τὸ ὑπὲρ πᾶν ὅ., 915
ὄπισθια, "τὰ ὀπίσθια αὐτοῦ", of Christ in the Transfiguration, 901 b
ὀπίσω, 891 b
ος, for ως, 966 a
οὐ, (?) wrongly translated by R.V. in Mk xiv. 36, 931 h, comp. 1010
οὐ μή (Epict. iii. 22. 33), 933 b
οὐ μὴ πίω (Jn xviii. 11), 933-6, 979 c, d, 1007

ω, interchanged with ο, 960 a, d, 966 a, 1015 c
ὠνείδισας, D's reading in Mk xv. 34, 1055
ως, written ος, 966 a

Papias, 995-8, 1147 foll.
Passover, "this P. is our Saviour," 630 b
Paul the Apostle, favours the subjective hypothesis of the Transfiguration, 880
Penuel, Jacob wrestling in, 961
Perfect participle, in Jn, 646 a
Peter the Apostle, his confession, 894; his saying (Mk ix. 5) "three tabernacles", 868 foll.; "not knowing what he said," 885 foll.; said by Papias to have had an "interpreter",

997; his vision, 1025; the "Second Epistle of P.," 1116-35, 1139
Phemé, compared with Bath Kol, 731, 733
"Philip", (?) meaning of the name, 1015 e, f
Philip the Apostle and Philip the Evangelist, 1015 c; early confusion between the two, 1015 a; Philip at Azotus, 1015 d
Pillar(s), name given to a Rabbi, 764 c, 943; to Apostles, 943; "the pillars of Caesarea wept," 764 c; "pillars" or "attendants", 764 d; confusable with "standing up" or "praying" or "with me", 943-4
Pittacium (Lat.), 784 a
Ploughs, and yokes, "restored by the Messiah," 704 b; "made by Christ as a carpenter," 558, 928 (iii)
Pluperfect, non-existent in Hebrew, 1068 b
Polycarp, his Martyrdom, 690
Power, "the power and the glory," 1021 a-b
Prayer, perh. implied in "oblation", 630; the Voice from Heaven an answer to prayer, 908-1028; Christ's One Prayer, 929-79; Lord's Prayer, the first clauses of, 965 foll., 971 (vii); the eighth clause, treated by Tertullian as an interpretation, 971 (i); the Long Johannine Prayer refers to the Synoptic Lord's Prayer, 970
Prayers, taught by Rabbis for use in travel and danger, 967
Praying, implied in "standing upright", 944; confusable with "pillars" and "with me", 943
Press, "I am pressed" confusable with "I press on", 1010 e
Prophecy, not quoted but implied, 703; confusable with "Vision", 853 a
Prophet, the term would include Joshua 797 e; not included by Justin in his 16 names of Christ 846 a; "Prophet" and "Messenger", 817-49; the Deuteronomic Prophet (Deut. xviii.

15, comp. xxxiv. 10), 817, 825 foll.,
846; prophets compared with sages,
757
Ptolemy Philopator, Seleucus said to be
an error for, 732 a
Purification of the temple, 862
παῖς, "boy", "son", or "servant",
806 a, comp. 805–11; interchanged
with δοῦλος, 807 d
παρά, meaning of π., in Celsus' account
of the Baptism, 610, 614
παραδίδωμι, 927 foll.
παράστασις, Lightfoot's interpretation
of, 1139 a
παραφέρω¹, 931 e, 975–7, 1007
παρεισφέρω, 1129 d

παρέλθῃ, pass by, i.e. surpass, outstrip,
conquer, 941 a
περιστερά (Lk. ii. 24); distinguished
from τρυγών, 594 a, 685 b
πίω, οὐ μὴ πίω, 933–6, 979 c, d, 1007
πλήν in Mt. Lk. = ἀλλά in Mk, 1010 c
πλήρωμα, 571 a, 665
πνεῦμα τοῦ θεοῦ (Is. xi. 2), exceptional,
669 a; πνεῦμα πληρώσεως (Jerem. iv.
12) means "wind of fullness", 674 a
προδίδωμι, 928 a
προδότης, 928 a
πῶς σὺ λέγεις; 939 a

φούρκα, 928 (vii) b foll.
φωνή = Heb. "word", 852–3
φωτίσθητε, 635 a

---

¹ (1) L.S. have "*to turn aside*, or *away from*, τὴν ὄψιν π. τινός Xen. *Cyn.* 5. 27; π. τὸν ὀφθαλμόν to look *aside*, Luc. *D. Meretr.* 10. 2; π. τοὺς ὑσσούς *to put* them *aside*, Plut. *Camill.* 41: *to avert, put away*, Ev. *Marc.* 12. 14 (? error for Mk xiv. 36, Lk. xxii. 42)." But see the passages. (*a*) Xen. ἡ ποδωκία πρὸς τὸ ἀμβλυωπεῖν αὐτῷ πολὺ συμβάλλεται, ταχὺ γὰρ ἑκάστου παραφέρει τὴν ὄψιν πρὶν νοῆται ὅτι ἐστί seems to mean "The hound's swiftness helps to make him still more dull of vision for *he lets slip past* him the sight of each object in turn before he perceives what it is" [less prob. "his swiftness carries the sight past him," as we should say of an express train]. (*b*) Luc. ἐκεῖνον δὲ ἐρυθριάσαντα κάτω ὁρᾶν καὶ μηκέτι παρενεγκεῖν τὸν ὀφθαλμόν, "[she reported that] the young man blushed and looked down and would no longer *let himself even glance* at her," Reitz "nec amplius eo oculum *adjecisse*." (*c*) Plut. Here π. seems at first sight to mean certainly "put aside." But see the passage. διὸ καὶ μεθιστάμενοι τῶν ἰδίων ὅπλων ἐπειρῶντο τοῖς ἐκείνων συστρέφεσθαι καὶ τοὺς ὑσσοὺς παραφέρειν ἐπιλαμβανόμενοι ταῖς χερσίν (?) "So [the Gauls], letting go their own shields [? arms], tried to grapple at close quarters with the shields [? arms] of the Romans, and to *give the slip to* the pila, catching hold [of the shields] with their hands." In view of the very freq. meaning "let slip", "let pass", this might mean that they tried to "*let* the javelins *pass* them" by "*dodging*" them with their *bodies*, and to catch hold of the shields of the Romans with their *hands*: and this view is confirmed by Plut. *Pelop.* 9 π. "let pass" (Field), (not "parry") [L.S. also refer to Plut. *Arat.* 43 "*let slip*", Xen. *Cyn.* 6. 24 (passive) "*slip away*", "*escape*"]. Even if π. in Plut. *Camill.* 41 means "twist aside *from oneself*," it could not shew that π. could mean "remove *from another person*."

Having regard to the fact that L. and S. can quote no better instances than these—and that so able a scholar as Field does not quote either these or any others—to shew that παραφέρω can mean "I *remove* [from some one]," the *onus probandi* seems to lie with those who maintain the customary interpretation of Mk xiv. 36, not with those who deny it.

(2) Athenaeus p. 380 d, e quotes a discussion on the use of παραφέρω in which a mention of the [passive] "things served *up* [on the table] (παραφερομένων)" leads to the question "where do we find (ποῦ κεῖται) the [active] *serve-up* (τὸ παραφέρειν)?" A guest gives four instances from *four comic poets*. The first is Aristophanes, π. τὰ ποτήρια "*hand* the *cups*". The second, Sophron, is said to use the word κατὰ κοινότερον [" communi magis notione", but (?) "more sociably", *one* bowl being "handed" or "passed round" among many guests *in common* (κατὰ κοινόν, see L.S.). κατὰ κοινότερον could hardly refer to the style "in a somewhat common fashion"] as follows: παράφερε Κοικόα (edd. κύκλῳ but ?) μεστὸν τὸν σκύφον. In two of these instances, spite of the context, scribes have substituted περιφέρω. These facts suggest that considerations of linguistic fitness may have had some part in inducing Mark to suppose that π., with ποτήριον, could not be used in this vernacular or comic fashion. Hence the text may have seemed to require amending by inserting ἀπ' ἐμοῦ "from me", converting the meaning from "*present* (*to*)" into "*remove* (*from*)".

Quotation, from initial words, 973 *a*

Ram, story of the (Gen. xxii. 13), 1069 (i) foll.
Ransom, "to give his soul a r.," 925
Red Heifer, the, 615 *a*
Reduplication, Hebrew, 1058
Refiner, the, 857–64; ambiguities connected with, 858–61
Remarriage, sanctioned by Bath Kol, 745–6
Rest, Jn prefers "abide" to "r." in describing the resting of the Spirit, 714
Rest(ing), confusable with "dove", 695–6; means "resting-place", 724 *c*; confusable with "[evening] oblation", 724 *d*; Solomon "a man of r.," 724 *b*
Resting Place, of Jehovah, the Temple, 724 *c*
Rod, Joseph's, 697–710
Rome or Edom, 961 *a*

Sabach, Mk xv. 34 &c. "forsake", means also "let alone", "pardon", "suffer", 1051–6 foll.
Sabbath, 738
Samaria, 1015 *d*
Samuel, anointing of David by, 650, 797
Samuel the Little, 735
Satan, accusing Jacob, 961; cast down from heaven, 922, 1003 *a*, 1015; enters into Judas, 986, 986 *a*; "S." a term applied to Peter, 891 *a*
Saul, Abba, 1022
Saul, "the chosen of the Lord," 783 *a*
Say, "some *say*" confusable in Heb. with "some *said*", 874 *a*, 1059, comp. 1002; "say" = "purpose", 744
Scent, "to have s.", said of the Messiah, 667
Scripture, used as *Sortes Biblicae*, 749
See, "s. the thunders of Sinai," 781 *d*
Seleucus, said to be an error for Philopator, 732 *a*
Seraphim, the, 1020
Seven, variously connected with "angels", "eyes", "lamps", "spirits", 668, 668 *a*; the s. deacons, 1015 *b*; the s. loaves and baskets, 1015 *b*
Seventy, s. angels, 668 *a*; nations, 668 *a*; tongues of the world, 781 *d*
Seventy (apostles), the return of, 922; (?) sent to the Gentiles, 1015
Sheba, transliterated, 1060 *c*
Shebna, brother of Hillel, 737
Shema, the, 783, 928 (ii) *a*, 928 (v)
Shechinah, 734; corresponds to "the Holy Spirit", 736; interchanged with "Name", 971 (iii)
Shemaiah and Abtalion, 738
Sibylline Oracles, 582 foll.
Simeon ben Eliezer, 969
Simon the Just, 732
Sinai, the Voice from, 781 *c*; "seeing the thunders of," 781 *d*
Siphra and Siphri, 743 *a*, 1078–9
Sit, might imply "pause before praying", 944; confusable with "sleep", 945 *a*; may mean "remain", 945 *d*
Six, spirits, 667–8; six, variously connected, 668
Slave (the word), not in O.T. except in Jer. ii. 14, 807 *b*
Slaves, 928 (vi); Philo on "the slavish race", 928 (iv) *a*
Sleep, confusable with "sit", 945 *a*
Snake, "the oven of a s.," 765
Snatch, "the Spirit snatched Philip," 1015 *d*
Solomon, "a man of rest," 724 *b*
Son, compared with "Name", 1005; "Beloved Son", 786–816; "son", in Heb., confusable with "fine [wheat]", 857; with "chosen", 860; a mistranslation of "servant", 805–11; "Son of God", 661; "Son of man", 661
Soul, "loving God with one's s.," 928 (v)
Sower, Parable of the, 1019; tradition about, 998
Sparrows, our Lord's saying about s. (Mt. x. 29) prob. not copied in Jewish tradition, 748 *a*

"*Specula*" (Lat.), *i.e.* "do the work of a *speculator*," "despatch", **748** *a*
Spirit, the Holy, "the whole fountain of," **665**; Jn's doctrine about, **671**; in j. Talm. corresponds to the Shechinah in b. Talm., **736**; Bath Kol said to be substituted for, **743**; "the Spirit" (absolutely), a title freq. in N.T., rare in O.T., **672**; the descent of, connected with Is. xi. 2, **666**; the resting of, **714** *a*; Is. xi. 2 "[the] Spirit of the Lord," mistransl. by LXX "[a] Spirit of the God," **669**; elsewhere mistransl. or om. by LXX, **675**; "Thy (or, the) Holy Spirit" substituted for "Thy (or, the) Name," **968, 971** (iii)
Spirits, "six" or "seven", **664–9**; called "the powers enumerated by Isaiah," **557** *a*; "seven s." connected with the "seven lamps" in the tabernacle, **668** *a*; "spirits, or winds, four," **668** *a*
Stand (Heb.), its local and metaphorical meanings, **945**; "standing upright" implies "praying", **944**; confusable with "pillars" and "with me", **943**
Stature, metaphorically used, **883** *c*
Stephen, **871, 1015** *c*
Stoic dogma, **920**; Stoic maxims, **1000**
Stream, *i.e.* river, confusable with N. Heb. "light", **635**
Successions, of the Apostles, **1136** foll., **1142** *a*
Sun, confusable with "Elijah" in Gk, **1057–60**, esp. **1060** *a*
Sword, metaph., **1015** *d*, **1018**

σανίς, **928** (vii) *c* foll., **928** (x) *a*
σειροῖς, **1129** *c*
στάσις, **928** (i) *e*
σταυροκόμιστος, **928** (vii) *e* foll.

σταυρός[1], **928** (i)–(x)
στήριγμα, στήριγξ, **928** (vii) *b*, foll.
συνεστώς, how used in Lk. ix. 32, **879** *b*; its meaning elsewhere, **879** *b*
συνέχομαι, parall. to ἀνέξω, **1010** *d*
σχῆμα, "fashion", contrasted with μορφή, "essential form", **810** *a*, **896** *d*
σχίζω, **641** *a*

Tabernacles, "the three T." (Mk ix. 5), **868** foll., **891–5**
Tabor, **867** *a*, **981** *a*
Talmud, Jerusalem contrasted with Babylonian, **762, 783** *c*, **785** *a*
Tamar, Bath Kol on, **740, 743** *c*
Targum, meaning of, pp. ix—x
Tatian, his Diatessaron, **556**
Tears, "strong crying and t." imputed to Jesus, **957–64** *a*
Temple, the, **1017–20**
Tempus (Lat.), "time of trial", **956** *a*
Teraphim, transliterated, **1060** *c*
Testament of the XII Patriarchs, **566**
"The" (Heb.) dropped before a noun defined by a genitive, **663**
They, *i.e.* God, the powers of heaven, **667** *a*, **738** *a*
Thirty (λ) perh. dropped, **587** *a*; "t. years old", applied to Mary and to David, **709** *c d*; "t. years old"= (Heb.) "son of 30 years," **709** *d*
Thunder(s), **727–9, 781** *c*; "seeing the t. of Sinai," **781** *c d*
Transfiguration, the, Physical Hypothesis of, unsatisfactory **865–7**; Voice at, why omitted by Jn? **865–907**; Origen's view of, subjective, **869–74**; in *Acts of John*, **877**; a Jewish comment on, **881**; tradition on, in Clem. Alex., **881**; the subjective hypothesis is favoured by St Paul, **880**; the Voice at, in "2 Pet.", **1131**

---

[1] As confirmation of the statement (**928** (x) *d*) that Jews would interpret "take up the cross" literally, see Dr Edersheim, *L. of Chr.* ii. 87 "*They*"—*i.e.* the disciples—"*knew the torture which their masters—the power of the world—the Romans, were wont to inflict: such must they,* and similar must we all, *be prepared to bear*, and, in so doing, begin by denying self": and he adds in a footnote, "*In those days the extreme suffering which a man might expect from the hostile power* (*the Romans*) *was the literal cross*; in ours, it is suffering not less acute, the greatest which the present hostile power can inflict: really, though perhaps not literally, a cross." I italicize the words that seem to confirm my thesis.

Transliteration, errors arising from, 1060 c
Tree, meaning Cross, 1020 a
Trouble, preceding prayer, 908-28; followed by "glory", 986, 1020 b; "freedom from t.", inculcated by Epictetus, 920

θεράπων, 807 c, 808

τί, (?) substituted for ὅ, 1010 c; τί prob. "why?" (not "what?") in Jn xii. 27
τί εἴπω, 938-40, comp. 933 a
τίθεται ἐπί, "is [a name] attached to," not "is placed on", 928 (vii) f
τίνα, meaning "what things", 1142-6
τίς, alleged to be used for ὅς, *931 f-h
τρυγών (Lk. ii. 24), distinguished from περιστερά, 594 a, 685 b

Uncovered, "with head u.", 883 c
Unfamiliar phrases corrupted, 789-90
Unveiled, "with u. face", 883 c
Upon, confusable with "go up", 707 b; with "came", 851; with "yoke", 928 (iii) c; "the word of the Lord u.," 850-2; "disquieted u. me" (Ps. xlii. 5), 918
Upright (Lev. xxvi. 13) = (Targ.) "with head uncovered", 883 c
"Ur-Marcus", p. xxxvi (c)

ὑπακούετε, 964
ὑποστάτης, 928 (vii) b foll.
ὑψοῦν, 1003 c

Variation of the Interrogative, 1146 c
Vaw (Heb.), "and" or "but", 937; "and" or "even", 818, 834; "for" or "but", 1068 a
Virtue, "the V. of God," 1126
Vision, confusion between v. and prophecy, 853 a
Voice, "the V. of the Lord" in the Bible, 727-9; how interpreted by Philo, 727; the V. at the Baptism, subjective, 864 a; John the Baptist calls himself a voice, 864; V. for "Daughter of Voice", 741 a; see *Bath Kol*.

Voices, *i.e.* "thunders", 728

Wait, "I have waited for thy salvation," 797 d
Walking, how interpr. by Philo, 727
Washing of feet, the, 928 (viii), 986
Water, "the water from heaven," 625; "the waters of the Law," 764 b
Weaving of the veil, explained mystically, 709 b
Well pleased, "to be w.", interchanged with "choose", 863
Wetstein on "the Dove", 686-7
"Why?" implies prohibition, 918; means also "How!" 918; in Heb. introduces what ought not to be said, 939
Will, God's Will, 1011; "Thy will be done," 931 foll., 955 foll.; Tertullian's treatment of the clause, 971 (v)
Wood, meaning Cross, 1020 a
Word, variously referred to as "Scriptures" or "Prophets", 953; "the word of the Lord came," 850; "according to thy, his &c. word," 949-54, 993, 1011 c; "words of life", 894
Works, good, meaning of, 1022 c
World, the, its double meaning, 1016
Writings, "the canonical writings", *i.e.* Bible or N.T., not Epistles alone, 1146

ξαίνω, "scourge", 928 (v) a, 928 (x) b
ξύλον, 928 (vii) b foll., 928 (x) b

Yoke 928 (i)-(x); "taking on oneself the yoke" = repetition of the *Shema*, 928 (ii); "the yoke of the Kingdom of Heaven," 928 (ii) a; the yoke, preparatory for martyrdom, 928 (v)
Yokes, and ploughs, "restored" by the Messiah, 704 b; made by Christ "as a carpenter", 558, 928 (iii)

Zalmon, 745 b
Zechariah, (Zech. ix. 9) "Behold, thy king cometh," 1018
Zion, the sons of, 1018

ζυγός = the bondage of the Jewish Law, 928 (vii)

FROM LETTER TO SPIRIT

III. HEBREW

The references are to paragraphs, indicated by black numbers, which, in this Index, run from **553** *to* **1149**]

1. "c. w." means that one Hebrew word has been *actually c(onfused) w(ith)* another; "perh. c." means "*perh(aps) c(onfused)*."
2. "cble w." means that one Hebrew word is *c(onfusa)ble w(ith)* another word, owing to similarity of letters.

אב "father", c. w. אם "if", 979 *b*
אבי " my father ", 979 *b*
אבי " O that ! " 979 *b*
אחד " one "
אחז " obtain " ⎱ perh. c., 891 *a*,
אחר " behind " ⎰ 1069 (ii)
אי, meanings of, 979 *b*
אי בי " I am able ", cble w. אבי, 979 *b*
אם " if ", c. w. אב " father ", 979 *b*
אם " if ", implying a wish, 985 *a*

בחירי " my chosen ", c. w. ⎱
ביחידי " in my beloved " ⎰ 803 *a*
בי, " I pray ", or " in me ", 979 *b*
בר, Bib. Heb. "lye", "purity", c. w. N. Heb. "son", 857 *a*
בר "son","lye",&c.,"chosen", 860
ברוח " with the Spirit " ⎱ (?) 857
ברית " soap " ⎰

גלה "reveal", used with אל or ־ל, not על, 971 (vii)

דבר " word ", or " hath spoken ", 954
ה־, see " Article "
הוי " woe ", cble w. ⎱ 985 *a*
היה " had been born " ⎰

הרפה "forsake", cble w. חרף "insult, reproach", **1055**

ו, see *vaw*

זקף " crucified ", 1003 *c*

חרף " reproach ", see הרפה

יון Javan, *i.e.* "Greece" ⎫
יונה " dove " ⎬ c. or cble,
ינה " oppress " ⎬ 696 *a*
ינוח " he will rest " ⎭
יקר, substituted for כבד, 915 *a*
יקר " be glorious ", c. w. קרא " call ", 915 *b*
יקרא, (Onk.) " the glory of ", (Heb.)
קרן " became horned ", 896 *c*
ישב " sit ", c. w. שכב " sleep ", 945 *a*

כבד, means "weight", "riches", " glory ", 660 *a*, 1021 *b*; altered to יקר, 915 *a*
כבודך or כבדך "thy glory", cble w. כדברך " according to thy word," 1011 *c*

ל־ " for ", rendered " to ", 927 *b*

לוֹ "to him", c. w. the rare לוֹ "not", 985 *a*; c. w. לֹא "not", 779 *a*

לָמָא "why?" cble w. מלא "there is fulfilled", 954 *b*

מָה "why?" implying negative, 918 *b*
מלא "fulfil", cble w. מלאך (*quod vid.*) "angel" or "messenger", 656 *a*, 954; cble w. לָמָא "why?" 954 *b*

מלאך "angel" or "messenger", c. w. מלך "king", 656 *a*; cble w. מלא "fulfil", 656 *a*, 954

מלאכדבר (?) "fulfilled according to the word," or "an angel hath spoken," 954

מלך "king", c. w. מלאך "angel" or "messenger", 656 *a*

מלכה "kingdom", cble w. מלך "king", 656 *a*

מנהו Ps. lxviii. 23 "from it", should be מנתו (R.V.) "its portion", 977

מנחה, see 627–39; "oblation" or "resting", 724 *d*

מנת "the portion of", 977

מנהר (?) (Targ.) מנהר "streamed with light", cble w. (Heb.) מנהר "from the river", 635

נצח "flower", c. w. } 708
נצר "branch"

עד "unto", c. w. על (*vid. infr.*), 918 *a*

על (*vid. infr.*) c. w. עד "unto", 918 *a*

על "upon", c. w. עלה "go up", 707; N. Heb. "came", Bib. Heb. "upon", 851; Bib. Heb. "yoke", cble w. "upon",

928 (iii) *c*; "upon us" (?) in old versions of Lord's Prayer, 971 (ii)—(vii)

עלה "go up", cble w. עַל "come" or "go", 637 *a*; c. w. עַל "upon", 707

עלו "they went up", "they went", "they entered", 637 *a*

עליון "O Most High" } cble 971 (vi)
עלינו "on us"

עלל, see עלה

עם "near" or "with", c. w. עם "people", 610–1

עמד "stand", 945

עמדי "with me", perh. c. w.
עמדים or עמודים "pillars" and } 943
עמדים "standing up"
עמדים, may mean "pillars" or "attendants", 764 *d*

ענה (root), "answer", "sing", "be afflicted", 923 *b*

פיליפי c. w. } 1015 *e*
פליטה

קרא "meet" or "call", 1069 *b*; c.w. יקר "be glorious", 915 *b*; c. w. קרב "draw near", 1069 *b*

קרב "draw near", c. w. קרא "call", 1069 *b*

קרן "became horned", cble w. יקרא "the glory of", 896 *c*

קרע "rend", cble w. רקיע "firmament", 644

שבע "seven", cble w. } 1015 *b*
שבעים "seventy"

שוב "(re)turn", also "return (an answer)", 946 *a*

שכב "lie down to sleep," c. w. ישב "sit", 945 *a*

PARADOSIS

I. NEW TESTAMENT PASSAGES

[*The references are to paragraphs, indicated by black numbers, which, in this Index, run from* **1150** *to* **1435**]

MATTHEW		MATTHEW		MARK	
	PAR.		PAR.		PAR.
4 12	1150, 1221	26 2	1151, 1206, 1215, 1289–1310	1 38	1376
5 46–7	1370 a–c			2 17	1371 a
6 7	1370 c			3 19	1221, 1355
14–15	1181	3	1296 b	5 41–2	1397**
10 4	1152 a, 1221, 1355	13	1400, 1411, 1411 a–c	6 3	1384 b
				46	1242 c
19	1221	21–4	1343–58, 1427–8	8 31	1248 a–b, 1297
39	1286, 1333 a			31–2	1252–4
40	1417	22	1359–60	32	1244 c, 1253 b, 1254 a, 1432–3
11 6	1236 a	23	1348 a		
13 55	1384 b	24	1312–4	35	1333 a
16 21	1297	25	1361	38	1371 a
21–2	1252–4	26	1319 foll.	9 9–10	1265
25	1333 a	28	1400	12	1248 a
17 9	1265	30–3	1234–44	27–32	1215 foll.
12	1248 a–b	32	1203, 1230, 1244	28	1215
18–23	1215 foll.			30	1204, 1220
22	1151, 1204	42–6	1385	30–2	1215–44, 1421–2
22–3	1215–44, 1265, 1421–2	45	1362–71		
		45–6	1362–7, 1429–30	31	1151, 1265
23	1272, 1273 b			32	1272, 1273 b
18 17	1370 c	46	1361, 1372–87	10 32	1253 a, 1273
20 17–19	1245–51, 1255–88, 1423–4	48	1366, 1378	32–4	1245–51, 1255–88, 1423–4
		49–50	1363–7		
18–19	1151	53	1383	33	1151
19	1206	61	1309 b, 1432	34	1264
26–8	1275–88	64	1382 a	43–5	1275–88
28	1214 a, 1275–82	67	1263	45	1214 a, 1275–88
		73	1432		
22 44–5	1382	27 26	1176–7	46	1246
24 10	1221	30	1262–3	11 25–6	1181
22	1225 a	49	1262 a	12 36–7	1382
25	1225 a	28 6–7	1216	13 4	1246, 1293 a
25 13	1293 a	7	1203, 1230–3	11	1221
14–30	1397		MARK	20	1225 a
21	1397			23	1225 a
24	1336 c–e	1 14	1150, 1221	33	1293 a
26 1–2	1289–1310	15	1310	37	1289–96 foll., 1425
1–4	1425–6	35	1242 c		

PARADOSIS

MARK		LUKE		JOHN	
PAR.		PAR.		PAR.	
14 1	1289–1310, 1425–6	18 31–4	1245 foll., 1255–74,	6 51–3	1214 a
				55–7	1340
9	1400, 1411 a–c		1423–4	57	1288 b, 1353
18	1215	32	1263	59	1340
18–21	1343–58, 1427 –8	34	1271	7 32	1388 a
		19 11–28	1397	39	1213
19	1359–60	13	1397 b	45–6	1388 a
20	1348 a	17	1397	8 59	1185 b
21	1215, 1312–4	21	1336 c–e	9 16	1371 b
22	1319 foll., 1358 b	20 42–4	1382	24–5	1371 b
		21 8	1293 a	31	1371 b
26–9	1234–44	37	1289	41	1371 b
27	1236 a	22 1	1289–98	10 11	1336 a
28	1203, 1230, 1244	1–2	1425–6	15	1336 a
		19	1319–25 foll.	17	1336 a
39–42	1385	[19 b]	1351, 1398–1419	18	1212
41	1361–71			11 7	1376 a
41–3	1362–7, 1429–30	20	1351	15	1226, 1376 a
		21	1341–58	16	1376 a
42	1361, 1372–87	21–3	1343–58, 1427 –8	39	1306
44	1366, 1378			50	1392
45	1363–7	22	1312–4	12 1	1298, 1425
58	1309 b, 1432	23	1359–60	3	1411 a
62	1382 a	26	1283 a	16	1213
65	1263	26–7	1275–88, 1353	23	1213
70	1432	28–30	1351 foll.	24	1336 e, 1338 a
72	1273 a	31–3	1234	30	1226
15 15	1176–7	32	1236	32	1212
19	1261–3	38	1361	38	1185 b
27	1183 b	39–40	1234–44	38–41	1210
34	1397*	46	1362	40	1185 b
16 6–7	1216	47–8	1362–7	13 10	1283, 1288 a, b, 1344
7	1203, 1230–3	48	1429–30		
		63	1260 b	11	1288 a, b, 1344
LUKE		64	1264 b	14	1286
		69	1382 a	15	1226, 1332, 1414 a
1 66	1350	23 16	1170		
2 41	1292	22	1170	18	1314 b, 1344
3 20	1150	25	1176–7	19	1226
4 43	1376	24 6	1204, 1216, 1219–33	21	1427, 1344
6 16	1355			22	1427, 1344
32–3	1370 a–c	6–7	1216–9 foll.	24	1359–60
7 23	1236 a	14	1246 a	26	1427
9 22	1297	19–20	1423	27	1361
24	1333 a	39	1326 d	33	1237
31	1356 a	42	1194 a	37–8	1237, 1336 a
36	1265			14 2	1204, 1226, 1229–43, 1393–7, 1434–5
43–5	1215–44, 1421 –2	JOHN			
44	1265	1 16	1339 a		
45	1271–3	29	1284 c	2–3	1213
12 37	1277 b	2 19	1309 b	4–6	1386
13 19–21	1338 a	3 15	1211	23	1294, 1393, 1413–4
32	1207, 1302, 1306–8, 1356	16–21	1339 a		
		24	1150	25	1413–4
17 33	1286, 1333 a	4 34	1353	26	1413–4
		6 51	1325	27	1384

NEW TESTAMENT PASSAGES

JOHN

		PAR.
14	28	1386
	29	1226
	30–1	1373
	31	1361, 1372–87
15	2	1288 a–b
	3	1288 a–b
	11	1226
	12–14	1338
	13	1226, 1336 a
16	1	1236
	4	1225 a
	10	1307
	16	1306
	17–18	1307
	21	1307
	22	1307
	26–7	1236
	28	1307, 1386
	32	1236, 1383
	33	1383
17	19	1226
	22–3	1386
	23–6	1383
18	3	1364–5, 1388 a
	12	1388 a
	14	1392
	18	1388 a
	22	1388 a
	30	1391
	35	1388–90
	36	1209 b, 1388–9
19	6	1388 a
	11	1209 b, 1371 b, 1390–2
	30	1214 c
	34	1262 a
	37	1259 a, 1262, 1336 b
20	18	1359 a

ACTS

2	23	1153, 1176, 1260 b, 1431
	25–7	1382
3	13	1153, 1431
	15	1153, 1431
4	28	1350
7	52	1153

ACTS

		PAR.
8	30–3	1158
9	4–6	1409 b
	15	1409 b
	40	1397**
10	4	1400, 1411 c
11	21	1350
13	35	1382
17	27–8	1381 a
	28	1241 a
19	9, 23	1250
22	7–10	1409 b
24	22	1250
26	17	1409 b

ROMANS

4	25	1155 a, 1156, 1181, 1187
5	6	1180
	15–20	1181
7	24	1326 d
8	32	1154
	33	1381 b
11	11	1236 a
	11–12	1181
	35	1209 c
12	1	1332

1 CORINTHIANS

4	13	1261 a, 1284 a, c, 1287 a
9	21	1176, 1182 a
11	23	1155, 1202, 1417
	24	1315–25 foll., 1332 foll.
	24–5	1398–1419
	26	1408
12	21	1307
13	3	1316 a, 1326 a, f
16	12	1220 a

2 CORINTHIANS

4	11	1340
5	19	1181
	21	1268 b
10	7	1307
11	16	1307

GALATIANS

		PAR.
1	4	1155 a, 1326 c
2	15	1368
	20	1154, 1326 c
6	1	1181

EPHESIANS

2	13	1386
	14	1386
	18	1386
5	2	1154, 1326, 1386
	25	1154, 1326, 1386

PHILIPPIANS

4	5–6	1381 a

COLOSSIANS

3	3	1338 a

1 THESSALONIANS

2	8	1330, 1340

1 TIMOTHY

2	6	1155 a, 1326 c

TITUS

2	14	1155 a, 1326 c

HEBREWS

9	14	1326 d
10	3	1411
12	15	1431**

1 PETER

2	21	1159
	22–5	1158 a–b
	23	1154
4	1	1159
5	1, 5	1283 a

2 PETER

2	8	1182 a

1 JOHN

2	8	1307
3	16	1336 a

REVELATION

1	7	1259 a, 1262
18	11–13	1327 b

PARADOSIS

II. ENGLISH AND GREEK

[*The references are to paragraphs, indicated by black numbers, which, in this Index, run from* **1150** *to* **1435**]

1. "c. w." means that one word has been *actually c(onfused) w(ith)* another.
2. "cble w." means that one word is *c(onfusa)ble w(ith)* another word, owing to similarity of letters.

Abraham, A. and Isaac going "together" or "as one," **1387** *b* ; s. also **1411** *b*
"Again," in Jn, meaning "on the other hand," **1307**
Akiba, R., connected with Is. liii. 12, **1198**
Alexandrians, (?) denoted by "Babylonians," **1261** *a*
Ananias, the baptizer of Saul, **1416-8**
Aramaic, confused with Hebrew, **1384***a*; uttered by Jesus, **1384** *a*; s. also **1397***, **1397****, and p. xxiii *c, d*
Ascension of Christ, the, **1307-8**
"Asham," see **1267-82, 1337**
"Authority," **1390-1**; "a. to lay down life," **1212, 1335**

ἄγνοια, **1270**
ἄγωμεν, **1372-7**
ἀθεσία, used by Aquila, **1182** *b*
-αι interchanged with -ε, **1260** *b*
αἴρω, parallel to θερίζω, **1336** *c*; antithetical to τίθημι, **1336** *c–e*
ἁμαρτωλός, **1370-1**, in Mk, **1371** *a*
ἀμνάς, "lamb" or "coin," **1396** *a*
ἀναβαίνω, c. w. συμβαίνω, **1246**
ἀνάμνησις, **1398-1419**
ἀνάστασις, analogous to מקום, **1244**

ἄνθρωποι, abbrev. as $\overline{ανοι}$, cble w. ἄνομοι, **1183**
ἀνισταμένους, v. r. for μετὰ παρρησίας, **1254** *a*
ἀνοήτοις, v. r. ἀνομία τοῦ, **1183** *d*
ἀνομίαι, "transgressions," distinct from παραπτώματα, "trespasses," **1181** *a–b*
ἄνομος, **1182**; implying unnatural crime, **1182**; οἱ ἀ. Ἰουδαῖοι, **1183** *c*; ἀ. cble w. ἀνοι, *i.e.* ἄνθρωποι, **1183**; s. also **1176** *a*, **1180** *a*, **1184**, and רשע
ἄρτοι εἰς ἀνάμνησιν, **1400**
ἀφανίζω, **1269** *b*, **1273** *b*

"Babylonians," (?) denoting Alexandrians, **1261** *a*
"Behold," in Jn, different from "see," **1307**; in Aramaic, הא, cble w. "this," **1321**
"Betray," s. προδίδωμι
Blood, not to be eaten, **1331-4**
Body, Aramaic original of "my b.," **1326-31**; b. of Christ, denoted by "Temple," **1309**; "b. of the Passover," *i.e.* the Paschal lamb, **1403** *a*; s. also σῶμα
"Bondservant," different from "minister," **1276**

ENGLISH AND GREEK

"Bone," in New Heb., = "self," Syr.
"soul," 1326 d; Lk. xxiv. 39 "flesh and bones," 1326 d
Bread, "the b. of affliction," 1358 a–b;
"the b. of the shewbread," 1400
Build, "b. the Holy Place," in Targum on Isaiah, 1195

Carpenter, "c. and son of a c.," 1384 b
Chrysostom, on 1 Cor. xi. 23–4, p. 9
"Cohort" (Jn xviii. 3), cble w. "sign," 1364-5; s. also σημαία
"Coincidences?" 1431**
Covenant, the C. with Noah, 1414 b; the New C., 1353; comp. 1331, 1334
Crucifixion, predictions of, 1216, 1219, 1258, 1303

καθαρισμός, for this and Gk words beginning with κ, see K

χείρ, ἐν χειρί, ambig., 1178; ἐπὶ χεῖρα, 1178 b

Dative, = "to" or "for," 1162 a–b, 1174
Days, s. "two," "three," "third"
Debts, "forgive us our d.," 1181
"Delivering up," the rendering of παραδίδωμι, in the Gospels, 1150-2; in the Acts and Epistles, 1153-6; in *The Suffering Servant* (LXX), 1156 foll. and *passim*; early Christian reference to, 1158-63; in the Targum on Isaiah, 1164-71, 1195-8; two kinds of, mentioned by Origen, 1179, 1222; "receiving and d. u.," 1315; 1 Cor. xiii. 3 "d. u. my body," 1316, 1326; "d. u. the soul," 1195, 1349 b; "the hand of him that delivereth me up," 1341-50; cble, through Heb., with "perfect," 1302 a; s. also παραδίδωμι, מסר, פגע, and 1185-94
Drinking, Lk. xxii. 30 "eating and d.," meaning of, 1351-2, 1357

δεῖ, 1248 a, 1252 a
δεῖγμα, 1414 a
δέκα, "ten," cble, through Hebrew, with "wealth" and "do (business)," 1397 a; s. עשׁר

διαπτύξαι, c. w. διαπτύσαι, 1264 a
διαπτύσαι, c. w. διαπτύξαι, 1264 a
δίδωμι, as distinct from παραδίδωμι, 1155 a; in the Eucharist, origin of, 1324; often = "appoint," "make," 1336 b

"Eat," the addition of, in the Eucharist, 1324; Lk. xxii. 30 "e. and drink," meaning of, 1351-2, 1357
Epictetus, on the Galilaeans, 1372-5
Eucharist, the, inadequacy of the Synoptic account of, 1339; "remembrance" in, 1407-19; s. also 1311-58

ἔ = "five," 1397
-ε, interchanged with -αι, 1260 b
ἐγγίζω, s. ἤγγικεν
ἐγκομβόω, 1283 a
ἐεπτυον, cble w. ετυπτον, 1261
ἐθνικοί, 1370 a–c
εἶπεν, cble w. εἶπον, 1233 a
εἶπον, cble w. εἶπεν, 1233 a; an illiterate way of writing εἰπών, 1360
εἰς, = Heb. ל, = (1) "belonging to," (2) "equivalent to," 1400 a
ἔκδοτος, 1153
ἐκκεντῶ, 1262
ἐμπαίζω, "mock," 1260; = (Nah. ii. 3) Heb. "scarlet," 1261 a
ἐμπτύσουσιν, in Mk x. 34 read by D as ἐνπτύξουσιν, 1264
ἐνέπηξαν, 1260 b
ενοχλη, c. w. εν χολη, 1431**
ἐνπτύξουσιν, s. ἐμπτύσουσιν
ἐξιλάσκομαι, construction of, 1160, 1174 a
ἐξουσία, 1390-1; s. also "authority"
ἐπιδίδωμι, 1316 a
ἔργα, through Heb., c. w. "wealth" and "ten," 1397 a
ἕτοιμον, -ασία, "place," 1244 b
ἕτοιμος, 1244 b, 1252 a
ετυπτον, cble w. ἐεπτυον, 1261
εὑρήσει, parall. το ζωογονήσει, 1286, 1333 a; with ψυχήν, 1333 a
εὐωδία, 1411 b

ζ, see below Z

ἤγγικεν, not used of persons, **1379**
ἡμῶν, error for ὑμῶν, **1199** a

θ, see below T

"Feared," parall. to "were very sorrowful," **1272**
"Finding" and "losing" the "soul," **1286, 1332, 1333** a
Flesh of Christ, the, how mentioned by Barnabas, **1214** a
"For" or "to," **1162** a–b, **1174, 1176**
Frankincense, **1399–1402**

φ, see below P

"Galilaean," inserted in Jer. Targ., **1240**; Epictetus on the Galilaeans, **1372–5**
Galilee, **1203–4, 1215–44**
"Galilee,"="circle," "district," "region," **1232**; "in, or into, G.," cble, through Heb., or Aram., w. "for your sakes," **1203, 1225–32**; s. גְּלִיל and **1432–5**

γέγραπται, different from ὡρισμένον, **1313**; γέγραπται ἵνα, parall. to μέλλει, **1248** a

Hand, "in(to) the h. of," **1178** b; "the h. of him that delivereth me up," **1341–50**; "his h. is with," meaning of, **1349–50**
"Heathen," the, **1370** a–c
Hebrew, confused with Aramaic, **1384** a; s. also **1397*, 1397****, and p. xxiii c, d
Hide, "your life is *hid* with Christ," **1338** a
Hillel, his usage in the Passover, **1406**; "in remembrance of H.," **1406**
'Honeycomb," cble, through Heb., w. "pour out," **1194** a–b
Hosea, his prophecy about "the third day," **1218, 1297**; Jewish comments on, **1306**
Humiliation, Messianic, the, details of, **1265**

Ignorance, **1270–4**; Gen. xxvi. 10 (LXX) "thou hast brought i. on us," **1270**
Intercession, s. "for," ἐξιλάσκομαι, and פגע
Isaac, sacrifice of, the, **1301-3**; I. and Abraham going "together" or "as one," **1387** b
Isaiah, his prophecy on the Suffering Servant, **1156–1214**; how quoted by St Paul, **1156, 1181**; by St Peter, **1158–9**; by Barnabas, **1159, 1214** a; by Justin, **1160–3, 1175**; by Clem. Alex. and Origen, **1163** b; the Targum on, **1164–71, 1195, 1198**; meaning of, obscured in LXX, **1164, 1172–4, 1195, 1199**; Greek and Hebrew renderings of, **1185–94**

ι = δέκα, **1397**
ἰδού and οὗτος, renderings of הוּא, **1321** c; s. also הא

Jacob, Gen. xxviii. 11 "He lighted upon the place," how interpreted, **1241**
Jericho, "going up from J.," **1246**
John, intervenes where Luke omits or alters Mark, Preface p. ix, **1225** a, **1236, 1281–8, 1309, 1311, 1325, 1344, 1373**; agrees with the Eucharistic doctrine of St Paul, **1339**; his comment not always distinguishable from his text, **1339** a
Justin, his double rendering of Is. liii. 12, **1161–2**

Kimchi, on Is. lii. 13, **1210**
"Kiss," in Heb., c. w. "seize," **1365**
Knife of Abraham, the, **1406** a

καθαρισμός, **1282** a
κατακρίνω, **1256** a
κατορχοῦμαι, **1260**
κεντῶ, **1262** a
κηρίον, **1194** b
κρύπτω, in Lk. xiii. 21, **1338** a

"Laying down," connected with "sow-

ENGLISH AND GREEK

ing" and "depositing," **1336**, s.
especially **1336** *e*
Legend, the growth of, **1185** *b*
"Lifting up," **1210–11**
Liturgies, the early, on Paradosis, **1387** *a*
"Losing" and "finding" the soul, **1286**, **1332**, **1333** *a*
Luke, wrote under Pauline influence, **1355**; his relation to John, s. John

λάβετε = הא, **1321**
λύτρον, **1275–88**, **1280** *a*

Mark, the character of his Gospel, **1281**, **1288**
Martyrdom, denoted by "delivering up the soul," **1195**
Martyrs, "the savour of m.," **1411** *b*
"Massora," or tradition, **1356**
Mean, "he meant" expressed by "he said," **1300**
"Memorial," **1399–1419**
Middle voice, in Heb., not easily distinguished from passive, **1197**
"Minister," different from "(bond)servant," **1276**
"Môad," "appointed time," **1293** foll.; various meanings of, **1304–6**
Moriah, Mt, Abraham's journey to, **1302**

μέλλω, meanings of, **1246–53**; μελλον, cble w. μελλων, **1247**; μέλλει parall. to γέγραπται ἵνα, **1248** *a*; Syr. equivalent of, **1248** *b*; comp. **1252** *a*, **1253** *a*
μνᾶ, **1395–7**
μνημόσυνον, **1399** *b*, **1400**, **1402** *a*, **1411**, **1412** *a*; in Hos. xiv. 7 (LXX) = Heb. זכר, R.V. "scent," marg. "memorial," **1411** *b*
μονάς, **1396** *b*
μονή, **1393–7**

Narrative, transmutation of, to words of the Lord, **1252–4**
Near, "the Lord is n.," **1380–1**; "made us n. in His blood," **1386**

"Nephesh," Heb. "soul," freq. rendered "self," **1326**; meaning "life-blood," "life," **1326** *e*, **1331**; = R.V. "desire" in Is. v. 14, **1326** *e*; rendered "body" in LXX Gen. xxxvi. 16, **1327**; = "tombstone," "memorial," **1329**, **1398** *a–c*; s. "soul" and ψυχή
Noah, the Law given to, **1331**; the Covenant with, **1414** *b*; s. also **1334**

νύσσω, **1262**

"Odour," = "memorial," **1411** *a–b*

ο used for ω, **1247**
ὁρίζω, see ὡρισμένον
οὗτος and ἰδού, renderings of הוא, **1321** *c*; s. also הא

ω written ο, **1247**
ὡρισμένον, different from γέγραπται, **1313**

Papias, **1243**, **1394**
Paraclete, the, **1413**
Paradosis, meaning of the term, **1150** *a*, **1356**; Christian mentions of, **1150–63**; in connexion with Isaiah, **1164–94**; in Jewish tradition, **1195–1214**; three views of, **1200**; references to, in ancient Liturgies, **1387** *a*; s. also "delivering up," παραδίδωμι, מסר, and פגע
Passive voice, the, in Hebrew, freq. has a reflexive meaning, **1197**
Passover, the, **1403–6**; "the body of the P.," *i.e.* the Paschal lamb, **1403** *a*; the Jewish P. service, **1358** *a–b*; "after two days the Passover," **1289–98** foll.
"Peace," **1384**, **1386**; "the man of my p.," **1346–8**; s. שלום
Perfect, to, **1308**, **1384**, **1386**; Lk. xiii. 32 "I am to be perfected," cble w. "delivered up," **1302**; s. τελειοῦμαι and שלם
"Pierce" in Zech. xii. 10, **1259–62**; "pierce" and "spit," **1261** *a*

Pilate, 1390-1; "by the hand of P.," 1177
Place, in New Heb., meaning " God," 1240-3; "to prepare a place," 1232-9, 1244 b, 1434-5
Pluperfect, non-existent in Hebrew, 1366
Pounds, Parable of the, 1336 c–e, 1397
Prayer of Jacob, the, 1241
Purity, the Johannine doctrine of, 1288 a–b
Put, lit. "putting the soul," 1336-8; s. τίθημι

παιδεία, " chastisement " or " instruction," 1170
παίζω, parts of, c. w. parts of παίω, 1260 a
παίω, parts of, c. w. parts of παίζω, 1260 a
παραδίδωμι, distinct from προδίδωμι, 1209 c, 1214 b; π. ψυχήν, 1214 c; s. passim, "delivering up," "Paradosis"
παρακαλυπτόμενον, 1273 a
παραπτώματα, "trespasses," distinct from ἀνομίαι, "transgressions," 1181 a
παρρησίᾳ, "openly," 1254 a, 1432-3; μετὰ παρρησίας, v.r. ἀνισταμένους, 1254 a
περικαθάρματα, 1261 a, 1284
περικαλύπτω, 1264 b
περιποιοῦμαι, 1333 a
περιπτύσσω, 1264 b
περιπτύω, used metaphorically, 1263
περίψημα, "offscouring," 1284; π. ὑμῶν, " your humble servant," 1284 b
πίνω, parts of, c. w. parts of ποιῶ, 1408 b
πλοῦτος, " wealth," cble, through Heb., w. " ten" and " make," 1397 a; s. עשר
ποιῶ, parts of, c. w. parts of πίνω, 1408 b
πόλις, "city," N. Heb. כרך, cble w. כבר which="region" or "talent," 1397; πολεῶ, cble w. πολλῷ, 1397
πολύς, επιπολλῶ, " over many things," cble w. επιπολεῶ, " over ten cities," 1397
πονηροί, c. w. πόρνοι, 1370 b

πόρνοι, c. w. πονηροί, 1370 b
προδίδωμι, " betray," why not used, 1209 c; distinct from παραδίδωμι, 1214 b
προδότης, 1153, 1355
προσπήξαντες, 1260 b
πτύω, s. ἕεπτυον
πυρ, ? dropped before προ-, 1400 a

φαγεῖν, "eat,"? c., through Heb., with ὑμῖν in Lev. x. 17 (LXX), 1324 a; c., through Heb., w. "go," 1324 a

χ, see under C

ψυχή, παραδίδωμι ψ., 1214 c; s. "nephesh" and " soul "

Ransom, " to give his soul a r.," 1275-81, 1337-40
" Receiving " and " delivering up," 1315; "receiving from the Lord," 1417
Redemption, hypotheses of, 1212
Reflexive meaning, the, freq. attached to the passive voice, 1197
Remembrance, 1399-1419; "our r.," in Jewish Prayer Book, 1401; " in r. of Hillel," 1406; " in r. of the knife," 1406 a
Resurrection of Christ, the, differently regarded by the Apostles and by their successors, 1294-5
" Right hand of God," the, 1382

ῥάπισμα, 1261 a

Sacrifices of human beings, 1284 c
"Said," in Heb. sometimes="meant," 1300
Sake, "for the s. of," how used in Gospels, 1225-6; cble in Heb. with " Galilee," 1226-30, 1240; s. גלל
Sanhedrin, the, called the " House of Judgment," 1256
Satan, " delivering up " to, 1222
" Savour," or " scent," used for " memorial," 1411 a–b; " the s. of Abraham, of martyrs," 1411 b; mean-

ing "reputation" in bad sense, 1411 b; Hos. xiv. 7 R.V. txt. "scent," marg.
"memorial," = LXX μνημόσυνον, 1411 b
Scapegoat, the, 1261 a
"Scarlet," in Nah. ii. 3 rendered by LXX "mocking," 1261 a
"See," in Jn, different from "behold," 1307
"Seize," in Heb., c. w. "kiss," 1365
"Self" = Heb. "soul," 1214a, 1326 b–c; sometimes = N. Heb. "bone" 1326 d
Seventy, the, Luke's account of, 1341
Shewbread, the, 1400-2
Simeon ben Jochai, the Mysteries of, 1185 a
"Sinners," 1370-1; use of the term "sinner" in Jn, 1371 b; "delivered up into the hands of s.," 1368-71
"Sin-offering," 1268 foll.
Soul, in Heb., *nephesh* = "self," 1214 a, 1326 b, c; = R.V. "desire" in Is. v. 14, 1326 e; once = "body" in LXX, 1327; = "tombstone" or "memorial," 1329, 1398 a–c; "drawing out the s.," 1200, 1285-6; "killing the s.," 1333 a; "losing and finding the s.," 1332, 1333 a; "laying down the s.," 1335-40; "delivering up the s.," 1195, 1349 b; Rev. xviii. 13 "souls of men," 1327 b; a soul attributed to God, 1331 a; s. "nephesh"
"Spitting," the prediction of, 1258; "spitting and piercing," 1261 a
"Stumbling (for a time)" and "stumbling (so as to fall)," 1236
Suffering Servant, the, s. Isaiah

σάρξ, applied to Jesus, 1159 a
σημαία, "cohort," cble w. σημεῖον, "sign," 1365
σπείρω, parall. to τίθημι, 1336 c–e
συμβαίνω, c. w. ἀναβαίνω, 1246
σύσσημον, סִימָא, 1365 a; condemned by Phrynichus, 1365 b
σῶμα, "person," 1326; in Gen. xxxvi. 16 (LXX) renders (Heb.) "soul,"

1327; in forms of sale of slaves, 1327 a

"Tabernacle of Testimony," 1304
Table, Lk. xxii. 30 "at my t.," meaning of, 1351-2
Talents, Parable of the, 1336 c–e, 1397
"Talitha" and "Tabitha," 1397**
Targum on *The Suffering Servant*, the, its tendency, 1198, 1285
Targums, 1339, 1416 a, comp. 1409 a
Temple, the, in Targum on Is. liii. 5, 1309 a; the T. of Christ's Body, 1309; the two Temples, 1306
"Testimony, Tabernacle of," 1304
Third, "on the t. day," 1297, 1301-2 foll.
Three, "after t. days," 1297, 1301-3
Thrones of the Twelve, the, 1351-2
"To" or "for," 1162 a, b, 1174, 1176
Together, Abraham and Isaac going "t." or "as one," 1387 b
"Trespasses," παραπτώματα, substituted for "transgressions," ἀνομίας, 1181-4; t. connected with forgiveness and confession, 1181; "for if ye forgive men their t.," 1181
"Trespass-offering," a, 1267-8
Two, "after t. days," 1289-98, 1301-10; "in t. days" (Ibn Ezra) means "in a short time," 1306 (comp. 1294); "t. days" cble, in Heb., w. "days," 1297

θέλημα, "the WILL," 1220 a
θερίζω, parall. to αἴρω, 1336 c

τάλαντον, cble, through Heb., with πόλις, 1397; s. ככר
τελειοῦμαι, in Lk. xiii. 32, 1302; applied to martyrdom, 1308
τελώνης, 1370 a–c
τίθημι, applied to ψυχή, meaning of, 1336; meaning "pawn," 1336 c; parall. to σπείρω, 1336 c–e; antithetical to αἴρω, 1336 c–e
τύπτω, s. ετυπτον

ὑμῖν, ? c. w. φαγεῖν, through Heb., in Lev. x. 17 (LXX), 1324 a
ὑμῶν, corrupted to ἡμῶν, 1199 a
ὑπέρ = ל, "for," 1322
ὑπηρέται, 1388 a
ὑπόδειγμα, 1414 a
ὑπόμνησις, 1411 d, 1414

"Veiled," meanings of, 1272-3

"Way," the, *i.e.* the Way of Life, 1250

"With," = " on the side of," 1350
Words of the Lord, transmutation of narrative to, 1252-4

Zohar, 1185 a

ζαφθανει, Mk xv. 34 (D), how explained, 1397*

ζωογονήσει, parall. to εὑρήσει, 1286, 1333 a

ω, see O

PARADOSIS

III. HEBREW

[*The references are to paragraphs, indicated by black numbers, which, in this Index, run from* 1150 *to* 1435]

1. "c. w." means that one Hebrew or Aramaic word has been *actually c(onfused) w(ith)* another; "perh. c." means "*perh(aps) c(onfused)*."
2. "cble w." means that one Hebrew or Aramaic word is *c(onfusa)ble w(ith)* another word, owing to similarity of letters.

אב "father," c. w.⎫
בוא "come" ⎬ 1341 *a*

אנומין, *i.e.* ἄγωμεν, 1377

אומן or אמון "artist"⎫
אומא "people"
אימא "mother" ⎬ c. or cble,
אמון "multitude" ⎪ 1384 *b*
אמנה "rearing" ⎭

אזכרה "memorial," 1402 *a*

אכל "eat," forms of,⎫
הלך "go," forms of, ⎬ c. or cble,
לכם "to you" ⎭ 1324 *a*

אסר "bind," forms of,⎫
יסר, Heb. "chastise," ⎬ cble,
Aram. "bind," ⎪ 1168–71
מסר "deliver up" ⎭

אשם "asham," meanings of, 1267–75;
c. w. שום τίθημι, 1273 *b*,
comp. 1336 *f*; c. w. שמם
ἀφανίζω, 1273 *b*; perh. c. w.
שמש διάκονος, 1278 foll.

ב "in" or "into," 1228, 1231;
c. w. מ, 1244

בגלוי "openly," 1432–3 ⎫
בגליל "in(to) Galilee," 1228, ⎬ cble,
1240 ⎪ s. גלל
בגלל "for the sake of," 1228 ⎪
בדיל "for the sake of," 1228; s. גלל

בוא "come," c. w.⎫
אב "father" ⎬ 1341 *a*

נבויין "tax-gatherers" ⎫
גוים "heathen" ⎬ c. or cble,
גרים "sojourners," also ⎪ 1370 *c*
(N. Heb.) πόρνοι ⎭

גבול "border" (Bib.) where Targums ins. "Galilaean" and "sake," 1240 *a*

גוים and גרים, s. נבויין

גליל "Galilee," means "circle," "region," 1232; cble w. (בגלל) "for the sake of," 1228, 1240;

perh. c. w. גבול "border," 1240 a

גלל " (for the) sake of," cble w. גליל "Galilee," 1228, 1240, and w. בגלוי "openly," 1244 c, 1432–3; Bib. Heb. בגלל = Aram. גלל or בגלל, 1228, and Targ. בדיל, 1228; s. also גליל

גרם "bone" = "self," 1326 d; s. עצם

דבר Aram. "guide," Heb. "speak," 1254 a

דין "judge," "judgment," 1256; "House of J." = Sanhedrin, 1256

דכא Heb. "bruise," Aram. "purify," 1167, comp. 1169

דקר "pierce," c. w.
רקד "mock" } 1259

הא Aram. "behold" or "this," 1321, 1358 a–c; rendered λάβετε "take," 1321

הוא rendered οὗτος, 1321 c

היה or הוה, w. ו, in Heb. and Aram., difference of meaning, 1290

היה "be"
חזה "see" } c. or cble, 1382 a
חיה "live"

הלך "go," forms of, c. w. forms of אכל "eat," 1324 a; c. w. הלל "boast," 1234 a

הלל, s. הלך

הערה "pour out," 1192–3; s. יער

ו "and" or "for," 1291

זכר "memorial," 1399 b; "scent" or "memorial," 1411 b

זעף, construction of, 1397*

חבא "hide." s. חוב(א)

חוב(א) N. Heb. or Aram. "debt" or "sin" = Heb. פשע "transgression," עון "iniquity," 1181, and חטא "sin," 1270 a; cble w. חבא "hide," 1273 d

חזה "see"
היה "be" } c. or cble, 1382 a
חיה "live"

חטא "sin," s. חוב(א)

חיה "live," causative of, variously translated, 1333 a; s. היה

חלל Heb. "wound" and "profane," Targ. only "profane," 1166 a, 1167

חרש "carpenter" or "dumb," 1384 b

ידע "know," forms of, c. w.
יער "appoint (a meeting)" } 1296 b

יחדו "together," 1387 b

ימים "days" or "two days," 1297

יסר, Heb. "chastise,"
Aram. "bind," } cble,
אסר "bind," forms of, } 1168–71
מסר "deliver up"

יער "appoint (a meeting)," s. ידע

יער "honeycomb," cble w. הערה "pour out," 1194 a, comp. 1194 b

כון "establish," "prepare," 1244 b

ככר "region" or "district," also "talent," cble w. N. Heb. כרך "city," 1397

ל "to" or "for," 1160, 1162 b, 1175, 1370; "belonging to" or "equivalent to," LXX εἰς, 1400 a; rendered ὑπέρ, 1322

לכם "to you,"
אכל "eat," forms of, } cble, 1324 a

מ. c. w. ב. 1244

מוֹסָר "chastisement" or "instruction," 1168-70, cble w. מֹסַר "deliver up"
מוֹסָר from אָסַר "bind," 1169
מוֹסָר "caused to go back," 1314 a
מוֹעֵד "appointed time," 1293 foll.
מָכוֹן "an established [place]," from כּוּן, 1244 b
מָנָה = "portion," "mina," "time(s)," 1393-7
מָסַר "deliver up," 1164-6, 1168-71, 1195-1200, 1207, 1314 (s. also παραδίδωμι and "soul"); the only Bib. instance of, 1196; middle and passive of, 1197; = Syr. שְׁלֵם which in Heb. = "perfect," "accomplish," 1207, 1302 a; cble w. מוֹסָר, s. above
מָקוֹם "place," "standing place," from קוּם "stand up," "arise," 1244; analogous to ἀνάστασις, 1244; in Aram. "official place," "rank," 1243; in N. Heb. a name of God, 1240-3; c. w. a form of קוּם "arise," 1244 a
מְשַׁמֵּשׁ "minister," "pupil," s. שָׁמַשׁ

נַגָּר "carpenter," a title for eminent teachers, 1384 b
נֶפֶשׁ s. "nephesh" and "soul"
נָשַׁק "kiss" or "seize," 1365

סְחִי = (Delitzsch) περίψημα, 1287 a
סִימָא "cohort," cble w.
סִיסְמָא "token" } 1365 a

עָוֹן "iniquity" = Targ. (א)חוּבָא "debt" or "sin," 1181; rendered by Aq. ἀνομία, 1182 c; contrasted w. פֶּשַׁע by Yepheth ben Ali, 1182 d; s. also 1191, 1193
עֶצֶם "bone" = "self," 1326 d; s. גֶּרֶם
עָשָׂה "do (business)"
עָשַׁר "wealth" } c. or cble, 1397
עֶשֶׂר "ten"
עָתִיד, meanings of, 1248 b, 1252 a, 1253 a; referring to "die Messianische Zeit," 1252 a

פָּגַע, (lit.) "go to meet," 1173-4, 1241, hence "make intercession," "entreat," 1162, 1173-4, 1189; with לְ, meaning "to" or "for," 1162 b, 1174-5; in connexion with Jacob at Bethel, 1241-2; how rendered, or paraphrased, in *The Suffering Servant*, 1185-94; rendered (LXX) παραδίδωμι "deliver up," 1162, 1172-4; s. παραδίδωμι and מָסַר
פֶּשַׁע "transgression" = Targ. חוּבָ(א) "debt" or "sin," 1181; variously rendered, 1182 b; distinguished by Yepheth ben Ali from עָוֹן, 1182 d; s. also 1180 a, 1256 b

קוּם "arise," 1239, forms of, c. w. } 1244 a
מָקוֹם "place"
קָרוֹב "near," 1379 b

רֹק "spittle," 1261
רָקַד "mock," c. w. } 1259
דָּקַר "pierce"
רָשַׁע freq. ἄνομος, 1180 a, 1256 b; הִרְשִׁיעַ = κατακρίνω, 1256 b

שָׁאַל "ask," c. w.
שָׁלִי "neglect," "forget" } 1273 c
שׂוּם = τίθημι "put," 1336, δίδωμι
"give," *i.e.* "appoint," 1336 b,
"put [in the ground]" *i.e.*
"sow," 1336 d; c. w. אָשָׁם,
1273 b, comp. 1336 f; cble
w. שָׁמַשׁ "minister," 1278;
s. "Asham," and "soul";
שָׁלוֹם or שָׁלַם, "peace," 1347, "the
man of my peace," 1346-8;
Syr. "deliver up," but Heb.
"perfect,". "accomplish,"
1207, 1302 a, 1384; comp.
1356 a, 1383-7, and s. παραδίδωμι and τελειοῦμαι
שָׁמַשׁ "minister," diff. from "bondservant," 1276-9; forms of,
cble w. תָּשִׂים אָשָׁם (lit.)
"put an *asham*," 1278

JOHANNINE VOCABULARY

I. NEW TESTAMENT PASSAGES

[*The references are to paragraphs, indicated by black numbers, which, in this Index, run from* 1436 *to* 1885. *To save space, the thousand figure is not printed.*]

MATTHEW		MATTHEW		MATTHEW	
	PAR.		PAR.		PAR.
1 20	749 c	4 16	710 c, 863 a	6 28	859
21	865	18	725 b	29	864
23	728 l_2	5 3–11	859 e	7 1	714 d, 859 a
24	865	4	674	3–5	851 d
2 2	641 b	6	750 b, 854 b	7–8	852 b
3	644, 727 b	8	857 c	13	764, 810 a
4	863	11	554	16	864
6	682 j, 862	12	851 b	22	478 a
7	749 c	14	748	22–3	484, 764 a
8	644, 675 b, 751	14–16	715 g	25	862
9	725 d	15	858	27	862-3
11	644, 754	16	728 h	27–9	573–4
13	749 c	18	860	28	865 b
16	686	19	708 i	29	562
18	674	22	682 a	8 2	644
19	749 c	23–4	851 d	4	695 b, 833 e,
23	860	25	565, 714 e,		885 a
3 2	690 a		719 h, 852 c	5–6	862 b, c
3	726	37	753	8	862 a, b, c
6	678 a, 861 a	44	856, 885 f	9	574 a, 718 c, 855
8	852	47	753	10	477 b, 673 d
9	851 a	6 9	851 a_1	11	851 a, 856
10	858	14–15	711 a	13	477 a, 862 b, c
11	686 f, 833 d	17	728 a	14	834 a–b
16	866 (iv)	19–20	858	17	679 d, 724 a,
4 1–11	854 a	23	864 a, 866		853
6	863	24	854 d	19	839 foll.
9	565, 643	25	865	20	452–8, 609 b,
10	643	26	856		839 foll.,
15	714 b	27	856, 862		858 a

This Index extends from 1436 *to* 1885 (*printed* 436—885).

68   JOHANNINE VOCABULARY

MATTHEW		MATTHEW		MATTHEW	
	PAR.		PAR.		PAR.
8 22	720 *f*	11 6	859 *e*	13 58	673 *d*
24	680 *a*	7	604 *a*, 689 *e*,	14 5	708 *c*
26	477 *b*		856	14	763 *b*
34	755	8	755	20	692 *c*
9 2	834 *a–b*	10	681 *a*	21	693 *c*
6	562, 575, 594 *c*	11	683 *b*	22	735 *a*
8	575	13	860	23	718 *i*, 813 *a*
9	604 *a*	16	861	24	813 *a*, 833 *b*,
11	718 *a*	17	857		864
16	815 *d*	19	775 *a*, 854, 864,	25	718 *i*
17	751 *b*, 853 *a*		866 *b*	26	727 *b*
18	644, 765 *a*,	20	708 *c*	27	713 *h*, 811 *e*
	852 *c*	22	859 *b*	33	644, 727 *j*
22	477 *b*, 864 *b*	23	851, 866 *a*	15 2	728 *a*
23	852 *c*	24	859 *b*	3	714 *h*, 824–31
27–30	742	25	678 *a*, 852, 860,	14	861
28	477 *a*		864–5	17	817 *a*
29	477 *b*	26	852	22	713 *b*
30	713 *e*, 811 *b*,	27	810 *c*, 852	24	723 *j*
	885 *a*	28	810 *c*	25	644
36	708 *c*	29	865 *a*	28	477 *b*, 533
38	853	12 13	728 *e*	16 9	721 *h*, 728 *l*
10 1	580 *a*	14	695 *c*	18	709 *a*
2	709 *a*	15	810	23	864 *b*
3	714 *c*	16	752 *b*	24	792 *b*, 842
5	863	18	674	27	712 *i*
6	723 *j*	19	752 *b* foll.	28	530 *a*, 710 *c*
8	751 *a*	20	689 *e*, 751	17 8	855
10	852	21	855	11	634 *b*
11	707 *a*, 751	30	863	14	862 *d*
13	853 *a*	34	864	18	862 *d*
15–16	859	41	859 *b*	20	477 *b*
18	695 *b*, 725 *c*	42	859 *b*, 864	26	712 *e*, 751 *b*
20	720 *k*	45	856 *a*, 858	18 2	793
21	679	48–9	749 *a*	3	676 *a*, 865 *a*
22	713 *f*	50	728 *g*	4	865 *a*
24	723 *h–i*	13 10	720 *a*, *b*, 802 *a*	6	686 *b*
24–8	775 *a*, 784–92	11–13	721 *c*	8	734 *b*
25	723 *h–i*	13	612–3, 724 *f*	9	682 *a*
26	716 *i*, 738 *a*,	15	683 *e*	11	692 *e*
	852, 859 *d*	16	560, 859 *e*	15	851 *d*, 852 *a*,
27	863 *a*, 866	19	854 *a*		855
28	565–6	21	811 *f*	16	696 *e*, 707 *c*,
32	861 *a*	22	676		725 *e*
34	854 *e*	24	692 *i*	20	793
35	860	28–48	864	21	779 *a*, 781,
36	787 *a*, 792 *a*	31	692 *i*		852 *a*
37	450, 792 *a*,	35	721 *c*	26	644
	866 *b*	39	854 *a*	31	720 *f*
38	792 *b*	46	753	19 1	865 *b*
40	671 *b*, 721 *f*	53	865 *b*	4	708 *d*
40–1	825–31	54	696 *d*, 720 *h*,	8	708 *d*
42	728 *b*		864	16	852 *c*
11 1	865 *b*	55	714 *c*, 777	17	714 *h*
3	632, 856 *a*	57	720 *h*	28	859 *a*

This Index extends from 1436 to 1885 (printed 436—885).

MATTHEW			MATTHEW			MATTHEW		
		PAR.			PAR.			PAR.
20	4	691 e	23	34	678, 854 c	26	25	696 e
	11	449 a, 718 a, 853		35	860		28	690 a
				37	674, 682 f, 859		30	794
	19	678		39	633		31	862
	20	644	24	6	719 a, 728 l		33	438 a
	21	712 i, 753		7	680 a, 687 a, 718 d		34	718 i
	22–3	678 c					36	634
	25	570–1		8	708 d		38	707 a
	26	717 d-e-f		9	713 f		39	716 b, 728 g
	27	717 f, 723 h		12	716 c, 851 c		40	634
	28	579		14	695 b		44	695 e
	30	737 a, 813		21	708 d		45	634
	32	725 b-c		23	477 a		48	716 g, 866 b
	34	477 b		26	477 a		50	862
21	1	775 e		27	866		51	738 b, 866 c
	2–7	861 b		30	712 i		54	722 d
	5	456 a, 634, 754 a, 757		31	682 f		55	857
				38	680 b, 710 h, 755 a		56	722 d
	8	720 f					59	695 c
	9	633, 816 b		42–4	634 a		61	675 c
	12	812 b		43	858		64	713 i
	15	816 b		45	862 e, 866		67	737 e
	16	860		46	859 e		71	860
	19	712 d		47	865		73	716 b, 727 j
	21	467		49	752	27	1	754
	23–7	562		50	856		6, 9	755
	24	857 b		51	860		11	725 c-e
	25	477 a	25	1	720 f, 755		15	711 e, 735 b
	27	841		4	720 f		19	745, 750
	32	477 a		7	720 f		27	814 c, 815 c
	42	722 c, 811 e		9	852		28	805–6
	43	687 a, 718 d		19	634 b		29	689 e, 734 a, 805–6, 814 b
22	7	861		21	862 e			
	8	853		23	862 e			
	11	604 a, 853		24	754		30	689 e
	12	853		24–6	856		33	807, 810
	15	695 c, 723 b		35	750 b		40	675 c
	16	727 d, m		36	810 b		44	817 c
	24	721 e		37	750 b		45	710 b
	27	866		38–44	810 b		48	689 e, 813 c
	29	722 d		40	749 a		49	756
	32	851 a		41	854 a		50	752 d
	36	860		42	750 b		51	707 e
	44	680, 856		44	750 b		52	693 a, 858
23	3	714 h	26	1	865 b		53	716 h
	6–7	866 b		2	678		54	727 j
	11	717 d-e		4	723 b, 811		59	716 a, 857 c, 866 (i)–(iv)
	12	865 a, 866 a		5	711 e			
	23	477 b, 697, 716 c, 851 c, 859 b		8	810 a		62	717 h
				9	742 a, 814 a		66	754
				10	728 j	28	1–2	680 a, 832 b
	26	857 c		12	734 e, 751 c		5	681 d
	27	861		18	834 e		6	858
	28	753		24	653, 713 a, 816 a		7	802 a
	31	859					8	675 b

This Index extends from 1436 *to* 1885 (*printed* 436—885).

JOHANNINE VOCABULARY

MATTHEW			MARK			MARK		
		PAR.			PAR.			PAR.
28	9	644	4	11–12	612–13, 721c	7	4	689c
	10	749		15	854a		5	677b
	13	858		17	811f		6	688a
	15	713m		19	676i, 833c		9	714h, 824–31
	17	644		21	715g		13	824a
	18	562, 590		22	686c, 716i,		22	811
	19	485c			738a, 859d		23	677b
	20	793		26–8	515		26	713b
				30	686a		29	477b
		MARK		33	721c		33	693d, 737b
1	1	708f		34	720a–d, 721c		35	852b
	2	681a		39	832c	8	6–7	692i
	4	690a, 734c		40	477b, 728l		17	728l, 737c
	5	678a, 861a		41	681c		18	721h
	7	686f, 833d	5	6	644		21	728l
	10	852b, 866(iv)		12	723d		23	693d, 737b
	15	467, 480a		14	675b		32	712f, 744(xi)a
	16	725b		19	653, 675b		34	792b, 842
	19	716b		22	765a, 852c		35	720f
	20	736b		29	736c		38	697, 711a, 712i
	22	562		33	727m	9	1	530a, 710c
	22–7	572–4		34	477b, 653,		12	634b
	24	835			728e, 854c		17	862d
	30	834a		36	477a, 507a,		18	735e
	39	884c			533		23	533
	43	713e, 811b–c		41	728l₂		24	862d
	44	653, 695b,	6	1	634a, 720h		34	570d, 683b
		833e, 885a		2	696d, 864		35	717d–g
	45	738		3	686, 714c, 777		36	721g, 793
2	1	884c		4	720f, h		37	721f, 826–31
	4	834a, 884a		6	673d		40	885f
	4–12	673, 736a, 834a		7	562, 580a		41	691b, 728b
	10	525a, 562,		10	707a		42	686b
		575, 594c		11	695b		43, 45	734b
	11	653		19	735b	10	1	634a
	12	575		20	832		6	708d
	14	604a		21	738		15	865a
	15	834b		26	832a		17	852c
	16	718a		30	675b		21	716d, 744(i)–(xi)
	21	815d, 853a		31	716b, 810c			
	28	525a		34	763b		34	686
3	3	793		37	710e, 734d		37	712i
	6	695c		41	692i		38–9	678c
	7	810, 834c		42	692c		42	570–1, 594a
	8	834c		45	735a		42–3	683a
	15	562, 580a		47	718i, 813a		43	810
	16	709a		48	634a, 718i,		43–4	717d–g
	18	714c, 726			735b–c,		44	723h
	20	634a			833b		45	579
	29	712d		50	713h, 727b,		46	737a
	31	725a, 737			811e		49	725b–c
	33–4	749a		52	737c		51	737d
	35	728g		55	673, 736a		52	477b
4	10	720a–b, 802a	7	2	677b	11	1	775e
	11	530a		3	713m, 728a		2	653, 728l

This Index extends from 1436 *to* 1885 (*printed* 436—835).

NEW TESTAMENT PASSAGES

MARK		MARK		MARK	
PAR.		PAR.		PAR.	
11 2-7	861 b	14 6	728 j	16 11	604 a, 856
7	720 f	8	734 e, 751 c	12	597 b, 686 c,
9	816 b	11	686		687 e, 716 i,
10	633 a, 816 b	13	653, 728 b,		738 a, 856 a
12	717 h		834 e	14	597 b, 686 c,
14	712 d	17	634 a		708 c, 716 i,
15	812 b	21	653, 713 a,		738 a, 856
17	675		816 a	16-17	477 a, 487
18	739-40	26	794		
22	467	29	438 a		**LUKE**
25	697, 711 a,	30	718 i		
	725 a, 737	34	707 a	1 2	708 f, 719 h
28	594	35	716 b	3	707 e
28-33	562	36	697, 711 a,	6	734 c
29	857 b		728 g	9	770
31	477 a	37	634 a	12	727 b
32	688 a	41	634 a, 695 e	13	708 b
12 2	723 h	44	716 g, 866 b	17	501 a
4	723 h, 832	47	738 b	30	775 c
10	722 c	49	722 d foll.	31	865
11	811 e	51-2	810 b	33	712 d
13	723 b	54	711 f, 715 g,	47	774 a, 851 b
14	727 d, m		735 d	51	766
17	687	58	675 c, 679 b	52	865 a
22	866	62	713 i	53	768
24	722 d	63	696 e	55	712 d
26	684, 837 a,	65	737 e	57	708 b
	851 a	67	735 d	59	709 c
30-33	716 d	70	716 b, 727 j	69-77	774 b
32	727 m	15 1	815 b	75	854 b
36	680, 856	6	711 e	79	710 c
37	739-40	12	707 g	2 3	720 f
40	834 d	16	814 c, 815 c	8	862
44	715 f	17	734 a, 805-6,	11	774 a
13 2	679 b		814 b	21	709 c
7	719 a, 728 l	19	644, 689 e	22	833 e
8	680 a, 687 a,	20	686	25	734 c
	708 d, 718 d	22	728 l₂, 807, 810	34	764
9	695 b, 725 c	29	675 c	36	734 c
11	720 k	31	686	39	720 f
12	679	32	817 c	40	775 c
13	713 f	33	710 b, 864 a	41-2	711 e
19	708 d	34	728 l₂,	43	774 c
20	592, 709 b	36	689 e, 813 c	44	767
21	707 a	38	707 e	46	857
26	712 i	39	727 j	52	775 c
27	682 f	46	691, 716 a,	3 2	764 b, 857
32	697, 711 a		857 c, 866	3	690 a
34	723 h, 728 h		(i)—(iv)	6	592
14 1	723 b, 811	16 1	832 b	8	851 a, 852
2	688 a, 711 e	2	815 a	9	858
3	736 d, 834 b	6	858	12	690 f
4	810 a	7	802 a	13	772 b
5	710 e, 738, 811	9	815 a	14	690 f, 852
	a-c, 814 a	10	802 a	15	885 b

This Index extends from 1436 *to* 1885 (*printed* 436—885).

JOHANNINE VOCABULARY

	LUKE			LUKE			LUKE
	PAR.			PAR.			PAR.
3 16	686 f, 833 d, 899		6 28	885 f		9 1	580 a
18	674		32-4	775 c		4	707 a
19	855		35	856		5	695 b
21	866 (iv)		37	714 d, 859 a		8	749 c
22	767		38	769		12	858 a
4 1	772 a		39	861		14	693 c
2-13	854 a		40	723 h, 775 a,		16	692 i
6-7	565			784-92		17	692 c
7-8	643		41-2	851 d		23	792 b, 842
11	863		43	707 g		26	712 i
16	778		44-5	864		27	530 a, 696 a,
17-19	690 b		7 1-10	862 b			710 c, 727 i
19	768		2	862 b		29	767, 769
20	719 h		3	713 m		32	802 a, 865
21	722 c		5	687 a, 718 e		35	833 a
22	775 c, 777-8,		7	862 a, b		38	771, 862 d
	857 a, 859		7-8	718 c, 855		42	862 d
23	778		9	477 b, 673 d,		47	793 a
24	720 f, h			864 b		48	717 e, 721 f,
25	727 m		12	771, 775 e			826-31
29	606 a		13	779 a		50	885 f
32	562		19	632, 779 a,		55	864 b
32-6	572-4			856 a		56	692 e
34	835		23	859 e		57	839 foll.
38	834 a		24	604 a, 689 e,		58	452-8, 609 b,
5 1	725 b, 769			856			839 foll.,
2	736 e		25	769			858 a
2-6	763		27	681 a		60	720 f
3	716 b		28	683 b		10 1	779 a
4	763 a, 775 e		32	857, 861		2	853
6, 8	834 c, 835 b		34	775 a, 866 b		3	859
14	695 b, 833 e,		35	854, 864		6	853 a
	885 a		37	834 b		7	707 a, 852,
19	884 a		38	768 a			860
24	562, 575, 594 c		44	728 b, 768 a,		8	692 j
25	834 a			864 b		12, 14	859 b
26	575		47	560 a		15	851, 866 a
27	604 a		8 9	720 a, b, 802 a		16	671 b, 825-31,
29	834 b		10	612-3, 721 c			832 a
30	449 a, 718 a,		12	854 a		17	478 a
	853		13	811 f		17-20	589
36-7	853 a		14	676, 715 f		19	567, 580 a
37	751 b		17	716 i, 738 a,		21	678 a, 851 b,
8	793			859 d			860, 864-5
11	695 c		19	884 a		21-2	852
13	833 a		21	728 g, 749 a		22	810 c
14	709 a		24	832 c		23	560, 859 e,
15	726		25	477 b			864 b
16	714 c		28	644		26	860
17	725 b		29	833 b		32	770
20-2	859 e		41	765 a, 852 c		38	771 a
21	750 b, 854 b		42	771		39	717 b, 771 b,
22	554		48	477 b			779 a
25	768		50	477 a, 507 a,		40	717 a, e, 771 a
27	856			533		41	771 a, 779 a

This Index extends from 1436 to 1885 (printed 436—885).

NEW TESTAMENT PASSAGES 73

		LUKE			LUKE			LUKE
		PAR.			PAR.			PAR.
10	42	709 b, 771 b, 833 a	12	58	565-6, 569 d, 714 e, 775 e, 852 c	17	8	712 g
							9	775 c
11	2	851 a_1					10	723 h, 861
	6	692 j		59	566		24	866
	9	852 b	13	1	862		27	710 h
	10	852 b		4	773		32	721 h
	21	720 f		14	728 j		34	718 i
	22	771 c		15	779 a, 861 b	18	6	779 a
	23	863		19	720 f		11	725 d, 866
	26	856 a, 858		20	707 g		13	720 f, 725 d, 760
	28	859 e		24	764			
	31	864		27	764 a		14	865 a, 866 a
	31-2	859 b		28	851 a		18	852 c
	35	864 a, 866		29	856		35	737 a
	36	775		32	774 c		37	860
	39	779 a		34	674, 682 f, 720 f, 859		40	725 b, c
	41	857 c					42	477 b
	42	477 b, 697, 716 c, 851 c, 859 b		35	633	19	7	718 a
			14	1	765 a		8	779 a
				7	833 a		9	774 b
				11	865 a, 866 a		10	692 d
	49	854 c		21	861		11	531, 693 e
	51	860		25	864 b		13	720 f
12	2	738 a, 852, 859 d		26	450, 713 f, 720 f, 792 a		17	862 e
							20	760
	3	784, 863 a, 866		27	720 f, 792 b		21-2	856
				29	686		23	772 b
	4	565, 723 i, 775 a, b, 784-92		33	720 f		29	775 e
			15	2	718 a		30-5	861 b
				12	715 f		36	720 f
	5	565		20	720 f		38	633 a, 816 b
	8	861 a		30	715 f		42	719 b, 859 c
	11	567 a, 569 a	16	4	720 f		48	739
	20	718 i		5	720 f	20	2-8	562
	21	884 c		6	767		3	857 b
	23	865		7	767		5	477 a
	24	856		8	715 g, 720 f, 782-3, 866		11	672, 832
	25	856, 862					12	672
	27	859, 864		11	727 f, 764		17	722 c
	33	858		12	851		20	567 a, 569 a, 723 b
	35	712 g, 858		13	854 d			
	37	712 g		16-17	860		21	727 d, m
	39	858		20-5	770		29	721 g
	42	779 a, 862 e, 866		22-3	769		32	866
				24	728 b, 765		37	771, 775 e, 851 a
	43	859 e		25	674, 715 f, 719 b			
	44	696 a, 727 j, 865					43	680, 856
			17	2	686 b		46	866 b
	45	752		3	851 d		47	834 d
	46	856, 860		3-4	852 a	21	3	696 a, 727 j
	48	692 j		4	781		4	715 f
	51	854 e		5	781, 779 a		9	719 a
	53	860		6	467, 477 b, 779 a		10	687 a, 718 d
	55	862					11	680 a
	57	691 e, 714 e, f		7	862		12	725 c

This Index extends from 1436 to 1885 (printed 436—885).

LUKE		LUKE		JOHN	
	PAR.		PAR.		PAR.
21 13	695 b, 763 b	23 48	760	1 11	624 a, 637 a,
15	720 k	49	767		720 d, 735 f
16	679	51	544, 713 m	12	481, 483-7,
17	713 f	53	716 a, 719 a,		576, 676 a,
20	770		728 l, 857 c,		721 f
27	712 i		866 (i)–(iv)	13	484, 708 k,
36	725 d	56	832 b		728 g
22 1	711 e	24 1	765, 832 b	14	604, 712 j,
2	723 b	3	779 a, 801 b		744 (x) a,
3	692 b, 765	4	832		771, 772 a,
5	774	5	858 a		885 e, 885
6	678 a	9	802 a		(ii) c
10	728 b, 834 e	12	600 b, 673 e,	14-17	727 n, 775 c
15	833 c		716 a, 726 b,	15	635, 885 g
17	721 f		772, 798-	16	727 n
19-20	885 f		804, 866	18	604 b, 605, 769,
22	653, 713 a,		(iii) a		771, 884 c
	816 a	13	798 foll.–804,	19	688, 770
23	772 b		864	20	679-80
25	570-1, 594 d	17	725 d	21	885 d
26	717 e, f, 810	20	765 a	22	723 e, 885 d
30	859 a	23	802	23	696 c, 728 f,
31	779 a	24	802 a		885 (ii) a
32	695 h	25	477 a	25	680, 885 d
33	438 a, 843	26	722 e foll.	26	725 a, g, 737,
37	770	27	722 e foll., l		796
42	728 g	29	858 a	26-7	635
45	713 d, 771, 858	32	722 e foll., l,	27	635, 686 f,
47	716 g, 866 b		775 e		833 d, 852
50	738 b	34	560	28	708 g
51	738 b, 866 c	35	769	29	607, 635, 717 h,
53	567	36	725 b, 793-7,		885 (ii) a
55	711 f		804 a, 884 c,	30	635, 885 g
56	711 f, 715 g		854 e	31	684 c, 716 j
59	727 m	36-43	794-7	32	604, 707 a
60	693 e	38	727 b	33	707 a, 723 e
61	779 a, 864 b	39	713 j, 861	34	606, 676 c
63	737 e	40	804 a	35	717 h
66	692	41	796 a	36	885 (ii) a
70	713 i	43	768 b	37	720 m
23 2	687 a, 718 e	44	724 f, 722 e	38	604, 694 c,
7	567 a	45	722 e, l		720 m,
11	676 d, 806 a	52	644		728 d, l₂,
13	765 a				864 b
15	772 b	JOHN		39	598, 609 a, 610,
20	707 g				885 d
22	695 e	1 1	708 f	41	717 c, 720 e, i,
23	769	1-5	443		m, 728 l₂
28	864 b	5	735 e-h, 885	42	439, 675, 709 a,
29	708 b		(ii) c		714 a, 728 l₂
33	807, 810	6	734 c, 885 e	43	717 h, 720 m
35	676 c, 765 a	7	464, 481-2	45	720 m, 778
41	772 b	8	708 k, 748 a	46	598 a, 609
44	710 b	9	635, 727 g, 775	47	702 a, 713,
46	692 j	9-11	483		727 l, 811

This Index extends from 1436 *to* 1885 (*printed* 436—885).

NEW TESTAMENT PASSAGES

	JOHN			JOHN			JOHN
	PAR.			PAR.			PAR.
1. 47–50	610		3 16	693 b, 716 e, 744		4 24	647
48	885 i			(vi) foll.,		25	635, 717 c
49	684 c			771		27	673 a
50	464, 481, 488,		16–18	498		28	885 (ii) c
	598, 885 i		16–21	497 a		31	860
51	524, 598, 672,		17	581–5, 677 d,		34	456, 774 c
	852 b, 866			692 f		35	604, 608, 674 b,
	(iv), 884 d		18	486, 502, 582–			885 (ii) c
2 1	686 d, 695 d,			5, 677 d,		36	691 b, 727 a
	853			771		36–7	693
2	675, 686 d,		19	582–5, 710 a,		36–8	856
	853			716 e, 728 h,		37	727 i
4	719 a, 728 l			744 (vi) a,		39–42	503–7
5	717 d			859 b		42	727 k, 774 a
6	833 e, 885 (ii)		20	728 h, 772 b,			777–8
	b, c			885 (ii) c		43	720 h, 755, 777
7	707 d, 728 b,		21	728 h, 772 b		44	–8
	885 (ii) c		22	481, 493, 885		45	606 a, 689 c,
8	719 d, 885 (ii) a			(ii) a			721 f
9	717 d, 885 (ii) a		23	707 f, 721 n		46	885 (ii) a
10	752, 885 (ii) a		24	438 b, 688		47	683 e
11	464, 489–90,		25	713 l, 833 e,		48	464, 508–9,
	712 j			885 (ii) b			524 a, 533
14	885 (ii) b		28	681 a		49	676 b, 885 (ii) a
15	686, 751 b, 812 b,		29	860		50	508–9
	885 (ii) a–c		30	684, 885 (ii) a		51	862 a
16	885 (ii) a		31	635, 707 e		52	863, 885 (ii) a, b
17	721 i, 860, 885		32	606		53	464, 509, 684 a
	(ii) b		33	727 d foll., 754		5 2	708 h, 713 g,
18	885 d		35	716 e			885 (ii) a–c
19	679 b, 708 i,		36	501, 885 (ii) a		2–7	720 n
	722 k		4 1	780		3	685 c, 834 a, c
20	675 c, 885 d		1–3	493		4	728 e
21	507		2	481, 853 a		5	683 d
22	491, 721 i, 722		5	687 c, 726		6	610, 834 a
	a, l, 860		6	885 (ii) b		6–15	728 e
23	483–4, 493 a,		6–14	736 c		8–11	673, 736 a
	598		8	865		10	683 d–e, 685
23–4	464, 481		9	713 l, 863, 885		13	683 e, 885 (ii) a
24–5	626			(ii) c		14	852 a
3 1	734 c, 765 a,		10	682 g, 885 (ii) a		16	854 c
	852 c		10–15	728 b		18	673 b, 708 i
2	544, 718 j		11	765, 885 d		19	607
3	676 a, 685 a,		12	683 c, 885 (ii) b		20	596, 673 b, c,
	707 e		14	712 d, 885 (ii) a			716 e, 728 p
4	885 (ii) a		16	652 a		21	716
5	685 a, 728 b		18	719 d		21–3	581–5
7	673 a, 707 e		19	598		24	614 b, 710 d,
8	614 b, 655, 728		20	647			860
	c, d, 862		20–4	640, 647–51		24–47	510–11
10	684 c		21	464, 503–7		25	719 c
12	464, 494, 520 a,		22	647–8, 713 m,		25–8	614 c, 710 d
	885 (ii) a			774 b		26–7	576–8, 581
14	494, 524, 728 f,		23	719 c, 885 (ii) b		27	581–5
	866 a		23–4	640–51, 727 p		28	673 a

This Index extends from **1436** *to* **1885** *(printed* 436—885*).*

JOHANNINE VOCABULARY

JOHN		JOHN		JOHN	
	PAR.		PAR.		PAR.
5 29	585 a, 772 b, 859 b, 885 (ii) c	6 35	517, 684	7 21	673 a
		36	512 b, 532, 605	22	709 c
		37	752 f	23	708 i, 709 c, 728 e, 885 (ii) c
30	581–5, 691 e, 728 g	38	728 g		
		39	721 e		
34	692 g	40	517, 598, 721 e	24	691 e, 714 f, 859 a, 885 (ii) b
35	685 d, 748 a, 851 b, 858, 885 (ii) c	41	718 b		
		42	624, 719 d, 777, 857 a	26	727 k, 765 a, 885 b
36	774 c	43	718 b		
37	605, 614 b, 767	44	517, 710 g, 721 e	27	624–5, 635
38	520 a, 707 a			27–8	728 c
39	492, 722 g, 885 (ii) a	45	885 e, 885 (ii) a	28	624, 727 h, 752 f
		46	605, 885 e		
43	720 i	47	518 a	30	728 l
44	885 e	49	717, 728 f	31	464, 521
45	855	50	710 f	33	655, 716 b
46	492	51	712 d	35	702, 713 b, 728 d
47	492, 767	51–63	712 b		
6 1	726 e, 811 d	52	885 (ii) b	37	683 a, 725 f, g
2	598, 605 a, 606 a	54	518 a, 721 e	37–8	521, 722 k
		54–8	710 h	38	728 b, 885 (ii) c
3	885 (ii) a	55	727 e, 885 (ii) b	39	521 a, 637 b
5	604, 608	56	707 a	40	614 c, 727 k
6	695 a	57	884 b	42	635, 679 a, 692 h, 696 b, 722 k, 853
7	710 e, 734 d, 852	58	712 d		
		59	694 b, 777		
9	708, 885 (ii) b	60	754		
10	765	61	694 a, 718 b	43	815 d, 884 a
11	735 b	62	885 d	44	735 b
12	768	63	519, 716	48	520, 765 a
13	708, 885 (ii) a	64	520 a	49	885 (ii) a
14	635, 727 k	64–70	464	51	765 a
15	810	67	652 a, 695 i, 835 b	52	885 (ii) a
16	718 i, 813 a			8 3–4	735 h
17	710 b, 718 i, j	68	519	4	694 c
18	683 a, 832 c, 862	69	519, 629, 835	5	726 a
		70	695 i, 709 b, 854 a	9	884
19	598, 833 b, 864			11	852 a
20	681 d, 713 h, k, 811 e	71	695 i, 724 c	12	748 a
		7 2	885 (ii) c	14	624, 637 a, 655, 728 c–d
21	652 a, 721 f, 735 b, c	3	652 a, 860		
		5	520	15	581–5, 714 f, 859 a
22	885 (ii) c	6	688, 719 a, 728 l, 862		
23	726 e, 736 e, 780			16	661, 714 f, 727 h
		6–8	695 f		
24	736 e	7	728 h	17	696 e, 707 c, 715 b
26	692 c	8	719 a		
26–36	512–16	10	738	18	522
27	707 a, 754	12	682	19	624, 626
29	512–13, 547	13	681 c	20	728 l
30	513	14	885 (ii) b	24	522, 713 k, 885 d
31	717, 728 f	15	673 a, 767		
32	727 h	18	720 i, 727 d foll., 764 a	25	708 e
33	512 a			26	727 d foll.

This Index extends from **1436** *to* **1885** (*printed* **436—885**).

NEW TESTAMENT PASSAGES

	JOHN			JOHN			JOHN	
		PAR.			PAR.			PAR
8	28	713 k, 866 a	9	21	719 d, 856	11	3	716 e, 728 o–p
	29	885 (ii) a		22	726, 774, 861 a		4	529, 710 d,
	30	464		23	672 c, 856			712 j
	30–1	523		24–5	693		5	728 p, 744 (vi)
	31	707 a, 727 l		28	885 (ii) b			foll.
	32	727 q–r		29	625, 728 c		8	527 a, 652 a,
	32–6	712 e		30	728 c, 811 e			719 g, 726 a
	33	692 h, 854 d		31	693, 885 (ii) b		9	607, 863
	33–6	751 b		32	672 a, 728 k		10	718 h, 863
	33–58	851 a		35–8	524–5		11	652 c, 693 a,
	34–5	723 i		38	464, 647			858
	35	684 a, 712 d		39	581–5, 594,		12	693 a, 858
	36	885 d			637 a		13	710 d, 865,
	37	692 h, 817 a		39–41	607			885 (ii) b
	38	885 d		41	707 a, 719 b		14	528
	39	676 a, 728 h	10	1–5	721 a		15	528, 545
	40	719 b		1–10	858		16	710, 885 (ii) c
	41	728 h		3	601, 614 a, c,		18	864
	42	637 a, 856			852 b		19	885 (ii) b
	43	614		4	601		20	636, 771 b
	44	708 e, 711 d,		5	682 c		21–2	529, 719 e
		725 a,		6	594, 721 a		23	534
		727 p, 737,		9	692 g		23–6	529–34
		833 c,		10	637 a, 753		25	534
		854 a,		11	715 d		26	507 b, 529 a,
		885 (ii) a, c		12	682 c, 736 b,			710 f, 712 d
	45–6	522			863		27	464, 636
	47	614 b, d		13	736 b		28	535, 862
	49	832		14	626, 885 j		30	696 b
	50	582		15	626, 715 d		31	684 a, 885 (ii) b
	51–2	710 d, 712 d,		16	614 a, c, 723 j,		33	466, 610, 713 e,
		714 h			862			727 b,
	53	683 c, 885 c		17–18	587–9, 715 d			811 b, c
	55	624, 686 a,		18	576–8		34	609
		714 h, 861,		19	815 d		35	885 (ii) a
		885 (ii) c		20	885 (ii)		36	716 e, 728 p
	56	478, 610, 851 b		21	679 c		38	636, 713 e, 769,
	59	726 a, 859 c		22	885 (ii) a			811 b, c
9	1	610, 687, 813,		23	864, 885 (ii) c		39	885 (ii) b, c
		885 (ii) a		24	770		40	529–34, 598,
	2–3	852 a		28	712 d			712 j
	4	718 h, 735 a		29	683 c		41	608
	5	748 a		31–3	726 a		42	528, 885 (ii) b
	6	693 d, 737 b,		33	674		43	683 a, 752 a, f
		885 (ii) b, c		34	715 b, 722 k		44	652 a, 760,
	6–15	709		35	708 i, 722 k			885 (ii) b
	7	652 a, 720 n,		36	674, 835 a		45	604
		728 l_2		37–8	526		47	692
	7–11	773		38	626		48	536, 702, 718 f,
	7–25	607		40	537			721 k
	8	737 a, 885 (ii) b		42	527		49	768
	9	686 a, 861	11	1	696 b, 734 c,		50	688 a, 718 f,
	11	652 a, 885 (ii) a			770, 771 a, b			770
	16	693, 815 d		2	734 c, 768 a,		50–2	885 h
	18	526			780		51	768

This Index extends from **1436** *to* **1885** (*printed* 436—885).

JOHANNINE VOCABULARY

JOHN		JOHN		JOHN	
PAR.		PAR.		PAR.	
11 51–2	718 f	12 35	657, 716 b, 735 e,	13 18	884 d, 885 (ii) b
52	676 a, 682 f		748 a,	19	545–6
53	536		775 d	20	671 b, 721 f,
54	710, 728 f	36	539–40, 715 g,		723 e,
55	885 (ii) a		748 a,		826–31
57	695 c, 771		775 d, 782–	21	727 b, 811 c
12 1	717 h, 770		3, 859 c,	22	607, 832
2	717 a, e, 771 a		866	23	596 a, 744 (vi)
3	684 a, 717 b,	37	540		foll., 769
	736 d, 753,	38	766, 852	24	885 (ii) b
	768 a,	38–40	673 b	25	744 (x), 760
	771 b,	39	540	26	724 c, 765
	885 (ii) b	39–40	612–13	26–30	724 e
4	810 a	40	683 e, 737 c,	27	692 b, 885(ii)c,
5	710 e, 738,		813,	29	885 (ii) a
	814 a		885 (ii) c	30	544 a, 710 b,
6	858, 885 (ii) a	41	610, 712 j		718 j
7	734 e	42	464, 726, 765 a,	33	658, 676 a,
8	688 b		861 a, 884 a		716 b, 843,
9	652 b, 739–40,	42–3	540–1		885 (ii) c
	884 a	43	744 (vi) a	34	843
11	537–8, 652 b,	44	752 f	36	658, 719 c,
	884 a	44–5	598		728 d, 866
12	636, 739–40	44–6	543–4	37	692 a, 715 d,
13	633 a, 635–6,	44–8	825–31, 832 a		843, 885 h
	674, 684 c,	47	614 c, 637 a,	38	679, 692 a,
	752 a, 755,		692 g		715 d, 843,
	816 b,	47–8	582–5		885 h
	885 (ii) a, c	50	885 d	14 1	546, 727 b
14	861 b, 885 (ii) b	13 1	680 c, 720 d,	1–12	464
15	456 a, 636,		744 (vi)	2	682 h, 684 a
	674 b, 677,		foll., 860	2–3	661, 688 c
	678 d,	1–3	657–8	3	637
	754 a, 756,	2	724 c, 854 a	4	658, 696 c
	861 b	3	637 a	5	728 d
16	721 i, 860	4	712 g, 885(ii) b	6	696 c, 727 q
20	647, 713 b	5	674 a, 712 g,	7	605, 626
20–1	538, 702		768 a,	8	852
21	677 a		885 (ii) b	9	605, 626 b
23	639 b	6	636	10	546, 707 a
24	681, 692 h	7	626	11	546
25	450, 713 f,	8	860	12	546, 662
	716 e, 728 p,	10	728 a	15	714 h
	866 b	10–11	545 a, 857 c	16	708 a, 712 d,
26	717 d	14	861, 885 d		720 j
27	639 b, 692 g,	15	885 (ii) c	17	627, 727 p
	719 f, 727 b	16	672, 683 c,	17–19	598
29	672		723 i, 775 a,	18	637
30	692 a		784 foll.	19	716 b
31	719 f, 859 b	17	784 foll., 859 e	21	597 b, 716 h,
32	517, 710 g,	18	680 b, 709 b,		885 j
	866 a		710 h,	22	714 c, 716 h
33	710 d, 724 b		722 k,	23	637 b
34	538–9, 704,		755 a,	26	720 j, 723 e
	866 a				

This Index extends from 1436 *to* 1885 (*printed* 436—885).

NEW TESTAMENT PASSAGES

	JOHN			JOHN			JOHN	
		PAR.			PAR.			PAR.
14	28	637, 658, 662, 683 c	16	21	721 h, 811 f, 865	18	13	764 b, 768, 885 (ii) b
	29	546		22	598, 719 c, 885 d		14	688 a, 885 h
	31	627		25	675 b, 694 d, 712 f		15	767, 885 (ii) c
15	1	684, 727 h		25–9	721 b		16	767
	2	674		26	708 a		18	711 f, 735 d, 885 (ii) c
	2–6	885 (ii) b		27	548, 596 a, 637 a, 716 f, 728 p		20	672 b, 694 b, 712 f
	3	857 c						
	4–5	674, 707 a						
	6	674, 682 a, 858, 864		28	637 a, 662–3		22	737 e
				29	662–3		24	764 b
	9–10	707 a		30	464, 548, 637 a		25	679, 735 d
	12	843		31	464, 548		26	680, 709 d, 734 b, 738 b, 866 c
	13	715 d		32	639 a, b, 674 b, 863			
	14	596, 775 a, b, 784–92		33	549, 771 c, 811 e, f		27	679
	15	596, 717 g, 723 i, 775 a, b, 784–92	17	1	639 b		28	745 a, 814 c, 815 b, 885 (ii) b
				1–2	590–2, 608			
				2	576–8		29	885 (ii) b
	16	659–60, 676 c		3	627		31	685, 715 b
	19	716 f, 728 p		4	774 c, 884 e		32	710 d, 724 b
	20	683 c, 721 h, 723 i, 775 a, b, 784–92, 854 c		5	712 j, 719 f		35	713 l, 718 f
				7	719 f		36	685 a, 713 m, 719 b, h, 764
				8	464, 550, 637 a, 727 l			
	21	625, 626 c, 692 a		9	708 a		37	614 c, 727 r
				12	591, 722 k, 810 a		38	727 r
	22	719 b, 834 d					40	752 a
	24	605, 719 b		13	719 f	19	2	676 d, 734 a, 805–6, 814 b, 885 (ii) b
	25	715 c, 751 a		15	708 a			
	26	720 j, 723 e, 727 p		17	727 q			
				18	723 g		3	737 e
	27	708 e		19	692 a, 885 h		4	707 g
16	1	545, 694 a		20	708 a		5	674 b, 734 a, 755, 805 a, 885 (ii) b
	2	679, 726, 885 (ii) b		20–1	464, 550			
				22	712 j			
	3	626 c		23	627, 774 c, 884 c		6	721 g, 752 a
	4	708 e, 721 h					7	861
	5	658, 728 d		24	712 j, 853		8	614 b
	5–7	662		25	629 a, 691 e		9	728 c, 814 c
	6	713 d, 771	18	1	885 (ii) b, c		10	577, 593
	7	720 j, 723 e		3	815 c, 885 (ii) b, c		11	570 c, 577, 707 e, 884 f
	8	582–5						
	8–10	854 b		5	860		12	752 a, 764, 788 a
	9	464, 547		6	885 (ii) c			
	10	658		7	672 c, 860		12–16	593–4
	11	582–5		8	652 a, 885 d		13	614 b, 713 g, 745, 750, 885 (ii) b
	13	727 p, 861		10	680, 709 d, 710 g, 734 b, 738 b, 885 (ii) b			
	16	597					15	752 a
	16–19	598 c, 716 b					17	713 g, 792 b, 807, 810
	19	735 b						
	20	857		11	508, 678 c, 885 (ii) b		18	796
	20–22	713 d, 771		12	738, 815 c		19	860, 885 (ii) c
	21	676 b, 708 b,						

This Index extends from **1436** *to* **1885** (*printed* **436—885**).

JOHANNINE VOCABULARY

	JOHN			JOHN			JOHN
	PAR.			PAR.			PAR.
19 20	689 a, 713 c, g, 721 l, 885 (ii) c	20	14 15 16	725 f, 728 d, 885 (ii) b 694 c, 713 g,	21	9 10 11	607, 711 g, 763, 769 719 g, 723 b 683 a, 710 g,
23	707 e, 885 (ii) a, c		17	737 d 695 g, 719 a, 728 l, 749		12	712 a 602, 751, 780,
24	679, 722 k, 769–70		18	599 a, 601,			810 c
25 26	885 (ii) b 596 a, 610, 744 (vi) foll.		19	694 d, 885 (ii) a 636, 681 c,		12–13 14	636 597 b, 686 c, 695 e, 716 j,
26–30	752 f			725 f, 796–			738 a
27 28	721 f 722 k, 750 b, 774 c			7, 804 a, 813 a, 854 e, 858, 884 c		15 15–17	714 a, 728 p, 885 (ii) a 437–41, 714 a,
28–30	865 b		20	780			728 p
29	813 c, 864, 885 (ii) c		21 22	723 e–g, 854 e 721 f, 885 (ii) a		16 17	862, 885 (ii) b 624 b, 695 e,
30	451–8, 462 a–c, 839 foll., 858 a		23	682 d, 691 a, 721 j			728 p, 885 (ii) b
31	683 a, 885 (ii) c		24 25	695 i, 710 465, 552–8,		18	693 g, 712 g, 735 b, 843,
31–3	751			885 (ii) b, c			885 (ii) a
32	678 b, 817 c, 885 (ii) c		26	636, 725 f, 796 –7, 854 e,		19	710 d, 712 h, 724 b, 843
33	775 d, 885 (ii) c			858, 884 c		20	596 a, 607, 638,
34	756		27	681 b, 862 e			695 h, 744
35	465, 551, 606, 727 h		29	465, 554–60, 599, 601,			(vi) foll., 760
36	722 k, 861			749 b, 859 e		20 foll.	638–9
37	687 e, 722 k, 856 a, 885 (ii) a		30 31	768 b 465, 553, 561		22 23	735 a 708 j, 735 a
38	541, 681 c	21	1	597 b, 686 c, 716 j, 726 e,		25	885 (ii) b
39	544, 718 j, 754, 885 (ii) a, b		2	738 a, 811 d 710, 727 a	1	4	ACTS 794 a
40	600, 716 a, 734 e, 751 c, 832 b, 866 (i)–(iv)		3	544 a, 652 a, 718 j, 719 g, 723 b		14 15 16–20 25	749 d 708 j 722 h 720 i
20 1	607, 710 b, 718 j, 815 a		3–8 4	736 e 725 b, f, 754, 884 c	2	1 14	727 a 725 e
2	596 a, 728 d, p		4–9	763		17	592
3–11	798–804		5	676 b, 796 a, 885 (ii) b		38	485 c
4	727 a, 885 (ii) c		6	691 d, 693 f,	5	15	736 a
5	600–1, 607, 716 a, 726 b			710 g, 712 a, 763 a, 834 c	6 7	20 3 43	725 e 772 a 645 a
7	760, 866 (ii)–(iv)		7	596 a, 602,		55	772 a
8	465, 552–60, 722 a foll.			712 g, 744 (vi) foll.,	8	55–6 16	725 h 485 c
8–10	673 e			780, 810 b		19	594 a
9	491, 722 a–l		7–8	560		27	645 a
11	466, 560, 600, 726 b, 775 d		8	712 a, 734 d, 736 e, 862,	9	32–5 33	772 h 736 a
12	672, 858			885 (ii) c		42	476 a
13	728 d						

This Index extends from **1436** *to* **1885** (*printed* 436—885).

NEW TESTAMENT PASSAGES

ACTS

		PAR.
10	10	735 b
	25	645 a
	43	476 a
	48	485 c
11	17	476 a
	24	772 a
	28	724 b
12	4	723 c
	21	745 a
13	41	507 b
14	2	708 j
	13	735 b
	17	853 a
	23	476 a, 692 j
16	19	710 g
	31	476 a, 507 a
	34	692 j
17	3	692 j
	22	725 e
	27	617, 804 b
18	12, 16, 17	745 a
19	4	476 a
	5	485 c
	32	504 b
	33	735 b
20	28	720 i
21	30	710 g
22	19	476 a
	23	752 a
23	13, 21	504 b
	35	814 c
24	11	645 a
25	6, 10, 17	745 a
	27	724 b
26	19	501 a
27	12	504 b
	21	725 e
28	23	504 b

ROMANS

		PAR.
1	30	501 a
2	1-27	714 g
	8	501 a
	17	648
3	4	771 c
	20-8	478
4	2-6	478
	3	474, 722 h
	5, 24	474
6	3	475 a
	6	517
7	19	772 b

ROMANS

		PAR.
8	17	844
	35, 37	744 (iv)
9	11	478
	17	722 h
	21	583 a
	32	478
	33	474
10	9-11	541
	11	474, 722 h
	14	474
	21	501 a
11	2	722 h
	6	478
	32	722 i
12	21	771 c
13	1	569 b, c
14	3-22	714 g
	4	725 a
15	24	604 b
16	5	722 j

1 CORINTHIANS

1	13, 15	485 c
	22	479
2	11	727 o
4	5	714 g
	11	842
5	3	714 g
6	12	594 a
	19	740
7	31	570 c
8	10	834 b
9	1-5	594 a
	18	570 c
10	2	475 a
	27	692 j
11	18	507 b
12	13	475 a
13	2	478
	7	474 a, 507 b
14	25	645
15	3-4	722 e
	5	560, 802
	5-8	597 b, 716 j
	6	504 b
	24	569 a
16	13	725 a
	22	630-1, 728 q

2 CORINTHIANS

3	17	727 q
11	32	723 c

GALATIANS

		PAR.
1	6	673 d
2	4	884 a
	9	720 c
	16	474, 722 i
	20	517, 744 (iv), (x)
3	6	474
	8, 10, 22	722 i
	27	475 a
4	10	648 b
	19	598 b
	20	735 b
	30	722 h
5	1	725 a
	12	709 d, 734 b
	13	717 f

EPHESIANS

2	4-5	744 (iv) a
3	10	569 a
	19	629
5	2	744 (iv)
	8	715 g, 782
	25	744 (iv)
6	12	569 a

PHILIPPIANS

1	14	744 (iv) b
	19	763 b
	29	474
2	15	748 a, 749 c
3	12	735 f
4	13	744 (iv) a

COLOSSIANS

1	4	475
	13	568, 569 d, 570 e
	16	569 a
2	5	475
	9	772 a
	10, 15	569 a
	16	648 b
4	12	725 d

1 THESSALONIANS

1	9	727 f
2	7	662
4	8	828 a, 832 a
	14	474 a
5	5	715 g, 782-3

2 THESSALONIANS

2	11, 12	474 a
	16	744 (iv) a

This Index extends from **1436** *to* **1885** (*printed* **436—885**).

1 TIMOTHY		JAMES		1 JOHN	
	PAR.		PAR.		PAR.
1 12	744 (iv) a	4 4	716 f	5 10–13	487 a
16	474 c	5	722 h	13	553 a
18	692 j			16	609
4 13	638, 735 a	1 PETER		17	764 a
5 18	722 h	1 8	475	20	627, 856
6 3	677 a	12	600 b, 726 b, 800 b		
2 TIMOTHY		21	475	3 JOHN	
1 12	474 c	24	592	14	609
2 2	692 j	2 4	677 a		
12	844	6	722 h	JUDE	
3 2	501 a	4 19	692 j	6	800 b
		5 3	594 a		
TITUS		"2 PETER"		REVELATION	
1 16	501 a	1 13	832 c	1 1	724 b
3 1	569 a	20	722 i	4	639
3	501 a	3 1	832 c	5	696 e
8	474 c			13	794
15	728 q	1 JOHN		2 1	794
PHILEMON		1 1	604, 804 b	13	696 e
5	475	1–5	616–20	17	711 h
		9	764 a, 848, 861 a	26	564, 594 b
HEBREWS				3 7–14	727 f
1 6	645	2 1	720 j	9	744 (iv)
2 9	712 h	3, 5	628	14	696 e
12	794	7	687 d	19	728 q
15	811 c	8	727 g	20	725 h
4 3	476 b, 853 a	9–10	539	5 6	794
5 8	845	11	656	6 8	563, 594 b
6 4	485 a	12	553 a	10	727 f
7 2	728 l_2	18, 29	628	7 17	794
23	504 b	3 1	609	9 3, 10,	
8 2	727 h	8, 12	728 h	19	563
9 24	727 h	17	603 a	20	646
10 7, 9	637 a, 856	18	728 h, 744 (v)	11 3	696 e
32	485 a	19	628	6	563, 594 b
11 1	478 c	23	487 b, 553 a	12 10	563
6	476 b	24	628	13 2–12	564 a
18–19	722 e	4 2	628	7	594 b
21	645	3	722 k	8, 12	646
34	858 a	6	628, 727 p	14 9, 11	646
12 2	475 b	7	628	18	564, 594 b
		9	498, 723 g	16 9	564 b, 594 b
JAMES		10	723 g	17 6	696 c
1 25	600 b, 726 b, 800	12	604	12, 13	564
2 8	722 h	14	604, 723 g, 774 a	18 1	564
17	478	16	629	19 20	723 c
19	476	17	585 a, 859 b	20 4	646
23	476, 596 a, 722 h, 790 b	18	651, 681 c	6	564
		5 6	637 a, 727 p	22 14	564 c, 594 b
		10	491 b	15	728 q
				17, 20	631

This Index extends from 1426 *to* 1885 (*printed* 436—885).

JOHANNINE VOCABULARY

II. ENGLISH

[*For Synoptic and Johannine words not in this Index, see the English alphabetical lists in* 1672—96 *and* 1707—28]

Aaron, "the holy one of God" 835 *a*
Abide 707; "abiding in" 659-60; "abiding," higher than "believing" 547
Above, from, 707
Abraham, God's "friend" 596 *a*, 789 *a*, 790; his faith 472-8
Adders, deaf 614 *d*
Allusiveness, in Jn 438-9, 446; specimens of 450-8, 762-3, 797, 804, 831
Alone, "the linen cloths alone" 804
Ambiguities, verbal 444-5, 529, and see Index to "Johannine Grammar"
Annas 764
Aphesis, the sabbatical "release" 690
Apostles or Missionaries in the first century 594 *a*
"Appeared to" or "was seen by" (ὤφθη) 597 *b*
Apprehend (καταλαμβάνω) 735 *e*
Authority 562-94; "receiving authority," explained by Origen 484

Baptism, baptizing 485, 487, 493
Baptist, see "John"
Begin (vb.), only once in Jn 674 *a*
Beginning (n.) 708 *d*

Beholding (θεωρέω) 597 foll., 723; sometimes unintelligent 598
Belief or faith, not used by Jn as noun 467; Mk's doctrine of 467; meaning of, influenced by Christianity 473; "thy faith hath saved thee," unique agreement as to, in the Triple Tradition 477; insignificance of "faith" in the teaching of Epictetus 479; a lower and a higher 505; inferior to "knowledge" 559
"Believe" or "trust," a key-word in the Fourth Gospel 463—561
Benefactor, a name assumed by several Eastern kings 571
Blood and water, the fountain of 606
Bowing the head 451 foll.
Bread 699; "the true bread" 513
Break (bread) 675
Brother (metaph.), not used in Jn till after the Resurrection 701; "the brethren" 708; "my brethren" 748-9
Burial of the Lord, the, verbal differences as to 866 (i)—(iv)

Child 676; "authority to become children of God" 579; "receiving little

This Index extends from 1436 *to* 1885 (*printed* 436—885).

JOHANNINE VOCABULARY

children" 698; "children of light" 782
Coming, vbs denoting 630-9; the coming of the Lord 630 foll. ; "come and see," a Talmudic formula 609; "He that cometh," a technical Jewish term 633; "thy king cometh" 634; s. also 624 a
Compassion 677
Cross, the, taking up, bearing etc. 792 b, 842; in connexion with "following" Christ 843
Cry aloud 752 a foll.

Darkness 710; degrees of 544
Dative w. πιστεύω 470-90
Deaf, the, not mentioned in Jn 614
Debts, remission of, in the sabbatical year 462, 690; Mt. has "debts" for "sins" in the Lord's Prayer 462
Destruction, parall. to "Judas Iscariot" 810 a; "the son of destruction" to be "destroyed" 591
Devils, authority to cast out 580 a
Diminutives, Jn's use of 736 e, 738
"Disciple that Jesus loved, the" 744 (x); at Christ's tomb 600
Double Tradition, defined 447 foll.

Edition, a second, hypothesis of in Lk. 871 a
Elenchos, the convicting Logos or Spirit 609 a
Enemies, "a man's enemies shall be they of his own household" 792 a
Enlightened, "those who were once enlightened" = "baptized" 485 a
"Eternal," applied by Jn to nothing but "life" 705
Euergetes and Kakergetes 571
"Eyes, lifting up the," symbolical 608

Faith, see "Belief"
Family of Heaven, the 698
Father, divine 711
Fear (i.e. worship) the Lord 643 a, 651

Fellowship 619, 700
Fire of coals 711
Five Thousand, Feeding of the 512
Flesh, metaph. 699; "all flesh" 592
Following Christ 840-3
Forgive, forgiveness 682; authority to forgive 575
Free (adj.) 712; "I am free and a friend of God" 788 a
Freedom 727 q; Epictetus on "freedom" and "slavery" 717 g
Friend, "my friends" 775 a, 784; distinction between "friends" and "servants" 789-91; "a friend of Caesar" 788 a; "I am free and a friend of God" 788 a

Galilaeans, the, described differently by Lk. and Jn 606 a
Galilee, the sea of 811 d
Glory, glorifying 712; in Jn, of a spiritual nature 489-90
God, "knowing God," "not knowing God" 622
Going, vbs denoting 652-64; "go and bear fruit" 659-60
Golgotha 807
"Government, the," Jewish traditions on 570
Greater, of persons 683
Greek, classical, fails to represent Semitic traditions about trust in God 470; low-class 732, 736, 737
"Grow in the understanding of God" 627

"Hating one's own life" 450, 713 f, 761, 792 a
Head, "bow the head," meaning of 451 foll., 839
Hearing, the Johannine and the Synoptic view of 612
Heaven, the opening of 530 b, 866 (iv)
Hebrew, "believing" or "trusting," meaning of, in Hebrew 469-71

This Index extends from 1436 *to* 1885 (*printed* 436—885).

Hell, "destroying in hell," parallel to "casting into hell" 566
Hillel, abrogated the Remission of Debts 462, 690
"Holy One of God, the," 835
Hosanna 807
Household, "they of his own household," Heb. "men of his house," Syr. "sons of his house,"="friends" 787

I AM [HE] 522
"Israelite, an" 727 *l*

"Jews, the," the term how used in Jn 647, 713
John, St, the Baptist 482
John, St, the Evangelist, see "Johannine Grammar" Contents, *passim*, and, in Index, "Allusiveness," "Ambiguity," "Emphasis," "Metaphor," "Mysticism," "Narrowing down," "Quotation"
"Joseph, son of" 776-8
Jubilee, the,=the Sabbatical Year 690*b*
Judas Iscariot, parall. to "destruction" 810*a*
Judging, judgment 714; not in Triple Tradition 714*d*; "judgment," not used by Mk 585; "day of j." not mentioned in Jn 585*a*; "authority to do judgment" 581-5
"Judgment seat, *a*" or "*the*" 745

Kingdom, antithesis between k. and "authority" 568; "the k. of God, of heaven" 685*a*
Knowing, vbs denoting 621-9

"Law, your" 715
Life, "hating one's own life" 450, 713*f*, 792*a*; "authority to lay down one's life" 594
Light, children (or sons) of 782; the Light of the world 748

Logos, the, described by Philo as "standing" 725 *g*
Look, "stoop (?) and look in" 798
Loosing the shoe 833 *d*
"Lord, the," meaning "Jesus" 779 foll.
Love, different words for 436, 596, 716, 728 *m—p*; the n. not used by Mk 697
Luke, a compiler of traditions in various styles 758; hypothesis of a second edition in his gospel 871*a*; his view of "authority" 565-71; avoids ὑπάγω 653; Jn differs from 606*a*, 778; where Lk. omits, Jn intervenes 792

Manifest (vb) 716
Maran atha 630-1
Mark, his doctrine of belief or faith 467
Marvel (see "Wonder") rebuked by Jesus 673 *a*
Mary Magdalene at Christ's tomb 601
Meant (ἔλεγε) 491 *a*
"Meek," an epithet om. by Jn in quoting Zechariah 456
Metaphors, Johannine 699, 867
Midst, "standing in the midst," used of Jesus 793-7
Might, mighty 686; "mighty work" 686*e*
"Minister" and "slave," apparently used by Mk as parallel terms 717 *g*
"Multitude, the great" 739-40

Name, the, believing in 483
"Narrowing down" 481
Nathanael, his profession of belief 488; the calling of 671 *b*
"Nazareth where he was brought up" 778
Nicodemus, the dialogue with 493-6; "a ruler of the Jews" 765*a*
Night (metaph.) 718
"Nos qui cum eo fuimus" 802*a*
"Now," different meanings of 719

"Own, his" 720

This Index extends from 1436 *to* 1885 (*printed* 436—885).

Parable, see "Proverb"
Paraclete, the 720
Paul, St, his view of "belief" 475, 478
Perfect belief, knowledge etc. 629
Peter, St, at Christ's tomb 600
Phantasm, phantom, or spirit 813 a
Praetorium, not in Lk. but in Acts 814 c
Praying (προσεύχομαι) not mentioned by Jesus in Jn 649
Prepositions in the Four Gospels 881-5
"Privately," not used by Jn of Christ's teaching 672 b
"Proverb" and "parable" 721

"Qui cum eo fuimus" 802 a
Quotation, Johannine, of Zechariah, inaccurate 456, 757; from Scripture, how introduced 722 h

Rebelling 502
Receiving (persons) 689, 721; "receiving little ones" 829
Recognising 629 a
"Reigning with Christ" 844
Rejection, Mk, Lk., and Jn on 823 foll.
Remission of sins 690
Resurrection, Christ's, revealed differently to different persons 600
"Retaining sins" 721
Revelation, "God revealed Himself by degrees" 600 a
Righteous, only once in Jn 668; applied to God 691 e
"Rising again," an ambiguous term 529

Sabbatical Year, the 690 b foll.
Salim 721
Samaritan Woman, the, dialogue with 647-51
Scripture, "believing the s." 491-2; "another s." 722; "the s.," "this s." 722; "the scriptures" 722
"Sea of Galilee, the" 811

Seeing, vbs denoting 597—611, 723; Philo on Gen. i. 31, "God saw (εἶδεν) his works" 611 a
Sending, vbs denoting 723; "He that sent me" 723
Serpent in the Wilderness, the 495, 517
Servant 723; bondservant 785; distinction between "servants" and "friends" of God 704, 789-91
"Signs,", i.e. miracles 521
Simon, father of Judas Iscariot 724 c;
Simon, in Heb. confusable w. "those with us" 802 a
Sing, Christ singing 794
Single Tradition, defined 447
Sins, remission of 690; Mt. substitutes "debts" for "sins" in the Lord's Prayer 462
"Slave" and "Minister," used by Mk as parallel terms 717 g
Sleep, "He giveth unto his beloved in sleep" 515
"Son of man" 525 a, 539 a, 704; the Eldest Son "looking at the Father's acts" 607; Sons of Light 782
"Spirit, a," = phantasm, or phantom 813 a; a spirit or messenger, in Epictetus 727 o
Spirit, the, "the Spirit of truth" 720 l, 727 p; Spirit or wind, πνεῦμα 655
Standing, applied to Jesus 725, 793-7; to God, Wisdom etc. 725 g
Stretching out the hands 693
Stumbling 545-6
Synonyms, see note on next page

Talmud, the, on authority 569 c, 570 a
Testimony, see "Witness"
"The Lord (Jesus)," in narrative 779
Tradition, see Double, Single, and Triple Tradition
Transliteration 728 l_2
Triple Tradition, defined 447; does not agree in a single saying of Christ using the verb "believe" 477

This Index extends from 1436 *to* 1885 (*printed* 436—885).

Trouble **727**; "freedom from trouble" in Epictetus **706, 727** *c*
True, truly, truth **727**; "knowing truth" **703**
Trusting or believing **469-78**
Truth, see "True"
"Twelve, the," how mentioned by Jn **671** *b*

Understanding (God or man) **624-9**; implies sympathy **626**

"Verily" and "Verily verily" **696** *a*
Vine, metaphor of the **660**

Water **699**
Wind or Spirit, πνεῦμα **655**
With, "those with us," confusable in Heb. w. "Simon" **802** *a*
Witness **696**; believing witnesses **522**; witness = testimony **703**
Wonder, in a bad sense **671** *a*, **673** *a—e*; "I saw and wondered," a phrase used by Greek tourists **673** *e*
Worshipping **640-51**; different from "prostration" **643**; "we worship that which we know" **647**

This Index extends from **1436** *to* **1885** (*printed* **436—885**).

Addendum on "Synonyms"

By "synonyms" are meant (**1595**) "words so far alike that at first the reader may take the thought to be the same, though it is always really different." A more exact term—if it were English—would be "*homoionyms*." Strictly speaking, some might say that *there are no "synonyms" in John*, i.e. no words that convey precisely the same shade of meaning.

JOHANNINE VOCABULARY

III. GREEK

[*The main object of this Index is to guide the reader to some paragraph in "Johannine Vocabulary" where a characteristic Johannine word is mentioned or discussed. It does not contain e.g.* ἄρτος, σάρξ, *or* ὕδωρ, *because these words are not characteristically Johannine. But "bread," "flesh," and "water," in the English Index, will guide the reader to passages illustrating the Johannine characteristic use of these common words.*

For conjunctions, prepositions, pronouns etc., the reader is referred to Index III. of "Johannine Grammar."]

Ἀβραάμ 851
ἀγαθός 682
ἀγαλλιάω 851
ἀγανακτέω 684
ἀγαπάω and φιλέω 436, 596, 716, 728 *m—q*, 744 (i)—(xi)
ἀγάπη 716, 851
ἀγαπητός 674
ἀγγελία 620
ἀγγέλλω 885 (ii)
ἄγγελος 672
ἀγιάζω 835 *a*, 851
ἅγιος, ὁ ἅ. τοῦ θεοῦ 835
ἁγνίζω 885 (ii)
ἀγωνίζομαι 764
ἀδελφός, οἱ ἀδελφοί 708, ἀδελφός σου 851
ᾅδης 851
ἀδικία 764
ἀθετέω 823-32
αἰγιαλός 750
Αἰνών 707
αἴρω, ἁ. ὀφθαλμούς 608, ἁ. σταυρόν 792 *b*
αἰών 672 *a*, εἰς τὸν ἁ., εἰς τοὺς ἁ. 712 *d*, 728 *k*
αἰώνιος 710, 715
ἀκάθαρτος 695
ἀκάνθινος 734, 805 *a*

ἀκούω, w. accus. and w. gen. 614 *a—c*
ἀκυρόω 824 *a*
ἀλήθεια 727
ἀληθής 727, 810, d. and ἀληθινός 727 *h—i*
ἀληθινός 727, 764, d. and ἀληθής 727 *h—i*
ἀληθῶς 727
ἁλιεύω (Jn xxi. 3) om. in 885 (ii)
ἀλλά 708, ἀλλ' εἶς and ἄλλος 756
ἄλλομαι 885 (ii)
ἄλλος, and ἀλλ' εἶς 756
ἀλλότριος 851
ἀλόη 885 (ii)
ἁμαρτάνω 852
ἁμαρτία, ἄφεσις ἁμαρτιῶν 690
ἁμαρτωλός 693
ἀμήν 696
ἀμνός 885 (ii)
ἀμπελών 696
ἀναγγέλλω 616, 620
ἀναγινώσκω 689
ἀνάκειμαι 689 *d*
ἀνακλίνω 689
ἀναπίπτω 689 *d*
ἀνάστασις 529 *c*

ἀνατρέπω 885 (ii)
ἀναχωρέω 810
ἄνεμος 696
ἀνέρχομαι 885 (ii)
ἀνθρακιά 711
ἀνθρωποκτόνος 885 (ii)
ἀνίημι 752 *b*
ἀνίστημι tr. 721, intr. 672
Ἄννας 764
ἀνοίγω 852, 866 (iv)
ἀντιλέγω 764
ἀντλέω 710
ἄνω, -θεν 707
ἄξιος 852
ἀπαγγέλλω 616, 675
ἀπαρνέομαι 679
ἀπειθέω 501, 885 (ii)
ἀπέχω 679
ἀπιστέω, -ία, -ος 681
ἀποβαίνω 763-4
ἀποδίδωμι 687
ἀποθνήσκω 710
ἀποκαλύπτω 738 *a*, 852
ἀποκόπτω 709 *d*, 734
ἀπόκρισις 765
ἀπολύω 679
ἀπορέω 832
ἀποστέλλω 723 *d*
ἀπόστολος 672

This Index extends from 1436 to 1885 (*printed* 436—885).

GREEK

ἀποσυνάγωγος 726
ἅπτομαι 695
ἀπώλεια 810
ἄρα 695
ἄραφος 885 (ii)
ἀργύριον 686
ἀρεστός 885 (ii)
ἀριθμός 765
ἀριστάω 765
ἀρκέω 852
ἀρνίον 885 (ii)
ἁρπάζω 750
ἄρτι 719, 750
ἀρχή 708, 810
ἀρχιτρίκλινος 885 (ii)
ἄρχομαι 674
ἄρχων 765, 852
ἄρωμα 832
ἀσθένεια 679 d, 724, 853
ἀσθενέω 724
ἀσθενής 724, 750
ἀτιμάζω 832
ἀταραξία 727 c
αὐξάνω 684
αὐτόματος 515 a
ἄφεσις 682, d. ἀμαρτιῶν 690
ἀφίημι 682; ἀ. φωνήν, 752 e
ἀφοράω εἰς 475

Βαθύς 765
βαΐον 885 (ii)
βάλλω, βεβλημένη 834 a
βαπτίζω 485 c
βάπτισμα 673
βαπτιστής 673
βάπτω 765
βασιλεία 685
βασιλικός 885 (ii)
βαστάζω σταυρόν 792 b
Βηθανία...πέραν τοῦ Ἰορδάνου 708
Βηθζαθά, v.r. Βηθσαιδά etc. 708
Βηθλεέμ 853
βῆμα 745, 750
βιβρώσκω 885 (ii)
βίος 694
βλασφημέω, -ία 674
βλέπω 600, 607, 723
βοάω 752 e
βουλεύομαι 766
βοῦς 766
βραχίων 766
βραχύ 766
βρέφος 676
βροντή 734

βρῶσις 746, 750

Γαββαθά 712
γαζοφυλάκιον 832
γαμέω, -ος etc. 686, 853
γάρ 712
γε 853
γέεννα 683
γείτων 766
γεμίζω 832
γενεά 682
γενετή 885 (ii)
γεννάω 708
γέρων 885 (ii)
γεωργός 684
γηράσκω 885 (ii)
γίνομαι 734, γ. and ἦν 734 c
γινώσκω 621-9, 715, 738 a
γλωσσόκομον 885 (ii)
γνωρίζω 766
γνωστός 767
γογγύζω 689 b, 718, 853
γογγυσμός 718
Γολγοθά 810
γράμμα 767
γραμματεύς 692
γραφή, sing. and pl. 692, 722
γράφω, τὸ γεγραμμένον τοῦτο 722 c
γρηγορέω 696
γυμνός 810
γυνή (wife) 696

Δαιμονίζομαι 679
δαιμόνιον 679
δακρύω 885 (ii)
Δαυείδ 679
δεξιός 691
δέομαι 853
δεῦτε 810
δέχομαι 689, 721 f, 825-31
δέω 866 (iii)
διά 692 a, διά τινα 652 b, 884 ab
διάβολος 665 a, 854
διαγογγύζω 689 b
διάγω 794 a
διαδίδωμι 767
διαζώννυμι 712
διακονέω 717
διάκονος 717, 810
διακόσιοι 734
διαλογίζομαι, -ισμός 689
διαμερίζω 679
διασπορά 713 b, om. in 885 (ii) a

διατρίβω 885 (ii)
διδακτός 885 (ii)
διδάσκαλε (voc.) 694
Δίδυμος 710
διεγείρω 832
δίκαιος 691, 727 f
δικαιοσύνη 854
δικαιόω 854
διψάω 750
διώκω 854
δόλος 811
δόξα 712
δοξάζω 712
δουλεύω 854
δοῦλος 717 f, 723, 790 foll.
δύναμις 669, 686
δυνατός 686
δώδεκα, οἱ δ. 695
δωρεά 885 (ii)
δωρεάν 746, 751
δῶρον 682

Ἑαυτοῦ, -ῶν 720 f
Ἑβραϊστί 713
ἐγγίζω 687
ἐγγύς 718
ἐγώ and εἰμί 713
ἔθνος 687, 718
ἔθος 767
εἶδον 610-11, ἰδεῖν 609, ἰδών 599
εἶδος 767
εἰμί 707, 713, ἦν and ἐγένετο 734 c
εἰρήνη 854
εἰς for ἐν 884, w. βαπτίζεσθαι 475 a, w. πιστεύω 470 foll.
εἰς? ἀλλ' εἰς read as ἄλλος 756
εἰσάγω 767
εἰσέρχομαι, parall. to προσέρχ. 801 a, b
ἑκατοντάρχης 676
ἐκβάλλω (δαιμόνια) 679
ἐκδύω and ἐνδύω 806
ἐκεῖ 527 a
ἐκκεντέω 885 (ii)
ἐκλέγομαι 709, 833
ἐκλεκτός 676
ἐκμάσσω 762, 768
ἐκνεύω 885 (ii)
ἐκτείνω χεῖρα(ς) 693
ἐκχέω 751 b
ἐλαιῶν (al. -ών) 687
ἐλαττόω 885 (ii)
ἐλάττων 885 (ii)
ἐλαύνω 833

This Index extends from 1436 to 1885 (printed 436—885).

JOHANNINE VOCABULARY

ἐλέγχω 855
ἐλεέω 677
ἐλεημοσύνη 855
ἔλεος 677, 727 n., 855
ἐλεύθερος 712, 751
ἐλευθερόω 712
ἕλιγμα 885 (ii)
ἑλκύω 710
Ἕλληνες, -ιστί 713
ἐλπίζω 855
ἐμαυτοῦ, -όν 718, 855
ἐμβριμάομαι 713, 811
ἐμός 718
ἐμπαίζω 686
ἐμπίμπλημι 768
ἐμπόριον 885 (ii)
ἔμπροσθεν 681 a
ἐμπτύω 693
ἐμφανίζω 597 b, 716, 751
ἐμφυσάω 885 (ii)
ἐν 881-2, w. πιστεύω 470, 480
ἐνδύω 689, é. and ἐκδύω 806
ἐνειλέω 866 (i) foll.
ἕνεκα 692, 884
ἐνθάδε 768
ἐνιαυτός 768
ἐγκαίνια 885 (ii)
ἐνταφιάζω 734 e, 751
ἐνταφιασμός 732, 734
ἐντεῦθεν 768
ἐντυλίσσω 855, 866 (i) foll.
ἐνώπιον 768
ἐξάγω 833
ἐξέρχομαι 637 a
ἔξεστιν 594 a, 685
ἐξετάζω 751
ἐξηγέομαι 769
ἐξομολογέομαι 678
ἐξουσία 562-94
ἐξουσιάζω 570 b
ἐξυπνίζω (Jn xi. 11) om. in 885 (ii)
ἑορτή 711
ἐπαίρω 855
ἐπαιτέω 737 a
ἐπάρατος 885 (ii)
ἐπαύριον 811
ἔπειτα 769
ἐπενδύτης (Jn xxi. 7) om. in 885 (ii)
ἐπερωτάω 672
ἐπί 884, πιστεύω é. 470-77
ἐπίγειος 885 (ii)
ἐπιγινώσκω 685

ἐπιθυμία 833
ἐπίκειμαι 769
ἐπιλέγομαι 885 (ii)
ἐπιστρέφω 695
ἐπισυνάγω 682
ἐπιτίθημι, v.r. περιέθηκαν 805
ἐπιχρίω 885 (ii)
ἐπουράνιος 885 (ii)
ἑπτά, ἑπτάκις 692
ἐραυνάω 885 (ii)
ἐργάζομαι 513, 728
ἔργον 728
ἔρημος 679, 728
ἑρμηνεύω 713, 728 l_2
ἔρχομαι 630-9, ἔρχομαι and ἦλθον 624, ὁ ἐρχόμενος 633, ἐλήλυθα 637 a, ἐλήλυθεν ὥρα, ἔρχεται ὥρα 639 a—b
ἐρωτάω 708
ἐσθίω 680
ἔσχατος 685, é. ἡμέρα 715
ἕτερος 687, 856
ἑτοιμάζω, ἕτοιμος 688
εὐαγγελίζομαι, εὐαγγέλιον 670, 682
εὐδοκέω, -ία 696
εὐθέως 693
εὐθύνω 885 (ii)
εὐθύς (adv.) 693
εὐλογέω, εὐλογητός 674
εὐνοέω 714 e
Ἐφραίμ 710
ἐχθές 885 (ii)
ἐχθρός 680, 792 a, 856
ἔχω 796 a
ἕως conj. 735, prep. 884

Ζῆλος 885 (ii)
ζήτησις 885 (ii)
ζωή 715
ζώννυμι 712
ζωοποιέω 716

Ἥ 647 c
ἡγεμών 682
ἤθελον etc. s. θέλω
ἥκω 637 a, 856
Ἠλείας 680
ἡλικία 856
ἧλος 885 (ii)
ἤπερ 647 c

Θάλασσα 811
θάνατος 710
θανατόω 679
θαρσέω 811

θαυμάζω 671 a, 673 a—e
θαυμαστός 811
θεάομαι 604, 723, 856
θέλημα 728
θέλω, ἤθελον, -ησα, -α 735 b, c
θεός, ὁ 497 a
θεοσεβής 885 (ii)
θεραπεύω 683
θερίζω 856
θερμαίνομαι 735
θεωρέω 598 foll., 723
θήκη 885 (ii)
θλίψις 811
θρέμμα 885 (ii)
θρηνέω 857
θυγάτηρ 678
θυρωρός 735

Ἰάκωβος 684 d
ἰάομαι 683
ἴδε 674, 812
ἰδεῖν 609-11, s. εἶδον
ἴδιος 720, κατ' ἰδίαν 672, οἱ ἴδιοι and τὰ ἴδια 720 d; (τις) τῶν ἰδίων 630
ἰδού 674
ἱερεύς 688
Ἱεροσολυμεῖται 735
ἱκανός 683
ἱμάς 833
ἱματισμός 769
ἵνα 726
Ἰουδαῖος 713
Ἰούδας, οὐχ ὁ Ἰσκαριώτης 714
Ἰσραήλ 684
Ἰσραηλείτης 713
ἵστημι 725, σταθῆναι and στῆναι 725 b—e, ἑστώς of God 725 g, ἔστη εἰς μέσον or ἐν μέσῳ, of Jesus 793 foll.
ἰσχυρός, ἰσχύς, ἰσχύω 686, 693
Ἰωάνης (Peter's father) 714
Ἰωσήφ (Mary's husband) 857

Κἀγώ 857
καθαίρω 885 (ii)
καθαρίζω 676
καθαρισμός 833
καθαρός 857
καθέζομαι 857
καθεύδω 693
Καιάφας 857

This Index extends from 1436 to 1885 (printed 436—885).

GREEK 91

καιρός 695
καίω 858
κακῶς ἔχων 679
κάλαμος 689
καλέω 675
Κανᾶ 709
κατά 884, κατ' ἰδίαν 688
καταβολή 858
κατάγνυμι 751
κατάκειμαι 834
κατακλίνω 689
κατακρίνω 677
κατακυριεύω 570
καταλαμβάνω 735
καταλύω 679
κατανοέω 800 a
κατεξουσιάζω 570
κατηγορία 885 (ii)
κατοικέω 858
Κέδρων (τῶν) 885 (ii)
κεῖμαι 858
κειρία 885 (ii)
κεντυρίων 676
κερδαίνω 682
κέρμα 686, 885 (ii)
κερματιστής 885 (ii)
κεφαλή, s. κλίνω
κῆπος 769
κηπουρός 885 (ii)
κηρύσσω 688
Κηφᾶς 709
κλάδος 674
κλάω 675
κλείω 858
κλέπτης 858
κλῆμα 674, 885 (ii)
κληρονομέω, -ία, -ος 684
κλίνω 858, κλίνω κεφαλήν 451–8, 462, 839
Κλωπᾶς 885 (ii)
κοιμάομαι 693, 858
κοίμησις 885 (ii)
κοινός 677 b
κοινόω 677
κοινωνία 700 a
κόκκος 692 h
κολάζω 723 c
κόλασις 723 c
κολλυβιστής 812
κόλπος 769
κολυμβήθρα 720
κομψότερον ἔχειν 885 (ii)
κοπιάω 859
κόσμος 728
κράβαττος 673, 736
κράζω 752 a—f
κρατέω 691, κ. ἁμαρτίας 721
κραυγάζω 752 a—f

κρίθινος 708
κρίνω 677 d, 714, 859
κρίσις 859
κρύπτω 859
κτήματα 694
κυκλόω 770
κύπτω, forms of 799 c
κυριεύω 570
κύριος (ὁ), of Jesus 770
κωφός 679

Λαγχάνω 770
Λάζαρος 770
λάθρᾳ 752
λαλέω 724
λαλιά 752
λαμβάνω 689 c, 721, 735 f, λ. σταυρόν 792 b
λαμπάς 746, 752
λαός 688, parall. to ὄχλος 733
λατρεία 885 (ii)
λέγω hist. pres. 804 a, ἔλεγε 491 a
λέντιον 885 (ii)
λέπρα, -ός 685
Λευείτης 770
λιθάζω 726
λίθινος 885 (ii)
λιθοβολέω 859
λιθόστρωτος 885 (ii)
λίτρα 885 (ii)
λογίζομαι 770
λόγος, s. Joh. Gr. Index
λόγχη 752
λοιδορέω 885 (ii)
λούω 728
λύκος 859
λυπέομαι 727 c, 812
λύπη 771
λύχνος, -ία 685
λύω 679 b

Μαίνομαι 885 (ii)
μακάριος 859 e
Μάλχος 885 (ii)
μανθάνω 812
μάννα 717
Μάρθα 717, 771
Μαριά(μ) (the mother of Jesus) 686
Μαριά(μ) (sister of Lazarus) 771
μαρτυρέω 703, 726, 859
μαρτυρία 695 b, 726, 834
μαρτύριον 695, 726
μάρτυς 696, 726
μάστιξ (disease) 692

μάχομαι 885 (ii)
μέγας 683
μεθερμηνεύω 728 l_2, 812
μεθύω 752
μείζων, of persons 683
μένω 707
μερίζω 679
μέριμνα 676
μέρος 860
μέσος, s. ἵστημι, 793 foll.
μεσόω 885 (ii)
Μεσσίας 717
μεστός 753
μεταβαίνω 860
μετανοέω, -οια 691
μεταξύ 860
μετρητής (Jn ii. 6) om. in 885 (ii)
μηδείς 885
μήποτε 885
μηνύω 771
μιαίνω 885 (ii)
μικρόν (adv.) 716, 812
μικρός 686
μιμνῄσκομαι 721 i, 860
μισέω 713
μισθός 691
μισθωτός 736
μνημονεύω 721
μονή 707
μονογενής 771
μόνος, τὰ ὀθόνια μόνα 804

Ναζωραῖος 860
Ναθαναήλ 718
νάρδος 736
νεύω 885 (ii)
νεφέλη 676
νήπιος 676, 860
νηστεύω, νηστεία, νῆστις 681
νικάω 771
Νικόδημος 718
νιπτήρ 885 (ii)
νίπτω 728, 813
νοέω 813
νομή (Jn x. 9) om. in 885 (ii)
νόμος 715, 860
νόσος 679, 724 a
νύμφη 860
νῦν 719
νύξ 718
νύσσω 753

Ξύλον 885 (i)

Ὁδηγέω 861

This Index extends from 1436 to 1885 (printed 436—885).

JOHANNINE VOCABULARY

ὁδοιπορία 885 (ii)
ὁδός 696
ὄζω 885 (ii)
ὀθόνιον 716, 772, 804
οἶδα 621–9, 715
οἰκία 684
οἰκοδεσπότης 684
οἰκοδομέω 675
οἶκος 684
οἶμαι 885 (ii)
ὀκτώ 772
ὀμνύω 694
ὅμοιος 861
ὁμοιόω 686
ὁμολογέω 678 a, 861
ὁμοῦ 727
ὀνάριον 885 (ii)
ὄνομα 553 a, πιστεύω εἰς τὸ ὄ. 483
ὄνος 861
ὄντως 834
ὅπλον 885 (ii)
ὅπως 695
ὅρασις 601
ὁράω 601, 605–6, 723, ὤφθη 597 b
ὀργίζομαι 861
ὅρκος 687
ὀρφανός (Jn xiv. 18) om. in 885 (ii)
ὀσμή 885 (ii)
ὀστέον 861
ὅστις 885
ὅτε 775 e
ὅτι 726, πιστεύω ὅ 476
οὐαί 696
οὐ μόνον 753
οὖν 883, 885
οὔπω 719
οὖς 680, 866 c
οὐχί 861
ὀφείλω 861
ὀφθαλμοὺς αἴρω 608
ὄχλος and λαός 739, ὁ ὄ. πολύς 739–40
ὀψάριον 712
ὀψία 813
ὄψις 885 (ii)

Παιδάριον 736 e, 885 (ii)
παιδίον 676
παῖς 862
παλαιός 687
παρά 885
παραβαίνω 824 a
παραβολή 669, 687, 721 a
παράγω 687, 813
παράδοσις 695

παρακαλέω 674
παράκλητος 720
παρακύπτω 600, 726, 772, 798—804
παραλαμβάνω 689 c, 735 f, 781 a
παραμυθέομαι 885 (ii)
παρατίθημι 692
παραχρῆμα 693, 862
πάρειμι 862
παρέρχομαι 631, 687, 735 c
παροιμία 669, 721
παρρησία 744 (xi) a, (ἐν) π. 712, 719
πάσχω 694
πατήρ 711
πεινάω 684
πειράζω, -ασμός 695
πέμπω 723, ὁ πέμψας (με) 723 e
πενθερός 885 (ii)
πεντήκοντα 834
πέραν τοῦ Ἰορδάνου 714, 813
περί 885, οἱ π. Πέτρον 802 a
περιάπτω 711 f
περιβάλλω 676, 806 a
περιδέω 885 (ii)
περιίστημι 885 (ii)
περιπατέω 656
περισσός 753
περιτέμνω 772
περιτίθημι 809, 813, περιέθηκαν v.r. for ἐπέθηκαν 805
περιτομή 709
πέτρα 691
πηγή 736
πηλός 709
πῆχυς 862
πιάζω 723
πιπράσκω 808, 814
πιστεύω pp. xi—xii, 463—561, 681, perf. 472, 519, 629
πιστικός 736
πίστις 478 c, 681, π. θεοῦ 467
πιστός 681, 736 d, 862
πλείων 504 b
πλέκω 809, 814
πλευρά 753
πλῆθος 834
πλήρης 772
πλήρωμα 814
πλησίον 687
πλοιάριον 736

πλούσιος 691
πλοῦτος 691
πνεῦμα 655, 720 k, ἐνεβριμήσατο τῷ π. 811 b
πνέω 862
πόθεν 728
ποιέω 513, 772
ποιμαίνω 862
ποίμνη 862
πολλάκις 814
πολύς, ὁ ὄχλος π. 739–40
πολύτιμος 753
πορεύομαι 652–64
πορνεία 814
πορφύρεος 885 (ii)
πόσις 885 (ii)
πόσος 683
πότερον (Jn vii. 17) om. in 885 (ii)
ποτήριον 678
ποῦ 728
πραιτώριον 809, 814
πράσσω 772
πρεσβύτεροι 680
πρό, π. μικροῦ 799 b, π. προσώπου 681 a, π. τοῦ (inf.) 863
προάγω 682
προβατική 885 (ii)
προβάτιον 885 (ii)
πρόβατον 723
προέρχομαι 682
προπορεύομαι 682
προσαιτέω 885 (ii)
προσαίτης 737
προσέρχομαι 649, 677, 801 a—b
προσευχή 688
προσεύχομαι 649, 688
προσκόπτω 863
προσκυνέω 640–51
προσκυνητής 885 (ii)
προσφάγιον 796 a, 885 (ii)
πρόσωπον, πρὸ π. 681 a
πρότερον, (τό) adv. 708
προτρέχω 773
πρόφασις 834
πρωί 815
πρωΐα 754
πρῶτος 682
πτέρνα 885 (ii)
πτύσμα 885 (ii)
πτύω 693 d, 737
πτωχός 688
πυνθάνομαι 863
πῦρ 682
πῶλος 677
πωρόω 737

This Index extends from 1436 to 1885 (printed 436—885).

GREEK 93

'Ραββεί 694 c, 815
'Ραββουνεί 694 c, 737
ῥάπισμα 737
ῥέω 885 (ii)
Ῥωμαῖοι, -αϊστί 721

Σαδδουκαῖος 692
Σαλείμ 721
Σαμαρείτης 863
Σαμαρεῖτις 885 (ii)
Σαμαρία 773
Σατανᾶς 692
σεισμός 680
σημαίνω 724
σημεῖον 669
Σιλωάμ 773
Σίμων (father of Judas Iscariot) 724
Σιών 754
σκανδαλίζω, -ον 545, 694
σκέλος 885 (ii)
σκηνοπηγία 885 (ii)
σκηνόω 885 (ii)
σκληρός 754
σκορπίζω 863
σκοτία, -ος 710, 863, 864
σμύρνα 746, 754
Σολομών 864
σουδάριον 773
σοφία, -ός 696, 864
σπεῖρα 809, 815
σπείρω 693
σπέρμα 692
σπλαγχνίζομαι 677
σπόγγος 815
σπόρος 692
στάδιος 864
σταυρός, -όω 678, 792 b
στέφανος 815
στῆθος 773
στήκω 725, 737
στοά 885 (ii)
στόμα 864
στρέφω 864
σύ 726
συγγενής 773
συλλέγω 864
συμφέρω 754
συνάγω 682 f
συναγωγή 694
συναλίζομαι 794 a
συνανάκειμαι 689
συνεισέρχομαι 885 (ii)
σύνεσις, συνετός 695, 865
συνέχω 834 a
συνήθεια (Jn xviii. 39)
om. in 885 (ii); see 2464 b
συνίημι 695
συνμαθητής 885 (ii)

συνσταυρόω 678, 817 c
συντίθεμαι 774
σύρω 885 (ii)
Συχάρ 726
σφραγίζω 754
σχίζω 866 (iv)
σχίσμα 815
σχοινίον 885 (ii)
σώζω 692
σῶμα 674
σωτήρ 774
σωτηρία 774

Ταπεινός, -όω 865
ταράσσω 727
τάχειον 885 (ii)
ταχέως 774
τε 865
τεκνίον 676 a, 885 (ii)
τέκνον 676
τελειόω 774
τελέω 865
τέλος 680
τελώνης 689
τέρας 816
τεταρταῖος 885 (ii)
τετράμηνος 885 (ii)
τηρέω 714, 816
Τιβεριάς 726
τίθημι 659 a, τ. ψυχήν 715
τίκτω 865
τιμή 746, 755
τίτλος 885 (ii)
τότε 695
τριακόσιοι 733
τρίτον, ἐκ τρίτου 695, (τὸ) τρίτον 834
τρίτος 695
τροφή 865
τρώγω 680 b, 710, 755
τύπος 885 (ii)
τυφλόω 885 (ii)

Ὑγιής 728, 816
ὑδρία 885 (ii)
ὕδωρ 728, 834
ὑμεῖς 728
ὑμέτερος 774
ὑπάγω 652-64, 713, 816
ὑπάντησις 755
ὕπαρξις θεοῦ 476 b
ὑπάρχοντα, τά 694, 865
ὑπέρ 692 a, 885
ὑπηρέτης 719
ὕπνος 865
ὑπό 885
ὑπόδειγμα 885 (ii)
ὑποκρίνομαι, -κρισις, -κριτής 684
ὑπομιμνήσκω 775

ὕσσωπος 885 (ii)
ὕστερον 866
ὑφαντός 885 (ii)
ὕψιστος 683
ὑψόω 711 c, 866

Φαγεῖν 680 b
φαίνω, ἐφάνη 749 c, 885 (ii)
φανερός 686
φανερόω 597 b, 716, 738
φανερῶς 738
φανός 885 (ii)
φαῦλος 885 (ii)
φεύγω 682
φιλέω and ἀγαπάω 436, 595-6, 716 d—f, 728 m—q
φιλία 716 f
Φίλιππος 720
φίλος 775, 866
φοβέομαι 643 a, 681
φόβος 681
φοῖνιξ 885 (ii)
φορέω 755
φραγέλλιον 885 (ii)
φρέαρ 775
φρόνιμος 866
φυλακή 688, 696
φωνέω 752 e
φῶς 715, 866, φ. κόσμου 748
φωτίζω 485, 775

Χαμαί 885 (ii)
χάρις 775
χείμαρρος 885 (ii)
χειμών 816
χιλίαρχος 738
χολάω 885 (ii)
χορτάζω 692
χωλός 685
χωρέω 816
χωρίον 816

Ψεῦδος 885 (ii)
ψεύστης 885 (ii)
ψηλαφάω 617, 804
ψῆφος 711 h
ψύχος 885 (ii)
ψωμίον 724

Ὦ 687
ὧδε 683
ὡς (when) 775
ὡσαννά 816
ὡσεί 693
ὥσπερ 866
ὥστε 693
ὠτάριον 736 e, 738, 866 c
ὠτίον 866

This Index extends from 1436 to 1885 (printed 436—885).

JOHANNINE GRAMMAR

I. NEW TESTAMENT PASSAGES

[*The references are to paragraphs, indicated by black numbers, which, in this Index, run from* 1886 *to* 2799. *The thousand figure is not printed. An asterisk distinguishes numbers up to* [2]000.]

MATTHEW			MATTHEW			MATTHEW		
		PAR.			PAR.			PAR.
2	2	782	9	2	559 b	14	7	536 f
	6	670 b		9	394 b		15	428 a, 746 a
	23	292		21	270 a		21	009–10
3	11	899*, 981*,		28	239		23	962*
		998*, 401 a	10	11	437 a		25–6	341–6
4	8	962*		14	437 a		26	220
	13	292		19	532		27	914 a*, 220–2,
	18	342 f		22	322, 499			699
	23	709 a		23	532 a	15	2	532
5	3	679 c		27	709 b		6	799 (iii)
	11	499 b	11	3	940*		11	959*, 646
	12	689 d		8	216 b		14	513 c, 534 c
	14	539		13	477		18	646
	15	948*, 275 b		18	253 a		29	724 a
	22	708 c		25	689 p	16	9–10	708 b
	23	513 c, 534 c		25–7	165		18	782
	25–6	520		27	586 d, e		19	517–19
6	4	377 a	12	14	173		23	566 c
	26	144		25	261 b		24	437 a, 496 c, 515
7	4	767		29	517 d		28	576
	7	536		32	553 c	17	1	962*
	11	743		46	395		17	364 a
	16	702 d		50	799 (iii)	18	8–9	592
	21	263, 680 b	13	2	342 f		18	517–9
	22	335 a, 409		13–14	093 b	19	3	379
	24–6	580 a		14	144		9	677
	27	915*		19	799 (iii)		26	649 a
8	6	584 b		21	039	20	1	708 c
	8	559		56	364 a		12	272 a
	27	162 a	14	3	460 a, 517 d		18	265 b

This Index extends from 1886 to 2799. Before numbers with * supply 1, e.g. [1]999*; before others, 2, e.g. [2]000.

NEW TESTAMENT PASSAGES

MATTHEW		MATTHEW		MARK	
	PAR.		PAR.		PAR.
20 28	593	27 13	737 b	4 26	917 a*
21 1	310 a	15	464 b-c	36	272, 570 d
7	537 (ii), 781 c	19	294 a, 537 (ii) b,	41	162 a, 694 b
11	292		732	5 11	962*
12	558 e	27	570 d	22	558 d
22	536	30	558 a	27	270 a
23	971*, 342 e	33	738	28	270 a
25	906*, 953*	48	623	30	270 a, 563 b
42	356, 396 b, 621	55	318	35	482 b
22 12	253 a	57	291, 769	36	237 a, 439 b
18	563 b	62	087-8	37	586 d
46	586 d, e	63	732	41	679 b
23 8	784 c	28 1	310	6 3	363 a, 364 a
25	329 a	6	171 e	10-11	437 a
30-2	950 a*	7	186 a	17	460 a, 517 d
32	439 (v) b	10	307 b	22-4	536 f
24 3	707	18	742 b	32	020
5	220 a, 585 a-b			36-7	428 a
8	197 a		MARK	37	512, 690 a
13	322, 499	1 5	670 b	38	745 a
14	709 a	7	899*, 043,	45	089 a
18	711 b		558 d	46	962-3*
23	439	8	981*, 998*,	48-9	341-6, 472
25	186 a, 585 a-b		401 a	49	220
26	439	9	292, 706 a	50	914 a*, 220-1,
30	317 f	16	342 f		699
35	255, 580 a	21	709 a	52	449 a
26 5	918*	27	694 b	7 13	799 (iii)
7	607	32	425 b	15	959*
14	928 a*	39	709 a	18	261 b
18	364 a	2 1	711 a	8 17	449 a
20	483 b	4	294 a	19-20	708 b
21	945*	5	559 b	32	917 (iii)-(vi)*
22	702 d	7	155 a	34	437 a, 496 c, 515
23	945*	13	394 b	38	580 a
25	702 d	19	235 a	9 1	576
28	721 a	27	959*	2	962*
29	532 b	3 3	710	11	155 a
30	307 c	6	173	19	363 a, 364 a
39	679 b	9	294 a	21	696 b
40	432 d	13	962*	24	782
47	928 a*	25	261 b	25	679 c
50	575 a	26	593	28	155 a
51	558 a	27	517 d	37	398, 593
56	111, 478 a	29	593	43-7	513 a, 592
61	331	31	395	45	534 c
63	734 d	35	799 (iii)	47	534 c
64	915 (vi) a*,	4 1	342 f	10 2	379 a
	220 a, 245 a	12	093 b	10	711 a
65	270 b, 563 c	14	799 (iii)	11	677
72	960 b*	17	039, 593	21	649 a
74	914*, 960 b*	21	948*, 275 b,	23-4	592
27 2	969*		372 a, 593 d,	26	366 c
12	537 a		702 d	27	593, 649 a

This Index extends from **1886** to **2799**. Before numbers with * supply **1**, e.g. [1]999*; before others, **2**, e.g. [2]000.

JOHANNINE GRAMMAR

MARK		MARK		LUKE	
	PAR.		PAR.		PAR.
10 33	265 b	14 63	270 b, 563 c	6 39	513 c, 702 d
45	167, 593	71	960 b*	42	767
11 1	310 a	72	914*	43	649 (i) c
7	537 (ii), 781 c	15 1	969*	46	680 b
8	047	4	736, 737 b	47	580 a
15	558 e	6	464 b–c	49	915*
23	521 a	14	068 a	7 1	709 a
24	536	16	570 d	2	584 b
25	532 a	19	558 a	6	559
27	342 e	22	738	19	940*
28	971*	23	380 b	33	253 a
30	906*, 953*	36	623	44	563 a
32	466 (i) a	40	318	47	178 a
12 11	356, 396 b, 621	42	043, 087–8	48	781 c
12	366 c	43	291	8 1	374 a
15	563 b	16 2	310	10	093 b
25	593	6	171 e	11	799 (iii)
28	665 b			13	039
37	468 b		LUKE	16	948*, 275 b,
41	333 a				372 a
13 3	707	1 3	904*	19	294 a, 395
6	585 a–b	37	356 a	21	799 (iii)
8	197 a	45	356 a	25	162 a
10	709 a	2 30	473	32	962*
11	532	41	715 d	46	563 b
13	322, 499	3 16	899*, 981*,	50	237 a, 439 b
16	711 b		998*, 043,	51	586 d
20	078 a, 441 b–c		401 a, 558 d	54	679 b
21	439	18	335 a, 414 f	9 4	437 a
23	585 a–b	19–21	460 a, 480 a	5	437 a
31	255, 580 a–b	20	517 d	13	428 a
35	678	4 1	072	17	329 (i) a
14 2	918*	14–15	374 a	23	437 a, 496 c, 515
3	563 a, 607	16	292	26	580 a
7	533	30	542–3	27	576
10	928 a*	31	709 a	28	962*
17	483 b	36	694 b	37	331 e
18	945*	40	425 b	41	364 a
19	702 d	44	709 a	10 21	689 p
20	945*	5 1	342 f, 354	21–2	165
24	721 a	2	354	11 2	532 a
25	532 b	3	342 f	7	711 b
26	307 c	14	593 b	9	536
31	513 a–b	19	294 a	13	743
36	679 b	20	559 b	21	533
37	482 d	27	394 b	22	517 d
43	911*, 928 a*	6 6	983 a*	36	532 c
46	575 a	8	710	39	329 a
47	558 a	11	173	41	760
49	111, 363 a,	12	962*	42	033 a
	364 a	20	679 c	12 3	709 b
58	331, 451	23	689 d	11	532
61	537 a	25	679 c	24	144
62	220 a, 245 a	33	513 d	32	679 c

This Index extends from **1886** *to* **2799**. *Before numbers with* * *supply* **1**, *e.g.* [1]999*; *before others,* **2**, *e.g.* [2]000.

NEW TESTAMENT PASSAGES

	LUKE			LUKE			JOHN
		PAR.			PAR.			PAR.
12	58–9	520	23	5	737 a	1	15–34	601–2
13	3	521–2		9	537 a		16	146 a, 414 h
	5	521		33	738		16–18	pref. p. vii
	26	335 a		34	318 b		17	301, 411 e
	28	532 b		36	623		18	938 *, 964 *,
14	12, 13	532 a		38	339, 347			275 a, 308–
	33	261 b		48	317 i, 318			9, 382, 615,
15	30	781 c		49	318 a			706 foll.
16	6	781 c		51	291		19	481
	16	477		53	257 b		19–21	766 (i) b
	18	677		53–4	087–8		20	189, 401, 598
17	20	736 c	24	1	310		20–1	600
	31	711 b		12	664 b		21	940 *, 965 *,
	33	739		21	472 b			248 c, 498 a
18	5	322		36	307		22	113
	31	265 b		36–42	483 a		23	401
19	2	374 a		39	220–1, 269 d,		24	214, 481
	28–9	310 a			699–700		26	998 *, 399
	31	513 d		41	703 a, c		26–7	401
	35	537 (ii), 781 c		43	335		26–33	552
	42	539		47	709 a		27	094 a, 104 a,
20	1	342 e						558 d, 687
	2	971 *			JOHN		28	968 c *, 172,
	4	906 *, 953 *						648
	10	690	1	1	937 *, 994 a *,		29	938 *, 509, 624
	18	397 a, 622 a			308, 363–8,		30	896 *–900 *,
	23	563 b			395			927 *, 330,
21	1	333 a		1–2	386			860, 369–
	8	220 a		1–8	594–7			71, 401,
	12	197 a		3	301, 440, 478			478 b, 571,
	18–19	322		3–4	996 *			666, 718
	33	255, 580 a		5	141			foll.
22	3	928 a *		6	937 *, 277, 358		31	064, 387
	14	483 b		7	302–4, 525–8		31–3	401
	19	721 a		7–8	063		32	952–5 *, 458,
	20	721 a		8	105–7, 112, 382			473
	27	593		9	277, 508		32–4	572
	33	643		9–11	508 c		33	947 *, 981 *,
	39	307 c, 799 (ii)		10	301			336, 382,
	42	679 b		11–12	570			509
	45	482 d		12	268–9, 448 a,		34	386 a, 401, 473
	47	928 a *			799 e		35	624
	48	072		13	268–9, 371 a,		36	649
	50	983 a *, 985 a *,			654, 722 c		38	279 a, 649
		558 a		14	946 *		41	901 b *, 985 *
	53	111, 364 a		14–17	284–7		42	456 a, 649
	54	575 a		14–18	180		43	471, 624
	58	960 b *		15	896 *–900 *,		43–5	970 *, 636
	60	914 *, 960 b *			925–7 *,		44	289
	61	649 a			330, 371,		45	931–2 *, 418 a,
	67	220 a			478 b, 479,			643
	69	915 (vi) a *			507, 571,		45–6	289
	70	220 a, 245 a			665–6, 722,		46	932 *, 245,
23	1	969 *			799 a			248 c

This Index extends from **1886** *to* **2799**. *Before numbers with* ***** *supply* **1**, *e.g.* [1]999*; *before others*, **2**, *e.g.* [2]000.

A. 7

JOHANNINE GRAMMAR

JOHN		JOHN		JOHN	
	PAR.		PAR.		PAR.
1 47-51	765	3 10	966*, 248	4 7	482 c
48	995 a*, 278,	11	428	8	310, 480, 746 a
	372, 491 c,	12	256, 554	9	pref. pp. viii-
	552	13	931-2*, 141,		ix, 066, 273
49	966*, 669		211, 265 a,	9-10	536 (i) a
50	189, 236, 241,		275, 503	10	980 a*, 400,
	248 c, 372,	15	636 c		553 a, 743
	552	15-21	pref. pp. vii-	11	258
51	953*, 265 a,		viii, 066	12	374 a
	275, 336,	16	917 a*, 986*,	13	553 c
	626 a		203, 262,	13-14	574
2 1	985*, 624		697	14	039, 255, 314-
1-2	461	17	301, 606		16, 405
3	031	18	986*, 181,	16	437-8
4	229-30, 642,		187, 253,	17	552
	647		475 a,	18	894*, 915(ii)*
5	414, 437, 516 b		477 b, 484,	19	439 (ii) a
5-7	632		695	20	245
6	070, 281-3	19	092, 181	21-3	019, 061, 485 a
7-8	437-8	19-20	568 c	23	167, 398
9	939*, 016-8,	20	574, 584 a, 606	23-4	603
	069 a, 281-	21	185 a, 574,	24	994 a*
	3, 459,		584 a	25	939*, 382
	506 a, 607	22	670 b	25-6	205, 221 b
10	424	22-3	277 a	26	940*
11	386 (i)	23	424	26-8	633
12	374, 394, 395	23-4	480	27	231 b foll., 338
13	553 b	23-5	633	28	310
14-16	553 a	25	349-50	29	702 b, d
15	929*, 558 e	27	496	30	465
16	437	28	189 c, 330, 401	31	668
16-18	633, 639	28-31	602	34	994*, 095, 298
18	179, 183 a, 400	29	939*, 571	35	185, 230 (ii)-
19	439 (iii)-(v)	30-6	pref. p. viii		(iii), 246 a,
19-20	331	31	904*, 555 a		437, 616,
20	021-4, 146,	32	451		762 a
	248 c	32-3	501, 568 b, 628	36	287 b, 313
21	382, 467-9	33	270 c	36-7	392
22	406, 469	34	324, 654, 714	37	980 a*, 795
23	069 a, 569,	35	334 c	38	477
	654, 670	36	576 d, 598	39	041, 273
23-4	466, 644	4 1	198, 459	40	465, 655
24	995 a*, 254	1-2	628	42	929 a*, 989*,
24-5	959*, 374,	1-3	635 (i)		450
	491 c, d	2	374 a	43	994 b*
25	094 a, 104 a,	3	440 b, 649 (i),	43-4	067
	607		670 b	45	167, 273, 460,
3 1	071 a, 290 a	4	272 a, 635 (i)		692
2	933*	4-5	482 c	46	071 a, 198,
3	576 d	5	970*, 198, 310,		649 (i)
3-5	573, 603		368 a, 405	46-53	584 b
3-7	903-8*, 612	6	916*, 198,	47	567 b
5	316 a		272, 751	48	232, 366 b,
8	614	6-9	631		456 a

This Index extends from 1886 to 2799. Before numbers with * supply 1, e.g. [1]999*; before others, 2, e.g. [2]000.

NEW TESTAMENT PASSAGES

JOHN		JOHN		JOHN	
	PAR.		PAR.		PAR.
4 50	406, 459	5 38–9	439 (i), (ii)	6 30	400, 525–8, 553 a
52	465 c	39	383 a		
52–3	013, 025–6, 206	39–40	141	31	552
53	374 a	41	605	32	455 a
5 1	951 a*, 394	42	032–40	33	974*, 503
2	216, 670	43	145, 554, 677	34	553 c
3	930*	44	895*, 923*, 145, 399 b, 496, 664	34–6	056
4	334 d, 348			35	255, 507, 625
5	071 a			36	161, 189
6	248 c, 279 a	45	973*, 235 a, 442–3, 474	37	507
6–7	206 a			38	952 a*, 552 a, 605
7	093 b	46	339		
9	914*	47	989*, 256	39	921–2*, 213, 262
11	380 b, 438 a	6 1	045		
11–12	206	1–15	963*	39–54	609 a, 715 b
13	031, 460, 466 (i), 541	2	417	40	093, 096
		3	707, 751	41	504
14	456 a, 478 b	3–5	616, 633	41–2	552 a
15	466 (i)	4	931*, 654 d	42	932*, 970*, 427 a, 552 a
15–18	389	5	279 a, 366 b, 428, 512, 642, 745–6		
16	537, 715 c				
16–18	464			43	349
17	915 (vi)*, 226 b, 537	6	374, 467–8	44	715 b
		7	643	44–5	548 a
18	468 b, 733 a	9	056, 412 b	45–6	218–19, 357–9
19	148, 382, 516, 537, 605, 617 a, 739 a	10	009–11, 070, 437, 632 b	46	386, 552
				48–50	504–5
		11	198	48–51	574, 608
20	114, 375	13	985*, 267, 329 (i), 419	49	950 a*, 552, 553 e
21	148, 741 a				
21–3	066 b	14	940*, 553 d	49–51	956–7*
23	128	15	198, 375, 649 (i), 724 foll.	50	530
24	477 b, 799 (iii)			51	074, 076, 504–5
25	485 a, 499, 603, 799 (i)	16	336	51–5	567
26	039, 148, 741 a	17	031	53	039
26–7	066 b	18	929 a*	54	715 b
28	485 a, 603	19	909*	54–7	613
29	499, 584 a	19–21	340–6	56	124 a
30	514 (i) e, 605	20	205, 220–2, 699	56–7	297–300
31	514 (i)	21	909*, 914*, 472, 478 b, 498, 716–7	57	957*, 124, 151
31–2	972*			57–8	504–5
32	384, 675, 730, 791–5	22	417, 466 (i)	58	949–50*, 952–7*, 122 b, 553 e
		22–4	417 a		
34	605	24	466 (i), 482 c, 752	60	041
35	275 b, 471, 655, 689 k			61	248 c, 279 a
		25	478, 758	62	172 a, 192, 210–12, 265 a, 515, 739 b
36	230 a, 384, 453, 604, 686–7	27	931*, 312–13, 438		
		28	493, 512		
37	450 a	29	968 b*, 096, 382, 405 a, 526–8	63	975–7*, 257 b, 545 c, 606
37–8	038–40, 259				
38	178, 382, 764–6, 799 (iii)				

This Index extends from **1886** *to* **2799**. *Before numbers with* * *supply* **1**, *e.g.* [1]999*; *before others*, 2, *e.g.* [2]000.

7—2

JOHANNINE GRAMMAR

JOHN		JOHN		JOHN	
	PAR.		PAR.		PAR.
6 6₃₋₄	056 b	7 34	487 a	8 29	449, 614
64	251 a, 254, 510	34–6	171 d, 190 a, 578, 605	30–1	470
64–5	470, 636	35	046, 179, 248 b, 607, 645	31	366 b, 506, 514
65	548 a			35	263 e–g
67	235	37	168, 479, 618	36	192
68–9	226 c	37–8	039, 129	37–8	193–4
69	442–3, 475	38	921–2*, 315–16, 421, 626 a	38	027, 355, 357–9, 439 (v) c
70	441 a–d			39	078–9, 213 a, 698
71	928*, 931*, 945*, 467–8	39	407, 468, 499	40	934–5*, 412 a, 451
7 1	498	40	213		
	931*, 951*	41–2	068, 289, 552	41	932*, 194 c
2	114, 147, 569, 690, 727	42	932 a*	42	326, 382, 457
		44	138, 472, 498, 575	43	251
4	917 (i), (vi)*, 202, 375 a, 727	45	991 a*, 385	44	932*, 194 b–c, 326, 378–9, 498, 535, 728
		48	057		
5	395 a, 466	49	924*, 253, 266, 417	45	177 a
6–8	989*, 605			47	389, 553 b
8–10	264–5, 629	51	960*	50	973 a*, 600
9	458	52	185 a, 439 (i) a, 492	50–1	978*
10	202, 375			51	989*
11	385, 732	8 6, 9	348	51–2	514–15, 552 b, 576, 657 b
13	917 (i), (vi)*	11	915 (vi) a*		
14	264–5	12	608, 625	52	017
15	253	13–14	554	53	923*, 413
16	989*, 629	14	457, 490, 514 (i), 549, 736 c, 739 a, 759	54	927 a*, 979*
16–17	250			55	160, 613
17	498, 515 a, 586 a			56	935*, 097, 688–9
18	386	15–16	628		
19	248 b, 455 a	16	074–6, 159, 207, 515 a, 600, 614	57	146, 248 c
21–2	388			58	221 b, 625
22	949–50*, 218–19			59	072, 538–43, 646
		16–17	428		
22–3	961*, 552, 715 c	17	988*, 558 e, 588 foll., 626	9 2	098
23	244, 248 c	18	794	3	063, 106–7, 112
24	438	19	148, 566 b, 739 d	4	089, 428 b–e
26	917 (vi)*, 057, 139 a			5	531 c, 608
		20	138, 333–4, 481	6	569 c, 784 b
27	531, 535, 736 c	21	487 a, 545, 552, 578	7	305, 437, 456 a, 583 c, 706
27–8	142				
28	200 a, 479, 600, 618, 736 c	21–2	190 a, 605		
		22	185 a, 702 d	8	466 (i)
		23	399, 553 c	9	189, 205, 221 b, 265 (i)
29	151, 613 a	24	189, 192, 221 b, 552		
30	138, 472, 481, 575			11	305, 381, 583 c, 706 a
		24–5	223–8		
31	074–5, 405 a	25	154–6, 413		
32	991 a*	26	062, 451	12	732
33–4	489	27	468	13	931*, 018, 351 b
33–5	082	28	221 b, 605 a		

*This Index extends from 1886 to 2799. Before numbers with * supply 1, e.g. [1]999*; before others, 2, e.g. [2]000.*

NEW TESTAMENT PASSAGES

JOHN		JOHN		JOHN	
	PAR.		PAR.		PAR.
9 14	071 a	10 26–7	987*	11 32	465, 565–6, 558 d–e
16	386 b	27	491 c		
17	018, 183, 274	28–9	139, 586 d–e, 767	33	198, 614 c
18	931*, 018			34	441
19	248 c	29	053 b, 496 b, 744	37	496
21	723			38	198
21–3	577	32	441, 486, 606	39	437
22	480	34	190 c	40	189, 545
24	425 a, 427 a	35	143, 799 (iii)	41	052, 452, 552 c, 617
25	274, 351, 381	35–6	921*, 244, 248 c		
27	498	36	190 b	42	058, 294, 525–8
27–8	558 e	37	256	44	437
28	554	38	893*, 511	45	941–4*
29	400, 427 a, 737 c	40	968 c*, 172, 458, 649 (i)	45–6	380
				47	991 a*, 493–4, 512, 766 (i)
29–30	068, 142 a	40–2	647		
30	218 c, 393, 683	41	075 a, 169	48	559 a, 645
		11 1	071 a, 290	50	104, 645
33	079 b, 698	2	276	50–1	645
34–5	248 c	4–6	633	52	664 b
35	242, 456 a, 459	6	198, 458	54	917 (vi)*, 199, 352 a, 724
36	113, 157, 381, 525–8	7	394		
		7–8	649 (ii)	55	646, 686–7
37	980 a*, 163, 456 a	8	146, 248 c	55–7	687
		9	514	56	184, 349, 766 (i) a
		11	394, 642		
40	215, 351	11–12	586 c	57	991 a*, 173, 480, 635
41	190 b	12–14	632 c, 634		
10 1	265 b–c	13	382, 464 a, 467–8, 481	12 1	172, 199, 288, 624, 635, 648
2	669				
2–9	608	14	917 (i), (ii)*		
3–12	267	14–15	099–102	3	168, 329, 607
3–27	420	15	525 foll.	4	928*, 945*, 586 a
4	330 a	16	928*		
4–5	558 e	17	198	5	945*
5	255	17–19	480	7	103, 352 b, 456 a
6	251, 382	18	670		
8	361–2, 798 d	18–19	941–4*	9	941 a*
10	606	19	990–1*, 360	9–12	992*
11	484, 608, 625	20–1	565–6	10	147
12	704	22	915 (i)–(v)*, 536 (i) a, c, 660 b	10–11	464
12–13	179			11	041, 294 a
14	608			12	278, 417
14–15	125–6, 491 c	25	456 a, 625	13	966*, 047, 669
15	484, 552	26	242, 248 c, 262, 545 a	14	461, 537 (ii), 756
15–18	612				
16	151	27	940*, 475, 553 d	15	537 (ii)
17	391, 552			16	339, 360, 396–7, 469, 621–2, 757
18	606	29	902 b*, 465, 565–6		
22	670				
23	969 a*	29–31	902 b*, 554 b	18	152–3, 386 b
24	917 (vi)*	30	480	19	439 (ii), 494, 645, 753 a–e
25	186 a, 604	31	902 b*, 941–4*, 686–7		
25–6	605				

This Index extends from **1886** *to* **2799**. *Before numbers with* * *supply* **1**, *e.g.* [1]999*; *before others*, **2**, *e.g.* [2]000.

JOHANNINE GRAMMAR

JOHN		JOHN		JOHN	
	PAR.		PAR.		PAR.
12 20	046 b, 686–7	13 10	263, 265 (i), 659	14 7	915(vi)*, 243 a,
21	289	11	190 a, 263,		477 b, 491,
22	418, 482 c		265 (i), 510		566 b, 739 d,
23	537 d, 604 a	12	243, 248 c, 270,		760 foll.
24	948*, 375, 725		477, 564, 649	8	437 b
25	313 b, 485		(iii), 762	9	248 c, 609
26	487, 515, 552 c	13	051 d, 195, 680	10–11	579
27	057, 231 b, 325,	14	931*, 195, 441,	11	080, 238, 727
	389 a, 437,		477, 564	12	151
	512 b–c,	15	127 a	12–14	536 (i)
	614 c	16	550 b	13	414, 516
27–8	052, 053 c, 659	17	514 (i)	13–14	604, 625
28	958*, 162, 441,	18	105–12, 263,	15	987*, 515 b,
	768 foll.		441		609
30	110 b, 478 b,	19	915 (vi)*,	16	931–2*, 630,
	611 c		995 a*, 221 b,		793–5
32	642, 739 a		526–8, 585	16–17	352–3
33	467–8	20	507, 609, 739 a	17	243 a, 491 c,
34	642, 645	21	945*, 614 c		496, 762
35	923*, 201,	23	277, 308	18	600
	342 h, 438	24	249, 252,	19	149, 177,
35–6	201, 696 c		465 c–d		230 (i),
36	238, 342 h, 538,	25	917*		241 a,
	646	26	537 d		762 a
37	031, 466	27	918*, 437,	21	980*, 987*,
37–40	390		439(v), 486,		373
39	466, 496		554 e	22	928 b*, 265 (i),
40	093 b, 114,	28–9	464		478 b, 694,
	449 a–b	29	926 b*		766 a
43	092, 369	30–2	914*	23	515 b, 609
44	072, 479	31	446, 522 b	23–4	569 a, 580
44–50	618	33	082, 127 a, 190,	24	799 (iii)
45	609		489 b, 545,	25	625
46	933*, 262, 457,		578, 605	26	931–2*, 411 c
	608	33–7	915 (vi)*	27	957 a*, 993*,
46–7	159	34	894 b*, 094,		122 b, 609 b
47	395, 606		116, 127 a,	27–9	525–8
48	978*, 799 (iii)		130, 412,	28	550 a, 739 c
48–9	179		441, 609	29	186 a, 585
49	293 b, 375,	34–5	036 b, 612	29–30	915 (v)*
	586 a, 606 a,	35	332, 393, 515 b	30–1	106–8
	742 a	36	082, 578, 605,	31	428, 742 a
49–50	195		642	15 1–5	608, 625
13 1	319–23	36–7	497, 555	2	920–2*, 421
1–4	279	37	565 a, 643	2–5	921*
3	327, 334 c	37–8	248 c	3	353, 799 (iii)
4	270	38	537 d	4	208, 437 c
6	200, 236 a,	14 1	889*, 236–40,	4–6	521
	248 c, 483,		555	5	386
	486, 564,	1–3	080–6, 186	6	919*, 266, 426,
	784 c	3	159, 486–7,		445, 755
7	394 a		649 (ii)	7	514, 516 a,
8	564	4–6	614 c		536 (i),
8–9	208–9, 564	6	301 a, 625		660 b, 739

This Index extends from 1886 to 2799. Before numbers with * supply 1, e.g. [1]999*; before others, 2, e.g. [2]000.

NEW TESTAMENT PASSAGES

	JOHN			JOHN			JOHN
	PAR.			PAR.			PAR.
15 8	114, 393, 446		16 20	058		17 11–12	408–11, 568
9	127, 437		21	948 a*, 535		12	584, 742, 744 c
9–11	988*, 581		21–2	149, 196–7		14	552
9–12	987*		22	915 (vi) c*,		15	325
10	131, 514, 568			077, 169		16	552
12	096, 131, 529 a,		23	516, 630 c,		17	661
	609			739 a		18	127, 132, 444,
13	095		23–4	536 (i), 604			554 a
15	901*, 441, 447,		24	915 (vi) b*		19	369, 376 a
	451, 477,		25	917 (i), (ii),		19–24	529 a
	550			(vi)*, 485 a		20	074–5, 304,
16	120–1, 313, 414,		26	536 (i), 630			500, 799 (iii)
	441 a, d,		27	931 a*, 246,		20–4	118–9
	516, 536 (i),			326–8,		21	208 b, 308,
	604			442–3,			376 a,
16–20	426			475–6			526–8, 554,
17	529 a		28	326–8, 457,			614, 740
18	896*, 901*, 243,			649 (ii)		21–2	127 b, 132 a
	666, 762		29	917(i), (ii), (vi)*,		21–5	052–3
19	387, 441 a, d			643		22	455
20	405–6		30	104 a, 246, 327,		23	306, 554, 614
20–1	059			332		24	151, 422, 455,
21	582		30–1	248 c			487, 495,
22	213 a, 698		31–2	475			740 e, 744 a
24	161, 213 a, 442		32	246, 485 a, 487,		25	164–5
	–3, 475, 698			604 a, 614,		26	014, 164 b,
24–5	105–12			629, 799 (i)			529 a
25	799 (iii)		33	058, 477		18 1	374 a, 671–4
26	931–2*		17 1	958*, 456 a,		1–2	799 (ii)
27	074			604 a, 617,		1–3	634
16 1–7	060			647		3	994 b*
2	093 b, 485 a,		1–2	455		4	200, 605 c, 635,
	499, 799 (i)		1–11	052			649 d
2–11	999*		2	921*, 936*, 114,		5	189, 205, 221 b
3	448, 582			117, 266,		5–6	634
4	254 a			422, 552,		5–8	625
5	139 a			690, 740–4		6	205, 221 b
7	104		2–24	742 b		7	605 c, 649 d
8	367, 614		3	936*, 095, 114,		8	189, 191, 205,
8–11	182			168, 491 c,			221 b
9–10	074–5			664 a		9	190, 742 b,
9–11	077, 169		4	340, 687 b			744 c
11	477 b		4–5	915 (v)*		10	985*, 558 a,
12	497		5	995 a*, 027,			563, 637
13–16	614			355, 405,		11	232, 377, 456 a,
14–15	488, 583, 629			768 foll.			742 b
15	189		6	455, 568, 798 a		14	104
16	190 d, 642		7–8	448, 455 a		16	931–2*, 986*,
16–19	583, 613		8	246, 328, 376 a			368
17	190 d, 213,		9	405 a, 455, 630		16–17	985 b*
	423, 468 b		9–12	744 c		17	381
19	248 c, 349,		10	332, 477		18	351 a
	466 (i), 472,		11	376 a, 529 a,		20	917 (vi)*,
	498			661, 740			251 b, 440 a

This Index extends from **1886** to **2799**. Before numbers with * supply **1**, e.g. [1]999*; before others, **2**, e.g. [2]000.

JOHANNINE GRAMMAR

JOHN		JOHN		JOHN	
	PAR.		PAR.		PAR.
18 21	381, 450 a	19 28	115, 394, 626 a	20 28	679 foll.
22	245, 248 c	28–30	279 a, 632	29	236, 241, 248 c,
24	462	29	425		475, 499
25	425	29–30	623	30	335, 414 f
27	914*	30	456 a, 644 (i)	30–1	431–5
28	048, 646	31	048,087–8,115,	31	526 foll.
29	969*		267, 419	21 1	917 a*, 340–6,
30	277, 566 b, 646	31–4	564 b		620
31	969 b*	32	607	2	418
33	234, 248 c,	33	336	3	486
	649 (i),	34	914*, 586 a	4	137, 307 a, 336,
	766 (i) b	35	151 a, 383–4,		341 a
33 foll.	649 (ii)		526–8, 607,	5	235 b–d, 701–3
34	090–1, 245 a,		611, 731	6	684, 703 c
	248 c, 250 b	37	317–18, 675–7	7	632 a
35	702 d	38	291, 394	8	020, 288
36	988*, 566 b	39	461	9	703
37	185 b, 233–4,	41	257 b	10	213, 405, 441,
	245 a, 248 c	20 1	310–11		703
	457	1–2	425, 482 c	10–12	437
38	553 d, 737	1–18	482 c	11	281, 283 c
39	094 a, 248 c,	2	367, 441	12	924*, 273, 466
	464 b–c	3	418	12–13	483
39–40	209	3–4	465	13	335 a
40	969 a*, 070	3–11	664 b	14	619–20
19 3	465 b	4	918*	15–17	248 c, 456 a,
4	553 d	6–7	377		584 c
5	960*, 200, 645	7	305	18	211 c, 796–7
6	553 d	10–11	638	19	468, 552, 564 a
7	403, 733	11	073, 368	19–21	209
8	586, 733 a	12	171–2, 216 b,	20	509
9	403–4, 537 c,		368	21	209, 386 c
	733 foll.	13	050, 185 d	22	229–30, 552,
10	231 a, 606, 645	14	137		564 a
11	904*, 213 a,	15	377, 649	22–3	089, 495, 498,
	698	16	586 b		515 a
12	969 a*	17	265 a, 307 b,	23	074–5, 185 b,
13	537 (i)–(ii),		489		486, 530 d,
	586, 707	18	925–6*, 190 c,		600, 642
14	048, 088		482 c, 586 b	24	166, 386, 427–
15	245, 248 c, 645,	19	031, 200, 307–		35
	737 c		9, 482	25	335 a, 414–16,
16–17	570 d	20	384 a		430–5,
17	738	21	127, 132, 453		660 b, 739
17–18	171	22	411 c		
19	347	23	473 b, 517–20,		ACTS
21	966 a*, 439,		558 e, 739 a	1 3	331 c, 620, 715
	645, 732	24	928*, 073	7	759 d
22	473	25	255 a, 607	8, 9	781 a
23	904 a*, 071,	25–7	567 a	12	673
	270, 632 d	26	307–9, 331 d,	18–20	781 a
24	270, 335 a		482	2 22	709 a
25	928*, 217, 355,	27	384 a	3 12	537
	418, 586 b	27–8	049–51	13	385 a

This Index extends from 1886 to 2799. Before numbers with * supply **1**,
e.g. [1]999*; *before others*, **2**, *e.g.* [2]000.

NEW TESTAMENT PASSAGES

ACTS			ROMANS			2 CORINTHIANS		
		PAR.			PAR.			PAR.
3	17	915 (i) *	13	11	559 a	7	9	915 (ii) a*
4	5	559 a	15	15	691 b	8	9	243 a
5	28	732	16	20	741		23	721 b
6	11–13	451		27	664 a	9	4	523 a
7	19	949 a*				10	12	723
9	2	739 a	1 CORINTHIANS			11	1	784 d
10	14	913 a*, 759 e					4	676
	16	913 *	1	7–8	322		16	784 d
	36–8	292 a	2	8	566 a	12	4	414 e
	41	335 a		11	959 *		10	534 a
11	8	913 a*, 759 e	3	4	534		17–18	440
	10	913 *	4	9	530 d	13	9	534 a
	22	709 b		19	569 b			
14	1	917 a*, 203 b		21	332 a			
16	22	270 b, 563 c	5	1	784 b	GALATIANS		
17	11	171 c		9–11	691 b			
	20	709 a	6	14	162 c	1	6–7	675–7
	29	759 d	8	12	563 b		12–15	559 d
19	14	409	9	4	702 b		18	364 b
	25–6	439 (ii)		11	783	2	5	364 b
20	22–32	915 (i) c*		15	691 b		13	694 c
21	20	439 (ii)		18	690	3	7	243 a
23	30	691 c		22	440	4	9	904 *
24	12	759 d	11	22	702 b		15	698
25	7	335 a		27	759 f		20	472 a, 717 b
	24	439 (ii)		30	746 a		24–6	413
26	5	904 *	12	3	680		25–6	906 *, 907 c*
	24	784 b		8–10	676	5	17	697 b
	27	242	13	1	522 a	6	9–12	114
	32	698		11	478 b		10	696
28	7	665		12	915 (vi) c*, 511 a		11	691 a–e, 78
				13	313 a			90
ROMANS				14 26	534 b			
1	11	784 b	15	6–8	619	EPHESIANS		
	20, 21	558 b		19	474 a			
2	14	534		20	901 *	2	4	014
3	19	606 a		22	530 b		13	909 *
	24, 25	558 b		24	531	4	8	744 b
	27	265 (i) a		47	906 *, 953 a*		26	439 (iii)
4	13	759 d	16	10	364 b	6	3	114
	18	689						
7	7	698	2 CORINTHIANS			PHILIPPIANS		
8	18	709 a						
	23	723	1	9	530 d, 723			
	29	897 b*, 901 *		10	474 a	1	7	721 b
9	11	759 d		14	559 d		25–6	559 d
	27	158, 721 b		23–4	219 b	2	1–2	036 b
10	1	559 d	3	12	917 (ii) a, (v) *		2	783
	11	262 a		14	449 a		9	409
	18	702 b	4	13	443		22	243 a
11	7–8	449 a–b	5	3	523 a	3	20	559 a
	23	522		8	364	4	12	162 b
	36	294		10	584 a		14	783

This Index extends from **1886** *to* **2799**. *Before numbers with* * *supply* **1**, *e.g.* [1]999*; *before others,* **2**, *e.g.* [2]000.

JOHANNINE GRAMMAR

COLOSSIANS

PAR.
1 15   897 b*
  16   294,   440,
       747 a
  18   897 b*
  24   915 (ii) a*
2 5   783
  15   917 (i)*
4 18   783

1 THESSALONIANS

1 7-8 991*
2 16   322
  19   558 b
3 7   515 (i)
  10   559 a
  13   559 a
4 9   379 a
5 1   379 a
  2-3 531
  3   534 b
  4   697 b
  23   322, 559 a

2 THESSALONIANS

2 1   721 b
  5-6 915 (ii)*
  10   033 a
3 5   033 b
  17   691 e

1 TIMOTHY

3 14   554 d
4 10   474 a
  13   089
5 25   539

2 TIMOTHY

2 12   322 b

TITUS

3 5   558 b

PHILEMON

18-19 691 b
19   219 a

HEBREWS

1 1   949*, 553 e
  14   265 (i)

HEBREWS

PAR.
2 4   558 b
  6   694
  9   576 b
  10   294
  12   307 b
4 8   566 a
  11   784 b
5 6   675
6 5   016 a
7 4   439 (ii) a
  6   751
  18   558 c
  25   322 c
8 7   566 a
  11   763
  12   255
  13   477
10 17 255
  37   230 (i)
11 17 751
  23   539, 543 a
  28   751
12 23 901*
13 6   203 b, 731
  19   918*, 554 d
  23   918*,   243 a,
         554 d

JAMES

1 11   445
  17-18 904 a*, 907 a*
  18   558 b
  24   753 c
2 14   522 a, 523 a
  17   522 a
  19   242 a
  24   439 (ii)
3 15   904 a*
  17   904 a*
4 2-3 536 g
  4   034 a
5 11   322 b

1 PETER

1 1   046
  3   907 a*
  6-9 689 c, l
  20-1 304 a
  23   907 a*, 313 a
  25   709 a
2 9   558 b
4 8   036 b

1 PETER

PAR.
5 10   377 a
  12   691 b, 710 a

"2 PETER"

3 1-2 783 a
  9   586 d

1 JOHN

1 1   427, 450
  1 foll. 399 c, 610
  3   074, 450
  4   399 c, 691 b
  5   181, 450
2 1   159, 399 c, 630 h
  2   075, 159
  3   392, 515
  4-5 569, 580 a
  5   033-40, 516
  6   132 b, 382
  7   254 a, 412
  7-8 594 b*
  8   412
  12   610
  12-14 691 b
  15   034 a
  16   262 b
  18   915 (iii)*,
         450 a
  19   106,   110,
         263 c-d
  21   262 b, 691 b
  23   262 b
  24   254 a
  24-7 922*
  26   691 b
  27   104 a,   201,
         558 b,
         569 a
  27-8 915 (iii)*
  28   427,   437 c,
         528 b
  29   243 a, 515 (i)
3 1   391, 454 a
  2   915 (iv)*,
         427 a, 434 b
  3   132 b, 382
  5   382
  6   262 b, 491
  7   132 b, 382
  9   262 b
  10   262 b
  12   957*

This Index extends from **1886** *to* **2799**. *Before numbers with* * *supply* **1**,
e.g. [1]999*; *before others*, **2**, *e.g.* [2]000.

NEW TESTAMENT PASSAGES

1 JOHN		1 JOHN		REVELATION	
	PAR.		PAR.		PAR.
3 14	178 a, 427 a,	5 13	399 c, 691 b	1 5	897 b*, 901*
	434 b	14	181, 536 (i)	7	317 e
15	039, 262 b	15	121 a, 159,	17	900*
16	035 foll., 382		427 a,	2 2	497
17	035 foll., 516 a		434 b,	7	920*
20	409 a, 414		515 (i),	9	781
21	522 a, 523 a		536 (i)	17	409
21-2	536 (i) b	16	121 a, 536 (i),	19	781 d
22	335, 516, 660 b		630 f, i	3 1	624
23	454 a, 528	18	262 b, 502 a	3	013
23 foll. 035 foll.		19	427 a, 434 b	10	175 a
24	454 a	20	936*, 114,	12	920*
4 2	243 a		427 a,	16-17	175
2-8	491 d		434 b,	21	920*, 421
3	915 (iv)*,		454 a,	4 11	681
	262 b, 450 a		491 c	6 8	332 a
9	297, 304			10 9	781 b, d
9-10	218, 440		2 JOHN	12 7	350 b
10	476 a	5	915 (iv)*	14 18	781 b
13	454 a	6	450 a	15 4	664 a
14	473	9	262 b	18 4-5	781 b
16	036 b, 475			7	175 a
16-19	036		3 JOHN	9	531
17	382, 528 b			19 7	689 i
5 2	037, 535	9-10	569	11	362 a
3	037	10	258	12	409
6-8	610			13	409
8	306, 383		JUDE	21 6	377 a
10	187			22 3-4	409
11	454 a	25	664 a		

This Index extends from **1886** to **2799**. Before numbers with * supply **1**, e.g. [1]999*; before others, **2**, e.g. [2]000.

JOHANNINE GRAMMAR

II. ENGLISH

Abba 679
Abide, abiding 915 (iii)*, 352, 437, 458, 514, 521; Origen on 649 e; imperat. 437; "a. in the house" 263 e–f; "a. (?) unto eternal life" 312 foll.; "a. alone" 375
Aboth, the, quotations in, how introduced 470 a
Above, "from a.," in Jewish literature 906*; "born from a." 903* foll.
Abraham, his love of man, Philo on 935*; his "laughing," Philo on 097, 689 e; Origen on 689
Abruptness of style 932*, 996* foll., 136–40, 766 (i) b
Accent (Greek) 960 a*, 190 a, 429–35, 671–4, 762 a–b
Accusative, absolute or suspensive 012; adverbial 009–11; cognate 014, 036 a; (?) of respect 267, 419; of time 013, 678; accus. and infin. 375 a, 495; for accus. w. special verbs, see the several verbs in Index III
Active (voice) and middle 563 c, 689 i
Adjectives, predicatively used 894*; special 895*–901*, 664–7, s. Index III, also Article 982–9*, Ellipsis 216, Emphasis 982* foll., 993*
Adverbs, how emphasized 902*, 554 b, 668; their position 636 c; intensive, rare in Jn 902*; special 903–18*, s. Index III
Adversative particles, s. Conjunction and Connexion
Advocate, s. "Paraclete"
Afterthought, in Jn 461; how introduced 633–4; expr. by pluperf. 480; s. Self-correction and Impressionism
"All that thou hast given me (or, him),"="the future Church" 921*, 262, 422, 444, 454, comp. 740–4
Allusiveness, in Jn 901 b*, 966 a*, 992*, 009 foll., 211 b, 265 b, 269, 275 b, 372 a, 517–20, 537 (ii), 584 b, 689, 764–5; s. also "John, intervention of," and Mysticism
"Alone," applied to God 895*, 664, comp. 168; "by himself alone" 375, 724–6; adv. 664 b
Ambiguity, causes of 886*, 893*
(i) in the meaning and reference of words: "first," "before," or "chief" 901*, 665–7; "from above" 903* foll.; "and now" 915 (i)* foll.; "thus" 916*; "boldly" or "plainly" 917 (i)* foll.; "(more) quickly" 918*; "the Jews" 941*; "the fathers" 949–50*; "the heaven" 952–8*; "the man" 959–61*; "the prophet" 965*; "taste" or "taste that" 016; "that" or "because" 083, 181–6, 219; "they went out [as our soldiers, *or*, as deserters]" 110 a–b, 263 c; "and" or "and yet" 141 foll.; "and" or "also" 149 foll.; "[in] the beginning" or "at all" 154; "and if" or "even if" 159; "and," "both," or "also" 166; "that" used for inverted commas 189 foll.; "lifted up" for "crucified" 211 c; "why?" or "what?" 231 b; "from the beginning" 254; "blood" pl.

This Index extends from **1886** *to* **2799**. *Before numbers with* * *supply* **1**, *e.g.* [1]999*; *before others*, **2**, *e.g.* [2]000.

ENGLISH

268; "we all" 287; "out of" and "from" describing extraction and domicile 289 foll.; "because of" or "for the sake of" 294 foll.; "through him" or "through it" 302 foll., comp. 378-9; "to" or "into" 310; "looking to" (in hope or fear) 317; "to the end" or "to the utmost" 319 foll.; "keep out of" or "take out of" 325; "in front of" or "superior to" 330; "on the sea" or "near the sea" 342; "along with" or "against" 349; "questioning" or "quarrel" 350; "in" or "among" 353 a; "before me" 361 foll.; "he knoweth" or "He (*i.e.* the Lord) knoweth" 383-4, 731; "that," "because" or "whatever" 413; "if" or "soever" 414; "at feast time"="at that feast" or "at any feast" 464 c; "apprehend" *i.e.* "understand" or "take captive" 596; "again" *i.e.* "a second time" or "back" 635 (i), 649 (i)–(ii), "another" or "Another (*i.e.* God)" 793 foll. (comp. 384, 730)

(ii) in forms or inflexions: indic. or imperat. 889*, 915 (iii) *b**, 079, 193, 194 *c*, 236 foll., 240 *a*, 439 (ii), 491, 760; particip. = "because" or "though" 924 *a**, 273; particip. pres. w. ἦν 277; "he that received" or "he, who received" 501-2; present, ordinary or prophetic 484 foll.; "hid himself" or "was hidden" 538-43; dat. of time 021; genit. subjective or objective 032 foll., voc. or nom. 049 foll.; 1st pers. pl. inflexion, "we," meaning of 427 foll.

(iii) in connexion or arrangement: 921*; apposition 928*, 933*, 937* foll.; asyndeton 996* foll.; connexion of "for" (conj.) 067 foll.; "but" adversative or consecutive 071 foll.; "because" 099 foll.; "accomplished in order that" or "saith in order that" 115; "in order that…in order that" 116 foll.; "even as" suspensive or explanatory 122-32; "because" suspensive or explanatory 175 foll.; "because" or "I say this because" 178 foll.; "I should have told you that" or "I should have told it to you, because" 186; "not …all" *i.e.* "not any" or "not every" 260 foll.; connexion of participle 277; "leaping to life" or "leaping, to life" 314 (comp. 312-13); "filled [full] of fragments" or "baskets of fragments" 329 (i); "for this cause [above mentioned, or, now to be mentioned]" 387 foll.; "everyone that cometh" or "the light…coming 508; "and they did" or "and [that] they did" 757; words of Christ and words of the evangelist (or others) not clearly distinguished 917 *a**, 936 *, 957 *, 066, s. Speech

(iv) in omission of words (s. also Asyndeton): "the [one] that is descending 974*, 503; "that [? spirit] which giveth life" 975* foll.; "but [? it was ordained] in order that" 105 foll.; "[I say this] because" 180 foll.; "This man what [shall he do? less prob. shall become of him?]" 209; "If therefore…[what then will ye do?]" 192 and 210 foll.; "[some] from" *i.e.* "some of" or "[sent] from" 214-15; "[daughter] of" or "[wife] of" 217; "[I do] not [say] that" or "[I say this] not because" 219; "I AM [HE] 220 foll.; omission of interrogative particle 236 foll., and see especially 240 *a*; comp. 142 *a*; "his own [family, or possessions]" 378, 728

(v) miscellaneous 372 *b*, 570 *b*
Anacoluthon 919-27*, 957*; w. subj. suspended 920-2*, 421, (?) 422
Anaphoric article, the 670 *a*
Anew, s. "New"
Anointing of David, the 502 *b*
"Another," meaning God, in Epictetus 791-2; connected with the Paraclete in Jn 793
"Answered and said," a Johannine phrase 271; "made public answer" 537
Antithesis 209, 263 *f*, 553 *a*, 568; s. Emphasis
Aorist: imperat. aor. and pres. 437-9; indic. aor. and imperf. 465 *c*, 584; aor. and perf. 440-9, 753; aor. for Eng. pluperf. 459-62; infin. aor. and pres. 496-8, 767; particip. aor. 276, 499-505; subjunct. aor. and pres. 511-35; aor. of experience or habit 443 *c*, 522 *b*, instantaneousness 443 *c*, 522 *b*, 755, persistence 443 *c*; anticipatory 635 (ii), epistolary 691 *a* foll., 785-90; "gnomic" and "instantaneous" distinguished 754-5; aor. of special verbs, see Index III

This Index extends from 1886 *to* 2799. *Before numbers with* * *supply* 1, *e.g.* [1]999*; *before others,* 2, *e.g.* [2]000.

Apocalypse, the, s. Revelation
Apodosis, ellipsis of 192; see also Index III ἄν, ἐάν, εἰ, ἵνα, καθώς, καί, ὅταν, ὅτι
Aposiopesis, s. Ellipsis
Apposition, w. proper names 928*; in subdivisions 929-30*; explaining or defining 931-6*; w. particip. 937-45*; noun repeated in 946*; pronoun in appos. w. preceding subject 947*, 386
Aramaic, s. Hebrew
Arimathaea, Joseph of 291
Arrangement and Variation 544 foll.
Artemidorus (*Oneirocritica*) quotations from 907 *d**, 211 *b*, *c*, 216 *b*, 642 *b*
Article, the, w. nouns in general 948* (s. also 194 *b*); w. "fathers" 949-50*; "feast" 951*; "heaven" 952-8*; "king" 966*, 669; "man" 959-61*; "mountain" 962-3*; "only begotten" 964*; "prophet" 965* (comp. 492); "teacher" 966*; "the woman [of the house]" *i.e.* "wife" 948*; w. names of persons 967-70*; w. names of places 670 foll.; in "the [? daughter] of " 217; w. "God," Philo on 594 *a*; "the love" (like "the Name," "the Will") 035; w. adjectives 982-9*; w. infin. 995*; w. particip. 275-6, 507; w. particip. and "is" or "are" 971-81*; quasi-vocative 049 (comp. 679 foll.); omitted or misplaced 990-4*; reduplicated 982* foll.; in Codex B 652; "Teuphilus [the] Jew" 683 *a*
Ascending 211 *a* foll., 489; "a. to heaven" 211-12, 275
Asking 516, 536 foll.; "a." and "requesting" 630
Asyndeton 996* foll.; instances of, classified 000-8; used by Jn w. historic pres. 482; introducing parenthesis 639
Attraction of relative 405-7
Authority 250; "I have a." 644; Epictetus on 798-9

B *i.e.* Codex Vaticanus, readings of, rejected by W.H. 650-62; pausespaces in 663; important readings of, in special passages 053 *c*, 079, 166, 401, 407, 428 *b*, 455 *a*, 507 *a*, 521, 530, 768; its authority great on πιστεύω 528 *a*; its weak points 895*, 925 *a**, 961*, 968 *a**, 530 *c*, 650-2; interchanges -αι and -ε 658 *e*
Baptist, John the, 898* foll., 927*, 303, 330, 350, 371, 479, 480 *a*, 501-2; his "testimony" 401; twofold repetition in his teaching 601 (comp. 927*)
Before (ambig.) 330, 361
Began to do, to say etc., expr. by imperf. 463, 470
"Beginning, from the" 251 *a*, 254
Beholding 318, 473, 516 *a*; in a bad sense 212
Belief 475
Believe, believing etc., 302-4, 438-9, 466, 475, 496, 499, 506, 695; aor. and pres. 438-9, 524 foll.; imperf., ambig. 466; perf. meaning "have fixed belief" 442, 474-5; "believe ye," ambig. 238 foll.; "believe" and "know" in juxtaposition 226 *c* (see also *Joh. Voc.* 1463—1561)
Bethany, connected w. Lazarus 290; twofold mention of 641; beyond Jordan 648
Bethlehem 289
Binding and loosing 517 *e* foll., 517-9
Blending two constructions 923*, 189 *c*, 468 *b*, 482 *c*
Blinding (metaph.) 449 *a*
Blood, of Christ 269 *b* foll.; of the circumcised 269 *e*; of the passover 269 *e*
Boldness of speech, Christ's, why emphasized 917 (i)* foll.
Bread, the, that descended from heaven 503 foll.; "buying b." 745-6
Brethren, Christ's 395; "He is not ashamed to call them b." 307 *b*
Bridegroom, the 371
Buying (metaph.) 745-6; "buying food," Origen on 746

Cana, the "sign" at 281-3; meaning of the name 386 (i)
Case, s. Accusative, Dative, Genitive etc., also Contents p. xv
Causation, notion of, prominent in Jn 174; expr. by conjunct. 174 foll.; by particip. 271-3; by prepos. 295
Cedars on Mt of Olives 671
Chiasmus 544, 554-7, 568
Choosing, God's 441 *b* foll.
Chronological order, not always followed by Jn 632
Chrysostom, compared with Origen 757 *e*; ?alluded to by Jerome 786; quoted or referred to 897*, 903*, 916*, 934*, 942*, 020, 062 *b*, 066, 083, 091-2, 102 *a*, 115, 122 *b*, 124-5, 154-6, 163, 169, 181, 184 *a*, 195, 199, 207, 209, 211, 212 *b*, 214 *a*, 215, 218 *a*, 231 *b*,

This Index extends from 1886 *to* 2799. *Before numbers with* * *supply* 1, *e.g.* [1]999*; *before others*, 2, *e.g.* [2]000.

ENGLISH

232, 240 a, 263 g, 264 a, 268, 281 a, 290, 300 a, 308 a, 322 c, 323 a, 329 (i), 331 c, 338, 342 h, 350 d, 351, 355, 357, 362, 372 c, 384–5, 386 (i), 396 b, 397 b, 398 a, 401, 403, 408, 412 b, 433, 439 (i), 452, 461 a, 465 c, 466 (i) a, 472 a, 478, 479 a, 489 a, 491 b, 508 c, 512 c, 514 (i) e, 515 e, 520, 537 (i) c, 540–1, 543 c, 549 a, 554 d, 566 b, 570 b, 573, 620 a, 630 b, 635 (ii), 649 (i) a; 649 (iii); 675–6, 686–7, 689 k, m, 691 d, 692, 694–5, 697, 701 a, 703 b, d, 707 a, 714, 716, 718, 722, 724–5, 727–8, 730, 732, 734, 736, 739 a foll., 740 b, 745, 753 e, 756, 757 d–e, 758–9, 762 b, 764, 767, 786, 788, 793 b, 794, 797, 799 (ii), 799 (iii)

Clean, man made clean by the Logos 799 (iii)
Codex Bezae, s. D
Codex Vaticanus, s. B
Come, applied to Christ 440, 482, 490; aor. 457; imperf. 465; pres. 482–6; "he that is to come" 940*; "he that cometh after me" 507; "coming into the world" 508; "came" and "have come" 440; "the hour cometh" and "hath come" 485 a, 604 a
Comparative degree 896*—901*, 918*, 092, 772, 775 b; comp. 733 a
Concessive particles 158–60
Conditional sentences 078–86, 158–9, 513–5, 517–23
Conjunctions: for most, s. Contents pp. xv–xvii; for others, s. Index III; for omission of conjunctions, s. Asyndeton
Connexion of sentences or clauses 996*, 278–9, 628 foll.; adversative or consecutive 069–76; with "and" or "and yet" 136–45; with "that" or "because" 174–86; doubtful instances 278, 414, 636–40, s. also Conjunctions and Pronouns
Consecutive particles 191—200, 203, 694, 697
Constructio ad Sensum, s. Anacoluthon
Convicting Spirit, the 649 b, d
Corrective manner, a Johannine characteristic 939*, 380, 628–30
Correspondence between the visible and the invisible 122 foll., 148
Crasis 150, 151, 383, 769
Cross, taking up the 515
Crucified, "the crucified feeds many" 211 c, 642 b
Crucifixion 211 b–c

Crying and crying aloud 479, 618

D, *i.e.* Codex Bezae, corrects irregularity 926*, 990*, 014, 258, 422; alters pres. to aor. subjunct. 524, 530 a; some readings of 942*, 053 c, 422, 428 b, c, 637 a, 664, 797 c
Dative, of instrument 020; of time (completion) 021–4; of point of time 025–6; of advantage, 776, 784 a; w. special prepositions 027, 338, 355, 357–9; w. special verbs 019, 506
Daughter (or wife?) ellipsis of the word 217
Day, "three days," "third day" etc. 331; day of judgment, the 521–2, 535 a
Dead, the, (?) prayer for the intercession of 630 i
Death, "tasting of d." and "beholding d." 576
Decalogue, the, second half of 676
Deliberative subjunctive 512, 766 (i)
"Delivering over to Satan" 520
Demonstrative, s. Pronouns
Descending from heaven 275; of the Son of man 503
Digression, causes anacoluthon 923–4*
Diminutives 235 d (s. *Joh. Voc.*)
Disciple, the beloved, Origen on 545 c
Dispersion of the Greeks, the 046
Distributive use of ἀνά 281 foll.
Domicile and birthplace, how denoted 289–93
Double Tradition, the, parallels between, and Jn 026, 165; "laying the head to rest" 644 (i)
Dove, "as a d." 955*
Dreams, Artemidorus on 211 c, 642 b
Drinking and eating at the Lord's Supper 759 f
Dying 530, 576

Eating in the presence of Christ or the disciples 335; "eating and drinking" at the Lord's Supper 759 f
Ellipsis, of two kinds 204; contextual 205–9; idiomatic 213 foll.; of apodosis 210–12; of "some" 213–5; (?) of "gate" 216; of "daughter" or "wife" 217; of copula 229–30; w. "I am" 220 foll.; between "but" and "in order that" 063–4, 105–12; s. also 386 c, 698
Emphasis, caused by insertion of word not needed for sense, *e.g.* of pron. 375, 399; of "is" 972*; of redupl. article with adj. 982* foll., 993*;

This Index extends from **1886** *to* **2799**. *Before numbers with* * *supply* **1**, *e.g.* [1]999*; *before others*, **2**, *e.g.* [2]000.

caused by unusual position 515, 553, *e.g.* of pron. 552 *c*, 553 *a*, *c*, 692; of "this" 553 *c*; of adverbs 554 *b*, 668 (comp. 902*); of "is" 353, 553 *b*, 555 *a*, 579; caused by chiasmus, 555; by antithesis 564 *b*, 566 *c* (which may be expressed or implied 399); on two pronouns in juxtaposition 564, 783, 784 *c*; on contingency 566; diverted from possessive genit. to noun 558, 569, 776–84; confusable w. contrast 399; s. also 902*, 979 *a**, 983*, 993*, 267, 555, 566 *a*, *b*, 605 *a*
Entering the Kingdom of God 496
Ephesians, Diana of the 743
Epictetus, quoted or referred to 907 *c**, 917 (v)*, 960 *c**, 049, 228 *a*, 229–30, 297 *c–e*, 305 *a*, 334 *d*, 404, 439 *b*, 439 (iv), 473 *a*, 493, 532 *d*, 570 *b*, 664 *b*, 683, 695, 697 *b*, 702 *b*, 705, 717 *b–d*, 719 *a*, *c–d*, 728 *d*, 736 *b*, 743 *a*, 755 *a*, 758 *a*, 763, 766 (i), 778–80, 791–2, 798–9, 799 (ii), 799 (iii)
Epistle, of St John, the first: general "duality" of its style 610; its use of "now" 915 (iii–iv)*; of "we" 399 *c*; of "He" absolutely to mean Christ 382; of "the true [One]" 936*; of "the love of God" to mean "God's love for men" 032 foll.; its emphasis on "confidence" 917 (ii)*; its universal negations 262 *b*; on "asking" and "requesting" 121 *a*, 630 *f–g*; peculiarities of construction or meaning in 159, 392, 515–6, 528
Eucharist, symbols of 746
Exclamatory Tone, s. Interrogation

Face of God, the 765
Father, ambig. 193, 359; "*the* fathers" and "*your* fathers" 949–50*, 553 *e–f*
Feast, "the [principal] feast [of the Jews]" 951*; "at feast-time" ambig. 464 *c*
Feminine, in Heb. and LXX, a cause of error 621–2; s. also "sheep-gate" 216
First, different meanings of 899* foll., 665–7
Fish, a symbol 703
Following 497
Form of God, the 765 *a*
Fruit (metaph.) 120
Future regarded as past 444; included in pres. partic. 507; fut. partic. a corrupt reading 500; fut. in apodosis 515 *b*; fut. and subjunct. w.

οὐ μή 255; w. ἵνα 114, 690; s. also 484, 660 *c–d*, 762 *a* and 960 *a**

Galilee, "from out G." 289; "out of G....no prophet" 492; "sea of G." 045
Gender, 216, 378, 621–2, 738
Genitive, absolute 028–31; objective 558 *e*; objective or subjective 032–40; partitive 041–2; before nouns 043; in special passages 044–8; possessive 558–69; unemphatic or "vernacular" possessive 563 *d*, 776 foll.; emphatic possessive 558 *b*, 563 *d*; ordinary possessive 558, 563 *d*, 779, 781 *a–b*; for gen. w. special verbs, s. the several verbs in Index III
Gennesar 045 *a*
Gennesaret supplanted by "Tiberias" 045
Giving 454–5; Hebraic use of "I have given" 444; "g. by measure" 714; "g. commandment" 742 *a*; "giving," in Jn, parall. to "grace" in the Pauline epistles 742–3; "all that thou hast given" 740–4, 798 *a*
Glorify, "glorifying God" 117; "the Father was glorified" 393, 446
Glory 211 *a–b*; connected with spiritual unity 946*, 455
Gnomic aorist 754–5
God, "the face of" 765; "the form of" 765 *a*; "the word of" 799 (iii)
Gods, "I said ye are g." 799 (iii)
"Going up to the feast" 265; to Jerusalem 265 *b*, s. "Ascending"
Golgotha 738
"Grace and truth" 286, 415; "grace" corresponds to the Johannine "giving" 742–3
Greek, non-classical, disuses the optative 252; uses μή with particip. 253 *a*; literary as distinct from vernacular 799 (ii); later Greek introduces other developments not found in Jn 694, 697, 702, 718–22; the futility of judging Jn's Gk as Byzantine 747–53
Greeks, "the Dispersion of the G." 046

Hardened, confusable with "blinded" 449 *a*
Harvest, waiting for 230 (iii)
Hate, "hating one's father" 228 *a*; "I hated," meaning "I steadfastly hated" 443; "I have hated" 475
He = HE 382 foll.
Head, "laying the head to rest," Origen on 644 (i), 713

This Index extends from 1886 *to* 2799. *Before numbers with* * *supply* 1, *e.g.* [1]999*; *before others*, 2, *e.g.* [2]000.

ENGLISH 113

Healing at a distance 026
Hearing 450 foll., 586
Heaven, "the h. opened" 958*; "from h." and "from the h." 952* foll.
Hebrew or Aramaic, influence of, in N.T. 915(v)*, 920*, 938*, 019, 041, 133–4, 137, 145, 260 foll., 277, 332, 347, 443–5 (see especially 445 a), 482 a; Hebraized Gk 216, 666, 671, 793
Hellenistic, s. Greek
Herod the Great and Herod Antipas 737 a
Hide, "Jesus hid himself" 538 foll., 724
Hireling, the years of a 230 (ii)
Historic present 482
Holy 411 c, d
Homoeoteleuton 490 a, 549 a, 654 c, 657 c, 659 e, 736 a, 759
Hoping 474, 476
Horse, allegorized by Origen 362 a
Hour, the, "cometh," "cometh and now is," "hath come" etc. 485 a, 604 a; the hour of trial 523 a (see also 770 and 799 (i))
House, allegorized by Origen 329; mention of, peculiar to Mk 711-13

I emphatic 401; in the Baptist's testimony 401; Epictetus on "the I" 228 a
I AM and "I am" 205, 220 foll., 487 a
Illuminating 532 c
Imperative, aor. and pres. 437–9; imp. pres. confusable w. indic. 439 (ii), with interrog. 238–44 (especially 240 a, 243 a); first aor. imp. authoritative 437; differently used by different writers 437 a; (?) "concessive" 439 (iii–v), might be called "judicial" 439 (v); implied by prohib. conjunct. 208–9; expressed or implied before "but if not" 080; s. also 233
Imperfect 463–6; imperf. and aor. 584; of special verbs 467–70; with neg. = "would not" 466; "it was" or "it had been" 466 (i)
Impersonal, s. Subject
Impressionism, results in anacoluthon 925* foll.
"In you" may mean "among you" 353 a
Inaccuracies, so called, deliberate 629
Indefinite "they" 424 a
Indicative: tenses of 440–94, and see Contents p. xxii; interrog. or noninterrog. 238–44; confusable w. imperat. 193, 194 c, 439 (ii–iii), 760; for subjunct. 114, 515 (i), 771
Indirect interrogative 249–51
Infinitive, aor. and pres. 496–8, 767; compared w. ἵνα and subjunct. 495; accus. and infin. 375 a, 495; infin. w. article 995*
Instantaneous aorist 755
Instrument, expr. in Hebrew by "in" 332; instrumental dative 020
Intercession of dead for living, (?) prayer for 630 i
Interrogation expr. by particles 231–5; without particles 236–48; sometimes exclamatory 142, 146, 486; confusable w. imperat. and affirmation 238–44 (esp. 240 a); indirect 249–51
Iota subscript 515 (i) b, 772–5
Irony, in Jn 960*, 046, 570 d, 643–5
Isaac, *i.e.* "laughter" 689
Ishmael, (?) alluded to 263 e
Israel = "seeing God" 765

Jacob, described as seeing God 765
Jerome, (?) alludes to Chrysostom 786; mentions Origen 789 a
Jew, "a Jew" 350; "the Jews" (?) = citizens of Jerusalem 942*; "many of the Jews," ambig. 941* foll.
Jewish canons of repetition 588, and of negation 591; Jewish Prayer-Book, repetition in 587 a; s. Hebrew
John the Baptist, s. "Baptist"
John the Evangelist, style of (see Allusiveness, Ambiguity, Anacoluthon, Asyndeton, Emphasis, Epistle, Impressionism, Irony, Metaphor, Mysticism, Narrowing Down, Parenthesis, Quotation, Repetition, Self-correction, Symbolism, Variation) shews traces of more than one writer 891–2*; intervention of, where Lk. omits or deviates from Mk 917* (iii) foll., 918*, 945*, 963*, 039, 045, 047, 048, 088, 173, 293, 346 a, 396, 464 b, 480 a
Joseph (husband of Mary), Jesus called "son of J." 289, 643
Joseph (son of Jacob) seeking his brethren 649 b–c
Josephus, his rendering of Heb. names 673
Judges, addressed in the words "I said ye are gods" 799 (iii)
Judging, judgment, 334 b, 695, 799; how regarded by Christians 182 a

Kidron 671–4

This Index extends from **1886** *to* **2799**. *Before numbers with* * *supply* **1**, *e.g.* [1]999*; *before others*, **2**, *e.g.* [2]000.

A.   8

King, "a k." and "the k." 245 a, 669;
the natural k. 798
Knowing 491 foll., 511, 515, 760 foll.;
"knowing" in juxtaposition w. "believing" 226 c; "I know" 448 a;
"they have not known" 448; "know
ye" ambig. 243, 762 foll.; "know
thyself" 126, 763

Latin versions 895 a*, 901 a*, 926 a*,
118 d, 154 d, 168 a, 190 a, 210 a,
289 a, b, c, 290 a, 331 b, 343 a, 350 c,
491 a, 569 c, 687, 702 a, 711 a, 715 d,
727 a, 767 a; infin. and subjunct. in
687, s. also 688 a
Latinisms 213 a, 258, 288
Law, the 286; "Present of Law" 484
Life, hating, loving, losing one's life 485
Lifted up=crucified 211 b, c; double
meaning of 642 b
Lifting up the eyes 616-7
Logos, the 269 b, 308, 410; action or
agency of 296 a, 301; titles of 938*,
964*, comp. 410
Looking to 317
Loosing sins 517; binding and loosing
517 foll.
Lord, used by Epict. in a bad sense
799 d; meanings of "my lord" 050
Losing one's soul 228 b
Love, "love of God," two meanings of
032 foll.; "the Love," like "the
Name," "the Will" 035
Loving 476, 529 a; loving one another
529
Luke, literary style of 781, 799 (ii);
various styles in his Gospel and the
Acts 913*, 563 a, 677, 686, 759 e;
peculiarities of 737 a; optative in
252; differs in construction from Jn
972*, 995*, 191 a, 307, 593, 799 (ii);
deviates from Mk, or omits what is
in Mk, where Jn intervenes 917 (iii)*
foll., 918*, 945*, 039, 045, 047, 088,
173, 276, 293, 346 a, 396, 464 b, 480 a

Man, emph. 412 a; "the man" 959-60*;
"the new man" 959*; perh.="husband" or "bridegroom" 371, 722;
the ideal, in Philo 649 b; in Epictetus
960 c*
Manifestations of Christ 331 c foll., 414 f,
619 foll., 699, 701-3, 715
Mark, style of 065, 380 b, 513 b, 649 (i) f,
686; his use of hist. pres. 482; of
article 967*; of the word "house"
711; Mk regarded as a Petrine

Gospel 913*; similarities in Mk and
Jn 917 (vi)*, 112, 238, 240, 380 b, and
s. "John, intervention of"
Mary "those that had come to M." 380
Master, the natural m. of men 798 c
Matthew, John agrees with 026, 537 (ii) b;
Mt's use of "this is come to pass"
478 a, 758; s. also *Joh. Voc.* 1745-57
Mean, "he meant to say" 467 foll.
Messiah, Talmudic Traditions about
736 c
Metaphor 948*, 955-8*, 120, 197 b,
211 a foll., 230 (ii-iii), 281-3, 300,
329, 346 a, c, 355, 449 a, 520, 642 b
Middle voice 536 foll., 660 d, 688, 689 i–l
Mis-spelling, s. Spelling
Mood 889*, 252; see also Imperative,
Indicative etc., Tense, and Contents
p. xxi foll.
Moses, Chrysostom on 745 a
Motion, implied without verbs of
motion 305
Mountain, the, meaning of 962*
Mysticism, 890*, 985*, 134, 168, 265,
281-3, 329, 384, 426, 483 a, 543, 587–
627, 611 a, 641-9, 702-3, 712-3, 731,
736-7, s. also Metaphor

Name, God's 409-10; "my n." 411 b;
"a new n." 409, 412; "thy n." and
"thy Son" 769; "thy n. that thou
hast given me" 744 c
Names: Proper names in apposition
928*; article with 967* foll.; indeclinable, with article 968*; declinable
and indeclinable 672 foll.
"Narrowing down" 290 (esp. 290 b);
908*, 303, 310, 629, 636 c
Nazareth 289; "Jesus from N." 292
Negation, repetition through 591, 593
Negative particles 253-65, 704; double
negative 257; negative w. imperf. 466
Net, of the Gospel, the 703 c
Neuter plural 267, 419-20
New 907*; the word in Aramaic and
Greek 906*; "the n. birth" 906* foll.;
"the n. man" 959; "a n. commandment" 412; "a n. name" 409, 412
Nicodemus in *Acta Pilati* 461
Nominative 049-51, s. Subject
Nonnus, quoted or referred to 156 a,
235 c, 338 a, 350, 384 a, 386 c, 386 (i) n,
419 b, 435 a, 461 a, 478, 487 a, 489 a,
508 c, 514 a, 515, 537 (i) c, 540 a, 586 c,
635 (i) a, 642 a, 649 (iii), 657 d, 664 a, b,
666, 668 a, 682 b, 683, 687-8, 689 k,
692, 694, 701 b, 702, 703 c, 704, 714,

This Index extends from 1886 *to* 2799. *Before numbers with* * *supply* 1,
e.g. [1]999*; *before others*, 2, *e.g.* [2]000.

ENGLISH

716, 722, 724-5, 727, 728 a, 730-2, 733 a, 734, 736, 739 b, 740 c, 742 a, 743, 744 c, 745, 753 d, e, 756, 757, 758, 759, 760, 762, 766 (i) a, 767, 768-9, 793 b, 796 b, 799 (ii), 799 (iii)
Nouns, indeclinable 968*, 970*, 673 c; neut. pl. 267, 419-20; repeated in apposition 946*; genitive before 043, 558 foll., 776 foll.; with article 948* foll.
Number, sing. and plur. 266-70
Numbering the people, under the Law 010
Numbers, mystically allegorized 281-3; "perfect" 283 c

One, meaning unity 118 b
One, meaning "anyone" 379
Only, "the o. man of Italy" 895*
Only begotten, with and without article 964*
Openly, confidently, or plainly 917 (i-vi)*, 727, comp. 798 f
Optative 252, 514 (i) b
Oratio Obliqua 189
Order, chronological, broken 460; of words 544-86, 776 foll., s. Emphasis and Variation
Origen, compared with Chrysostom 757 e; mentioned by Jerome 789 a; quoted or referred to 895*, 897*, 903 a*, 934*, 942-4*, 965*, 022 a, 079 c, 110 b, 118 b, c, 184 a, 209, 218 a, 222 a, 263 d, 269 a, 275 a, 283 c, 285-6, 304 b, 307 d, 316 b, 324 c, 329, 329 (i), 335 a, 338, 346 a, 357, 362 a, 386 (i), 396 b, 397 b, 412 a, 414 b-h, 428 b foll., 430, 434 e, 439 a, 439 (i), (iii), (v) a, 452, 464 b, 479, 489 a, b, 490 a, 492 a, 507 a, 508 c, 540 b, 543, 545 c, 549 a, 553 f, 573, 584 c, 586 c, 622, 635 (i), 644 (i), 649 e, 649 (iii), 659 e, 664, 666-7, 668 a, 680, 682 a, 685, 688 a, 689, 692, 695, 703, 713, 716 b, 722, 724, 725, 726, 728, 730, 736 a, 740-2, 744, 746, 756, 757 c, e, 758, 759, 765 a, 766 (i) a, 767, 770, 793 b, 799 (ii), 799 (iii)
Orthography 114, 691; Augustus, negligent of 790

Papyri, quoted or referred to 049, 114, 173 a, 235 d, 252, 282 a, 332 a, 334 d, 386 a, 414 a, 416 a, 465 d, 479 a, 520 a, 554 c, 630 d, i, 640 e, 642 b, 665 a,

667, 678 a, 683 a, b, 690, 691, 693, 696, 697 c, 698 a, 708 c, 711, 717, 729, 771, 775 a
Paraclete, the 932*, 352-3, 793
Parallelism, as distinct from Chiasmus 544 a
Parenthesis 070 foll., 164, 168, 180, 631 foll.; w. Asyndeton 639; avoided by SS 631; comp. 018
Participle 271-9; in apposition 937* foll.; w. negative 253-4, comp. 704; aor. 499—505; fut. a false reading 500; fut. comprehended in present 500; perf. 506, 517; pres. 351, 507-10; probably expressing cause 924 a*, 273; see also Article and Genitive Absolute
Partitive Genitive 041 foll.
Passive voice, avoided by Jn 373; passive and middle 538-43
Patriarchs, the 949-50*
Paul, St, the Apostle, his handwriting 114, 691, 785-90; his view of God's preordinance 689 j
"Pause-spaces" in Codex B 663
Penuel, meaning of 765
Perfect tense, as result of Johannine style 473-5; as result of Johannine thought 476-7; compared with aorist 440 foll.; meaning "it is on record that" 758; denoting instantaneousness and permanence 517-20; in Heb. 443; second perf. 478-9; some act. perfects in Gk seldom used 441, 747-53; perf. partic. 506; s. also 683 a, b
Personal, s. Pronoun
Pharisees 214-5; chief priests and P. regarded as one council 991 a*
Philo, on the "laughing" of Abraham 097; quoted or referred to 890*, 895*, 905*, 907 c*, 917 (v)*, 935*, 964*, 097, 223, 275 b, 281, 283 b, c, 285, 295-6, 307 d, 346 a, 386 (i), 410, 414 h, 494, 535 a, 579 a, 588-90, 594 a, 602, 616, 617 a, 647 (n.), 649, 665, 676, 689 e, 743, 765
Philosophers and kings 799
Phrynichus on ἧς 772 foll.
Pilate's judgment 799 f
Plato, on "knowing" 763 a-b; his use of the "vernacular genitive" 776
Pleonasm for emphasis 606
Pluperfect 480-1; aor. for Eng. p. 459-62; no p. in Heb. 480; no p. partic. in Gk 506
Plural 417; pl. vb w. sing. noun 278;

This Index extends from 1886 to 2799. Before numbers with * supply 1, e.g. [1]999*; before others, 2, e.g. [2]000.

pl. referring to sing. 266; neut. pl.
  267, 419-20
Position of words, 544-86; see also
  Emphasis and Variation
Possessive adjectives 987-9 *
Possessive genitive 558-69, 776-84
Prayer 452; the Lord's Prayer, reference
  to, in Jn 053
Praying 536; the Son not described as
  "praying" to the Father 630 h
Predicate, when before subject 994*;
  p. in one clause subject of next 596;
  "such" used as p. 398
Preordinance, divine 093, 102-5, 109-10
"Preparation of the Passover," meaning
  of 048
Prepositions 280 foll., and see Contents
  pp. xix-xx
Present, imperat. 437-9; indic. 482-94;
  historic 482-3; of prophecy and of
  law 484-94; infin. 496-8; aor. and
  pres. infin. in LXX 767; particip.
  507-10; pres. part. w. "was" 277;
  subjunct. 511-35
Privately, Christ does not teach privately
  202, 348, 251 b
Pronouns, demonstrative 374-98;
  personal 399—404; relative 405-16;
  ins. for emphasis 399 foll.; in appos.
  to preceding subject 947 *; ambiguous
  378-9; emphasized by juxtaposition
  784 c; see also possessive genit.
  558-69 and 776-84
Proper names, s. Names
Prophecy, "present of p." 484, 509
Prophet, "a, or the, p." 492 a; "the p."
  940*; "art thou the p.?" 940*, 965*
Prophetic present 484, 509
Proselytes 907-8 *
Punctuation 996*, 186, 225 a, 243 a, 278,
  314, 372 b, 414, 508, 799 (i), s. Connexion of Sentences
Purpose, how expressed in Jn 093, 097,
  173, 524-9, 686-90, 693, comp. 995 *

"Question" (vb) meaning interrogate
  498, 577
"Questioning" (n.) meaning discussion
  or dispute 349-50
Quotations and repetitions 190 a-c, 275 a;
  variation in 544; of Christ's words by
  Himself 545; conformed to txt. rec.
  269 a, 357 b; introduced in Aboth
  470 a; s. also 079 c, 412 b, 745 a

Rab, root of "Rabbi," two meanings
  of 899 *

Rachel, regarded by Justin, Iren., and
  Orig. as type of the Church 944 *
Reception of Christ 448 a
Recognition 491, s. "knowing"
Regeneration 903 * foll., 268 foll.; "from
  above" 573
Relative (Pronoun) 405-16; attraction
  of 405; s. also 738
"Remembering" after the Resurrection
  469
Repetition, or Refrain 587 foll.; variation in 544 foll.; in Jewish Prayer
  Book 587 a; Jewish Canons of 588;
  through negation 591, 598; in
  Synoptists 592; of Vocatives 592 a;
  twofold, in the Baptist's teaching
  601-2; in Christ's words 603 foll.;
  in narrative 607; twofold or threefold
  608-11; threefold 396, 612-23; sevenfold 624-7
Resumptive clauses 633
Resurrection, manifestations after the
  335, 699-700, 703 b, d; the period of
  331 c, comp. 715
Retaining sins 517-20
Revelation of St John, the 890*, 892*,
  964*, 011, 176, 270 c, 288, 329, 349,
  624, 640, 781, 799 (ii)
"Right side of the ship, the" 703 c

Samuel, the call of 307 d
Saul, Abba 227
Saying, vbs of 456, 469, comp. 251 b;
  "began to say" 467, 470
Scripture 339; difficulty of identifying
  129; Orig. on lit. interpretation of
  545 c; Christ's quotations from 626;
  "searching the scriptures" 439 (i)
Sea, "on, or near, the s." 340-5; Jesus
  standing "by the s." 354
"Searching the scriptures" 439 (i)
Seeing = experiencing 576 e; s. and
  beholding 572; s. and knowing 491,
  764-6; s. the kingdom of God 573
Self-correction 628 foll., 635 (ii)
Sending 277, 440, 453
Sentences, connexion of 628 foll.
Septuagint, variety of styles in 349 a,
  536, 649 (i) f, 689 d, comp. 911 *
Serving 515
"Seven," the number, in Revelation
  624; sevenfold repetition 624 foll.,
  comp. 411 a-b, 529 d
"Sheep-gate, the," an error 216
Singular number 418; referred to as pl.
  266

*This Index extends from 1886 to 2799. Before numbers with * supply 1,
e.g. [1]999*; before others, 2, e.g. [2]000.*

ENGLISH

"Six," the number 283 b; six days, mystically implied 647
Slave, the, does not "abide in the house" 263 e
Son of God 410, 798–9
Sower, Parable of the, "word" how used in 799 (iii)
"Speaketh of his own" 728
Speaking, vbs of, see "Saying"
Speech, direct or reported 926*, 189; speech confusable w. narrative or comment (see Preface, pp. vii–ix) 936*, 949*, 956–7*, 066, 128, 203, comp. 925*; speech assigned wrongly by Chrys. 734 d, 745 (see esp. 745 a), by Cyprian 737 c, by Aphraates 768, comp. 061; change of "him" to "me" in 695 c
Spelling, St Paul's 691; Augustus's 790; misspellings freq. in Mk 513 b
Spirit 315 foll., 407; different meanings of 976 a*; not given "from a measure" 714; "the Holy S." 488; "the S. of truth" 352
SS (see p. xxv) 926 a*, 942 a*, 944 a*, 977*, 990*, 079, 083, 186 b, 235 a, 329 (i) b, 448 a, 517 d, 632 a, b, c, 739 b, 756, 760, 769; its avoidance of parenthesis 631, 632 a, 639 a
Stand, "Jesus stood" 307 a foll., 703, 710
Stone (metaph.) 397; "a white s." 409; "the s. that the builders rejected" 622
Style, Johannine 891–3*, 112, 132, 134, 455; its abruptness 135; contrasts 140 a; rarely resembles that of Lk. 335 a; s. "Ambiguity," "Epistle," "Hebrew," "Speech"
Subject 417 foll.; collective or noun-group 417–8; neut. plur. 419–20; suspended 421–2; omitted in partitive clauses 041–2, 213–5; "they" non-pronominal 424–6; "we" non-pronominal 427–35; "[any]one" 379
Subjunctive aor. and pres. 893*, 511–35; deliberative 512, 766 (i); in final clauses 093 foll., 524–30, 687–9; in conditional clauses 513–5, 517–23; in temporal clauses 531–5; after the indef. relative 516; in strong negation 255
Suspensive sentences 122 foll., 175 foll.
Symbolism, s. Metaphor and Mysticism
Synonyms (on the meaning, see p. 645 n.) 630 h; juxtaposition of 570, 576–7, 584 a–c, s. *Joh. Voc.* p. 151

Tabernacles, the feast of 265 a
Talmud, the 196
Tautology, Philo on 588 d
Teacher, "thou art the t. of Israel" 966*
Temple, the, rebuilding of 021 foll.
Tense 893*, 436, 753, s. Contents, p. xxi—xxiii, also Aorist, Future etc.
They, non-pronominal 424; THEY 426
Third day, the 982*
This, "this is he" etc. 957 b*; "this [thing] is the Lord's doing" 396
Thomas, his confession of faith 049–51
Three Witnesses 588–9
Threefold repetition 612–23, comp. 411 c; thr. rep. of "remembering" 639; twofold or threefold rep. 608–11
Tiberias, the sea of 045
Time, completion of 021 foll.; duration of 013 b, comp. 678; interval of 331 c, 715; point of 013, 025, 331; simultaneousness of 531
Transliteration 216, 666, 671 a, 793
Transposition 915 (ii), (iii); s. Emphasis and Variation
Treasury, the 333
Two, "t. witnesses" 588; "t. or three firkins" 281–3
Twofold attestation 589; twofold meanings and events 641–9, comp. 172; twofold repetition: in the Baptist's teaching 601–2; in Christ's teaching 603–6; in narrative 607; twofold or threefold rep. 608–11

Understanding, or knowledge, moral 491 d

Variation in repetition or quotation 544 foll.; in sympathy w. meaning 565; miscellaneous 570 foll.
"Vernacular genitive, the" 558 foll., 776–84
Vernacular and literary Gk 781, 799 (ii)
Vocative 052–3; expr. by article 679 foll.
Voice, middle 536–7; passive 538–43; s. also 563 c, 689 c foll.

Walking 342; = "teaching" *ib.*
Water, connected with "life" 314; "rivers of w." 316 b
"We," meaning of 287; non-pronominal 427
"Which" and "who" in A.V. and R.V. 273 a
Wife (?) ellipsis of the word 217

This Index extends from 1886 *to* 2799. *Before numbers with* * *supply* 1, *e.g.* [1]999*; *before others*, 2, *e.g.* [2]000.

"Will of God, the," parall. to "the word of God" 799 (iii)
"With" = "in the sight of" or "in the house of" 355; ambig. 363, 799 (ii); "questioning w." 349
Witnesses, "two" and "three" 588; "three" 306
Witnessing 383–4
Wonder, in bad sense 338
Word, "the word," "the word of God," "my word" etc. 799 (iii)

Worshipping 019
"Would" = "was minded to" 471; "would not," how expr. 463; "would have liked" 472, 498

Year, the agricultural, how divided by the Jews 230 (iii); "forty and six years" an error 021–4

This Index extends from **1886** *to* **2799**. *Before numbers with* * *supply* **1**, *e.g.* **[1]999***; *before others,* **2**, *e.g.* **[2]000**.

JOHANNINE GRAMMAR

III. GREEK

[*This Index deals mainly with conjunctions, prepositions and pronouns. Nouns and verbs in it are regarded mainly in their grammatical and syntactical aspects and not so much with reference to their separate meanings—for which the reader is referred to Index III of "Johannine Vocabulary." If a word, e.g.* ἀγαπάω, *is occasionally mentioned in a non-grammatical aspect, it is because of a desire to supply some defect in "Johannine Vocabulary," e.g. the testimony of Origen to the difference between* ἀγαπάω *and* φιλέω (2584 c).]

Ἀ- privative expr. by οὐ 143, 248, 256
Ἀββά 679
ἀγαλλιάομαι: w. ἵνα 097, 688–9; -αθῆναι v. r. -ασθῆναι 655 a; active form of 689 i
ἀγαπάω: aor. 323, 515 b; aor. and perf. 443; perf. 476–7; ἡ ἀγάπη ἣν ἠγάπησάς με 014; Origen on ἀ. and φιλέω 584 c
ἀγάπη 581; rarely w. objective genitive 033 foll.; ἡ ἀ., in Jn, "the love of God revealed to men" 035
ἀγοράζω: ἀγοράσωμεν in Mk and Jn 428 a, 512, 745–6
ἀγρός: εἰς ἀγρόν 711 b
ἄγω: ἄγωμεν 428
ἀδελφός: τοῖς ἀ. μου 307 b
-αι interchanged w. -ε 428 b, 514 a, 658 e
αἷμα and αἵματα 268
αἰτέομαι, s. αἰτέω
αἰτέω: pres. and aor. subjunct. 516; ἀ. and αἰτέομαι 536; ἀ., αἰτέομαι, and ἐρωτάω 630 f foll.; προσεύχεσθε καὶ αἰτεῖσθε 536 a; αἰτήσασθε imper. or infin. 514 a

αἰτία, ἡ 295 b
αἰών: εἰς τὸν ἀ. 312; οὐ (or μή)...εἰς τὸν ἀ. 263 e–g
ἀκοαί = "ears" 709 a
ἀκούω: aor. and perf. 450–2; fut. act. 660 c–d; w. accus. and w. gen. 586
ἀληθεινός in Codex B 654
ἀλλά: = contrariety, "not this but that, or, something more" 055–7; = difference, "nevertheless" 058–9; in special passages 060–2; ἀλλ' ἵνα 063–4, 105–12, 387, in the Synoptists 111; ἀλλ' οὐχὶ πάντες 265 (i); οὐκ... ἀλλά 593; οὐ followed by καί instead of ἀλλά 598; οὔτε...ἀλλά in Papyri 683 a, b
ἀλλήλων: μετὰ ἀ. 349
ἄλλομαι 314–6
ἄλλος: ἄλλος ἐστιν 972*, 675 foll., 730; ἄλλος and δι' ἄλλον in Epict. 791 foll., 297 e; ἄλλα πολλά 335 a; ἄλλος and ἕτερος 675–7
ἀμὴν ἀμήν 611 a, b
ἄν: its omission 079, 213 a, 698; its position 566, before a pause[1] 739 c;

---

[1] To the instances of ἄν at the end of a sentence add Lucian *Hermotim.* § 24 (i. 762) ἴσως γὰρ ἂν αὐτὰ ἤδη ἀμφὶ τὰ προάστεια καὶ πρὸς ταῖς πύλαις ἦν ἄν.

*This Index extends from 1886 to 2799. Before numbers with * supply 1, e.g.* [1]999*; *before others,* 2, *e.g.* [2]000.

ὅστις ἄν, ὁ ἄν (or ἐάν) etc. 516; ὥστε ἄν...θέλω 697 c; ἄν and ἐάν interchanged 739; ἄν "if," only in Jn 739; s. also ἐάν
ἀνά 281-3
ἀναβαίνω 264 a, 265; with ἑορτή 264-5, 771; quoted as πορεύομαι 489 a
ἀνήρ: applied to Christ 371, 722 b, c; distinct from ἄνθρωπος 009, 571; θέλημα ἀνδρός 269; ἰδοὺ ἀνήρ in Zech. 662 a
ἄνθρωπος 386 b; emphatic 412 a; how used in Jn 934*; ὁ ἄ. 959-61*; ὁ ἄ. in Epict. 960 c*; ἄ. contrasted w. λόγος 277, distinct from ἀνήρ 009, 571; οὐκ ἄ. or ἄ. οὐ in LXX 586 d
ἀνίστημι in repetition 609 a
ἀντί 284-7
ἀντλέω 281 foll.
ἄνωθεν 903-8*, 403, 573, 734 d
ἀπάρτι, s. ἄρτι
ἀπέρχομαι: w. ἐν 334 d; ἀπελήλυθεν and ἀπῆλθεν 753 a foll.
ἀπό: transposed 288; ambig. 215 b, 291; ἀπό and ἐκ meaning "[some] of" 213-5, denoting domicile and birthplace 289-93, interchanged in LXX 293 a, w. λαλέω 293 b, 586 a; ἀπό, ἐκ, and παρά, w. ἐξέρχομαι 326-8
ἀποθνήσκω: οὐκ ἀποθνήσκει 486; ὁ ἀποθνήσκων "he that is under sentence of death" 530; ἵνα μὴ ἀποθνήσκῃ v.r. for ἀποθάνῃ 530
ἀποκρίνομαι: ἀποκριθεὶς 271; ἀπεκρίνατο and ἀπεκρίθη 537; ἀπεκρίθη ('Ιησ.) καὶ εἶπεν 611 a-c; ἀπεκρίθη w. 'Ιησ. (not w. ὁ 'Ιησ.) 968*
ἀπολύω: κατὰ δὲ ἑορτὴν ἀπέλυεν 464 b
ἀποστέλλω: aor. and perf. 440, 453; ἀπεσταλμένος παρὰ θεοῦ contrasted w. ἦν πρὸς τὸν θεόν 277; ά. and ἐξαποστέλλω 753 b

ἀποτινάσσω: ἀποτινάσσετε and ἐκτινάξατε 437 a
ἀριθμός: τὸν ά., adv. accus. 009
ἄρτι and νῦν 915 (i)-(vi)*, 246
ἄρτος: ὁ ἄ. ὁ καταβαίνων and ὁ ἄ. ὁ καταβάς 504; ὁ ἄ. οὗτος and οὗτος ὁ ἄ. 553 c
ἀρχή: τὴν ἀρχὴν ὅτι καὶ λαλῶ ὑμῖν 154-6; ἀ. τῶν σημείων 386 (i); ἐξ ἀ. and ἀπ' ά. 254 a
ἀσθενέω: ἀσθενούντων, ambig. 930*
ἀστραπή 532 c
αὕτη s. οὗτος
αὐτός 374-80, meaning "God" 731, change from to ἐκεῖνος 302; αὐτοῦ etc. possessive, emphatic and non-emphatic 558, om. or rep. 395; αὐτοῦ ambig. 378-9; αὐτόν ins. and om. 537 (i) a; αὐτὸς ὁ 931 a*; αὐτὸς μόνος and μόνος αὐτός 724-6; αὐτὸς περὶ ἑαυτοῦ 723; ἐγώ εἰμι αὐτός 220, 221 a, 224, 699—700; δι' αὐτοῦ ambig. 302, 595 a; αὐτοί ἐσμεν "we are by ourselves" 699; καὶ αὐτοὶ γάρ emph. 692; αὐτός v. τ. αὐτό 727; αὐτοὺς [ὁ] 'Ιησοῦς, why a doubtful reading 656 c

Βαΐα: τὰ β. τῶν φοινίκων 047
βαπτίζω: w. εἰς 706 a
βασιλεία: εἰσελθεῖν εἰς, or ἰδεῖν, τὴν β. τοῦ θεοῦ 573
βασιλεύς: with and without article 966*, 669; σὺ λέγεις ὅτι β. εἰμί 245 a; s. also 798-9
βασιλικός: ἐκ τῶν βασιλικῶν 215 b
βαστάζω: aor. and pres. infin. 497
Βηθανία: ἀπὸ B. 290
Βηθλεέμ: ἀπὸ B. 289
βῆμα 537 (ii) b
βλέπω: hist. pres. 482; βλέπετε, initial, imperat. 237 [1]

---

[1] In 2237 it was said that "βλέπετε would naturally be imperative." In N.T., βλέπετε—except with relative or negative—is almost always (abt 20) initial *and*, when initial, alw. imperative (1 Cor. i. 26 being no exception). In *Poet. Scen.* βλέπετε is only in Eurip. *Cyc.* 211 (imperat.). Initial ὁρᾶτε in *Poet. Scen.*, though possibly interrog., prob. always means "See!"—Aesch. *Prom.* 119 "See [me outraged because of my love for mankind]!," *Ag.* 1217 "See [these spectres]!," Soph. *El.* 1228-30 "See [Orestes restored to life]!" to which the Chorus replies "We do see," *Oed. Col.* 871—2 "See [these insults]!" to which Oedipus replies, "They do see," *Ant.* 806 "See [me led away to death]!," Eurip. *Fragm. Alcm.* 11 "See [the tyrant in exile]!" In Aristoph., too, ὁρᾶτε initial, or after a pause, is almost alw. imperative, or may be so taken. In N.T., ὁρᾶτε is alw. imperat. exc. perh. in Jas ii. 24 ὁρᾶτε ὅτι (after βλέπεις ὅτι) R.V. "ye see that"; and, even there—in view of Epictet. iii. 13.9 ὁρᾶτε γὰρ ὅτι, "videte enim" and the frequency

This Index extends from 1886 *to* 2799. *Before numbers with* * *supply* 1, *e.g.* [1]999*; *before others*, 2, *e.g.* [2]000.

GREEK

Γαζοφυλάκιον : ἐν τῷ γ. and κατέναντι τοῦ γ. 333-4
γάρ: Synoptic and Johannine use 065-6 ; sometimes an indication of evangelistic origin 066 b; in special passages 067-8, 683 ; καὶ γάρ 167, comp. 692 ; οὐ γάρ, not interrogative in Jn 683 ; various ellipses before 683 a
γεμίζω : w. ἐκ 329 (i)
γέμω : w. ἐκ 329 a
γεννάομαι 904-8*, 573
γεύομαι : w. accus. 016-18 ; γ. θανάτου 576
γῆ : εἰς τὴν Ἰουδαίαν γῆν 670 b ; γῆ Ἰούδα 670 b
γίνομαι : ἐγένετο contrasted w. ἦν 277, 506-7 ; γέγονα 396 b, 478 b ; γέγονεν ἵνα 478 a ; γέγονα and ἐγενόμην 440 ; γέγονας 758 ; γενάμεναι 472 b
γινώσκω : aor. and perf. indic. 448, 511 a ; aor. and pres. subjunct. 511 ; ἔγνων 328, 511 a, 582 ; ἔγνων = " I knew [at once]" 443 c ; γινώσκετε ambig. 243, 491, 760 ; γινώσκετε combined w. ἑωράκατε 491 ; γ. and οἶδα 491, 757 d, 763 ; γνῶθι σαυτόν and τὸ ἑαυτὸν γινώσκειν 763
γνωρίζω : aor. 447
Γολγοθά 738
γράμμα : πηλίκοις γράμμασιν 691 d-e, 785-90
γράφω : ἐπ' αὐτῷ γεγραμμένα 339 ; δ γέγραφα γέγραφα 473 ; ἔγραψα in letters 691 a foll., 785-90
γυνή : w. article 948 a * ; ? ellipsis of γ. or θυγάτηρ 217

Δέ : consecutive or adversative 069-73 ; third word, or later, in its clause 074-6 ; denoting antithesis 209 ; introducing parenthesis 633 b ; in doubtful connexion 636 ; a δέ-clause before an οὖν-clause 634 ; w. ἔλεγεν 468 ; w. pluperf. 480 ; καὶ...δέ 076 ; μέν...δέ 077 ; μέν ends Thucyd. iii. 116 foll. by δέ ib. iv. 1 638 ; s. also 635 (i) a
δεῖ : ἔδει 272 a, 635 (i) a ; δει written δι, confusable with δι' (prep.) 428 c
δεκάς 283 c

διά : w. accus. of pers. 294—300, 705 : w. gen. of pers. 301-4 ; w. gen. of time 331 c foll., 715 ; δι' ὅν...καὶ δι' οὗ 294 ; οὐ διὰ τοῦ θεοῦ ἀλλὰ παρ' αὐτοῦ 296 a ; διὰ τί ; 231 c ; διὰ τοῦτο 387 foll. ; (?) δι' ὑμᾶς 428 c ; διὰ σοῦ for διὰ σέ 729 a
διασπορά : ἡ δ. τῶν Ἑλλήνων 046
διδάσκαλος : w. article 966 *, 195, ? vocatively used 680
δίδωμι : aor. and perf. 454-5 ; imperf. 465 b ; pres. and perf. in LXX 444; δ δέδωκάς μοι 422 ; πᾶν δ δέδωκας 740-4 ; ἔδωκεν, v. r. for δέδωκεν 687 c ; late forms of, e.g. ἔδωσα 690 ; δός, v. r. in ch. xvii. 740
διώκω : ὁ διώκων " the prosecutor " 537
δοκέω : aor. and imperf. 464 a ; μὴ δοκεῖτε 235 a ; τί δοκεῖ ὑμῖν and τί δοκεῖτε 766 (i) a
δοξάζω : aor. 441 ; various meanings of ἐδοξάσθη 446
δοῦλος 263 g, 584 b
δραχμαί om., e.g. ἀραβῶνα (δ.) η "eight [drachmae] as earnest money " 729
δύναμαι : w. aor. and pres. infin. 496, 767 ; δύναται ἁρπάζειν and ἁρπάσει 767; δ. ins. by LXX = Heb. interrog. 767
δύο 281-3

Ε, Θ, Ο and C interchanged in B 650-2
-ε interchanged w. -αι 428 b, 658 e
ἐάν or ἄν : w. aor. and pres. subjunct. 511, 513-5 ; w. indic. in 1 Jn 515 (i), comp. 771 ; ἐὰν μή 521-3, w. pres. subjunct. in connexion w. the hour of trial 523 a ; ἐάν τις 580 ; ἐάν and τις separated 552 c; καὶ ἐάν 158-9 ; ἄν τινων κρατῆτε 517-20 ; ἐὰν οὖν θεωρῆτε 210-12 ; ὅστις ἐάν ambig. 414-6 ; ὅστις ἄν, ὃ ἄν (or ἐάν) etc. 516, 660 b ; ἄν and ἐάν interchanged 739 ; ἐάν for ἄν in Papyri 416 a
ἑαυτοῦ : ἐν ἑαυτῷ, -οῖς, how used in Jn 039 ; πρὸς ἑαυτούς 366 c ; αὐτὸς περὶ ἑαυτοῦ 723
ἐγγύς 909 *
ἐγείρω : προφήτης οὐκ ἐγείρεται 492

---

of ὅρα ὅτι in Epictet., as well as i. 3. 9 ὁρᾶτε οὖν καὶ προσέχετε—the meaning may be "see [and note] that." These facts bear on 2762 a, which rendered Il. i. 120 λεύσσετε imperatively, though rendered in Monro's *Hom. Gramm.* p. 190 "ye see." The scholiast says, "ὁρᾶτε, βλέπετε," perh. intending not only to explain the poetic λεύσσετε by a prose word, but also to shew that it was imperative, like initial ὁρᾶτε and βλέπετε.

*This Index extends from 1886 to 2799. Before numbers with * supply 1, e.g. [1]999* ; before others, 2, e.g. [2]000.*

ἐγώ 401 ; ἐγώ εἰμι 220 foll. ; ἐγώ εἰμι αὐτός 221 a, 224, 699 foll. ; ὅπου ὑπάγω and ὅπου ἐγὼ ὑπάγω 578 ; λέγω om. after ἐγώ 658 b, 660 ; ἐμοῦ, not in N.T. without (1) prepos. (2) antith. (3) v.r. or parall. 566 c ; μου emph. and non-emph. 559, 776 foll. ; μου, v.r. for μοι 563 ; μου and σου confused 768 ; με ταῦτα for μετὰ ταῦτα 659 ; s. also ἡμεῖς
ἐθέλω, s. θέλω
εἰ : written ι 659 e, comp. 428 c, 515 (i) e, 650 a, 654 b, 793 e ; corresponding to ἄν, in words of the Lord 078-9 ; εἰ w. fut. 514 (i) a, w. optat. 514 (i) b ; εἰ οὐ 256 ; εἰ δὲ μή 080-6, in LXX foll. imperat. 080
εἶδον : ἰδεῖν " to experience " 576 e ; ἰδεῖν τὴν βασιλείαν and εἰσελθεῖν εἰς τὴν β. 573 ; τεθέαμαι...ἐφ' ὃν ἂν ἴδῃς...ἑώρακα 572 ; ιδη and ειδη confused 515 (i) e, 798 e[1].
εἶδος θεοῦ 765 a
εἰμί : ἐγώ εἰμι 220 foll. ; ἐγώ εἰμι αὐτός 224, 699—700 ; ὅπου εἰμί (v.r. εἶμι) ἐγώ and ὅπου ἐγὼ ὑπάγω 190 a, 487 a ; πόθεν εἶ σύ 733-7 ; ellipsis of ἐστί 229-30 (i) ; ἐστί w. particip. 971-81*; εἰσὶν οἵ 971 c*; ἦν, contrasted w. ἐγένετο 277, 596-7 ; ἦν w. pres. particip. 277 ; ὅτι ἐστίν and ὅτι ἦν after εἶδον 466 (i) ; ὁ ὤν in various phrases 938*, 964*, 275, 308, 358, 711 foll. ; ὁ...οὐκ ὤν 704 ; ὤν referring to the past 274 ; ἵνα ὦσιν, seven times repeated in the Last Prayer 529 a ; forms of εἰμί emphasized 972*, 979 a-d*, 553 b, 555 a, 579 ; repeated for emphasis 606[2], ἐὰν σὺ ᾖσθα 515 (i) ; ἧς and ἦσθα 515 (i) b ; Phrynichus on the spelling of ης 772-5 ; ἔσσι 711
εἶμι : not used in N.T. 171 d, v.r. for εἰμί 190 a, 487 a ; εἰς Κόπτον εἶμι 711 ;
(?) εἶσι spelt εσσι 711
εἶπον 456 ; ὃν εἶπον v.r. ὁ εἰπών 925 a*,

507 a ; εἶπε, differently used by Lk. and Jn 456 a ; εἶπεν and ἔλεγεν 469 ; εἰρήκει 481 ; τί εἴπω ; τί σ' εἴπω ; 512 b ; εἰπόν and εἰπέ 658 c ; εἶπον ἂν ὑμῖν ὅτι 083-6, 186 ; εἶπον with and without ὅτι 189 foll. ; εἴρηχεν, in Pap., = εἶπεν 683 a, b
εἰρήνη : ἑ. τὴν ἐμήν 609 b
εἰς : without verb of motion 305-9, 706 foll. ; "to" or "into" 310-11 ; εἰς ζωὴν αἰώνιον 312-6 ; ὄψονται εἰς 317-8 ; εἰς τέλος 319-23 ; περιπατέω εἰς 342 h ; πιστεύω εἰς 506 (and s. πιστεύω) ; ὁ ὢν εἰς τὸν κόλπον 308-9, 706, 711 foll. ; εἰς and ἐπί 310, 316 b ; ἔστη εἰς v.r. ἐπί 307 a ; εἰς τό in St Paul's Epistles 689 j ; λέγω εἰς implying publicity 709 εἰς : used with dative 118 b ; εἰς καθ' εἷς 343 ; εἷς [ἐκ] 586 a ; ἐν "one" in juxtaposition with ἐν "in" 118 b ; οὐδὲ ἐν or οὐδὲν 660
εἰσέρχομαι : εἰσελθοῦσαι 311 ; ἑ. εἰς, or ἰδεῖν, τὴν βασιλείαν τοῦ θεοῦ 573
εἶτα, see below[3]
εἰώθα : εἰώθει parall. to imperf. 464 b
ἐκ : "from" or "(some) of" 042, 213-5 ; "native of" (but ἀπό "resident in") 289-93 ; ἐκ and ἀπό in LXX 293 a ; ἐκ and ἀπό w. λαλέω 293 b, 583 a ; ἐκ w. ἐξέρχομαι 326-8, w. πληρόω 329, w. γεμίζω 329 (i), w. σώζω and τηρέω 325 ; ἐξ ἡμῶν 110 a-b, 263 c foll. ; ἐκ μέτρου 324, 714
ἐκεῖ ἡ conf. w. ἐκείνη 687 d
ἐκεῖνος 381-5, 729 ; emph., change to from αὐτός 302 ; contemptuous 732 ; meaning "HE" 132 b, 382, 731 ; ἐκείνη conf, w. ἐκεῖ ἡ 687 d ; κἀκεῖνος 150-1
ἐκκεντέω 317 h
ἐκλέγομαι : aor. 441, and see esp. 441 b foll.
ἐκλεκτός : v.r. for υἱός 386 a
ἐκμάσσω : ἡ ἐκμάξασα 276
ἔκμετρος 324 d

---

[1] For ἴδε, see Joh. Voc., where it should have been added that ἴδε, foll. by nom. without verb, is pec. to Mk and Jn.
[2] Comp. Epict. i. 14. 13—14 μέμνησθε μηδέποτε λέγειν ὅτι μόνοι ἐστέ· οὐ γὰρ ἐστέ. ἀλλ' ὁ θεὸς ἔνδον ἐστί, καὶ ὁ ὑμέτερος Δαίμων ἐστί.
[3] εἶτα occurs Mk (2), Mt. (0), Lk. (1), Jn (3), comp. Mk iv. 28 εἶτεν (bis). In canon. LXX, εἶτα occurs only in Job (12, with v.r.), Prov. (2). It is one of several points in common between the style of Job and Mk. In N.T. (outside Gospels) it is only in 1 Cor. xv. 5 (txt), 7 (txt), 24, 1 Tim. ii. 13, iii. 10, Heb. xii. 9, Jas i. 15.

This Index extends from 1886 to 2799. Before numbers with * supply 1, e.g. [1]999*; before others, 2, e.g. [2]000.

GREEK

ἐκνεύω : ἐξένευσεν, v.r. ἔνευσεν 541
ἐκτινάσσω : ἀποτινάσσετε and ἐκτινάξατε 437 a
ελαιων : how accented 673
Ἕλληνες : ἡ διασπορὰ τῶν Ἑ. 046
ἐλπίζω : imperf. 472 b, 474 ; ἠλπίζαμεν 472 b ; perf. 442, 474
ἐμβλέπω : twofold use of ἐμβλέψας 649
ἐμός : ὁ ἐμός...and ὁ...ὁ ἐμός 987-9* ; ὁ ἐμός, ἡ ἐμή etc. emphatic 559, 581
ἔμπροσθεν 896*, 330
ἐν : temporal 025-6, 331, om. by B 661, ins. and om. before ἡμέρᾳ, ἑορτῇ, and σαββάτῳ 715 b–d ; instrumental and quasi-instrumental 332 ; = "into" 334 c, d ; ἐν τούτῳ 332, 392 ; ἐν τῷ γαζοφυλακίῳ 333-4
ἕνεκα 300
ἐντέλλομαι 742 a
ἐντολὴ καινὴ...b 412
ἐνώπιον 335
ἓξ 281-3
ἐξεραυνάω 439 (i) a
ἐξέρχομαι 263 c foll., w. ἀπό, ἐκ, and παρά 326-8 ; aor. 457 ; ἐξῆλθον ambig. 110 a–b
ἐξουσία 798-9
ἑορτή : w. article 951* ; ἀναβαίνω εἰς ἑ. 264-5 ; κατὰ δὲ ἑορτήν 464 c ; ἐν ins. and om. before 715 d, comp. 771
ἐπαίρω τοὺς ὀφθαλμούς 616-7
ἐπεί and ἐπειδή 087-8
ἐπερωτάω and ἐρωτάω 577
ἐπί : w. accus. 336, 342 d, i ; w. dat. 337-9 ; w. gen. 340-7 ; ἐπί and εἰς 307 a, 310, 316 b ; ἐπὶ τούτῳ 338 ; ἐπὶ τὴν θάλασσαν and ἐπὶ τῆς θαλάσσης 340-6 ; ἔστη ἐπί 336 ; ἐπ' αὐτῷ γεγραμμένα 339 ; ἐπιγραφὴ ἐπ' αὐτῷ 339 ; ἐπὶ τοῦ σταυροῦ 347
ἐπιβάλλω χεῖρας 575 a
ἐπιβλέπω : ἐπιβλέψονται πρός με 317 c
ἐπιγινώσκω 511 a
ἐπιγραφὴ ἐπ' αὐτῷ 339
ἐπιεικῶς 233 a
ἐπικαθίζω : ἐπεκάθισεν v.r. ἐκάθισεν 756 a
ἐπιτίθεμαι : how used by Origen 412 a
ἐραυνάω : of "searching" the Scriptures 439 (i) ; ἐραυνᾶτε ambig. ib.
ἐργάζομαι 226 b ; ἐργάζεσθαι v.r. -θε 428 b
ἔρχομαι : aor. and perf. 326, 457 ; aor. and pres. 490 ; hist. pres. 482 ; ἤρχοντο 465 ; ἦλθαν 472 b ; ἦλθεν and ἤθελον 342 d, 346, 717 e ; ἐρχόμενος and ὁ ἐρχόμενος 940*, 277, 553 d ; ὁ ὀπίσω μου ἐρχόμενος 507 ; ἐρχόμενον (neut. or masc.) εἰς τὸν κόσμον ambig. 277,

508 ; ἕως ἔρχομαι 089 ; ἔρχεται...καί ἐλήλυθεν 604 a, 625 e ; ἔρχεται...καί νῦν ἐστίν 799 (i) ; s. also εἰς 310-11
ἐρωτάω 498, 630 ; ἐ., αἰτέομαι, and αἰτέω 630 f–h ; ἐ. and ἐπερωτάω 577 ; ἐ. in Alexandrian Gk 630 d ; (?) ερωτα υπερ ημων in Christian tombstone 630 i
ἑταῖροι in Aquila = φιλοῦντες in LXX 584 c
ἕτερος : ἕτερος and ἄλλος 675-7 ; πολλὰ... καὶ ἕτερα 335 a
ἔτι : ἔ. μικρόν 230 (i) ; ἔ. τετράμηνός ἐστιν 230 (ii) foll.
ἔτος : ἔτεσιν, dat. pl. of duration, when used 021
εὐθέως, εὐθύ, and εὐθύς 910-15*
εὑρίσκω : hist. pres. 482 ; εὑρών om. in xii. 14 756
εὐχαριστέω 614 c
ἐφάλλομαι 315
ἔχω : ἔχεις τι ; 235 b foll.
ἕως (conj.) 089 ; (?) ὡς for ἕως 201, 696 ; ἕως ἔρχομαι 089

Ζάω : w. διά and accus. of pers. 297, 705 ; w. πρός and accus. of pers. 366 ; σοὶ ζῶ, ἤτοι διὰ σέ 297 c
ζητέω 375 a, 398 ; w. infin. 575, 727 ; first use of in LXX 649 b ; forms of 748
ζήτησις 349, 350 a
ζωή : εἰς ζωὴν αἰώνιον 312-6

Ἤ 090-1 ; after negative (οὐ...καί and οὐ...ἤ) 549 a, 759 ; omitted 628 a
ἡ τοῦ 'Α.? the [wife, or, daughter] of A. 217
ἡμεῖς : perh. applied to Christ 428 b ; how used in 1 Jn 399 c ; ἡ. πάντες 287 ; ἡμῶν and ὑμῶν in v.r. 428 c
ἡμέρα : τρίτη ἡμέρα, διὰ τριῶν ἡμερῶν, ἐν τρισὶν ἡμέραις etc. 331 ; καθ' ἡμέραν, inserted by Lk. 515 ; ἐν ins. and om. before 715 b–d
ἤπερ 092, 685
Ἡρώδης 737 a

Θ, ε, ο and c interchanged in B 650-2
θάλασσα : ἐπὶ τὴν θ., ἐπὶ τῆς θ., and παρὰ τὴν θ. 340-6, 354, and see specially 341 and 344
θάνατος : w. γεύομαι, θεωρέω, and ἰδεῖν 576
θᾶσσον 918 a *
θεάομαι : twice applied to Christ 617 a ; τεθεάμεθα 473 ; τεθέαμαι...ἐφ' ὃν ἂν ἴδῃς...ἑώρακα 572

This Index extends from 1886 to 2799. Before numbers with * supply 1, e.g. [1]999* ; before others, 2, e.g. [2]000.

θέλημα ἀνδρός and θ. σαρκός 269 ; θ. τ. θεοῦ parall. to λόγος τ. θεοῦ 799 (iii)
θέλω: ἤθελεν of unfulfilled desire 716–7 ; (?) ἤθελεν, ἤθελον and ἤλθεν 342 d, 346, 716–7 ; ἤθελεν and ἠθέλησεν 471–2, 716–7 ; w. accus. and infin. 495 ; ἔθελες 717 b
θεός: the distinction between θεός and ὁ θεός 594 a ; παρὰ θεῷ 027, 355 ; ὁ ὢν παρὰ [τοῦ] θεοῦ 358 ; εἶδος θεοῦ 765 a
θεωρέω 210–12, 318, 576, 739 b ; θεωρεῖτε ambig. 439 (ii)
θυγάτηρ : (?) ellipsis of θ. in the phrase ἡ τοῦ Ἀ. 217

Ι: sometimes written ΕΙ, and ει written ι 659 e, comp. 428 c, 515 (i) e, 650 a, 654 b, 798 e
ἰδεῖν, ἰδών etc., s. εἶδον
ἰδίαν : κατ᾿ ἰδίαν 348
ἴδιος : τὸν ἀδελφὸν τὸν ἴδιον 985–6* ; ἐκ τῶν ἰδίων 378, 728 ; οἱ ἴδιοι 570 a–b
ἰδού 246
Ἱεροσόλυμα w. article 670
Ἰησοῦς : with and without article 968* ; in B written ΙΣ, liable to confusion 661 c ; Ἰησοῦν (ΙΝ) and Κύριον (ΚΝ) confused 662 b ; αὐτοῖς [ὁ] Ἰησοῦς, why a doubtful reading 656 c
ἱμάτιον : sing. and pl. 270 ; in ellipsis 216 b
ἵνα : freq. in Jn 686 ; expresses or implies purpose 093–6 ; special passages 097—103 ; ἵνα and subjunct. compared w. infin. 104, 495 ; ἵνα w. indic. 114, 690 ; w. aor. and pres. subjunct. 511, 524–30 ; omission of principal vb before ἵνα 105–12 ; dependent on vb implied in question 113 ; its connexion 115 ; ἵνα...ἵνα 116–21 ; ἀλλ᾿ ἵνα 063–4, 105–12 ; ἠγαλλιάσατο ἵνα ἴδῃ 097, 100, 688–9 ; ἵνα τί ; not used in Jn 231 c ; οὕτως... ἵνα 697 ; ἵνα εἰδῇς "to tell you the plain truth" 729 a ; ἔρχεται ὥρα...ἵνα 799 (i)
Ἰουδαῖος : οἱ Ἰουδαῖοι 941* foll. ; πολλοὶ ἐκ τῶν Ἰ. 941–2* ; εἰς τὴν Ἰουδαίαν γῆν 670 b
ἵστημι : ἔστη εἰς (v.r. ἐπί) 307 a ; στῆναι εἰς τὸ μέσον 710 ; ἑστῶτα, of God 307 d
ἰσχυρότερός μου in Synoptists 667, 799 a
ΙΧΘΥΣ 703
Ἰωάνης with and without article 968 c*
Ἰωσήφ with and without article 970*

Κἀγώ : in crasis 150 ; after καθώς 123–7
καθαρός in Jn, and καθάριος in Epictet. connected with ὁ λόγος 799 (iii)
κάθημαι : forms of 751 ; καθημένου εἰς 707
καθίζω : trans. and intrans. use 537 (i)–(ii) ; ἐκάθισεν εἰς 707 ; ἐκάθισεν v.r. ἐπεκάθισεν 756 a ; τὸ ὄνον (sic) καθίσαι 756 a
καθώς : suspensive 122, followed by κἀγώ or καί in apodosis 123–7 ; supplementary 128–32 ; ἵνα...καθώς... ἵνα 117–8
καί : in narrative (Hebraic) 133–4 ; connecting affirmation and negation 135 ; meaning "and yet," "but," 136–45, 265 (i) b, 439 (iii) ; parall. to μέντοι 137 ; exclamatory 146 ; meaning "[indeed] and" 157 ; meaning "also" 147, 152–6 ; in apodosis 123–7, 148 ; in crasis 150 ; omitted between two adjectives 168 ; καὶ ὑμεῖς 149 ; κἀγώ 123–7 ; κἀκεῖνος 151, 383 ; κἄν 160 ; καὶ γάρ 167 (comp. 692) ; καὶ ἐάν 158–9 ; καὶ νῦν, varies in meaning 915 (iii) ; καί...δέ 076 ; καί...καί 161–6 ; οὐ...καί instead of οὐ...ἀλλά 598 ; τὴν ἀρχὴν ὅτι καὶ λαλῶ ὑμῖν 154–6 ; written ΚΕ and confused with ΚΕ i.e. κύριε 657 d ; οὐ...καί and οὐ...ἤ 549 e, 759 ; καί and ἤ interchanged 759 a foll.
καινός : ἐντολὴν καινήν 894 b* ; ἐντολὴν καινήν...ὅ 412
καιόμενος 275 b
κἀκεῖνος 151, 383
καλέω and λέγω 468 b ; καλέω foll. by accus. and voc. 680 b
καλῶς ποιήσεις 729 a
κἄν 160
κατά 348 ; εἰς καθ᾿ εἷς 348 ; κατ᾿ ἰδίαν 348 ; κατὰ δὲ ἑορτήν 464 c
κατάγνυμι : ἵνα κατεαγῶσιν αὐτῶν τὰ σκέλη 267, 419
κατάθεσις : inscr. on Christian tombstone 630 i
καταλαμβάνω 596
κατευθύνω 033 b
Κεδρών : how accented 671–4
κλάδος 047
κλάσματα 329 (i)
κλίνω κεφαλήν 644 (i), 713
κοιμάομαι : double meaning of 586 c
κόκκος : w. article 948*
κόλπος : ὁ ὢν εἰς τὸν κ. τοῦ πατρός 308, 706 foll.

This Index extends from **1886** *to* **2799**. *Before numbers with* * *supply* **1**, *e.g.* [1]999* ; *before others,* **2**, *e.g.* [2]000.

GREEK

κομίζομαι 230 (i) a
κόπτω : κόψονται 317 c foll., v.r. ὄψονται 317 d
Κόρινθος : πλοῦς εἰς Κ.¹ 263
κόφινος 329 (i)
κόσμος 508 c ; ὁ κ. οὗτος and οὗτος ὁ κ. 553 c ; in connexion with χωρεῖν 414 b ; ἐρχόμενον εἰς τὸν κ. 508
κράβαττος 206 b
κράζω : thrice applied to Christ 618 ; κέκραγε 479
Κρανίου Τόπον ὁ λέγεται...Γολγοθά 738
κρατέω : how used in the Gospels 517 a foll. ; ἄν τινων κρατῆτε 517-20
κρίμα or κρίσις 799 f
κρίνω : κέκρικα, how used 473 ; κέκριται 695 ; κρίνει, unaccented, fut. or pres. 960 a*
κρύπτω : the meaning of ἐκρύβη as applied to Jesus 538-43, 724
κτίζω : ἐκτίσθη and ἔκτισται 440 ; forms of 747
κύριος : ὁ κύριός μου 049, 679 foll. ; παρὰ κυρίου 356 ; κύριε 680 foll., ins. or om. 565 a ; written κε and confusable w. καί (κε) 657 d ; κύριον (κν) confused w. Ἰησοῦν (ιν) 662 b ; used by Epict. in a bad sense 799 d
κώμη 746 a

Δαλέω and λαλιά 251 ; λαλέω w. ἐκ and ἀπό 293 b, 586 a ; ἐκ τῶν ἰδίων λαλεῖ 728 ; ταῦτα λελάληκα ὑμῖν, seven times repeated 625
λαμβάνω : ἔλαβον and παρέλαβον 570 ; λήμψεται and λαμβάνει 488, 583
λαοί (pl.) "peoples," used of the Jews 317 h
λέγω : imperf. 467-70 ; ἔλεγεν and εἶπεν 469 ; λέγω and καλέω 468 b ; σὺ λέγεις and ὑμεῖς λέγετε 234 b, 245 ; ὅταν λέγωσιν 531 ; λέγω om. after ἐγώ 658 b, 660
λίθος 396-7
λόγος : distinct from λαλιά 251 ; ὁ λόγος ἦν foll. by ἐγένετο ἄνθρωπος 277 ; ὁ λόγος in Christ's words (1) in the Synoptists and (2) in Jn 799 (iii) (1) and (2) ; ὁ λόγος μου, τ. θεοῦ, ὁ σός etc. in Jn 799 (iii) 2 ; λόγοι (pl.), in Christ's words, only once in Jn 580

λούω : w. εἰς 305 a
λύχνος : w. article 948 b* ; ὁ λ. ὁ καιόμενος 275 b

Μαθητής 545 c
μακάριος : μακάριοί ἐστε ὅταν 499 b
μᾶλλον 733 a, w. ἤ and w. ἤπερ 092
Μάρθα : τὰς περὶ Μάρθαν, v.r. for Μάρθαν 990*, 360
Μαρία and Μαριάμ 586 b
μαρτυρέω : perf. 473 ; μαρτυρεῖς σαυτῷ 514 (i) e ; ἄλλος...ὁ μαρτυρῶν 730
μαρτυρία 383
μάχαιρα : ἐν μαχαίρῃ 332 a
μέν 169-70 ; μὲν...δέ 077, in Mt.-Lk., where not in Mk-Jn 998* ; μέν ends Thucyd. iii. 116 foll. by δέ ib. iv. 1 638 ; μὲν οὖν 335 a
μέντοι 170, parall. w. καί 137
μένω 263 e-f, 312, 313 a ; aor. and imperf. 458 ; ἔμεινα 458 ; μένετε ambig. 915 (iii) * b ; μένετε and μείνατε 437 a-c ; μένει and μενεῖ 762 a ; ἐὰν μὴ μένητε and ἐὰν μείνητε 523 ; μ. μετά 352
μετά : w. accus. 349 ; w. gen. 349-53 ; μ. τοῦτο and μ. ταῦτα 349 a, 394 ; μ. Ἰουδαίου 349-50 ; οἱ μ. αὐτοῦ ὄντες 351 ; μένω μ. 352 ; μετά τινος compared w. παρά τινι 352-3, and σύν τινι 799 (ii)
μεσονύκτιον 678
μέσος : στῆναι εἰς τὸ μέσον and στῆναι ἐν μέσῳ 710
μετανοέω : pres. and aor. subjunct. 521-2
μεταξύ 668
μετρητής 281-3
μέτρον, μέτρῳ, ἐν μέτρῳ, ἐκ μέτρου 324, 714
μή (interrog.) 235 ; μή τι or μήτι 701-2
μή (neg.) : encroaches on οὐ 253-4 ; implies imperat. 208-9 ; w. particip. 499 b ; w. πᾶς 260 foll. ; ὅτι μή 187, 695 ; οὐ μή 255
μικρόν : ἔτι μικρόν 230 (i) foll.
μισέω : aor. and perf. 443, 475
μισθός 287 b
μονογενής 938*, 964*, 308
μόνον (adv.) 664 b
μόνος : applied to God 895*, 664, comp. 168 ; μόνους inserted paraphrastically

---

¹ Lucian *Hermotim*. § 27 foll. (i. 767) takes Corinth as the ideal city to which all the seekers of truth are journeying.

This Index extends from **1886** to **2799**. Before numbers with * supply 1, e.g. [1]999* ; before others, 2, e.g. [2]000.

762 b; αὐτὸς μόνος and μόνος αὐτός
375, 724-6

N dropped or inserted, ἐκεῖH confused
w. ἐκεῖH 687 d
Ναζαρέτ : τὸν ἀπὸ N. 239
νῦν and ἄρτι 915 (i)–(vi) *, 246; καὶ νῦν
varies in meaning 915 (iii) * ; καὶ τὰ
νῦν 915 (i) c *

O, ε, θ, and c interchanged in B 650-2
ο and ω interchanged in MSS. 928 a *,
114, 691
ὁ and ὅν, v.r. 925 * foll.
ὁ, ἡ, τό : see Index II "Article"
ὁ, δέ 684
οἶδα : οἶδα and γινώσκω 491, 757 d, 763;
οἴδαμεν "we know" (?) οἶδα μέν
429-35; καὶ ἐκεῖνος οἶδεν 384 b, 731;
ἐὰν οἴδαμεν 515 (i) ; ἵνα εἰδῇς "to tell
you the plain truth" 729 a; ειδη and
ιδη confused 515 (i) e, 798 e
οἰκία, οἶκος : Mark's use of εἰς οἶκον or
εἰς τὴν οἰκίαν 711 a
ὅλος and ὄχλος 753 e
ὄνομα : ἐν τῷ ὀ. σου ᾧ δέδωκάς μοι 408
(comp. 740-4); ΤΟΥΝ[ΟΜΑ], confusable w. ΤΟΥΝ "the Son" 768-9
ὅπου 171-2 ; ὅπου εἰμι (v.r. εἶμι), ὅπου
ὑπάγω, and ὅπου ἐγὼ ὑπάγω 190 a,
487 a, 578
ὅπως 173 ; ὅπως ἄν 693
ὁράω : perf. 475, ἑόρακεν and ἑώρακεν
651 ; τεθέαμαι...ἴδης...ἑώρακα 572 ;
ἑωράκατε and γινώσκετε 491; ὄψονται
εἰς 317 ; ὄψονται v.r. for κόψονται
317 d ; ὁρᾶτε, after pause, mostly
imperat. or interrog., see n. on
p. 678.
ὀρθογραφία 790
ὀρθότερον : meaning of 775 b
ὁρίζω : forms of 748
ὅρος : w. article 962-3 *
ὅς (demonstr.): ὃς δέ 380 b
ὅς (rel.) : in attraction 405-7 ; ἐν τῷ
ὀνόματί σου ᾧ δέδωκάς μοι 408-11 ;
ἐντολὴν καινήν...ὅ 412 ; Κρανίου Τόπον
ὃ λέγεται... 738 ; δι' ὅ, δι' οὗ, ὑφ' οὗ
etc. 294-5 ; ὃς ἄν and ὃς ἐάν 739 ;
v.r. οὕς, ὅ, ᾧ 740 foll., 744 c
ὅσος : ὅσα ἐάν 660 b
ὅστις 413 ; ὅ,τι ἄν (or ἐάν) 414, 516 ;

ἅτινα ἐὰν γράφηται 414-6 ; ὅστις ἄν
739
ὅταν : parall. to ᾗ ἂν ὥρᾳ 533 a ; w. aor.
and pres. subjunct. 511, 531-5 ; ὅταν
λέγωσιν "in the moment when they
are saying" 531, in Epict. "when, at
any moment" 532 d¹
ὅτε 799 (i)
ὅτι : (1) suspensive and (2) explanatory
174-7 ; suspensive, a characteristic of
Jn and Rev. 176, 236 ; in LXX
390 a ; (?) "that" or "because"
181-6, 219 ; introducing (1) cause of
action or (2) ground of statement
178-80 ; recitativum 189-90 ; not
used interrogatively in Jn 231 c ; ὅτι
after vbs. of seeing 762 a ; ὅτι v. r. τί
ὅτι etc. in LXX 231 d foll. ; ὅτι μή
187, 695 ; οὐχ ὅτι 188, 218-9 ; εἶδον
ὅτι ἦν 466 (i); τὴν ἀρχὴν ὅτι καὶ λαλῶ
ὑμῖν 154-6 ; ὅτι=ὥστε 694 ; οὕτως...
ὅτι 697 ; τί ὅτι and τί ἔστιν ὅτι, for
τί γέγονεν ὅτι 694 ; ὅτι...καὶ ὅτι 757 b
οὐ(κ) (interrog.) 231 ; οὐκοῦν 233-4 ; οὐ
μή 232 ; οὐχί 231 (and see οὐχί below)
οὐ(κ) (neg.) : encroached on by μή 253 ;
v. r. for οὔπω 264-5 ; οὐ and οὐκέτι
583 ; οὐ μή w. fut. and subjunct. 255 ;
εἰ οὐ 256 ; οὐ...μόνον 147 b; οὐ...οὐδεὶς
257 ; οὐ...οὐκέτι 257 a ; οὐ combined
w. πᾶς 260-3 ; οὐ followed by καί
instead of ἀλλά 598 ; οὐ(κ)...ἀλλά
593 ; Xenophon uses οὐκ, ἀλλά, but
Epictetus οὐ, ἀλλά 265 (i) c ; οὐχί
265 (i); οὐ=ἀ-privative 143, 248, 253 a,
256 ; οὐ γάρ, not interrog. in Jn 683 ;
ὁ...οὐκ ὢν 704; οὐ...καὶ and οὐ...ἤ
549 a, 759; οὐ...τις and οὐδεὶς 586 d, e;
ου confused w. συ 797 c
οὐδέ : v. r. for οὔτε 258; introducing parenthesis 633 b; ουδε εν or ουδεν 660
οὐδείς : καὶ οὐδεὶς 139 ; οὐ...οὐδεὶς 257 ;
οὐ...τις and οὐδεὶς 586 d, e ; οὐδέν,
emphasised by position 605 a ; ουδεν
or ουδε εν 660
οὐκέτι : repeated as οὐ 583 ; οὐ...οὐκέτι
257 a
οὐκοῦν 233-4
οὐ μή 232, 255
οὐ μόνον 147 b
οὖν : in Christ's words 191-7 ; in narrative of Christ's acts 198—200 ; after
parenthesis 631 foll. ; in LXX 640 ;

---

¹ Add Epict. i. 24. 20 ὅταν σοι φαίνηται...ἀπαλλάσσου.

This Index extends from 1886 to 2799. Before numbers with * supply 1,
e.g. [1]999* ; before others, 2, e.g. [2]000.

GREEK

in Papyri 640 e; "pause spaces"
before οὖν in B 663; v. r. τότε 637 a
οὔπω : v.r. οὐ 264-5
οὐρανός: with and without article 952-8*
οὔτε...καί 258-9; οὔτε...ἀλλά (in Pap.)
683 a, b
οὗτος 386-97; how emphasized 553 c;
οὗτός ἐστιν etc., used in testimony
957 b*; αὕτη "this [thing]" 396,
621-2; διὰ τοῦτο 387-91; ἐν τούτῳ
332, 392-3; ἐπὶ τοῦτο and ἐπὶ τούτῳ
338; μετὰ τοῦτο and μετὰ ταῦτα 349 a,
394; ταῦτα thrice repeated 396, 621,
ταύτην ἐποίησεν ἀρχὴν τῶν σημείων
386 (i)
οὕτως "unpremeditatedly" 916-7*;
οὕτως...ὥστε 917 a*, 203, 697; οὕτως
...ἵνα or ὅτι or ὡς 697
οὐχ ὅτι 188, 218
οὐχί: interrog. 231 a; ἀλλ᾽ οὐχὶ πάντες
265 (i)
ὄχλος 417; ὁ ὄχλος πολύς 153 a; ὄχλος
and ὅλος 753 e
ὀψάριον 235 d, 703
ὄψομαι s. ὁράω

Παιδάριον...ὅς 412 b
παιδίον 701-3
παῖς, παιδίον, and δοῦλος 584 b
πάλαι ἄν (?) confused w. πάλιν 698 a
πάλιν : double meaning of 635 (i), 649
(i)-(iii), 711 a; ? confused w. πάλαι
ἄν 698 a
παντέλειος : an epithet of the number
"ten" 283 c
παρά : w. accus. 354; w. dat. 352-3,
355, 363; w. gen. 356; w. gen. and
dat. interchanged 357-9; παρὰ τὴν
θάλασσαν 341, 344, 354; παρὰ θεῷ 027;
παρὰ τῷ θεῷ 355; παρὰ τῷ πατρί and
παρὰ τοῦ πατρός 357; ὁ ὢν παρὰ [τοῦ]
θεοῦ 358; οὐ διὰ τοῦ θεοῦ ἀλλὰ παρ᾽
αὐτοῦ 296 a; παρά, ἀπό, and ἐκ w.
ἐξέρχομαι 326-8
παραδίδωμι: παραδοῖ 252; ὁ παραδιδούς
510
παράκλητος 630 h, 791-7
παραλαμβάνω : used in Epict. 570 b; παρέλαβον and ἔλαβον 570
παρασκευή : π. τοῦ πάσχα 048; ἐπεὶ ἦν
π. 087 a
πάρειμι 225 a
παρέρχομαι 342 d
παρρησία 917 (i)-(vi)*, 727 ; connected
w. Epict. 917 (v)*, 798 f
πᾶς : combined w. οὐ or μή 260-3; πᾶν

ὁ δέδωκεν (δέδωκας) etc. 921-2*, 422,
740-4; περιπαντων, for περιπατων
651; οὐ...πᾶν Hebraic 759 e
πάσχα : παρασκευὴ τοῦ π. 048; τὸ πάσχα
ἡ ἑορτή 654 d
πατήρ : used vocatively, πάτερ, πατήρ,
and ὁ πατήρ, 052-3, 661 a, 679, v. r.
in B 659 b; παρὰ τῷ πατρί, παρὰ τοῦ
πατρός, and παρὰ τοῦ θεοῦ 355-9; οἱ
πατέρες 949-50*, 553 e; οἱ π. and οἱ
π. ὑμῶν 957*
πατριάρχαι 949 a*
παχύνω 449 a
πέμπω : ἔπεμψα, in letters 691 c
περα for περαν 656 a
περί 360, 370; τὰς π. Μάρθαν 990*; π.
and ὑπέρ 718, 719 b
περιπατέω 342 a foll., diff. from βαδίζω
342 b, = "teach" 342 e; περιπατων
corrupted to περιπαντων 651
περιρρήγνυμι : active and middle, w.
ἱμάτια 270 b, 563 c
πηγή 316 b
πηλίκος: πηλίκοις γράμμασιν ἔγραψα
691 a-e, 785-90
πιάζω: ἐπίασαν οὐδέν and οὐδένα ἔπεισαν
703 c
Πιλάτος : with and without article 969*
πιπράσκω, forms of 750
πιστεύω: w. dat., εἰς, ἐν, see Joh. Voc.
Index III and esp. 1470; πίστευε and
πίστευσον 439 b; πιστεύετε ambig.
237-40; perf. 442, 474; τοὺς πεπισ-
τευκότας αὐτῷ 506; οὐκ ἐπίστευον
466; οἱ πιστεύοντες, meaning of 500;
aor. and pres. subjunct. 525 foll.;
πιστεύσωμεν v. r. -εύωμεν 528; pres.
subjunct. altered by D into aor.
subjunct. 530 a; π. διά τινος 304 a
πίστις s. Joh. Voc. Index III
πιστός 304 a
πλήν : v. r. for πρὸ προσώπου 361 a
πληρόω : w. ἐκ 329
πλησίον "near" 368 a
πλοῖον : ἐδράξωμεν v. r. 346 c
πνεῦμα : τὸ π. ἐστι τὸ ζωοποιοῦν 975-7*
πόθεν: π. εἶ σύ; 403, 733-7 ; ποθεν, a
corruption of ποθι 759
ποιέω : π. and ἐργάζομαι 226 b; π. and
πράσσω 584 a; ἐποίουν 463-4; ποιεῖτε
ambig. 194 c, 359 ; τί ποιοῦμεν; τί
ποιῶμεν; and τί ποιήσωμεν; 493,
512, 766 (i); καλῶς ποιήσεις 729 a;
ἤκουσαν ὅτι ἐποίησεν 459
πολύς : πολλοί sometimes ambig. 941*;
πολλοὶ τῶν, not in Jn 041; πολλοί...
ἐκ τῶν Ἰουδαίων 941* foll.; ὕδατα

This Index extends from 1886 to 2799. Before numbers with * *supply* 1, *e.g.* [1]999*; *before others*, 2, *e.g.* [2]000.

πολλά 270 c; άλλα πολλά, πολλά...
καὶ ἕτερα and πολλά...καὶ ἄλλα 335 a
πονηρός: σώζω, τηρέω etc. ἐκ τοῦ πονηροῦ
(ambig.) 325
πορεύομαι and ὑπάγω 082¹; π. substituted for ἀναβαίνω 489 a
πόσος: ποσα v. r. οσα and τοσα 737 b
ποτέ 351 b
πότερον 250
πράσσω and ποιέω 584 a
πρό: πρὸ ἐμοῦ 361–2; πρὸ προσώπου 330, v. r. πλήν 361 a; πρὸ ἐξ ἡμερῶν τοῦ πάσχα 288; πρό corr. to πρός 651, 655
πρόβατα (pl.): collective and non-collective 420
προβατική 216
πρός: w. accus., w. vb of rest 363–6, w. vbs of speaking 366 b–c, repeated after vb of motion 367; w. dat. 368; εἶναι πρός τινα 363 a; ἦν πρὸς τὸν θεόν, contrasted w. ἀπεσταλμένος παρὰ θεοῦ 277; τί πρὸς σέ; 229; πρός a corruption of πρό 651, 655
προσάββατον 048
προσεύχομαι 630 h; προσεύχεσθε καὶ αἰτεῖσθε 536 a
προσκυνέω: w. accus. and w. dat. 019
προσφάγιον 235 d, 701–3
πρόσωπον: πρὸ π. 330, v. r. πλήν 361 a
προφήτης: with and without article 940*, 965*; προφήτης for ὁ προφήτης (?) 492 a; διὰ τοῦ π. 301
πρωι for πρωτον 901 b*
πρῶτον, s. πρῶτος
πρῶτος followed by genitive 896* foll., 665–7; πρῶτον ὑμῶν ambig. 901*; πρῶτος or πρώτιστος Hebraized 666
πρωτότοκος 897*
πύλη 216 a
πυνθάνομαι: aor. and imperf. 465 c–d
πωρόω: v. r. πηρόω 449 a; aor. and perf. 449 a–b

Ραββεί 680
ῥάβδος: ἐν ῥάβδῳ ἐλθεῖν 332 a

C, ϵ, θ and ο interchanged in B 650–2
σάββατον: σαββάτῳ and ἐν σαββάτῳ 715 c
σάρξ: θέλημα σαρκός 269; τὰς σάρκας ἀπολλύουσιν οἱ σταυρωθέντες 211 c

σημεῖον 386 b; ἀρχὴ τῶν σημείων 386 (i)
σκανδαλίζω: variations of ὃς ἂν σκανδαλίσῃ 513 b
σκέλος: ἵνα κατεαγῶσιν αὐτῶν τὰ σκέλη 419
σταυρόω: ὑψηλὸς ὁ σταυρωθεὶς καὶ πολλοὺς τρέφει...τὰς σάρκας ἀπολλύουσιν οἱ σταυρωθέντες 211 c
στήκω: στήκετε w. ἐάν and ὅταν 515 (i)
στιβάδας: v.r. στοιβάδας 047
σύ 400 a, 402–4; σὺ λέγεις 234 b; πόθεν εἶ σύ 733–7; σύ with vocat. and imperat. 734 e; σου and μου confused 768; σου unemph. 776 foll.; συ confused w. ου 797 c
συμφέρον: how used by Epict. 228 a
σύν 799 (ii)
συνειδός 798 e
συνζητέω 349
συνήθεια 464 b
σώζω: w. ἐκ 325

Ταράσσω: applied to Christ 614 c
τάχειον " more quickly " : not the same as ταχέως 918*, 439 (v) a, 554 c–e
ταχέως, ταχύ, ἐν τάχει 554 b–d
τε: how used in Jn 929*
τέλειος: applied to numbers 283 c
τέλος " eminence " 320 a; εἰς τ. 319–23
τετράμηνος: ἔτι τ. ἐστιν 230 (ii) foll.
τηρέω: w. ἐκ 325; pres. and aor. subjunct. 515; ἐτήρουν...καὶ ἐφύλαξα 584
τί, s. τίς
Τιβεριάς 045
τίθημι: late aor. of 690
τις: omitted 379 b; τινί supplied w. ἔξεστιν 379 a; ellipsis of τινές 213 foll.; ἐάν τις 580; ἐάν separated from τις 552 c; οὐ...τις and οὐδεὶς 536 d, e
τίς; τί; (direct interrogative) τί; διὰ τί; ἵνα τί; 231 b–e; τί; τί ὅτι; and ὅτι, in v.r. 231 d; τί ὅτι; τί ἔστιν ὅτι; and τί γέγονεν ὅτι; 694; τί λαλεῖς; ambig. 231 b; τί εἴπω; prob. = " what should I say? " 512 b, c; τί ποιοῦμεν; τί ποιῶμεν; τί ποιήσωμεν; distinction between 493, 512, 766 (i); τί ἐμοὶ καὶ σοί; 229–30; οὗτος δὲ τί; 209, 386 c; τί πρὸς σέ; 229; τίνα ἦν ἃ ἐλάλει 251; τίς ἐστιν ὁ παραδώσων 251 a; τί δοκεῖς; in Epict. 766 (i) a

---

¹ Add Epict. iii. 24. 44—7 θέλεις με...πορεύεσθαι;...διὰ τί μὴ ἀπέλθῃς;...τί οὖν ἔτι πορεύομαι; ἵνα ἀπέλθῃς.

This Index extends from 1886 *to* 2799. *Before numbers with* * *supply* 1, *e.g.* [1]999*; *before others*, 2, *e.g.* [2]000.

GREEK 129

τοιοῦτος 398; τοιαύτη "such a thing" 396 b
τόπος : ? ellipsis of τόπῳ 675
τοσοῦτοι v.r. 745
τότε : v.r. for οὖν 637 a
τρεῖς 281–3, s. "Three" and "Threefold"
τρέφω : ὁ σταυρωθεὶς πολλοὺς τρέφει 211 c, 642 b

'Υδρία 281 a
ὕδωρ: ὕδατα πολλά 270 c; ἐπὶ τὰ ὕ. 342 d
υἱός : ? interchanged w. παῖς 584 b; v.r. ἐκλεκτός 386 a; ΤΟΥΝ i.e. τὸν υἱόν, confusable w. ΤΟΥΝ in τουνομα 768–9
ὑμεῖς : Jn's use 399; καὶ ὑμεῖς 149; (?) δι' ὑμᾶς 428 c; ὑμῶν, unemph. 559 a; ὑμεῖς in LXX before ambig. forms in -ετε 243 a; ὑμ- and ἡμ- confused 428 c
ὑμέτερος : rare and emphatic 988*
ὑπάγω 486; distinct from πορεύομαι 082;
ὅπου ὑ. (and ὅπου ἐγὼ ὑ.) and ὅπου εἰμί (v.r. εἶμι) 487 a, 578 ; ὑπῆγον 464
ὑπέρ 369–71 ; ὑπὲρ οὗ 927 b*, 360 ; ὑπέρ τινος masc. and neut. 718–22 ; ὑπέρ and περί 719 a–c
ὑπεραγαπάω 323 b
ὑπό: w. accus. 372; w. gen. 373; ὑ. and ὑποκάτω 372
ὑποκάτω 372
ὑπομένω 322 b ; ὁ ὑπομείνας 499
ὑψηλός : applied to ὁ σταυρωθεὶς 211 c
ὑψόω : applied to Christ 614 b

Φανερόω : thrice applied to Christ's Resurrection 619
φέρω : "bear fruit" 120 b

φημί rare in Jn, freq. in Acts[1]
φιλέω 328, 584 c ; perf. 442, 476–7 ; Origen's distinction between φ. and ἀγαπάω 584 c
φοῖνιξ : τὰ βαΐα τῶν φοινίκων 047
φυλάσσω: ἐτήρουν...καὶ ἐφύλαξα 584
φυλή : αἱ φυλαὶ τῆς γῆς 317 e–f
φωτίζω 532 c

Χάρις : Philo on 285 b; Epictetus on 743 a
χείρ: in var. phrases w. εἰς and ἐν 334 c ; χεῖρα or χεῖρας w. βάλλω and ἐπιβάλλω 575
χόρτος 632 b
χρονίζω : forms of 752
χώρα : ἡ Ἰουδαία χ. 670 b
χωρέω 414 b foll.

Ψῆφος: δίδωμι ψῆφον 409 a

Ω and Ο interchanged 114, 691
ὠδίνες 197
ὥρα : combined with ἔρχεται and ἐλήλυθεν 604 a, 625 e ; τὴν ὥ. ταύτην "about this time" 013 ; (ἐν) ἐκείνῃ τῇ ὥ. 025 ; ὥ. ἐβδόμην 013, 206; ᾖ ἂν ὥ. parall. to ὅταν 533 a ; ὥ. ἵνα and ὥ. ὅτε 799 (i), s. also 770
ὡς : (?) for ἕως 089, 201, 696 ; "as it were" 202 ; ὡς δέ "so when" 069 ; ὡς ἄν 696 a ; οὕτως...ὡς, for οὕτως ὥστε 697
ὥσπερ 066 b
ὥστε 203, 694 c ; οὕτως ὥ. 917 a*, 697 ; in Egypt. Pap. 697 c
ὠφέλεια : how used by Epict. 798–9

---

[1] It should have been stated in 2456 a that Jn—who uses φημί only in i. 23, ix. 38, xviii. 29—never applies it (as the Synoptists do) to Christ. Mt. and Lk. agree (agst Mk) in applying it to Christ in His answer to Pilate, "Thou sayest it." It is a mark of classical style. In Pentateuch, of seven instances, five are in the prophecy of Balaam, Numb. xxiv. 3—15. In N.T., it occurs mostly in Acts, 24 times. In the Synoptists, Mt. uses it most freq. (17), Mk (6), Lk. (7). It is never used by three Synoptists in common. Lk. mostly uses it in traditions peculiar to himself.

This Index extends from 1886 *to* 2799. *Before numbers with* * *supply* 1, *e.g.* [1]999*; *before others*, 2, *e.g.* [2]000.

A. 9

NOTES ON NEW TESTAMENT CRITICISM

I. NEW TESTAMENT PASSAGES

[*Black Arabics refer to paragraphs* [2]800–[2]997 (*the* 2 *not being printed*). *Ordinary Arabics refer to the sections of* 2998–9, *the two "Longer Notes".*[1]]

MATTHEW			MATTHEW			MATTHEW		
		PAR.			PAR.			PAR.
1	8	882	10	24	32 e	17	2	28 w–x
	16	881		26	55 m		7	2 b*, 6 b–c*
	18	40		28	819		17	913
	18–25	880		41	886		20	851–6, 942*
	21	881	11	2–3	841, 888			(xxiv) b
	24–5	881		5	995		22	857, 23 d
2	1 foll.	17 b foll.		11	880		24–7 foll.	7* foll.,
	9	17 e, i		25	842, 23 a			12 b*
	15	883		25–7	50 c–e		27	8 b*
	18	883		27	27 f, 39 b		3–4	885
	22	942* (xxiv) b		28–30	844–9		10	824* (i) g, 15 b
3	7	937 f		29	842–9, 963–4		11	861
4	3	20 a	12	7	840		12	864 foll.
	6	20 a		10	961 (i) d	18	17	887
	24	2 b*		18	54 f		18	887, 979
5	1	887		28	6 e*		20	887
	3	888	13	9	29 b	19	4	984 c, 47
	6	888		13 foll.	913		8	984 c
	25	14 a*, 17 i*		31	852		10–12	888, 974
	41	887 a		33	55 k		20	834 a
	44–5	816		55	879		26	858
6	1–6	55 l	14	12	942* (xxii) b		28	8 b
8	14	17 g*		26	824* (i) b, 6 a*	20	23	935
	15	1 b*, 6 c*		29–30	979		28	829, 964, 996
	17	964		32–4	8 a* foll.	21	1 foll.	848
	21	872	15	11	841		9	24 f
9	6	44 a		24	860–71		15	874 c, 24 f
	13	837 c, 840	16	17	39 b, 44		16	840, 23 a, 24 f
	25	1 b*		19	887		18–21	873
10	6	861 foll.		24	841		20	875, 17 g*
	8	995		27	850, 24 e, 44		21	851
	10	888		28	25 a–b, 44,	22	1 foll.	45
	16	32 e			17 g–h*		14	914

[1] *Black Arabics refer to paragraphs* [2]800–[2]997, *ordinary Arabics to the sections of* 2998, *or, if starred, to the sections of* 2999. *For example,* 872=2872, 16=2998 (xvi), 16*=2999 (xvi).

NEW TESTAMENT PASSAGES

MATTHEW		MARK		MARK	
	PAR.		PAR.		PAR.
22 30	56 d	1 34	839	11 20	17 g*
44	22 b–c, 23 b, e	36	17 g*	21	875, 17 g*
23 35	51 b, 54 f	38	839 c	22–3	851 foll.
24 6	26 b	2 10	839	24	857, 873
8	874 d	17	837 c, 840, 54 i	25	840, 857, 873
15–16	874 e–f, and Pref. p. xii foll.	27	840	12 25	56 d
		3 1	961 (i) d	36	22 b–c, 23 b
		10–11	2 b*	13 7	26 b
16	942* (xiii) e	11	2 a*	8	874 d
21	984 c	17	969 foll.	14	837 (iii) d, 874 e–f, 942* (xiii) e, and Pref. p. xii foll.
28	942* (xxii) b	21	883		
29	16 a	4 12	913		
30	26 s, 31 a	22	55 m		
32	874	26–9	55 j		
25 1–11	942* (xv) c	28	876	19	984 c
31–46	850	5 35	859	26	31 a
26 26	891	6 3	879	28	874
26–8	828	8	888	14 22–4	828, 891
30	897–903	9	17 c*	26	897–903
39	6 b*	12	840	27	869
51	934, 17 g–i*	29	942* (xxii) b	35	6 b*
54	26 b	34	866, 869	36	858
61	985	49	824* (i) b, 6 a*	47	17 b–k*
64	23 b, 31 a, 32 a	51	8 a* foll.	50–2	17 b* foll.
71	12 a*	7 7	857	58	985
75	12*, 13*	15	841	62	23 b, 31 a, 32 a
27 45	910	27 foll.	859	68	12 a*
46	910, 917 foll.	8 34	841	72	13*
49	987	38	850	15 22	930 foll.
50	910, 917 foll.	9 1	25 a–b, 44, 17 g–h*	34	910, 917 foll.
53	909			37	910, 917 foll.
28 2	909, 5 b*	7	850	43	942* (xxii) b
5	909	8	2 b*	16 3	908–9
7	17 g*	19	913	4	5 b*
9	889, 979, 1 b*, 3*, 4*	23	858	7	17 g*
		29	851 foll.	8	878
16	3 a–b*	31	857	9	878
17–18	6 c*	33	12 b*	10	17 g*
18	23 d, 6 b*	35 foll.	857		
20	887	36	885–6		
		49–50	858		
		50	857		LUKE
	MARK	10 6	984 c, 47		
		13–14	859	1 1–2	980–4
1 3	839 b foll.	15–16	857, 885–6	13–14	881 a
4	839 c	20	834 a	16	936 a
7	839 c	21	857	26–35	880
11	850	27	858	2 8 foll.	13, 17 f foll.
14	839 c	39	935 foll., 28 a	9	17 i, 5 a*
15	839 a–d, 857	45	829, 857, 964, 996	13	16, 5 a*
22	839			14	24 g
29	17 g*	11 12–14	873	38	5 a*
31	1 b*, 6 b–c*	13	874 a, 878	40	840* g

Black Arabics *refer to paragraphs* [2]800–[2]997, *ordinary Arabics to the sections of* 2998, *or, if starred, to the sections of* 2999. *For example,* 872=2872, 16=2998 (xvi), 16*=2999 (xvi).

9—2

NOTES ON NEW TESTAMENT CRITICISM

LUKE		LUKE		LUKE	
	PAR.		PAR.		PAR.
2 41	961 (i) a	12 4	819	24 24	17 g*
48	883	58	14 a*	32	908
52	840* g	13 6–9	874	33	17 g*
3 7	937 f	21	55 k	34	17 f*
11	17 c*	14 1–2	961 (i) c–d	36	897–907
23	882, 994	15	56 c	37	824* (i) b
36	20 c	15 4	861 foll.	39–40	824* (i)
4 3	20 a	4–10	9*	44–9	903
9	20 a	17 6	851–6, 873		
18	839 a	21	996		
22	840* g, 879	18 17	885		
38	17 g*	21	834 a		JOHN
38–9	1 b*	35	6 a*		
39	5 a*, 6 c*	19 10	865	1 1–2	980
41	839	11	6 a*	3	27 f
42	17 g*	29, 37	6 a*	13	39–42
5 32	837 c, 840	38	24 f–g	14	942* (xii) a,
6 6	961 (i) d	41	6 a*		24 e, 28 f,
17	887	20 1	5 a*		44
19	2 b*	36	56 d	14–17	840* g
20–1	888	42	23 b	18	32 d
7 12	6 a*	43	22 b–c	29	32 d
13	6 d*	21 9	26 b	33	55 i
14	6 b–c*	20	837 (i), (iii) a,	39	977
19	841, 888		874 e–g, and	41	21 a
22	995		Pref. p. xii	45	979
8 10	913		foll.	49	20 a foll.
17	55 m	21	874 e–g, 942*	50	20 b
9 3	888		(xiii) e	2 19–21	942* (xii) a,
23	841	27	31 a		985
27	25 a–b, 44,	29	874	20	962
	17 g*	30	874	22	875
32	17 g*	34	5 a*	3 3	978
36	2 b*	22 17–20	828	8	26 d, 55 j
41	913	25	829	13	48
44	23 d	27	829, 963–4, 996	16	870, 23 e
45	908	30	8 b	29	806
46–7	12 b*	32	923 c, 936 a	4 7	968
47	885	44	986	18	961 (i)
55	942* (xvii)	49	875	24	27 q
59	872	49–50	17 g*, 17 i*	25	21 a
10 1	888	58	12 a*	35	961 a
3	32 e	62	12*, 13*	5 1	961 foll.
8	887	69	23 b, 32 a	2	800 a, 959–62
19	23 a	23 31	875	5	961 (i)
20	942* (viii) g,	45–6	910, 917 foll.	19	806, 858
	15 b	53	908	27	28 s, 45 b
21	23 a, 50 c–e	24 4	5 a–b*	30	858
22	23 d, 39 b,	6	4*, 5*	6 12	870
	50 c–e	9	17 g*	19	6 a*
40	5 a*	11	890	21	8 a* foll.
11 20	6 e*	12	17 g*	39	870
50	51 b	15	6 a*	64	984 c

Black Arabics refer to paragraphs [2]800–[2]997, *ordinary Arabics to the sections of* 2998, *or, if starred, to the sections of* 2999. *For example,* 872=2872, 16=2998 (xvi), 16*=2999 (xvi).

NEW TESTAMENT PASSAGES

JOHN		JOHN		ACTS	
	PAR.		PAR.		PAR.
7 24	28 w	16 22	874 d, 881 a, 942* (xii) b	1 13	8 f*
37	968			15	942* (viii) g
8 17	26 k	24	806	24	888
18	26 k	25	875	2 2	970
44	984 c	32	923	35	22 c
57	989–90	17 3	985	41	942* (viii) g
9 35	48	7	803	3 1	8 f*
10 1	985	11	54 j	13–15	54 f
1–18	871	12	870	18	54 f
10	870	13	806	26	54 f
11–12	985	21	28 i	4 13	879
28	870	24	806	27	54 f
36	20 a–b, 45 b	25	54 j	30	54 f
11 33	985	18 9	870	36	860
35	806, 985	10	17 g–j*	5 29	958
39	909	11	875	7 52	54 f
44	28 w	18	17 o*	55–6	25
48–52	962 a	22	17 j–k*	56	32 a, 44 a
12 16	875	32	927	9 7	890
23–4	856, 55 m	19 5	43 c	10 9	8 f*
27	985	28	806	9–16	841
28	26 c	30	923 d, 967	13	887
31	26 p	35	925, 987	41	895 foll.
33	927	37	26 s	11 2	8 f*
34	850, 21, 33, 49	20 3	17 g*	5–10	841
40	24 d	8	977	7	887
43	24 d	17	805 a, 979, 1 b*, 17 g*	12 1–2	937 b–c
13 5	963–4			13–15	15 b
21	985	18	17 g*	13 5	983–4
23	32	23	887	15 10	843
33	805 a, 978	26	892 b, 17 g*	16 25	898
34	858, 924	21 2	925, 978	17 23 foll.	996
14 2	942* (xiii) e	3	7*, 8*	18 25 foll.	942* (xxii) d
9	984 b	5	978	19 3	942* (xxii) d
18	805, 978	7	934, 977, 17 m*	20 27	984 a
20	28 i	10	8 d*	22 14	54 f
23	899, 27 f	11	7*, 8*	20	26 j
26	875	13	895 foll.	23 10	937 d
30	26 p	15	978, 32 b	26 14	984 d
15 3	985	17	978	16	826 a, 983–4
4	978	18	930 foll., 17 o*	28 23	3 a*
5	978	18–19	936 foll.		
6	877	18–23	962 b, 15 a*		
11	806	19	926 foll.		
12	858	20	925, 936 foll.	ROMANS	
26	26 c	23	941		
27	984 c	24	925, 941 foll.	1 1 foll.	823
16 4	984 c			3	26 o
17	881 a, 942* (xii) b	ACTS		3–4	35
				16	825
21	874 d, 881 a, 942* (xii) a–b	1 3	892 a foll., 904	16–18	942*
		4	892–5	17	54 e
				20	28 b

Black Arabics refer to paragraphs [2]800–[2]997, *ordinary Arabics to the sections of* 2998, *or, if starred, to the sections of* 2999. *For example,* 872=2872, 16=2998 (xvi), 16*=2999 (xvi).

NOTES ON NEW TESTAMENT CRITICISM

ROMANS

		PAR.
2	16	825
	19–20	49
4	3	825
	9	825
	13	839
	24–5	820
5	7	54 *j*
	14	814
6	6	841
7	7	815
	18	815
	22	55 *l*
8	13	30 *b*
	23	814
	28	826
	32	918
	35	814
9	3	823, 942* (xviii)
	27–9	820
	33	908
10	6	908–9
	20	820
11	2	826
	8	913
	26	942* (xviii)
	32–3	942* (xviii)
12	1	828, 11 *b**
	14	909
13	4	942* (xviii) *a*
	9	815
15	12	820
	13	814
	19	824

1 CORINTHIANS

1	17	825
	17 foll.	814
	25	883
2	3	824
	4	814
	7 foll.	55 *i*
	10	814
3	2	50 *a*
	16–17	811
4	1	983, 984 *e*
	9–13	811
	15	823
5	4	887
6	2–3	8 *b*
	5	28 *k*
	19	811
7	1	888

1 CORINTHIANS

		PAR.
7	1–40	888
	35	811
9	20	829
	22	829
10	1	30
	17	895
	27	887
	31	811
11	22	811
	23–4	827–8
13	12	826
14	20	887, 978, 24 *e*, 50 *a*
15	3–8	892 *b*
	4	823
	5	17 *f**, 17 *i**
	27	22 *a*, 24 *c*
	27–8	839
	35–45	824*
	54	820

2 CORINTHIANS

3	6	828
	14	828, 908
	17	824* (i)
4	7	883
	10	26 *i*
	16	55 *l*
	18	43 *b*
5	1	43 *b*
	1–2	824*
	2–4	17 *n**
	14	814
	15	841
	17	823
	21	924
6	3 foll.	811
	11	14 *d**
	16	28 *f*
	17	28 *h*
	18	27 *i*
11	2	942* (xv) *f*
	28–9	824
12	2–3	953
	5	824
	9	824
	10	824

GALATIANS

1	10	803
	11 foll.	826
	13–14	823

GALATIANS

		PAR.
1	15	984 *d*
	16	823
2	1	826
	2	984 *d*
	6	803
	9	941, 17 *h**
	20	841
3	6	825
	11	54 *e*
4	4	880, 23 *c*
	13	824
	19	805 *a*, 978
	24	828
	25	826
5	1	843
	12	823
	13	23 *e*
6	1	840
	2	840, 924
	14	841

EPHESIANS

1	19–22	22 *a*
	21	27 *l*
	22	839
2	6	43
3	16	55 *l*
4	1	811
6	10	814
	14	28 *l*
	19	14 *d**

PHILIPPIANS

1	17	823
	23	826
	25	997 *a*
2	6–9	23 *d*
	7	923 *b*, 23 *c*
	11	26 *e*
3	2	860
	5 foll.	823
	20–1	22 *a*
	21	839, 858
4	3	942* (viii) *g*
	13	814

COLOSSIANS

1	11	814
	28	11 *b**
2	5	884
4	14	879
	15–16	28 *e*

Black Arabics *refer to paragraphs* [2]800–[2]997, *ordinary Arabics to the sections of* 2998, *or, if starred, to the sections of* 2999. *For example,* 872=2872, 16=2998 (xvi), 16*=2999 (xvi).

1 THESSALONIANS		JAMES		REVELATION	
	PAR.		PAR.		PAR.
2 18	824	5 1–6	51 b	1 12	942* (xxii) a,
4 15	826	6	54 f		26 c–d
				13	26 a
2 THESSALONIANS		1 PETER		14	7 e, 27 h, 29 c
				15	26 a
1 8	942* (xviii) a	1 13	11 b*	16	28 n
11	811	19	11 b*	17	27 a–e, n
		24–5	839 b–c	20	28 e
		2 2	50 a, 11 b*	2 1	28 c, f, g, i, p
1 TIMOTHY		4	11 b*	6	942* (iii) b
		4–6	908	7	29 b
1 15	823	12	11 b*	8	27 a–b
6 15	27 h	3 4	55 l	10	26 n
		19	11 b*	12	28 t
		20–1	942* (i) k	13	942* (iii) c, 26
2 TIMOTHY		4 10–11	11 a*		i–j, n
2 4	811	12	948	14	942* (iii) b
4 7	824, 826	18	54 e	16	28 t
		5 1	954, 26 j, 28 a	17	942* (xv) a
		5	17 n*	18	26 a, 28 p
PHILEMON				20	942* (iii) b,
9	955				(xv) f
		"2 PETER"		23	27 e
		2 5	942* (i) f, k	24	942* (iii) b
HEBREWS		7–8	54 e	26–7	942*(xvii)
		3 4	984 c	27	942* (xiv)
1 3	27 g, 45 b			3 1	942* (iii) b,
13	22 c				(viii) i
2 6	24	1 JOHN		4	942* (viii) a, i
6–9	24	2 1	978, 54 f	14	26 i, n
8	839	7	984 c	17	942* (v) b, 28 h
12	898	12	978	18	28 h, 17 a*
13	978	14	978	19	28 h
14	978	18	962 a	20	899
4 11–12	28 t	19	12 a*	21	8 b, 28 i
5 14	942* (xii) b	3 12	54 f	4 1	26 b–c
7 23	997 a			4–7	33 a
8 4–5	28 d	JUDE		5	28 e
9 23–4	28 d			6	28 i
25	961 (i) a	9	27 p	7	942* (xiii) d
10 1	961 (i) a, 980–1	14	31 a	8	942* (i) j
3	961 (i) a			5 1	942* (i) h, 31 a,
11	26	REVELATION			32
11–12	32 a	1 1	27 q	2–7	32
13	22 c	1–2	26	2	26 c
38	54 e	4	27 f	2 foll.	27 q
11 1	980	4–7	26	5	26 f
4	54 f	7	29, 31 c	6	942* (i) j, 26 f,
23	978	8	26 p, 27		28 e, i, p
37	937 d	9	944	6–14	33 a
12 23	942* (viii) g	9–16	28	7	8 c
13 4	942* (xv) b	10	942* (iii) b	11–13	942* (i) j
15	11 a*			6 2	28 d, 29 c

Black Arabics refer to paragraphs [2]800–[2]997, ordinary Arabics to the sections of 2998, or, if starred, to the sections of 2999. For example, 872 = 2872, 16 = 2998 (xvi), 16* = 2999 (xvi).

NOTES ON NEW TESTAMENT CRITICISM

REVELATION		REVELATION		REVELATION	
	PAR.		PAR.		PAR.
6 6	942* (v) a, 28 i	12 1–17	942* (xi)–(xv)	17 14	26 n, 27 h
9	26 i	3	942* (i) c, i, (xv)	16	942* (xv) f
10	942* (iii) c, (xviii) a, 51 b	4	942* (xiii) b, 55 h	18 5–9	942* (xv) f
11	942* (iii) c	5	942* (xii) b, (xiv)	9	948
16	28 w	6	942* (xiii) e	18	948
7 2	942* (i) h	7	24 g, 27 p, 33 a	19 5–9	26 c
2 foll.	26 c, 28 n	9	942* (xiii) b	8	17 a*
2–8	942* (i) c	11	26 i	10	26 e, i, 27 n
4	942* (iv) c	12	28 g	11	26 n, 28 d, 29 c
15	28 f–g, j	14	942* (xiii) d–e	12	28 p
17	28 j	17	26 i	13–15	28 t
8 3–4	15 b	13 1	945	15	942* (xiv), 28 t
9 1	16	3–4	942* (i) j	20	942* (xx) a
3–11	942* (vi) a	6	28 f–g	21	28 t
12	942* (viii)	8	942* (iii) d	20 4	8 a, 26 i
14	51 b	11	942* (xx) a	10	942* (xx) a, 33 a
15–18	942* (viii)	16	942* (i) h	11	28 w, 29 c
10 1	27 q, 28 w, 31	18	942* (i) k–m	14	942* (xviii)
4	975, 29 a	14 2	28 r	21 1 foll.	942* (xx) c–d
8	26 c	3	942* (xv) c	3	942* (xii) a, 28 f, g
9	26 c	4	942* (xv) b–f	5–6	27 a, e–f
11	942 foll.	7	27 n	9	26 b, c
11 1–13	942* (ii) a, (x), (xix)–(xxii)	8	942* (xv) f	10	942* (ii) b
2	942* (iv) c, (vii) foll.	13	29 a–b	12	942* (xv) b
		13–15	29 foll.	14	942* (xv) b
3	942* (iv) b–c, 26 i	14	26 a	22	26 f, 27 h
4	942* (iv) b, (xxii) a	15 1–3	942* (xv)	23	26 f, 28 e
7	26 i	5	28 f	22 1	28 j, 32
8	942* (i) c, (ii) a–c, (iii) b, (xxii) b	6	28 l	2	28 i
		16 12	51 b	3	32
9	942* (xxii) b	13	942* (xx) a	4	28 w
11–12	30 a	15	17 a*	5	28 x
13	942* (vii) foll., (esp. (viii) c–i), (xiii) f	19	942* (ii) b	6	26 b, e, 27 h
		17 1	26 c	6–16	26 e
		1–4	942* (xv) f	8	26 e, 27 n
14	942* (viii)	1–15	28 r	11	54 f
19	942* (xii) a, (xiv)	3	942* (i) i, (iv) b	13	27 a–f
		5	942* (iv) b	15	860, 942* (xviii)
12 1	942* (xv)	6	26 i, j	16	26 g, 27 e
		7	942* (i) i	16–17	29 b
		9–11	942* (i) d foll., i	18	942* (xix) a
		11	942* (i) j–l	18–19	942* (xix)
				20	26 h

Black Arabics refer to paragraphs [2]800–[2]997, *ordinary Arabics to the sections of* 2998, *or, if starred, to the sections of* 2999. *For example,* 872=2872, 16=2998 (xvi), 16*=2999 (xvi).

NOTES ON NEW TESTAMENT CRITICISM

II. ENGLISH

[*Black Arabics refer to paragraphs* [2]800–[2]997 (*the* 2 *not being printed*). *Ordinary Arabics refer to the sections of* 2998–9, *the two* "*Longer Notes*"¹.]

Abbahu 18–19
Abel 54*f*
Abomination **942*** (i) *m*; of desolation, the **837** (iii), **874** *e*; s. also Pref. p. xvi foll.
"Above" and "below," mystically interpreted 7 *d–e*
Abraham **839**, **963**, 28 *v*, 54 *h*, 56 *d*; and Adam 37; superior to Noah 37 *d*; A., Isaac, and Jacob, the three feet of God's throne 14
Acts, the Son of Man in 24–5
Acts of John, the **902**, **988**
Adam, meaning "man" in Heb. but not in Aram. 2, comp. 20 *c*; son of A. 20, 23 *b*; A. and Abraham 37
Adjuration to scribes **942*** (xix) *a*
Ailam 28 *j*
Akiba **842**, 31 *b*
Almighty 27 *f–m*
"Alone," transposition of, error caused by 17 *c** foll.
Alpha and Omega 27 *a* foll.
Alphabet, Gk **942*** (i) *l*
Am, "I AM," applied to God 27 *e*
"Ambassador" and "elder" **954-5**
American revisers **840*** *f*
Ananus the high-priest **942*** (ii) *d*
Ancient of Days, the 28 *o*
"Angel" interch. w. "voice" 26 *c–d*; of great counsel 27 *l*, *q*; meant by "watcher" 17 *h*; the recording **942***, 28 *n*; "angel of God," substit. for "God" 3 *h**; "his angel" (Rev. i. 1) 26 *c–g*; s. also "Angels"

Angelology, influence of 15 *f*
Angels **942***, 26 *c* foll.; ascension of **909**; ascending and descending 13; opposing Moses 11 foll.; guardian 15 *b* foll.; interch. w. "sons of God" 16; at the right hand of God 31 *a*; associated with "stars" 28 *e*, comp. 16 foll.; song of the 24 *g*; myriads of 31 *a*; not to be worshipped 27 *n*; "three a." (Gen. xviii. 2, Targ.) 5 *b**; "a little lower than the a." 24, 42 foll.; "their a." (Mt. xviii. 2) called by Ephrem "orationes" 15 *b*
Anthropomorphic metaphors 45
Anthropos 34
"Anticipate" 4*–5*; Mt.'s unique use of 7* foll.
Antiochus Epiphanes **942*** (i) *e*, (xiii)
Antipas, Herod **942*** (xxii)
Antipas, the martyr **942*** (iii) *c*
Antithesis, the principle of **942*** (i) *g* foll.
Anytus, Socrates on **808**
"Aperuit" and "apparuit" 17 *d* *
Apocalypse, s. "Revelation"
Apollos **942*** (xxii) *d*
"Apparuit" and "aperuit" 17 *d**
"Appear" and "meet" 3*
"Appoint" and "shew" **888**; "were appointed" and "stood up" 17 *g* *
Aramaic 20, 23 *b*; how it expresses "man" 2
Ark of the Covenant, the **942*** (xiv)
"Army," parall. to "wing" **837** (i); s. also Pref. p. xvi foll.
Arrian **800-1**, **813**

---

¹ *Black Arabics refer to paragraphs* [2]800–[2]997, *ordinary Arabics to the sections of* 2998, *or, if starred, to the sections of* 2999. *For example,* 872 = 2872, 16 = 2998 (xvi), 16* = 2999 (xvi).

138 NOTES ON NEW TESTAMENT CRITICISM

Artemidorus, on "carrying" and "being carried" 931; on "dragon" and "serpent" 942* (xiii) *b* ; s. also 929
Article, the, in Revelation 942* (xix)–(xx) ; s. also ò in Gk Index, and 984
Ascension, to heaven 18; of angels 909; and resurrection of Christ, events between 892-907
Ass and colt 846-8 ; "Ass's Jawbone" 873
"Assembled with" 892-5
Astrologers, called "Chaldæans" 17 *a*
Ath (Heb.), meanings of 27 *c*
Atonement, the Day of 961 *a*
Authority and goodness, Philo on 28 *u*

"Babes and sucklings" 23, 24 *f*, 49
Babylon 942* (ii) *b–c*, (xv) *e–f*
Balaam's song 3, 4
Baptism, (metaph.) 935 ; (lit.) 27 *w*; a place of 961 ; of spirit or of fire 30
Baptist, the, s. "John the Baptist"
Barnabas, on the Son of Man 36 ; s. also 843, 890, 914, 942* (i) *a*, (iv) *c*, 994, 28 *o*
Beast, the 942* (xx) *a*; the number of 942* (i) *l* foll.
"Beasts," in Heb., identical with "living creatures" 33 *a*, 47 ; "the b. of the field" 840, 43 *d*
"Beginning, from the" 984 *c*
Bellerophon 37 *c*
"Below" and "above," mystically interpreted 7 *d–e*
Beryl, in Ezek. and Dan. 28 *m*
Bethesda, the pool of 959 foll.
Between 28 *j*; in Heb., ambig. 28 *i*; "b. [the two sides of]" 28 *k*; "judge b. his brother" 28 *k*
Bildad 10
Blood, Christ's, Justin on 39 *c*
Blotting out 942* (viii) *h*
Boanerges, the name 969-77, comp. 942* (ii)
"Bodiless," ambig. 824* (i) ; s. also 56 *d*
Body, resurrection of the 56 *a*; Enoch's, melts away 55 *b*; "a spiritual body" 824* foll.
"Bones, a spirit hath not" 824* (i) *d*
Book, of Life, the 942* (viii) *g*; the sealed b. 32
Bosom of the Father, the 32
"Bow" and "truth" 837 (ii)
"Branches" and "daughters" 837 (ii)
Bride, the 942* (xv) *c–f*
Brutus, Marcus, in Shakespeare 830 foll.

"Call" and "meet" 3 *g* *, 4*
Candlestick, in the Temple, the 28 *b* foll.; placed by Vespasian in the Temple of Peace 28 *e*
Candlesticks, the seven 28 *c* foll.; "seven" and "two" 942* (xxii) *a*
Capernaum, 12*, 13*; "village of consolation" 7 *b**
"Carrying" and "being carried," Artemidorus on 931
Catherine of Siena 966, 996
Cause, "*Beware of single causes*" 1*, s. also Pref. p. xi
Celibacy, ascetic 942* (xv) *b*
Chaldæans, *i.e.* astrologers 17 *a*
"Charioteer, the," Origen on 31
Cherubim, the 28 *u*
"Child," an error for "servant" 54 *f*; receiving as a little c. 885-6; little children 978
Christ, birth of 880-2 ; preexistence of 37 *c* ; blood of, Justin on 39 *c* ; titles of 44 *a*
Christians, the, mentioned by M. Antoninus 813, by Tacitus 807
Chrysostom 823, 849, 895, 917, 936 *a*, 980, 990, 995, 20 *a–b*
Churches, the Seven 942* (iii)
City, the great 942* (i) *c*, (ii) *a* foll.
Clemens Alexandrinus, on the yoke 843 ; on the ass and colt 847 ; on the Son of Man 42 foll.; s. also 824* (i) *g*, 837 (iii), 854, 865, 918, 937 *f*, 942* (i) *l*, (xv) *d*, 985, 996, 27 *f*, *u*, 55 *k*, 7 *a**, 10*, 17 *c**
Clemens Romanus 845, 26 *j*, 55 *j*
Clement, Recognitions of 837 (iii) *c*
Cloud, a white 29 ; were baptized in the 30; the pillar of 30, 31 ; Rashi on the pillar of 4 *c*
"Clouds" and "cloud" 30 *b*–31 *c*; Origen on 31 *a* ; of heaven, the 29; "with the clouds" 31 *c*
Coal fire, the 17 *o**
Colt and ass 846-8
"Comfort with food" 9 *a**
Compilation 942* (xix)
Confessors or martyrs 939 *a*
Conflation 837 (ii), 17 *j*, 3 *e**
"Convivo" and "convivor" 897
Creatures, s. "Living creatures"
Cross, the 926 foll.; stretch out hands on 926 foll.; "tree" *i.e.* "cross," Ephrem on 933, comp. 942* (ii) *b*; cross and yoke 842-9
Crucifixion, not a Jewish punishment 927 ; of Peter 926 foll.

Black Arabics refer to paragraphs [2]800–[2]997, *ordinary Arabics to the sections of* 2998, *or, if starred, to the sections of* 2999. *For example,* 872 = 2872, 16 = 2998 (xvi), 16* = 2999 (xvi).

Cry (n.) "three mysteries of the c." 55 *h*
Cry (vb.) *i.e.* "proclaim the gospel" 839 *b*
Cup, metaph. 935

Daniel, the Aramaic portion of 8; *ben adam* in 8; influence of, on Revelation 942* (i) *e*, (xviii), 26–33 *passim*
"Daughters" or "branches" 837 (ii)
David, son of 23 *b*, 36
"Dawn" (vb.) applied to God 27 *t*
Dead, first-born of the 26 *o*; "the dead are raised" 995
Delocalisation 28 *i*
Delos 942* (xi), (xiii) *b*
Denarius, a day's wage 942* (v) *a*
"Depart," ambig. 938–9
Desolation, the abomination of 837 (iii), 874 *e*, comp. 942* (i) *m*
Didaché, the, i.e. The Teaching of the Twelve Apostles 895, 26 *s*, 27 *w*
Didrachm 7 *b** foll., 9 *a**, 10*
Digamma 942* (i) *l*
Diogenes, in Epict. 814; Jerome on 824
"Disciples," "those with him" &c., parallels to 17 *g–h**
"Distrahitur," not "beheaded" 937 *d*
Divergence, caused by obscurity 837 foll.; caused by metaph. 17 *a** foll.; s. also Pref. p. xiv foll.
Divider, God as 28 *v*; the Logos as 28 *u*
Docetics, the 35
Domitian 942* (i) *a, b, e, m*, 27 *k*, 28 *a*; "a bald Nero" 942* (i) foll.; prohibits new vineyards 942* (v) *a*; on a white horse 28 *d*
Door, metaph. 985
Drachma, finding a 9*
Dragon, the 942* (xii) *c* foll., (xx) *a*
"Draw near" and "touch" 1*–2*; "draw near," "go to meet," and "go before" 4*–5*
Dropsical 961 (i) *c*

Eagle, the great 942* (xiii)
Earthquakes 942* (v) *b*, 946
Eating, attributed to Christ after the Resurrection 896–907; metaph. 56 *c*
Ebion and the Ebionites 867, 40, 41
Eclipse, an, Origen on 910
Egypt, "the iron furnace" 950
Eight hundred and eighty-eight 942* (i) *k* foll.
"Eighth," only twice applied to persons in N.T. 942* (i) *f*; "Noah the e. person" 942* (i) *f, k*

Elchasai 942* (xxiv) *a, b*
"Elder, the," meaning of 915, 954–5; "elders," mentioned by Irenæus 958; "twenty-four e." 942* (xv) *b*, 33 *a*
Elect, the 51
Elect one, the 51 foll.
Eliezer, the name 994
Elihu 10
Emmanuel 40
"End," parall. to "fig-time" 874 *a–b*
Enoch, the Patriarch 54 *c*; called the Son of Man 55
Enoch, the Book of 51 *a* foll.; a compilation 942* (xix); compared w. Revelation of John 942* (xix); quoted as Scripture 914; earlier part of 56
Enoch, the Similitudes of 19, 51; date of 51 *a* foll.; on the throne of judgment 8 *c*; doctrine of "hiding" in 55 *d* foll.
Ephod, the 17 *a–n**
Ephrem, on the "tree" *i.e.* "cross" 933; s. also 15 *b*, 24 *g*, 7 *e**, 8*, 17 *h**, 17 *o**
Epictetus, alleged lameness of 801; agreements of, with John 805–6; anecdote about 912; on the Galilæans 813; on repentance 815; on profit 816
Epictetus, Dissertations of:—
Bk. I. i. 7 (802), i. 10 (802), ii. 12 (802), ii. 19 foll. (801), ii. 21 (818), ii. 29 (801), iv. 11 (814), iv. 24–7 (913), ix. 10–12 (954), ix. 15 (801), ix. 29 (810), ix. 30–2 (814), x. 2 (8 *b**), xii. 3 (822), xii. 16 (804), xii. 24 (801–2), xiv. 7–10 (822), xiv. 12 (804), xiv. 15–17 (807), xvi. 1 foll. (822), xvii. 1–4 (822), xviii. 19 (913), xix. 6 (807, 824, 840), xix. 8–9 (801), xix. 11 (816), xix. 12–15 (807), xxii. 1 (807), xxiv. 1 foll. (825), xxiv. 6 (823, 840), xxiv. 15 foll. (913), xxv. 1 foll. (825), xxvii. 4–6 (813), xxix. 1 foll. (812), xxix. 3–4 (817), xxix. 4 (815), xxix. 9 foll. (801), xxix. 18 (808), xxix. 46 (811), xxix. 50 foll. (801), xxx. 1 foll. (812), xxx. 6–7 (801)
Bk. II. ii. 1 foll. (913), ii. 15 (808), ii. 22 (879), v. 15 foll. (828), v. 15–20 (913), vi. 10–13 (825), vi. 26 (840), vi. 27 (818), vii. 10–12 (814), viii. 2 (819), viii. 10 foll. (804), viii. 12 foll. (807, 811), viii. 18–20 (807), viii. 21 foll. (827), viii. 28 (818), ix. 1 foll. (801), ix. 3 (801,

---

Black Arabics refer to paragraphs [2]800–[2]997, *ordinary Arabics to the sections of* 2998, *or, if starred, to the sections of* 2999. *For example,* 872 = 2872, 16 = 2998 (xvi), 16* = 2999 (xvi).

997), ix. 19 foll. (812), x. 1 (997), xi. 1 (985), xii. 20-1 (819), xiii. 10 (913), xiii. 14 (801), xiii. 21-7 (801), xiv. 11 foll. (802), xiv. 15 (879), xv. 6 (939), xvi. 1 (812), xvi. 27 foll. (817), xvi. 33 (807), xvii. 19 foll. (827), xvii. 26 (827), xvii. 38 (818), xviii. 29 (814), xix. 20 foll. (827), xix. 23-4 (811 b), xix. 26 (807), xix. 32-4 (827), xx. 7 (827), xx. 22 (815), xx. 32 (807, 992), xxii. 15 (807, 816), xxiii. 13 (827), xxvi. 1 foll. (817)

Bk. III. i. 16 (913), i. 19 (913), i. 36 (818), iii. 2-4 (819), iii. 5 (913), iii. 6 (807), iii. 7 (913), vii. 4 (819), vii. 33-4 (825), vii. 34 (840), x. 13 (824), xii. 6 (813), xiii. 1 foll. (819), xiii. 4 (807), xiii. 13-15 (819), xiii. 23 (811), xv. 14 (822), xvi. 13 (813), xvii. 1 foll. (822), xxi. 11-12 (814), xxii. 5-8 (804), xxii. 21 (818), xxii. 23 (823), xxii. 30 foll. (801, 812), xxii. 35 (985), xxii. 45 foll. (801), xxii. 49 (884), xxii. 54 (811, 884), xxii. 56 (814), xxii. 58 (824), xxii. 69 (811), xxii. 72 (801, 820, 840), xxii. 73 (840), xxii. 78 (978), xxiii. 21 (808), xxiii. 30 (812), xxiv. 8 (818), xxiv. 14-20 (805-6), xxiv. 18 (913), xxiv. 18-20 (985), xxiv. 19 (804, 913), xxiv. 48 (801), xxiv. 64 foll. (814), xxiv. 64-8 (913), xxiv. 86 (55 j), xxiv. 91 (55 j), xxiv. 111-15 (804), xxv. 5 (813), xxvi. 22 (929)

Bk. IV. i. 79 (887 a), i. 103 (817), i. 153 (887), i. 169 (828), iv. 7 (815), v. 3 (913), v. 16 (801), v. 28 (818), vi. 5 (802), vii. 6 (813), viii. 35-6 (55 j), viii. 36-43 (876), ix. 6 foll. (817), ix. 12 (817), ix. 16 (814, 817), x. 14 foll. (801), x. 16 (803), x. 31 (818), xi. 4 (985), xii. 10-11 (803), xii. 19 (818), xiii. 4-19 (827)

Epictetus, Manual of (or *Encheiridion*) i. 3 (817), i. 5 (812), v. (817), viii. (817), x. (815), xi. (817), xv. (806), xvi. (913), xviii. (913), liii. 4 (808)

Epiphanes, Antiochus 942* (i) e
Epiphanius, on James the Just 17 c*; s. also 824* (i) b, 865, 942* (xxiv) b, 994, 17 b* foll.
Esdras, Fourth (or Second) Book of 942* (i) a, 993, 54 h, 55 g

Essenes, the 27 r-w
Eucharist, the, implies incorporation 895
"Euergetes," assumed as title 829
Euphrates, the 51 b
Eusebius, on "two tombs of John" 957; s. also 828, 837 (iii), 879, 915, 937 b-c, 939 a, 940 a, 942* (i) b, (v) a-b, (xiii) e, (xxii) c-d, 957-8, 960, 961 (i) a, 967 a, 984, 997 a, 25, 54 g, 17 c*, 17 h*
Evangelium Infantiae Arabicum 17 g, j
Exactors 14 a*
"Eyes of God (or the Lord)" 28 b, p; connected with "stone" 27 v
"Eyewitnesses" 984
Ezekiel 942* (viii) h, (xv) e, (xvi); influence of, on Revelation 942*, also 942* (iv) a and (xviii), and 28-33 *passim*; parallelism of, with John 942* (ii); *ben adam* in 7

Faith 992; as a grain of mustard-seed 851-6
Famine 942* (v)
"Favour," "grace," "kindness" &c. 840*
Feeding with (?) συναλιζόμενος 893
Feet, washing of the 963-5
Fever and Cholera, divinities 807, 824
Field, beasts of the 840, 43 d
Fifty, "thou art not yet f." 989
"Fig-time," parall. to "end" 874 a-b
Fig-tree, the barren 874-8
Finding a stater 7* foll.; a drachma &c. 9*
Fire, the Stoics on 819; martyrdom by, legends of 948-51; flame of 28 p; baptism of spirit or of fire 30; confused with "man" 7 c
First 7* foll., 16*; "First" and "Last" 27 a foll.
Firstborn of the dead 26 o
Fish, different symbolisms of 11*; the first 7* foll., 16*
Fishing 8*-9*
Flame, meant by "Ur" 949; of fire 28 p
Flesh, sons of 3
"Flocks" and "waking up" 17 g
Following, metaph. 936 a
"Footstool" 22 b-c, 31 b
Forsaking 917 foll.
"Forty-six years" (Jn ii. 20) 962
Fountain of righteousness 53
Four "beasts" and four "living creatures" 33 a

Black Arabics refer to paragraphs [2]800-[2]997, *ordinary Arabics to the sections of* 2998, *or, if starred, to the sections of* 2999. *For example*, 872 = 2872, 16 = 2998 (xvi), 16* = 2999 (xvi).

ENGLISH 141

Fulfilment, in Jn and Epict. 806
"Fuller, the," term given to a rabbi 837 (iii) c
"Fuller's club, a" 17 c*
"Furnace, the iron," i.e. Egypt 950

Gabriel and Michael 33 a
Galilæans, the 813
Galilee 4*, 5*
Garment, reaching to the feet 28
Garments, white 17 a* foll.
Genealogy, Christ's, in Mt. and Lk. 38 a
Genitive, defining, force of 20
Gird 926-34, 17 n* foll.
Girdle, the golden 28 l
Glorifying 23 e
Glory of God, the, "above the heavens" 12, 24 e, 50 c; "a living man" 28 b
Gnostics, the, on the Son of Man 34-6
Go, "going out" 12*; "going up" 8*; "going to meet," "going before," and "drawing near" 4*-5*
God, "is not as man" 4; why called "man" 45; "repents" 3; said "not to repent" 45 a; "meeting" man 3*; said to "dawn" 27 l; rendered by τὸ θεῖον 27 u; dividing 28 v; "hands" of 40 a; "the right hand of," s. "right"
Gold, metaph., meaning of 28 l
Golden girdle, the 28 l
Goodness and authority, Philo on 28 u
"Gospel," in Mk, referring to Isaiah 839 c; fourth, date of 962 a; s. also Hebrews
Gospels, Irenæus on the number of 916
"Grace," "favour," "kindness" &c. 840*
Great City, the 942* (i) c, (ii) a foll.
Greatness 992
"Greeks, are always boys" 888

Habit, Epict. on 813
Hadrian 942* (viii)
Hair, white 27 o, 29 c; as wool 28 o
Hand, "stretch out the hand" and "stretch out the hands" 928, 932-4; "upon the throne of Jah" and "hidden" 36 a
Hands, of God 36 a, 40 a, 43; of an idol 837 (iii) d; "stretch out the h. on the cross" 926 foll.; "spread abroad the h." 928; "works of God" and "works of God's h." 43 b
Hannah, the mother of Samuel 880

"Head, rested his" 967; "a h. of days" 52; s. also 8 c
"Heads," prophetic meaning of 942* (i) a, c
Healing 995
Heaven, hosts of 16
Heavens, glory above the 12, 24 e, 50 c
Hebrew, Matthew wrote in 916; parallelism, Matthew misunderstood 3*
Hebrews, Epistle to the 839; on the Son of Man 24
Hebrews, Gospel of the 824* (i), 17 d* foll.
Hegesippus, on James the Just 837 (iii), 25, 17 c*; s. also 967 a
"Heli," connected with "sun" 917 foll.
Heracleon 938; on martyrdom 941
Hercules, as a son of God 806
Hermas, author of the Shepherd 981, 28 m
Hermas, an imaginary character 838
Herod the Tetrarch 17 a
Hesperus 17 d
Hiding, the doctrine of, in Enoch 55 d foll.; a means to manifesting 55 m; Noah "was hidden" 55 e; "a hand hidden" and "a hand upon the throne of Jah" 36 a
High, the Most, a name of God 26 p
High priest, the, clothing of 27 t-v
"Him" and "sign" 54 c
Hippolytus 852, 920, 942* (xii) a, b, (xiii) d, (xxii) d, (xxiv) a, 27 f, t, v, 55 h
"Hold fast" and "draw near" 2*
Honour, two kinds of 43
"Hook" and "net" 8*
Horse, a white 28 d, 29 c
Hosts, of heaven 16, 27 m; the Lord of 27 m
"House" = "School" 12*
Husbands, five 961 (i)
Hymning 897-907

I AM, applied to God 27 e
Ignatius, on the Son of Man 35; s. also 824* (i), 891, 894-5, 942* (xv) d, 962 a, 17 d, 55 h, 17 g*
"Immolatur," how used by Tertullian 937 d
Incorporation, implied in the Eucharist 895
Infanticide, Tertullian on 911
Inkhorn, a writer's 28 m
Irenæus, mentions "elders" 958; on

Black Arabics refer to paragraphs [2]800-[2]997, *ordinary Arabics to the sections of* 2998, *or, if starred, to the sections of* 2999. *For example,* 872 = 2872, 16 = 2998 (xvi), 16* = 2999 (xvi).

the number of the gospels 916; on "Titan" 942* (i) *l–m*; on the Son of Man, misquotes Jn i. 13, 39–40; s. also 882, 895, 917, 920, 923a, 942* (i) *k, l, m, o*, (xii) *a*, 961, 984 *a, e*, 986, 989, 994, 996, 997a, 15, 27d, 28b, 34, 36a

Isaac, son of Sarah 880; metaph. "laughter" 881a, 942* (xii) *b*

Isaiah, and Mark, continuity between 839 *a–d*; *ben adam* in 5; in LXX, peculiarities of 27 *b*

Israel, house of 860; the name, meaning of 987

Jacob's Ladder, Jewish tradition about 14

James the Just, or Righteous 837 (iii), 54g, Hegesippus on 17c*; called the brother of the Lord 25; s. also 937 *d*

James the son of Zebedee 937 *d*, 942* (xxii) *c*

Jeremiah, *ben adam* in 6

Jerome, on John's old age 952; on Jewish interpretations 942* (i) *o, q*, (xiii) *f*; s. also 823, 824* (i), 960, 961 (i) *a*, 995, 997 *a*, 7 *d*, 22 *c*, 17 *c–d**, 17 *j–k**

Jerusalem, the fall of 942* (vii) foll.; the spoils of 28 *d*; the surrounding of 837 (i), (iii), 874 *f*; going up to 8 *e**

Jesus, the age of 989–90; not seen in the visions of Revelation 33; verbs of motion applied to 6*; s. also "Christ"

Jesus, the kinsman of Ananus 942* (ii) *d*

Jesus, the son of Nun 942* (ii) *b*

Jezebel 942* (iii) *b*, (xv) *f*

Job 10, 12

John the Apostle, son of Zebedee, confused with John the Baptist 937; tradition about 948; old age of 952; parallelism between, and Ezekiel 942* (ii); s. also "Revelation"

John the Baptist 942* (xxii) *b–d*, 995; confused with John the son of Zebedee 937; described by Origen as an "angel" 942* (xxii) *d*, comp. 15 *f*; the Spirit said to have "ceased" in 942* (xxii) *d*

John the Evangelist, intervenes in Synoptic Tradition 965, comp. 936; on the Son of Man 21; use of χάρις by 840* *g*

Joseph (husband of Mary), son of 979

Joseph (son of Jacob), Targumistic tradition on 837 (ii)

Joseph, The Prayer of, an apocr. work 15 *f*

Josephus, on the Galilæans 813; illustrated by Targums 837 (ii); interpolation in 837 (iii); illustrations of Revelation from 942* (vi) *a*; s. also 839, 890, 942* (ii) *d*, (ix), (xxii) *d*, 971, 27 *r–v*, 27 *w*, 28 *d–e*, 7 *c–d**

Joshua 36

Judah, Targumistic tradition on 837 (ii)

Judging 28 *s*

Judgment, the throne of 8 *b–c*

Justin Martyr, not a Samaritan by religion 37 *b*; on the Son of Man 37–9; s. also 846, 880, 882, 898–907, 917, 942* (and 942* (xxii) *d*), 986, 994, 28 *a*, 36 *a*

"Kindness," "grace," "favour" &c. 840*

Kingdom, the, is within 44

"Kings" and "kingdoms" interchanged 942* (i) *a*

Know s. "See"

Lamb, two Gk words for 32 *b–d*; *talitha* in Heb., not in Aram. 32 *c*; "lambs" parall. to "sheep" 32 *e*

Lamb of God, the 32 *d*; in the bosom of the Father 32; the sacrificial aspect of 32; the throne of 32; the Bride of 942* (xv) *c*

Lamech 54 *d*

Laodicea 942* (v); the Church of 28 *h*

Last, "first and last," applied to God 27 *b–c*

Latona 942* (xiii) *b*

Laughter, meant by "Isaac" 881 *a*

Law, the, at the right hand of God 31 *a*

Leaven 55 *k*

Leper, the Messiah to be a 995; "cleanse the lepers" 995

Letters, ignorant of 879

Life, the Book of 942* (viii) *g*

"Lifting up" 23 *e*

"Likeness," of a son of man, meaning of 33

Linen 17 *a** foll.

Living creatures, the four 942*, 33 *a*

Loaf, one 895

"Locusts with the hair of women" 942* (vi) *a*

Logos, the, between Goodness and Authority 28 *u*; the universal

Black Arabics refer to paragraphs [2]800–[2]997, *ordinary Arabics to the sections of* 2998, *or, if starred, to the sections of* 2999. *For example,* 872 = 2872, 16 = 2998 (xvi), 16* = 2999 (xvi).

divider 28 *u*; comes forth from silence 55 *h*
Lord, of hosts 27 *m*; of Spirits 51
Lord's Day, the 942* (iii) *b*
Lost, ambig. 863; save the 861 foll.
Love (n.), never mentioned by Mark 924
Loving-kindness 840* *d–e*
Lucifer 16
Luke, "inseparable from Paul" 984 *e*; his use of χάρις 840* *g*; his tradition about Christ's eating 897–907; his omission of "Why hast thou forsaken me?" 917 foll.; his preface to his gospel 980–4; on Christ's genealogy 38 *a*
Luther, on repentance 800 *c–d*
Lyons, the Martyrs of 939, 942* (xxii) *d*

Maccabean princes 51 *a*
Magi, the 17
Malchus, the name 17 *i*
"Man" and "the man" 43 *c*; dominion of 47; God is not as 4; God meeting 3*; ?"man" or "Adam" 20 *c*; "man" and "men" 23 *c*, 37 *c*; Son of Man, definite or indefinite 19, 37–45; s. also 998 *passim*
Man-child, the, birth of 942* (xi) foll.
Manna, the hidden 942* (xv)
Marcion 824* (i) *d*, 55 *i*
Mark, Papias on 915, 965, 983–4; never mentions love (n.) 924; his gospel, how concluded 924; continuity of, with Isaiah 839 *a–d*
Martyr, or witness 935, 26 *h–k*; or confessor 939 *a*; s. also "Martyrs"
Martyrdom 940 foll., 28 *a*; by fire, legends of 948–51
Martyrs 942* (iii) *c*, 25 *a*; variety of 937 *d*
Mary, 881–2, s. also "Virgin"
Matthew, misunderstands Heb. parallelism 3*; literalises 15*; on Christ's genealogy 38 *a*
"Meant" and "said" 837 (iii) *a*, 874 *f*
Measures, three 55 *k*
Measuring for the Temple 942* (ii) *a*, (iv)
"Meet," and "appear" 3*; and "call" 3 *g*, 4*; God "meeting" man 3*; "meeting" Moses 3*–4*; "go to meet," "go before," and "draw near" 4*–5*
Meeting, the tabernacle of 3*
Mercy 840* *a–f*
Messiah, the, birth of 942* (xi) foll.; to be a leper 995; in N.T. 21 *a*; to go forth from Rome 28 *v*
Metaphors, converted to prose 837 foll.; anthropomorphic 45; cause divergence 17 *a** foll.; s. also Pref. p. xiv foll.
Methuselah 54 *d*
Michael 27 *p*; and Gabriel 33 *a*
Midst, standing in the 897 foll.; walking in the 28 *f–k*
Ministers, in N.T. 983; of Christ 984
Miriam, the song of 27 *s*
"Mirror, the enigma of the" 826
Mistranslation 830 foll.
Moon, the, a witness 26 *n*
Moses 942* (xiii), (xv), 28 *v*; opposed by angels 11 foll.; being met by God 3*–4*; the song of 27 *s*
Mother, the Berecynthian 942* (xi)
Motion, verbs of, applied to Jesus 6*
Mountains, an uprooter of 873; seven 942* (i) *d*
Mouth, the, a sword 28 *t*; "opening the mouth" 14 *b–d**
Muratorian Fragment, the 956
Musonius Rufus 810, 944
Mustard-seed, faith as a grain of 851–6
Myriads of angels 31 *a*
"Mysteries of the cry, three" 55 *h*
Myth, springing from verbal corruption 17 *c**

Nakedness, lit. and metaph. 17 *b** foll., comp. 28 *h*
Name, "for my name's sake" 816; s. also below
Names, variations of 942* (i) *q*; "names of men"? used for persons 942* (viii); "men of name(s)" 942* (viii) *i*
Nebuchadnezzar, the dream of 15; "the true N." 24 *e*
Nero 942* (i) foll.; said to be "avenged" 942* (i) *e, m*
"Net" and "hook" 8*
Nicolaitans, the 942* (iii) *b*
Nile, the 942* (xiii) *c*
Noah, "the eighth person" 942* (i) *f, k* inferior to Abraham 37 *d*; hidden 55 *e*; Philo on 54 *h*
Number, the of the Beast 942* (i) *l* foll.; of a man 942* (i) *m*
Numbering 942* (viii) *g*
Numbers, antithetical 942* (i); mystical 942*, 942* (i) *d* foll., (vi)–(x), 994; stress on 28 *k*

Black Arabics refer to paragraphs [2]800–[2]997, *ordinary Arabics to the sections of* 2998, *or, if starred, to the sections of* 2999. *For example,* 872=2872, 16=2998 (xvi), 16*=2999 (xvi).

Obscurity, causes of **837** (ii); divergence caused by **837**; s. also Pref. p. xv foll.
Offerings, bringing 17 *b*
Oholah and Oholibah **942*** (xv) *f*
Olive-tree, the sacred, in Acropolis **820**
Omega, Alpha and 27 *a* foll.
"Omnitenens," Origen's use of 27 *g*
"Opening the mouth" 14 *b–d**
Oracula Sibyllina **942*** (i) *a*, (ii) *b*, (v) *b*, **946**, 27 *w*
Origen, on ἀσώματος **824*** (i) *e*; quotes interpolation fr. Josephus **837** (iii); on the ass and colt **848**; on mustard-seed **853** foll.; on the fig-tree **878**; on little children **885–6**; on an eclipse **910**; on the forsaking of Christ **919–23**; on the sword 28 *t*; on the removing spirit 30; on clouds 31 *a*; on the Son of Man 43–5; refers to Philo 45 *a*; s. also **801**, **805** *a*, **824*** (i) *a–f*; **845**, **857**, **867**, **874** *d–f*, **881** *a*, **890**, **892** *a–c*, **896**, **909**, **937** *c*, **941**, **942***, **942*** (i) *c*, (ii) *c*, (viii) *h*, (xii) *b–c*, (xiii) *d*, (xv) *d*, (xvii), (xviii), (xxii) *c–d*, **961** *a*, **961** (i), **963–4**, **967**, **972**, **974–5**, **978**, **980**, **982**, **984** *b–c*, **989**, **995**, 7 *d–e*, 13, 15 *b*, *f*, 16, 17 *a*, 20 *b*, 22 *c*, 23 *e*, 24 *e–f*, 26 *k*, *m*, 27 *f*, *g*, *l*, *q*, 28 *a*, *m*, *o*, *t*, *w*, *x*, 30, 32 *d*, 34 *a*, 48, 49 *a*, 50 *b*, 54 *c–g*, 55 *h–k*, 7 *a–b**, 7 *e**, 9*, 10*, 11 *a–b**
Orphans, in Epict., Jn, and Talmud **805**
Osiris **856**
Oulai 28 *j*

Papias, on Mark **915**, **965**, **984**; s. also **879**, **937**, **941**
Papyri, the **811** *a*, **875**, **879**, **923** *d*, **942*** (viii) *b* foll., **982**, **997**, 32 *b*, 44 *b*, 17 *m**
Parables, anthropomorphic 45
Parthians **942*** (xxiv) *a*, 51 *a* foll.
Patmos **942*** (xiii) *b*, **942–7**
Patriarchs, the 54 *h*; of promise 37; son of 37
Paul, "inseparable from Luke" **984** *e*; an "eyewitness" **984** *a*; mentioned in the *Recognitions of Clement* **837** (iii) *c*; does not mention the Son of Man in his epistles 22
Pella **837** (iii) *a*, **942*** (xiii) *e*
Peter, death of **926** foll.; martyrdom of 26 *j*; primacy of 7*; in Rome, legends of 15 *a**; the first to see the risen Saviour 17 *f**; the "reclothing" of 17*
Peter, the name, parallels to 17 *g–h**, comp. **875**
Peter, the Teaching of **824*** (i)
Pharaoh **942*** (xiii) *a*, *c*
Philo, referred to by Origen 45 *a*; on the Therapeutae 27 *r* foll.; on Noah 54 *h*; on "the half of the didrachm" 10*; s. also **806**, **880**, **881** *a*, **888**, **908**, **923** *b*, **942*** (i) *k*, (xii) *b*, **961** *a*, **965**, **987–9**, **994**, **996**, 4 (esp. 4 *b*, *d*), 26 *d*, 28 *d*, *e*, *j*, *n*, *u*, *v*, *x*, 30, 31 *b*, 54 *c*, *d*, *h*, *j*, 55 *k*, 56 *d*, 10*, 17 *o**
Philosophers, pretended **811**
Pillar, metaph., errors caused by 17 *h**; of cloud 30, 31; of cloud, Rashi on 4 *c*
Pinnacle, of the Temple **837** (iii); s. also Pref. p. xvii foll.
Planets, s. "Stars"
Plant of righteousness 55 *f*
Pleasing, Epict. on **803**
Pliny **944**, **946**, **960**
Plummet, metaph. 26 *m*, 28 *b*
Polycrates **958**
Pompey **942*** (xiii) *a*
Pool of (R.V.) Bethesda **959** foll.
Poor, metaph. **942*** (xv)
Porch, the, of the Temple 28 *j*
Power, the **824**
"Pray," "stand," and "with," confusable 27 *t*
Prayer, not entirely forbidden by Epict. **814**; prayers, perhaps personified 15 *b*
Prayer of Joseph, the, an apocr. work 15 *f*
Precocity, human, illustrations of **876**
Priests, metaph. 26 *r*
Proclaim, i.e. preach the gospel **839** *b*
Profit, Epict. on **807**, **816**
Promise of the Man, the **997**
Propator, the 34
Prophecy, adaptation of **942*** (i) *o*
Prose, substituted for metaphor **837** foll.
Psalms, the Son of Man in 9–10
Python **942*** (xiii) *b*

Quarries in Patmos **947**

Race, i.e. Gentiles, as opposed to Jews 37 *a*
Raising the dead **995**
Rashi, on the pillar of cloud (Deut. i. 31) 4 *c*
Receiving as a little child **885–6**

Black Arabics refer to paragraphs [2]**800**–[2]**997**, *ordinary Arabics to the sections of* **2998**, *or, if starred, to the sections of* **2999**. *For example*, **872**=**2872**, 16=**2998** (xvi), 16*=**2999** (xvi).

ENGLISH 145

Recorder, in Ezekiel, the 28 *n*
Regeneration 885
"Relegatio" 941, 944
Remnant, the faithful 942* (viii), (xiii) *f*
Repent, God does and does not 3, 45 *a*
Repentance 815, 992; Luther on 800 *c–d*
Rephaim 942* (i) *m*
"Rested his head" 967
Resurrection, the 56; of the body 56 *a*; different beliefs as to 56 *a*; and ascension of Christ, events between 892 foll.
Revelation of John the Apostle, the, date and authorship of 942* foll.; moral character of 942* (xvii) foll.; parallelism between, and Ezekiel 942* (ii); influenced by prophets 942* (i) *e*, (iv) *a–b*, (xviii), 26–33 *passim*; on the Son of Man 26 foll.
Right hand of God 23 *b*, 25 *a*, 32; the Law or the angels at 31 *a*
"Righteous," first use of in O.T. 54 *h*; Heb. (*tsaddîk*) used and disused 54 *i*; "the righteous one" 51 foll., 54 *c*, 55 *a*; in N.T. 54 *e, f*; the Righteous Servant, in Isaiah 54 *f*
Righteousness, fountain of 53; plant of 55 *f*
Ripeness 874
River 942* (xiii)
Roman Empire, the 942* (i) *h*
Rosh Hashanah 961, 961 (i)
Rufus, Musonius 810
Rufus, Tineius 942* (i) *q*
Rulers, oppressive 51 *b*

Sabaoth 27 *b*, *k* foll.
Sacrifice 963-4
Sadducees 51 *a*
Salt, metaph. 858
Samaritan, Justin not a, by religion 37 *b*
Samaritans 868, 37 *b*
Samson 837 (i)
Samuel, son of Hannah 880
Sapphire 7 *e*; s. and "writer" 28 *m*
Sarah 881 *a*; Isaac son of 880, 55 *k*
Scapegoat, the 28 *o*
Scorpion, the constellation 942* (xiii) *g*
Scribes, adjuration to 942* (xix) *a*
Scripture, *Enoch* quoted as 914
Scriptures, opening the 908
Sea, the 942* (xiii) *a*, 961, 992, 55 *g*
Sealing, the, of the faithful 28 *n*
See, "he that seeth" 987; "I know (οἶδα)" rendered "I saw (vidi)" 824* (i) *c*

Seer, a 942* (ii), (xiii) *c*, 26 *g*, 32; s. also "Vision"
Self-suppression, taught by Epict. 55 *j*
"Servant," in Is. l. 10 rendered "son" by Tertull. 54 *f*; the righteous, in Isaiah 54 *f*; the suffering, a leper 995; of the priest 17 *e**, 17 *i** foll.
Seven, mystically used 942* (i), 26 *m*, 28 *e*, *k*, *y*; angels, kings, hills, mountains, seals, spirits, stars, torches &c. 942* (i) *d*, *i*; churches, the 942* (iii); candlesticks 942* (xxii) *a*; signs 991; confused with "seventy" 26 *m*
Seven thousand 942* (viii), (xiii) *f*
Seventy, confused with seven 26 *m*; disciples, the 50 *e*
Shaddai 27 *j*
Shakespeare, misled by North's Plutarch 830 foll.
Shechinah, the 969–71, 27 *c*, 28 *f*
Sheep, the lost 860–71; parall. to "lambs" 32 *e*
Shekel of the sanctuary, the 7 *c**
Shema, the, recitation of 27 *t*
Shepherd, in the gospels 869–71
Side, "by the side of"=ἐπὶ χεῖρα 961 (i) *d*
"Sign," confused with "him" 54 *c*
Silence, the Logos comes forth from 55 *h*
Siloam 961
Similitudes, the, s. "Enoch"
Simon, the name, parallels to 17 *g–h**
Simon Magus 852
Simon the Righteous 54 *g*
Six 942* (i) *k* foll.
Six hundred and sixty-six 942* (i) *k–m*
"Snow" and "wool" 28 *o*
Socrates, on Anytus 808; saying the same things 809; zealots of 840
Solomon 942* (xv) *f*
Solomon, the Wisdom of 956
Son, in Heb., =specimen of a class 4; in classical Gk, metaph. 20 *d*; s. of David 36; of the Patriarchs 37
Son of God 36; "a" or "the" 20
Son of Man, the 998 *passim*; the term, why disliked 35; "one like a" 26 *a*, 28 *l–r*, 33; in *Enoch* 52 foll.; def. or indef. 19, 45; s. also "Man"
Sons, of flesh 3; of God, interch. w. "angels" 16; of men 20 *f*; of Zeus 880 *a*; "s. of oil" (Zech. iv. 14) 942* (xxii)
Song, of Miriam and Moses, the 27 *s*
Sophia, the Valentinians on 917, 923 *a*
"Soul," in Heb., ="self" 966

Black Arabics refer to paragraphs [2]800–[2]997, *ordinary Arabics to the sections of* 2998, *or, if starred, to the sections of* 2999. *For example,* 872=2872, 16=2998 (xvi), 16*=2999 (xvi).

A. 10

Sow, the congregation sown by God 55 *f*
Spirit, the, used absolutely 29 *b*; said to have "ceased" in John the Baptist **942*** (xxii) *d*
"Spirit," interch. w. "wind" **837** *a*, 30; the removing wind or spirit 30; baptism of spirit or of fire 30
Spirits, bodiless, evil **824*** (i) ; the Lord of 51 ; the seven 26 *m*; three, unclean **942*** (xx) *a*
Spiritual body, a **824*** foll.
"Spread abroad the hands" **928**
Springs, medicinal and intermittent **960**
Staff, perh. metaph. **888**
Stand 25; in the midst **897** foll. ; "stand," "pray," and "with," confusable 27 *t*; "stood up" or "were appointed" 17 *g* *
"Stars," and "angels" 16 foll., 28 *e*; and "sword" 28 *s–x*; singing 16; the seven s., *i.e.* the planets 28 *u*
Stater, finding a **7*** foll., **12*** foll.
"Staters, Samuel's," proverb about 9 *a**
Stephen **937** *c–d*, 24–5
"Stoic, a genuine" **811** *b*
Stone, meaning "plummet" 26 *m* ; connected with "eyes of God" 27 *v*; "rolled away" **909**
"Stretching out the hand(s)" **928**, **932–4**; on the cross **926** foll.
Subjecting 22, 24 *c*, 50 *e*
Suckling 49; confused with "sucker" 49; used by Jews = "pupil" 49; connected with "Son of Man" 50 *b*
Sucklings, s. "Babes"
Sun, the 28 *x*; one of the seven stars 28 *u*; worshipped **942*** (i) *m*, (xxiv) *b*; not worshipped by the Essenes 27 *r–v*; connected with "Heli" **917** foll. ; with "God" **920**, with "tabernacle" **918–20**, **942*** (xiii) *d*
Sunrise, a time of prayer 27 *t*
Sweat, metaph. **986**
"Sword," and "stars" 28 *s–x*; the mouth a s. 28 *t*; Origen on 28 *t*; two-edged **942***, **942*** (xvii), (xxii), 28 *n*
Symbolism **942*** and **942*** (i)–(xxiv) *passim*, 26–33 *passim*
Syrophœnician woman, the **862**, **867**

Tabernacle (n.) 28 *f*; of meeting or of testimony 3*; "in the sun he placed his t." **918–20**, **942*** (xiii) *d*
Tabernacle (vb) 28 *f*
Tacitus, on the Christians **807**

Talitha = (Heb.) "lamb," (Aram.) "young one" 32 *c*
Targums, **837** foll., **949–51**, 4, 28 *v*; s. also *Pref.* pp. vii–viii and xiii foll.
T(e)itan, Irenæus on **942*** (i) *m*
Temple, the **962**, metaph. **839**, **942*** (xv); measuring for **942*** (ii) *a*, (iv) ; destruction of **942*** (xi) *a*
Tertullian, on infanticide **911**; on the Son of Man 41 ; renders "servant" in Is. l. 10 "son" 54 *f*; s. also **824*** (i) *d*, **918**, **924**, **937** *d*, **939** *a*, **940**, **942*** (i) *b*, *m*, (xxii) *d*, **948**, **960**, **996**, 17 *c*, 41
Testimony, or meeting, tabernacle of 3*
Tetradrachm 7 *c** foll.
Theophany **998** *passim*
Therapeutae, the, Philo on 27 *r* foll.
Third part, a **942*** (viii), (xiii) *f*
Thirst, metaph. **966**; in Jn and Epict. **806**
Thirty, "a son of t. years" **994**
Thirty-eight, only twice in Bible **961** (i)
Three, measures 55 *k*; unclean spirits **942*** (xx) *a*
Three and a half years **942*** (i) *o*, (viii)
Threshold 28 *j*
Throne 8 *a*; metaph. **942*** (xv) ; of judgment 8 *b–c*; of God and the Lamb 32 ; of glory 8 *c*, 51 ; a white t. 29 *c*; the face of the 12; "a hand upon the t." 36 *a*
"Throne" or "thrones" 31 *b*
Thunder **972** foll.
Titan **942*** (i) *m*
Titus **942*** (i) *a*; the name, how used **942*** (i) *m*; in the Talmud **942*** (i) *m*, *q*
Tobit 15 *f*
"Touch" and "draw near" 1*–2*
Trajan, the third year of **942*** (xxiv) *a*
Transfiguration, the **942*** (i) *l*
Translations, Targumistic **837** foll. ; s. also "Targums"
"Travail, in" **942*** (xii), (xiv)
"Tree," *i.e.* "cross," Ephrem on **933**, comp. **942*** (ii) *b*
"Truth" or "bow" **837** (ii)
"Truth is always right" **828**
Turnus, *i.e.* tyrant **942*** (i) *q*
Twenty-four Elders, the **942*** (xv) *b*, 33 *a*
Two, divine powers, Philo on 28 *u*; witnesses, the **942*** (ii) *c–d*, (xix) foll.
Two-edged, s. "Sword"
Two hundred, perh. mystically used 17 *o**
Tyre **942*** (xv) *e–f*

Black Arabics refer to paragraphs [2]800–[2]997, *ordinary Arabics to the sections of* 2998, *or, if starred, to the sections of* 2999. *For example*, 872 = 2872, 16 = 2998 (xvi), 16* = 2999 (xvi).

Ulai 28 *j*
Ur, = "flame" **949**

Valentinians, the **917, 920, 942*** (i) *k–l*; on Sophia **923** *a*
Vespasian **942*** (i) *a*; placed the golden candlestick in the Temple of Peace **28** *e*
Vines, planting of, prohibited **942*** (v) *a*
Virgin, the **881-2, 942*** (xii), 37–9
"Virgin," in LXX, = Aq. "young woman" **880**
"Virgins," meaning of, in Rev. xiv. 4 **942*** (xv) *b–f*
Vision, mixed with fact **953**; s. also **942***, **942*** (i)–(xxiv) *passim*, 26–33 *passim* (esp. 26 *g*, 32), and *Apologia* pp. v–vi and 80
Visitation, Origen on **43** *a*
"Voice," interch. w. "angel" **26** *c–d*; "seeing the voice" **26** *d*
Vowel points, not written in anc. Scriptures **839** *a*

"Waking up," confused w. "flocks" **17** *g*
Walking, metaph. **890**; in the midst **28** *f–k*
Washing of Feet, the **963-5**
"Watcher," meaning "angel" **17** *h*
"Watchers by night," astrologers are **17** *f*
Water, by the side of **961** (i) *d*; "running w." **27** *w*
Waters **942*** (xiii) *c*, **961** (i) *d*, 28 *r*; gathering of **961** (i) *c*; many 28 *r*
"Week of years, a" **942*** (i) *o*

Weeping, in Jn and Epict. **806**
White, a symbol of purity **29** *c*; w. garments **17** *a** foll.
"Wind," interch. w. "spirit" **837** *a*; "the removing wind, or spirit" **30**
"Wing," in Dan. ix. 27 **837** (i), (iii); parall. to "army" **837** (i); s. also Pref. p. xvi foll.
Wisdom, Philo on **923** *b*
Wisdom of Solomon, the **956**
"With," "pray," and "stand," confusable **27** *t*; "those with him" **17** *g–h**
"Witness" and "martyr" **26** *h–k*; the faithful **26** *n–q*
Witnesses, the two **942*** (ii) *a, c*, (xix) foll.
Woman, born of a **880**
Wool, scarlet **28** *o*; and snow **28** *o*
Works, (1) of God, (2) of God's hands **43** *b*
Worship, of symbols, deprecated **27** *o*
"Written, it is" **914**
"Writer" confused with "sapphire" **28** *m*

Year, the New **960-1**; year by year, ambig. **961** (i)
Yoke and Cross **842-9**

Zealots of Socrates **840**
Zechariah, influence of, on Revelation **942*** (iv) *b*; "sons of oil" (Zech. iv. 14) **942*** (xxii)
Zeus, sons of **880** *a*
Zipporah **2*, 3***

Black Arabics refer to paragraphs [2]800–[2]997, *ordinary Arabics to the sections of* **2998**, *or, if starred, to the sections of* **2999**. *For example,* 872 = 2872; 16 = 2998 (xvi), 16* = 2999 (xvi).

NOTES ON NEW TESTAMENT CRITICISM

III. GREEK

[*Black Arabics refer to paragraphs* [2]800–[2]997 (*the* 2 *not being printed*). *Ordinary Arabics refer to the sections of* 2998–9, *the two* "*Longer Notes*"[1].]

Ἀγάπη : not in Epict. 814; not in Mk 924
ἀγγαρεία, -εύω : in Epict. and Mt. 887 a
ἀγγέλων and ἀγελῶν 17 g
ἀγνοέω : ἀγνοεῖσθαι μελέτησον 55 j
ἀγράμματος "unlettered" 879
αἰλάμ 28 j
Αἰλείμ 28 j
αἴνιγμα : ἐν αἰνίγματι 826
αἴρω ζυγόν 843
ἀλίζομαι and αὐλίζομαι 893–5
"Ἄλλος 17 o*
"Ἄλφα καὶ Ὦ 27 a foll.
ἀμνός and ἀρνίον 32 b–d
ἄν : dropped in LXX 889
ἀναβαίνω 7* foll., 8 a–f*
ἀναβλέπω : of "seeing visions" or "recovering sight" 909, 3 e*, 5 b*
ἀναιρέω "kill" 937 a–b
ἀναλαμβάνω : ἀναληφθῆναι 939 a, 942* (xxii) d
ἀνατέλλω "dawn," applied to God 27 l
ἀνήρ and ἄνθρωπος 942* (xii) b, 2 ; ἀνήρ and πῦρ 7 c
ἄνθρωπος : denoting the female parent 1 ; a human being, masc. or fem. 38; interpr. by Irenæus as the Virgin 39; with and without ὁ 43 c ; ἄνθρωπος and ἀνήρ 942* (xii) b, 2; ὡς ἄνθρωπος 4; υἱὸς ἀνθρώπου and ὁ υἱὸς τοῦ ἀνθρώπου 38 ; ἄνθρωπος ἐξ ἀνθρώπων 37 c
ἀνοίγω 14 b–d*, 17 d*
ἀπαντάω 3*
ἀπάντημα 3 d*
ἀπ' ἄρτι 29 a

ἀπερίσπαστος κ. ἀπαρενόχλητος 811 a
ἀποκαίω, καίω, and ξηραίνω 876–7
ἀποκαλύπτω : ἀποκαλυφθῆναι, how expressed, s. 3 f–j*
ἀπόλλυμι : ἀπολέσας, parall. to πλανηθῇ 864
ἀπορικός 942* (viii) e
ἅπτομαι, ἐγγίζω, κρατέω, προσεγγίζω, προσπορεύομαι &c. 1 a–b*, 2 a*, 6 c*
ἆρα : εἰ ἆρα 878
ἀρνίον and ἀμνός 32 b–d
ἄρρην : superfl. 942* (xii) b
ἄρτι : ἀπ' ἄρτι 29 a
ἀρχή : ἀπ' ἀρχῆς 984 c–e
ἀσώματος 824* (i) a–g, 56 d
αὐγή : how used by Josephus 27 u ; w. Διός &c. 27 v; pl. may mean "rays" or "eyes" 27 v
αὐλίζομαι 894
αὐτοκράτωρ 27 k
αὐτόματος 55 j
αὐτόπτης κ. ὑπηρέτης 983–4

Βαστάζω and φέρω 931
βοάω and κηρύσσω 839 a–c

Γαλιλαία 4*–5*
Γαλιλαῖοι, οἱ 813
γένος : i.e. Gentiles opposed to Jews 37 a
γίνομαι : "am born" 880 ; γενόμενα parall. to τέκνα 880 ; γ. ἐκ γυναικός 880
γνάθος : Ὄνου γνάθος 873
γναφεύς and γνάφος (κνάφος) 17 c*

---

[1] *Black Arabics refer to paragraphs* [2]800–[2]997, *ordinary Arabics to the sections of* 2998, *or, if starred, to the sections of* 2999. *For example,* 872 = 2872, 16 = 2998 (xvi), 16* = 2999 (xvi).

GREEK

γνάφος s. γναφεύς
γυμνός 17 ο*
γυνή: γενόμενον ἐκ γυναικὸς 880;
  γυναῖκα...τροφόν,?"wife" or "nurse"
  912; μετὰ γυναικῶν μολύνεσθαι,
  metaph. 942* (xv) b-f

Δαιμόνιον 824* (i) b
διά: w. gen. of time 892 a-b; διὰ
  'Ιωάννου, ambig. 937 f
διάγω 899 foll.
διαγωγή, δίαιτα, and διατροφή 905
διαζώννυμι: διασώσασθαι and διαζώσασθαι
  17 n*
δίαιτα s. διαγωγή
διάκονοι 983
διασώζω s. διαζώννυμι
διατροφή s. διαγωγή
δίδραχμον and στατήρ 7 b* foll.
δίδωμι and παραδίδωμι 828, 23 e
δίκαιος 54 j; ὁ δίκαιος 54 e foll.
δικαιώματα "claims" 942* (viii) c
δοξάζω: ταῦτά μοι δοξάσαντες 37 a
δραχμή 7 c*
δύναμις, ἡ 824; ἡ δ. μου 923 b; ἐν
  μυριάσι δυνάμεων αὐτοῦ 31 a
δωρέομαι: in Aq. 840*

Ἑβδομάς 28 d
ἐγγίζω 6* (esp. 6 a*, 6 d*); ἐ., ἅπτομαι,
  κρατέω, προσέρχομαι &c. 1 a-b*, 2 a*,
  6 a-d*
ἐγγύς 6 a*
ἐγκομβόομαι: ἐγκομβώσασθε 17 n*
ἐγκρύπτω: ἐνέκρυψεν v.r. ἔκρυψεν 55 k
ἐγκρύψαι "cakes" 55 k
ἔθος: ὑπὸ ἔθους 813
εἶδος s. ὁμοίωμα
εἰμί: applied to God 27 e
εἰς: προσεύχεσθαι εἰς "to pray towards"
  942* (xxiv) b
εἰς παρεστηκώς 17 j*
εἶτα (Epict.) and εἶπεν (Mk) 876
ἐκδίκησις 942* (xviii) a
ἐκεῖ "thither" 942* (xxiv) b
ἐκλείπω 910 a, 923 c
ἐκτείνω χεῖρα(ς) 926 foll.
ἔλεος, -έω 840*
ἐμπεριπατέω 28 f-h
ἐνιαυτός: κατ' ἐνιαυτόν 961 (i) a
ἐνοικέω 28 f
ἔνσαρκος 942* (ii) b
ἐξαίρω 30 b-c; ἐξαῖρον πνεῦμα 30
ἑξᾶς 942* (i) l
ἐξέρχομαι: ambig. 938-9; w. ἔξω 12*
ἐξομολόγησις and εὐχαριστία 11 a*

ἔξω s. ἐξέρχομαι
ἑορτή: appl. to Day of Atonement
  961 a; ἡ ἑ. τῶν 'Ιουδαίων 961 a
ἐπαγγελία 997
ἐπαείδω, ἐπαοιδός 17
ἐπάνω 17 i, 5 a-b*
ἐπένδυμα 17 n*
ἐπενδύομαι 17 n*
ἐπενδύτης 17 l* foll.
ἐπί: w. gen.=" referring to " 42; ἐ.
  and ἐπάνω 5*
ἐπιβάλλω 13*
ἐπικαλέω: ἐπικέκληται and προσκέ-
  κληται 3 g*
ἐπίκρισις 942* (viii) c
ἐπίσημος 942* (i) l foll.
ἐπιστρέφω: in Epict. 815; ἐπιστραφείς
  and ἐπιστρέψας 936 a
ἐπιτίθημι and προστίθημι 942* (xix) a
ἐπιφαίνω and ἀνατέλλω 27 t
ἑπτακέφαλος 942* (xiii) b
ἑτοιμάζω τόπον 942* (xiii) e
ἔτος: κατ' ἔ. 960, 961 (i) a
εὐημερία 27 s
εὐχαριστία and ἐξομολόγησις 11 a*
εὐχή 27 r foll.
ἐφίστημι: w. ἐπάνω and w. dat. 17 i; in
  Lk. 5* (esp. 5 a*), 6*
ἐφούδ 17 n*
ἔωθεν εὐχόμενοι 27 t
ἕως " dawn ": πρὸς τὴν ἕ. στάντες 27 r-t

Ζυγόν 843 foll.
ζῷα and θηρία 33 a, 47

Ἠλί, ἠλί 917 foll.
ἥλιος 917 foll.
ἡμέρα: ταξάμενοι ἡμέραν 3 a*
ἡνίοχος: used by Orig. in Ezek. i. 26 7 d
ἡσυχία θεοῦ 55 h

Θεῖος: τὸ θεῖον, when used for " God "
  27 u
θέλω: in Epict. and Jn 806
θεός: υἱὸς τοῦ θεοῦ, υἱὸς θεοῦ, and ὁ υἱὸς
  τοῦ θεοῦ 20 a-b; ὁ θεός, absol., alleged
  to mean "the sun-god" 27 v; w.
  ἀνατέλλω 27 t
θέρος "fruit-time" 874
θηλάζον 49 a
θηρίον: θηρία and κτήνη 840 a; and
  ζῷα 33 a, 47
θύρα: διὰ τῆς θ., κατὰ θ., παρὰ θ. &c. 985

Ἰαώ 27 d
'Ιησοῦς: the name 942* (i) l
'Ισαάκ: the name 881 a, 942* (xii) b

Black Arabics refer to paragraphs [2]800–[2]997, *ordinary Arabics to the sections of* 2998, *or, if starred, to the sections of* 2999. *For example,* 872=2872, 16=2998 (xvi), 16*=2999 (xvi).

Ἰσραήλ : interpr. as ὁρῶν θεόν 15 f
ἵστημι : ἑστηκότων ὧδε 17 h*
ἰσχύς : ἡ l. μου ἐξέλιπεν 923 b
ἸΧΘΎΣ 8*

Καίω, ἀποκαίω and ξηραίνω 876–7
καλέω 839 a foll.
κανών 28 b
κατά = ὅμοιος 26 a ; κατ᾿ ἔτος, κατ᾿
 ἐνιαυτόν 960, 961 (i) a
κεράννυμι : κραθέντες τῇ σαρκὶ αὐτοῦ 895 ;
 κραθῆναι and κρατηθῆναι 895
κηρύσσω 839 a foll.
κνάφος s. γνάφος
κόλπος 32
κρατέω 1 b* ; κρατήσας τῆς χειρὸς 6 c* ;
 s.-also ἅπτομαι and κεράννυμι
κρυπτός : ἐν κρυπτῷ 55 (esp. 55 l)
κρύπτω : ἔκρυψεν v.r. ἐνέκρυψεν 55 k
κτήνη and θηρία 840 a
κύριος and ὁ κύριος 26 e–f, 27 h

Λέγω : ἔλεγε "meant", or "said"
 837 (iii) a, 874 f
λέντιον 17 m–n*
λίμναι 960
λόγος, ὁ : ἀπὸ σιγῆς προελθών 55 h ;
 τομεύς 28 n, t, u
λούομαι 27 w
λυχνία, λύχνος 28 e foll.

Μάγος: "magician," in bad sense
 17 a foll.
μαθηταί, parallels to 17 g–h*
μαρτυρέω 26 h
μαρτυρία 26 i foll.
μαρτύριον 28 a ; and συνταγή 3 a*
μάρτυς 26 i foll.
μέγας : μεγᾶ (i.e. μέγαν) perh. read as
 μέγα 833 ; μεγάλη πόλις, how applied
 942* (ii) b
μέν : ἐδώκαμεν or ἔδωκα μέν 802
μέσος : ἀνὰ μέσον 942* (i) e, 28 j, k ; ἐν
 μέσῳ 942* (i) e, 28 i–k
μετανοέω, -νοια 800 c–d
μονώτατος ambig. 17 c*

Νεφέλη 30 a

Ὁ, ἡ, τό : ins. and om. with ἄνθρωπος
 43 c ; with κύριος 26 e, f, 27 h, with
 νεφέλη 30 ; υἱὸς ἀνθρώπου, υἱὸς τοῦ
 ἀνθρώπου, and ὁ υἱὸς τοῦ ἀνθρώπου
 24 b, 38, 45 b ; υἱὸς θεοῦ, υἱὸς τοῦ
 θεοῦ, and ὁ υἱὸς τοῦ θεοῦ 20 a–b ; s.
 also 942* (xix)–(xx), 984

ὀγδοάς 942* (i) l
ὄγδοος 942* (i) f, k
οἶδα rendered "vidi" 824* (i) c
οἰκτείρω 840*
ὅμοιος : parall. to κατά 26 a ; foll. by
 accus. 26 a
ὁμοίωμα ἀνθρώπου, ὁμ. ὡς εἶδος ἀνθρ. &c.
 7 c
ὀνειδίζω : ὠνίδισας in D 923 c
ὄνομα : ἐπίσημον ὅ. 942* (i) l foll.
ὀνόματα ? meaning "persons" 942*
 (viii) a foll.
Ὄνου γνάθος 873
ὄντως ? corr. of ὁ ὡς 825
ὁράω : ὁ ὁρῶν 987 ; "Israel" interpr. as
 ὁρῶν θεόν 15 f ; passive of 997 a,
 comp. 3 f–j*
ὀρφανός : in Epict. and Jn 805 a
ὀστᾶ 824* (i) b, d
οὐδέ = "on the ground" 837 (iii) d
ὄψις 28 w

Ξηραίνω, καίω, and ἀποκαίω 876–7

Παιδεύω : for τροποφορέω 4 d
παιδίον 49 a ; and τεκνίον 978
παῖς "servant" 54 f ; supplanted by
 υἱός 54 f ; ambig. 24 f
παντοκράτωρ 27 b, f–m
παρά as abbreviation 942* (viii) c
παραδίδωμι 828, 23 e
παρακαλέω 839 b
παράκειμαι 942* (viii) c
παραμένω 997 a, 27 t
παρθένια Μαρίας 55 h
παρθένος : ἐκ (or ἀπὸ) παρθένου γεννητός
 880 a ; παρθένοι appl. to men (Rev.
 xiv. 4) 942* (xv) b–f
παρίστημι : εἷς παρεστηκώς, εἷς [τις] τῶν
 παρεστηκότων 17 j*
πεδίον "field" 840 a
περί : οἱ περί, parallels to 17 g–h*
περιπατέω 28 f–g
Πέτρος, parallels to 17 g–h* ; οἱ περὶ
 τὸν Π. 17 g–h*
πιστός 26 n
πλανάω : ἀπολέσας parall. to πλανηθῇ
 864
πλήρης : vernacular use of 44 b
πληροφορέω 980–2
πληρόω 806, comp. 982
Πνεῦμα, τό, used absolutely 29 b, comp.
 824* (i) b
πνεῦμα "wind," "spirit," "breath"
 30 a ; v.r. φάντασμα 824* (i) b
ποδήρης 28 l–n

Black Arabics refer to paragraphs [2]800–[2]997, ordinary Arabics to the
sections of 2998, or, if starred, to the sections of 2999. For example, 872 = 2872,
16 = 2998 (xvi), 16ª = 2999 (xvi).

www.ingramcontent.com/pod-product-compliance
Lightning Source LLC
Chambersburg PA
CBHW060607230426
43670CB00011B/2002